WALKING ALONG A STREET IN A SMALL TOWN, I COME
TO A T-INTERSECTION AND TURN RIGHT. AT THE NEXT
T-INTERSECTION I TURN LEFT. I KEEP REPEATING THIS
PATTERN, WONDERING HOW FAR I'LL GET. FINALLY I END
UP ON A LARGE ROAD, WHERE I'M NOT GOING TO COME
TO ANY T-INTERSECTIONS FOR A LONG TIME, SO I TURN
AROUND AND HEAD BACK. BUT ON THE RETURN JOURNEY,
ALL THE T-INTERSECTIONS I'D TURNED AT HAVE BEEN
TRANSFORMED INTO PLAIN OLD SIDE STREETS. "THIS
IS A MYSTERY. THIS IS A TRICK!" I THINK, AS I ASK
PASSERS-BY FOR HELP GOING HOME. JUST ONE MEMORY
FROM A FOOLISH CHILDHOOD.
-TSUGUMI OHBA

Tsugumi Ohba
Born in Tokyo.
Hobby: Collecting teacups.
Day and night, develops manga plots
while holding knees on a chair.

Takeshi Obata was born in 1969 in Niigata, and is the
artist of the wildly popular SHONEN JUMP title **Hikaru
no Go**, which won the 2003 Tezuka Shinsei "New Hope"
award and the Shogakukan Manga award. Obata is also
the artist of **Arabian Majin Bokentan Lamp Lamp**,
Ayatsuri Sakon, and **Cyborg Jichan G**.

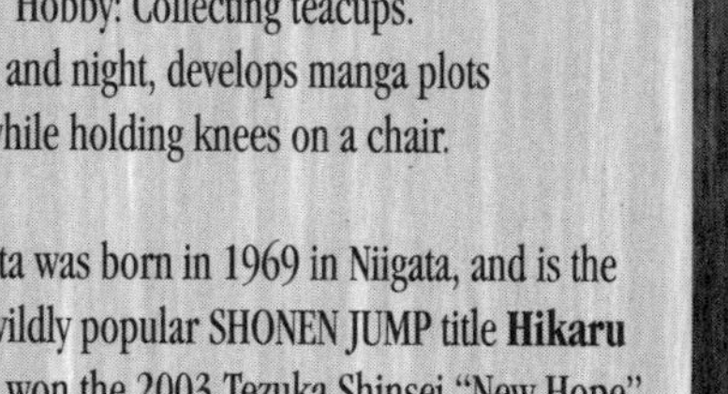

DEATH NOTE VOL 3
The SHONEN JUMP ADVANCED Graphic Novel Edition

STORY BY TSUGUMI OHBA
ART BY TAKESHI OBATA

Translation & Adaptation/Pookie Rolf
Consultant/Alexis Kirsch
Touch-up Art & Lettering/Gia Cam Luc
Design/Sean Lee
Editor/Pancha Diaz

Editor in Chief, Books/Alvin Lu
Editor in Chief, Magazines/Marc Weidenbaum
VP of Publishing Licensing/Rika Inouye
VP of Sales/Gonzalo Ferreyra
Sr. VP of Marketing/Liza Coppola
Publisher/Hyoe Narita

Printed in the U.S.A.

Published by VIZ Media, LLC
P.O. Box 77010
San Francisco, CA 94107

SHONEN JUMP ADVANCED Graphic Novel Edition
10 9 8
First printing, December 2005
Eighth printing, August 2007

THE WORLD'S MOST
CUTTING-EDGE MANGA

viz MEDIA
www.viz.com

SHONEN **JUMP** ADVANCED
www.shonenjump.com

SHONEN JUMP ADVANCED

DEATHNOTE
デスノート

3

激走

Vol. 3
Hard Run
Story by Tsugumi Ohba
Art by Takeshi Obata

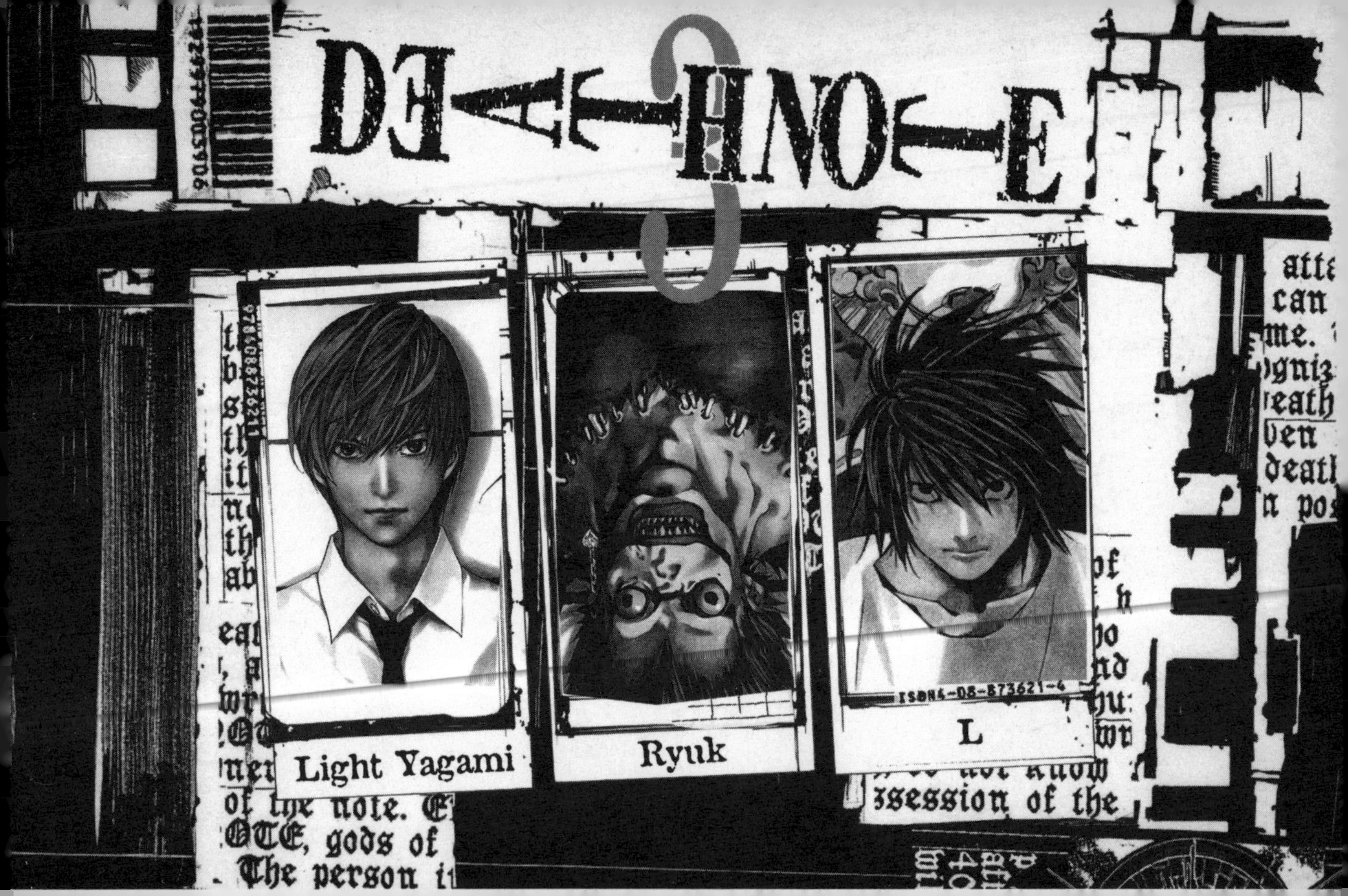
DEATH NOTE
3
Light Yagami
Ryuk
L
ISBN4-08-873621-4

Naomi Misora

Raye Penber

Sayu Yagami

Sachiko Yagami

Soichiro Yagami

specific, the person will cripple his of a heart attack

Watari

Mogi

Ukita

Aizawa

Matsuda

"THE HUMAN WHOSE NAME IS WRITTEN IN THIS NOTE SHALL DIE"... LIGHT YAGAMI, A STRAIGHT "A" HIGH SCHOOL HONORS STUDENT, PICKS UP THE 'DEATH NOTE' DROPPED BY THE SHINIGAMI RYUK INTO THE HUMAN WORLD. HALF DISBELIEVING, LIGHT USES THE NOTEBOOK, ONLY TO SEE THE PEOPLE WHOSE NAMES HE HAS WRITTEN DROP DEAD! INITIALLY HORRIFIED BY THE NOTEBOOK'S POWERS, LIGHT EVENTUALLY DECIDES TO USE THE DEATH NOTE TO PURGE THE WORLD OF VIOLENT CRIMINALS AND CREATE AN IDEAL SOCIETY. MEANWHILE, AS CRIMINALS WORLDWIDE START DYING MYSTERIOUSLY, THE ENIGMATIC L, WHO IS A SECRETIVE GENIUS WHO SPECIALIZES IN SOLVING UNSOLVED CASES, ENTERS THE PICTURE. HE USES A TV BROADCAST TO ANNOUNCE HE WILL CATCH WHOEVER IS RESPONSIBLE, SETTING OFF AN ALMIGHTY BATTLE OF WITS BETWEEN LIGHT AND HIMSELF...

IN RESPONSE TO L MOBILIZING THE FBI, LIGHT SKILLFULLY USES THE DEATH NOTE TO ELIMINATE ALL THE FBI AGENTS ON THE CASE IN JAPAN. THEN, ON A VISIT TO THE NATIONAL POLICE AGENCY, HE RUNS INTO NAOMI. AS THE FIANCEE OF RAYE PEMBER, ONE OF THE SLAIN AGENTS, NAOMI FIGURED OUT THAT THE BUS-JACKING RAYE WAS INVOLVED IN HAD BEEN MASTERMINDED BY KIRA (AKA LIGHT). WHEN LIGHT HEARS THIS, HE SMOOTH-TALKS HER INTO TELLING HIM HER REAL NAME, AND GETS RID OF HER. MEANWHILE, L HAS PLACED BUGS AND SECRET CAMERAS IN THE KITAMURA AND YAGAMI HOMES - BUT LIGHT NOTICES SOMEONE HAS ENTERED HIS ROOM, AND KNOWS ABOUT IT. L VS. LIGHT: THEIR CLASH-VIA-CAMERA IS ABOUT TO BEGIN...!

DEATH NOTE
Vol. 3

CONTENTS

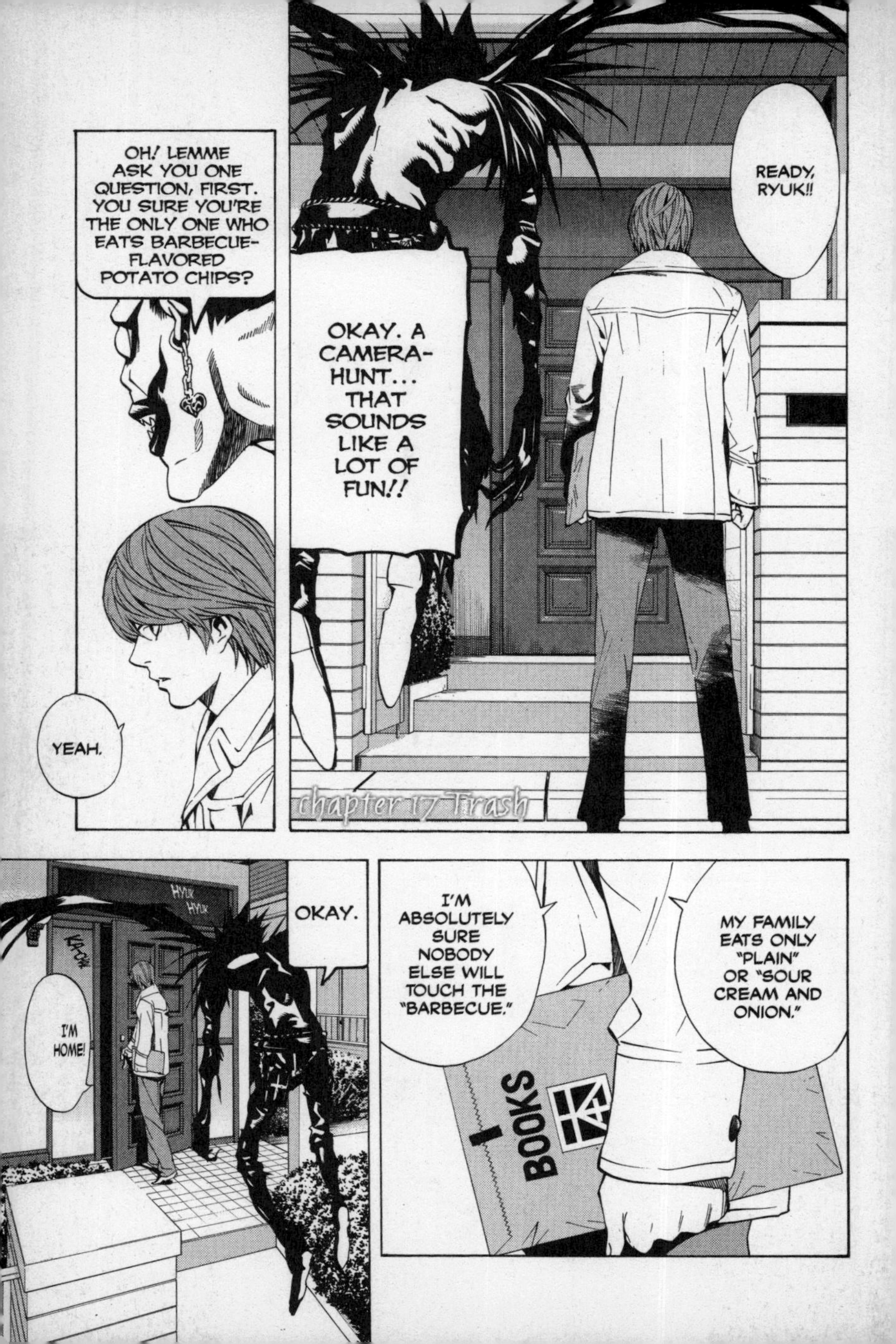
READY, RYUK!!
OKAY. A CAMERA-HUNT... THAT SOUNDS LIKE A LOT OF FUN!!
chapter 17 Trash
OH! LEMME ASK YOU ONE QUESTION, FIRST. YOU SURE YOU'RE THE ONLY ONE WHO EATS BARBECUE-FLAVORED POTATO CHIPS?
YEAH.
MY FAMILY EATS ONLY "PLAIN" OR "SOUR CREAM AND ONION."
I'M ABSOLUTELY SURE NOBODY ELSE WILL TOUCH THE "BARBECUE."
BOOKS
OKAY.
HYUK HYUK
I'M HOME!

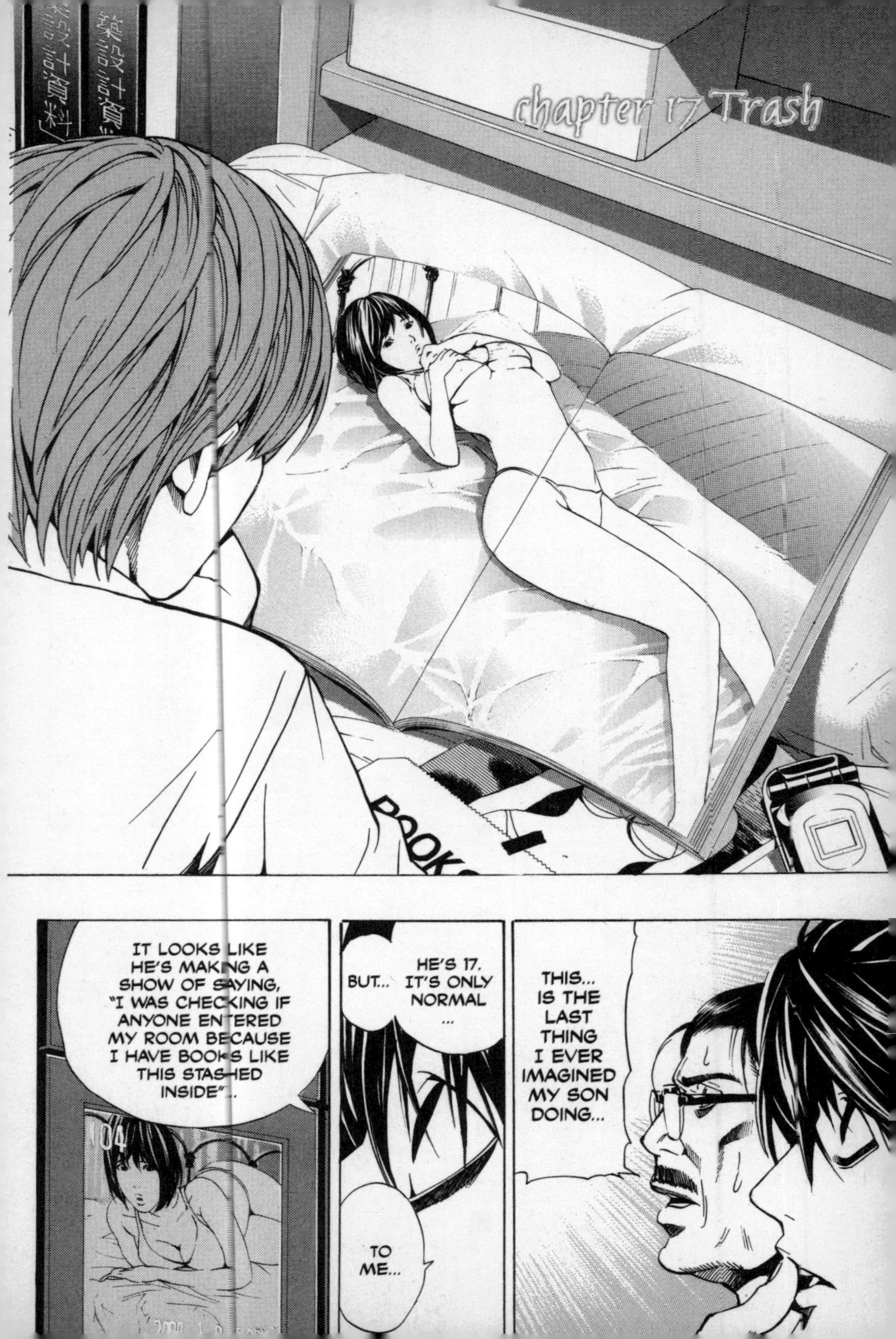
chapter 17 Trash
THIS... IS THE LAST THING I EVER IMAGINED MY SON DOING...
HE'S 17. IT'S ONLY NORMAL ...
BUT...
TO ME...
IT LOOKS LIKE HE'S MAKING A SHOW OF SAYING, "I WAS CHECKING IF ANYONE ENTERED MY ROOM BECAUSE I HAVE BOOKS LIKE THIS STASHED INSIDE"...

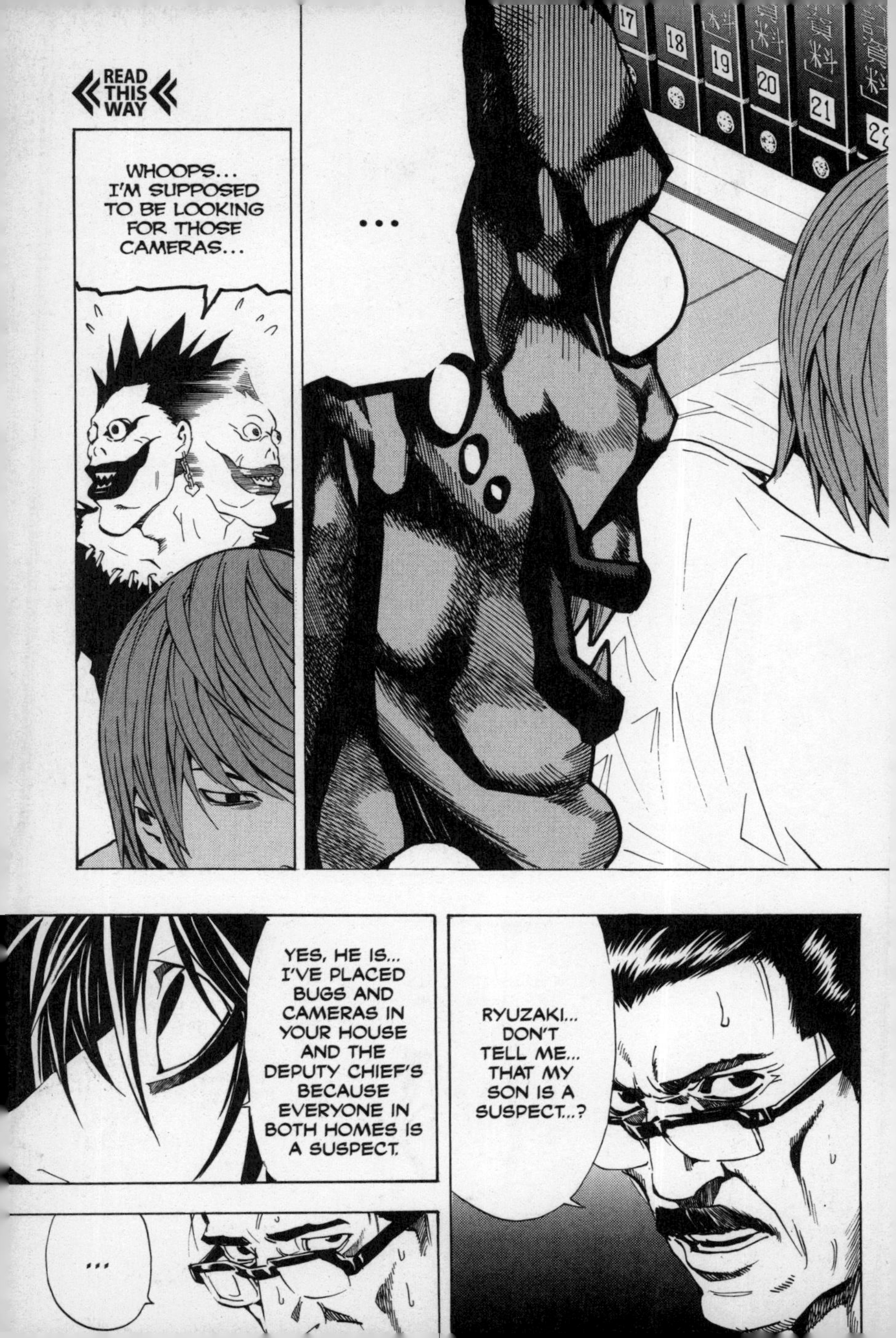
READ THIS WAY
...
WHOOPS... I'M SUPPOSED TO BE LOOKING FOR THOSE CAMERAS...
RYUZAKI... DON'T TELL ME... THAT MY SON IS A SUSPECT...?
YES, HE IS... I'VE PLACED BUGS AND CAMERAS IN YOUR HOUSE AND THE DEPUTY CHIEF'S BECAUSE EVERYONE IN BOTH HOMES IS A SUSPECT.
...

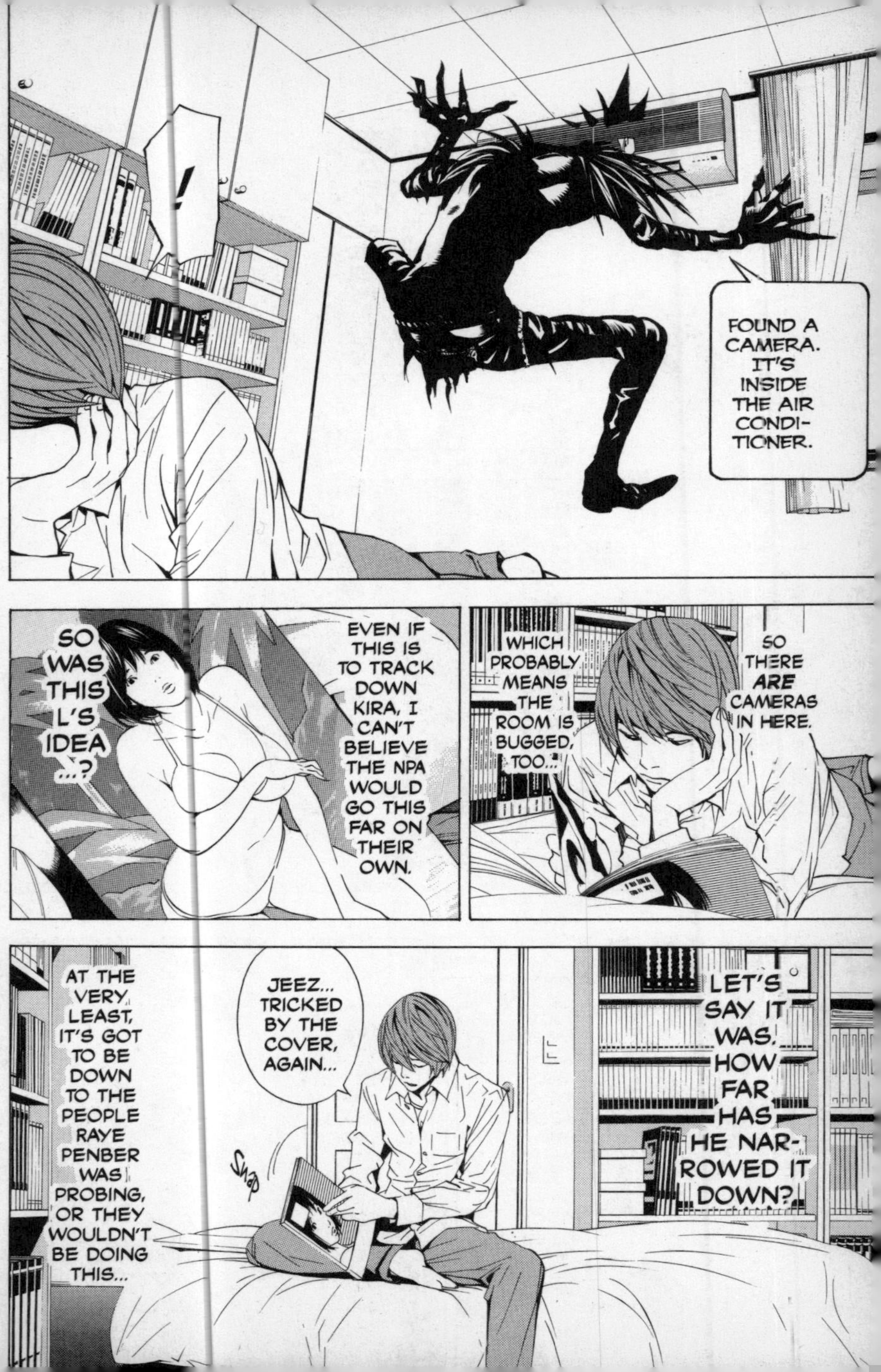
FOUND A CAMERA. IT'S INSIDE THE AIR CONDITIONER.
!
SO THERE *ARE* CAMERAS IN HERE.
WHICH PROBABLY MEANS THE ROOM IS BUGGED, TOO...
EVEN IF THIS IS TO TRACK DOWN KIRA, I CAN'T BELIEVE THE NPA WOULD GO THIS FAR ON THEIR OWN.
SO WAS THIS L'S IDEA ...?
LET'S SAY IT WAS. HOW FAR HAS HE NARROWED IT DOWN?
JEEZ... TRICKED BY THE COVER, AGAIN...
SNAP
AT THE VERY LEAST, IT'S GOT TO BE DOWN TO THE PEOPLE RAYE PENBER WAS PROBING, OR THEY WOULDN'T BE DOING THIS...

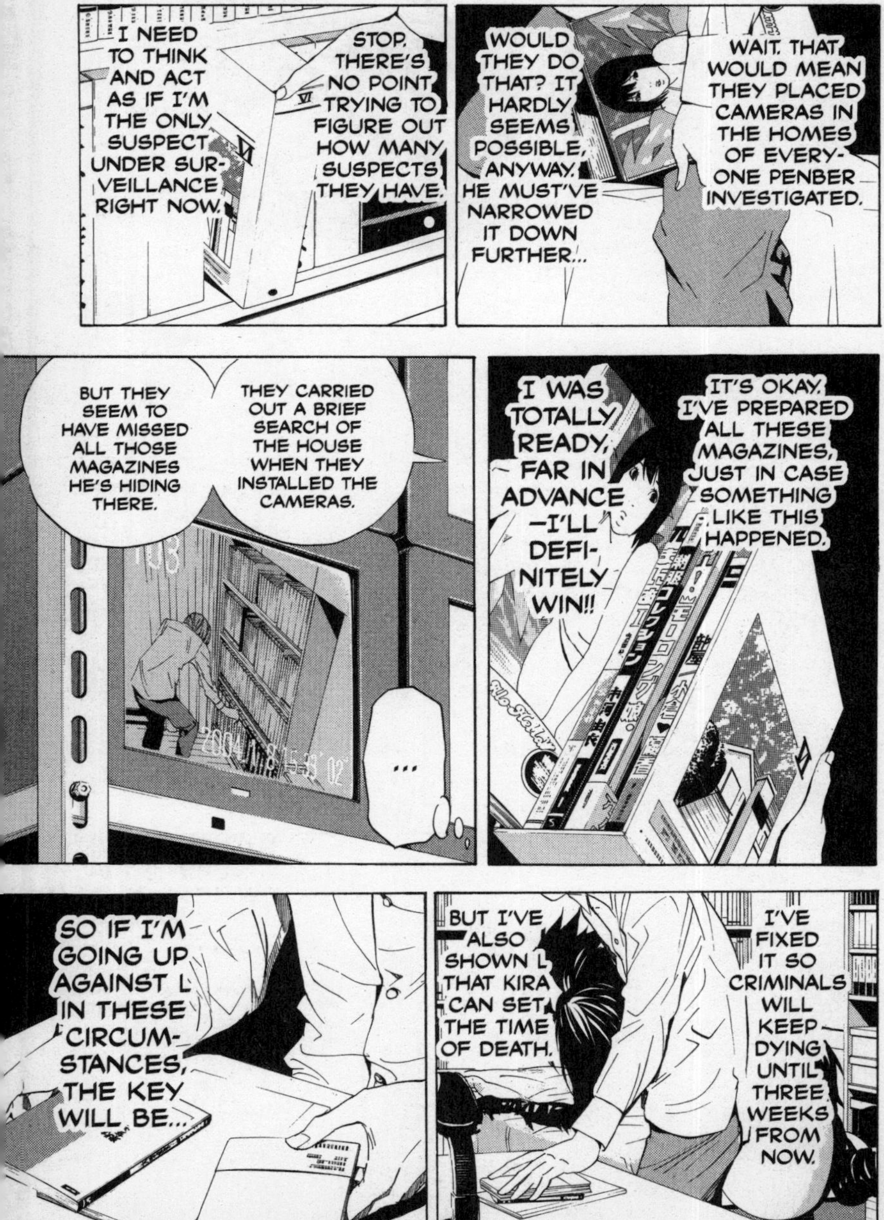
WAIT. THAT WOULD MEAN THEY PLACED CAMERAS IN THE HOMES OF EVERYONE PENBER INVESTIGATED.
WOULD THEY DO THAT? IT HARDLY SEEMS POSSIBLE, ANYWAY. HE MUST'VE NARROWED IT DOWN FURTHER...
STOP. THERE'S NO POINT TRYING TO FIGURE OUT HOW MANY SUSPECTS THEY HAVE.
I NEED TO THINK AND ACT AS IF I'M THE ONLY SUSPECT UNDER SURVEILLANCE RIGHT NOW.
IT'S OKAY. I'VE PREPARED ALL THESE MAGAZINES, JUST IN CASE SOMETHING LIKE THIS HAPPENED.
I WAS TOTALLY READY, FAR IN ADVANCE—I'LL DEFINITELY WIN!!
THEY CARRIED OUT A BRIEF SEARCH OF THE HOUSE WHEN THEY INSTALLED THE CAMERAS.
BUT THEY SEEM TO HAVE MISSED ALL THOSE MAGAZINES HE'S HIDING THERE.
...
I'VE FIXED IT SO CRIMINALS WILL KEEP DYING UNTIL THREE WEEKS FROM NOW.
BUT I'VE ALSO SHOWN L THAT KIRA CAN SET THE TIME OF DEATH.
SO IF I'M GOING UP AGAINST L IN THESE CIRCUMSTANCES, THE KEY WILL BE...

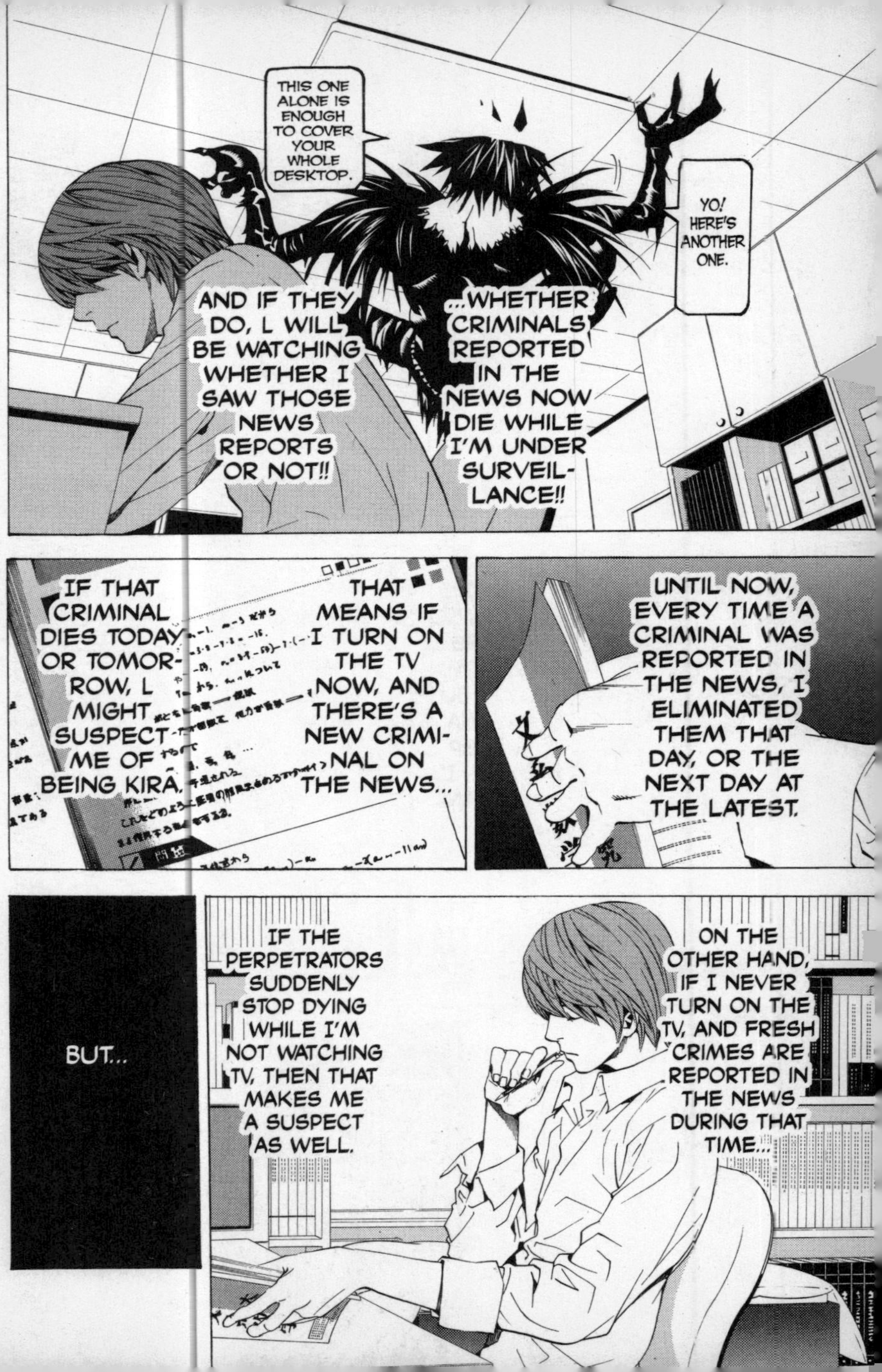
YO! HERE'S ANOTHER ONE.
THIS ONE ALONE IS ENOUGH TO COVER YOUR WHOLE DESKTOP.
...WHETHER CRIMINALS REPORTED IN THE NEWS NOW DIE WHILE I'M UNDER SURVEIL-LANCE!!
AND IF THEY DO, L WILL BE WATCHING WHETHER I SAW THOSE NEWS REPORTS OR NOT!!
UNTIL NOW, EVERY TIME A CRIMINAL WAS REPORTED IN THE NEWS, I ELIMINATED THEM THAT DAY, OR THE NEXT DAY AT THE LATEST.
THAT MEANS IF I TURN ON THE TV NOW, AND THERE'S A NEW CRIMI-NAL ON THE NEWS...
IF THAT CRIMINAL DIES TODAY OR TOMOR-ROW, L MIGHT SUSPECT ME OF BEING KIRA.
ON THE OTHER HAND, IF I NEVER TURN ON THE TV, AND FRESH CRIMES ARE REPORTED IN THE NEWS DURING THAT TIME...
IF THE PERPETRATORS SUDDENLY STOP DYING WHILE I'M NOT WATCHING TV, THEN THAT MAKES ME A SUSPECT AS WELL.
BUT...

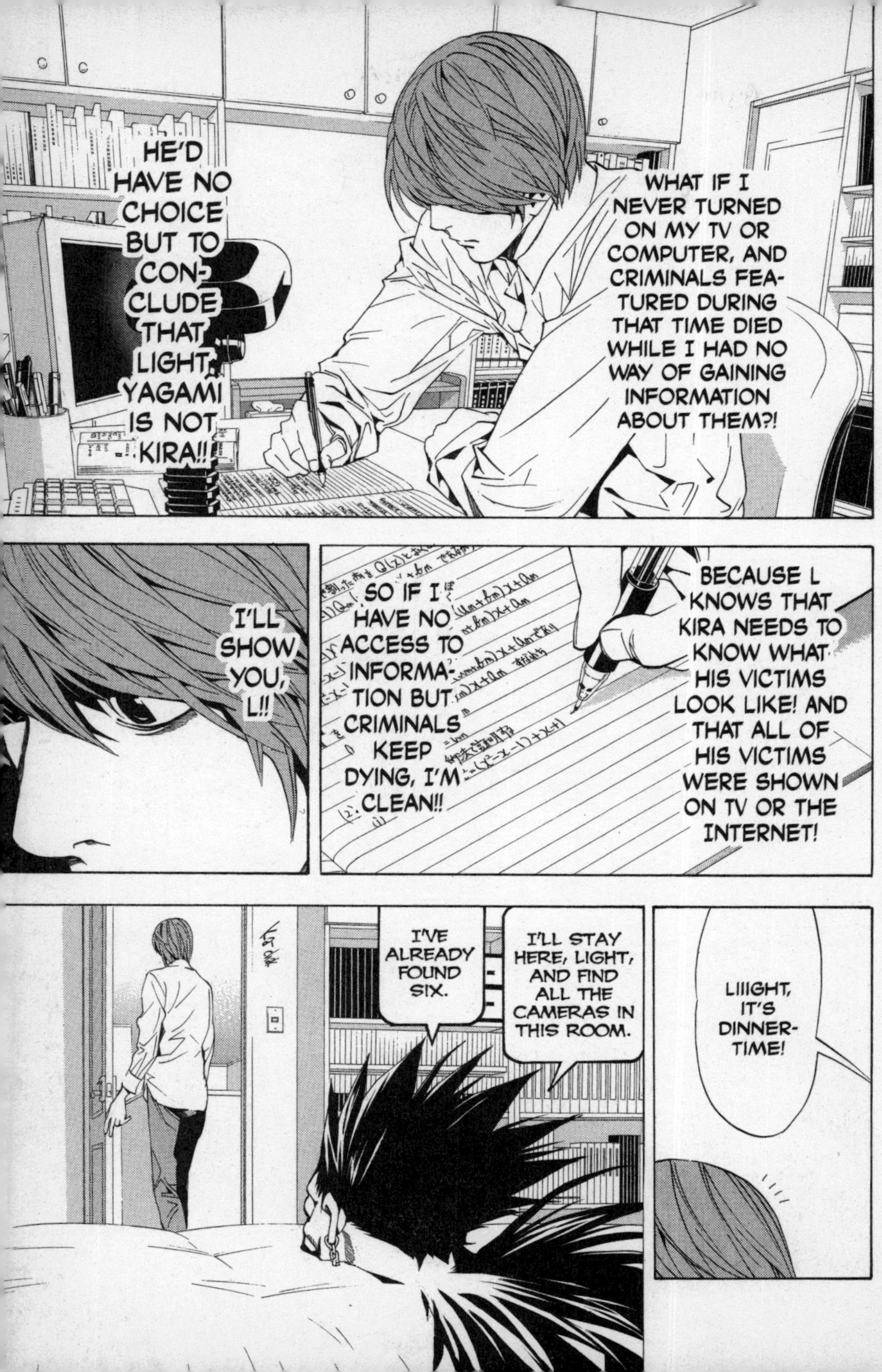
WHAT IF I NEVER TURNED ON MY TV OR COMPUTER, AND CRIMINALS FEATURED DURING THAT TIME DIED WHILE I HAD NO WAY OF GAINING INFORMATION ABOUT THEM?!
HE'D HAVE NO CHOICE BUT TO CONCLUDE THAT LIGHT YAGAMI IS NOT KIRA!!
BECAUSE L KNOWS THAT KIRA NEEDS TO KNOW WHAT HIS VICTIMS LOOK LIKE! AND THAT ALL OF HIS VICTIMS WERE SHOWN ON TV OR THE INTERNET!
SO IF I HAVE NO ACCESS TO INFORMATION BUT CRIMINALS KEEP DYING, I'M CLEAN!!
I'LL SHOW YOU, L!!
LIIIGHT, IT'S DINNER-TIME!
I'LL STAY HERE, LIGHT, AND FIND ALL THE CAMERAS IN THIS ROOM.
I'VE ALREADY FOUND SIX.

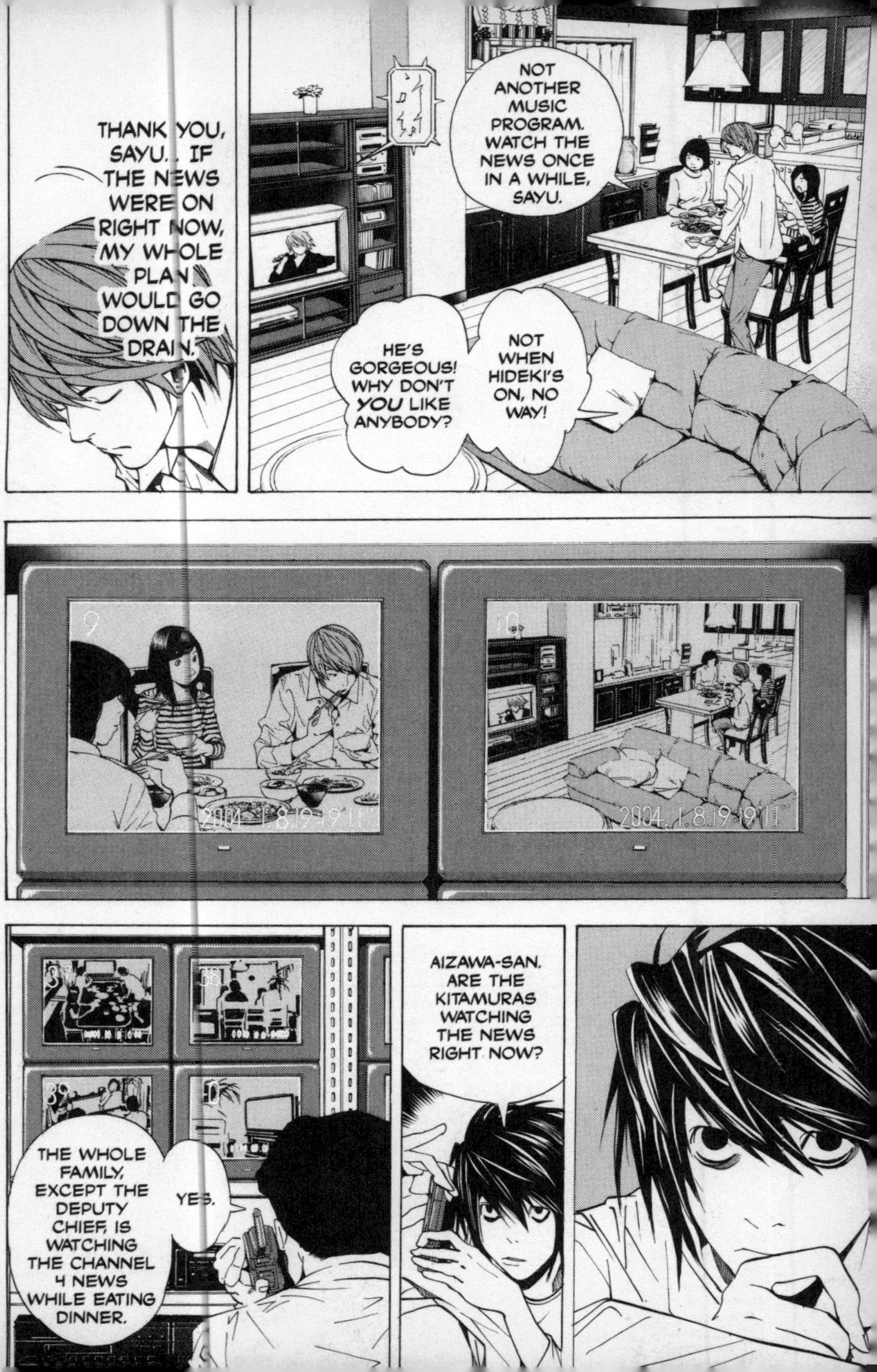
NOT ANOTHER MUSIC PROGRAM. WATCH THE NEWS ONCE IN A WHILE, SAYU.
NOT WHEN HIDEKI'S ON, NO WAY!
HE'S GORGEOUS! WHY DON'T *YOU* LIKE ANYBODY?
THANK YOU, SAYU... IF THE NEWS WERE ON RIGHT NOW, MY WHOLE PLAN WOULD GO DOWN THE DRAIN.
AIZAWA-SAN. ARE THE KITAMURAS WATCHING THE NEWS RIGHT NOW?
YES.
THE WHOLE FAMILY, EXCEPT THE DEPUTY CHIEF, IS WATCHING THE CHANNEL 4 NEWS WHILE EATING DINNER.

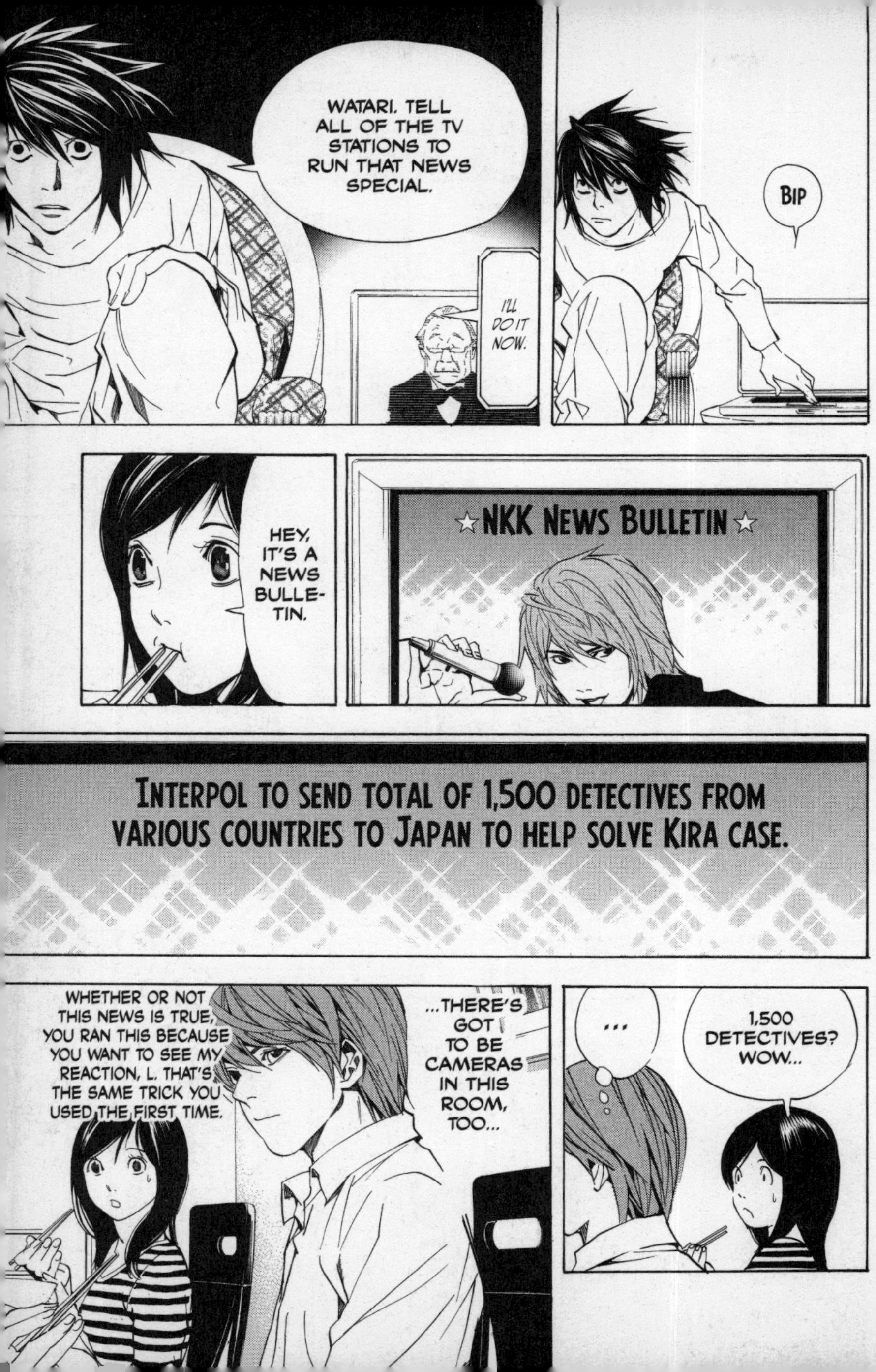
BIP
WATARI. TELL ALL OF THE TV STATIONS TO RUN THAT NEWS SPECIAL.
I'LL DO IT NOW.
★NKK NEWS BULLETIN★
HEY, IT'S A NEWS BULLE-TIN.
INTERPOL TO SEND TOTAL OF 1,500 DETECTIVES FROM VARIOUS COUNTRIES TO JAPAN TO HELP SOLVE KIRA CASE.
1,500 DETECTIVES? WOW...
...
...THERE'S GOT TO BE CAMERAS IN THIS ROOM, TOO...
WHETHER OR NOT THIS NEWS IS TRUE, YOU RAN THIS BECAUSE YOU WANT TO SEE MY REACTION, L. THAT'S THE SAME TRICK YOU USED THE FIRST TIME.

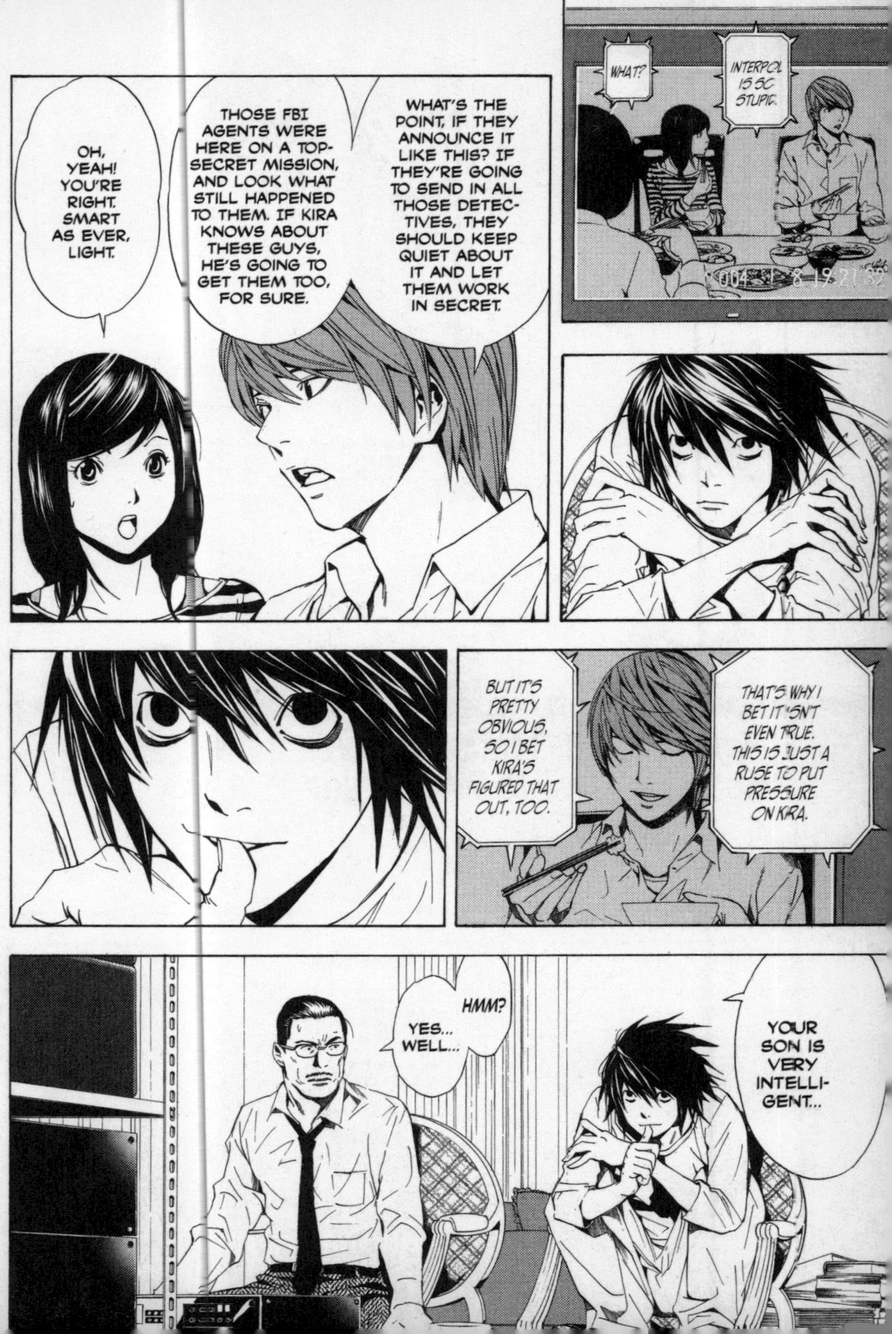
INTERPOL IS SO STUPID.
WHAT?
WHAT'S THE POINT, IF THEY ANNOUNCE IT LIKE THIS? IF THEY'RE GOING TO SEND IN ALL THOSE DETECTIVES, THEY SHOULD KEEP QUIET ABOUT IT AND LET THEM WORK IN SECRET.
THOSE FBI AGENTS WERE HERE ON A TOP-SECRET MISSION, AND LOOK WHAT STILL HAPPENED TO THEM. IF KIRA KNOWS ABOUT THESE GUYS, HE'S GOING TO GET THEM TOO, FOR SURE.
OH, YEAH! YOU'RE RIGHT. SMART AS EVER, LIGHT.
BUT IT'S PRETTY OBVIOUS, SO I BET KIRA'S FIGURED THAT OUT, TOO.
THAT'S WHY I BET IT ISN'T EVEN TRUE. THIS IS JUST A RUSE TO PUT PRESSURE ON KIRA.
YOUR SON IS VERY INTELLI-GENT...
HMM?
YES... WELL...

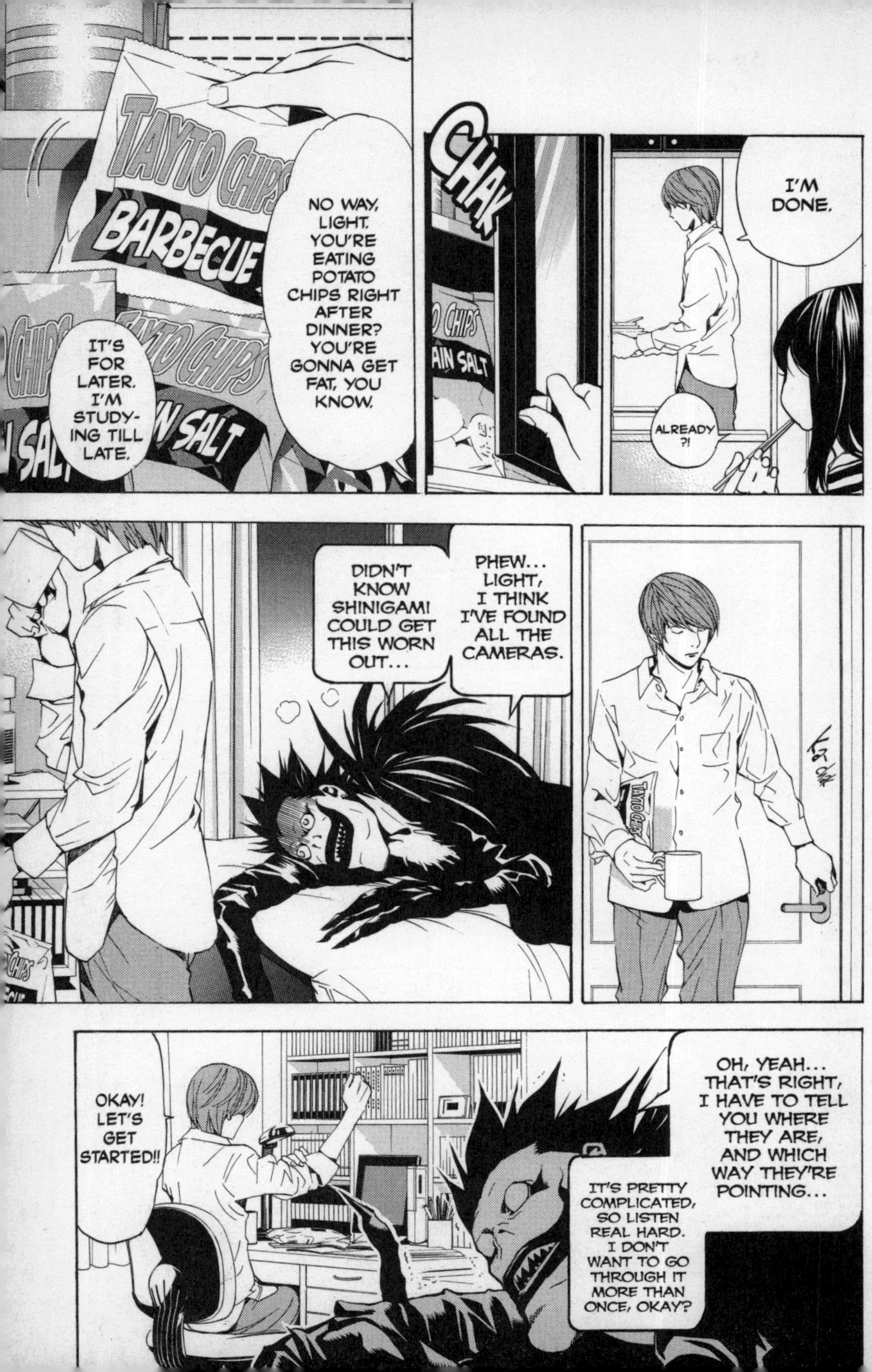
I'M DONE.
ALREADY?!
CHAK
NO WAY, LIGHT. YOU'RE EATING POTATO CHIPS RIGHT AFTER DINNER? YOU'RE GONNA GET FAT, YOU KNOW.
TAYTO CHIPS
BARBECUE
IT'S FOR LATER. I'M STUDYING TILL LATE.
chak
PHEW... LIGHT, I THINK I'VE FOUND ALL THE CAMERAS.
DIDN'T KNOW SHINIGAMI COULD GET THIS WORN OUT...
OH, YEAH... THAT'S RIGHT, I HAVE TO TELL YOU WHERE THEY ARE, AND WHICH WAY THEY'RE POINTING...
IT'S PRETTY COMPLICATED, SO LISTEN REAL HARD. I DON'T WANT TO GO THROUGH IT MORE THAN ONCE, OKAY?
OKAY! LET'S GET STARTED!!

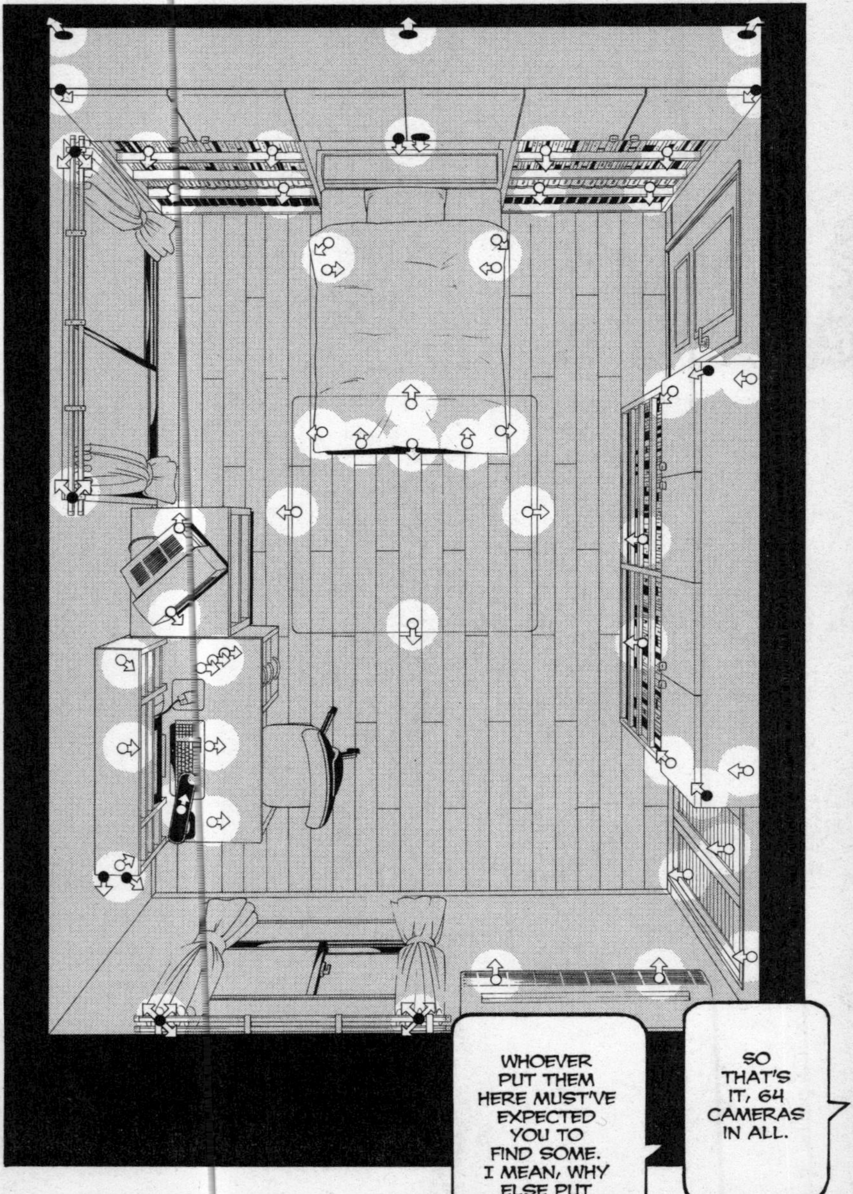
SO THAT'S IT, 64 CAMERAS IN ALL.
WHOEVER PUT THEM HERE MUST'VE EXPECTED YOU TO FIND SOME. I MEAN, WHY ELSE PUT SO MANY?

READ THIS WAY

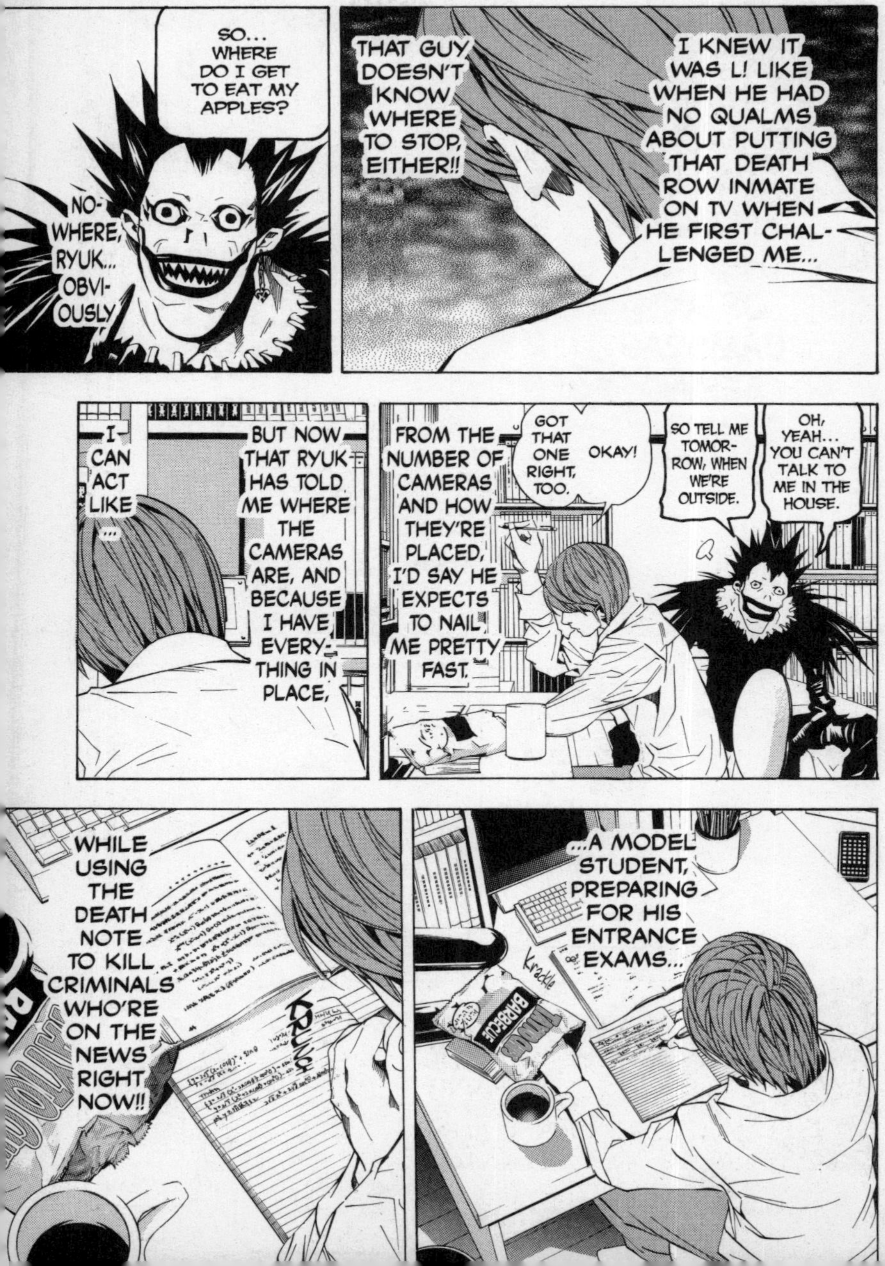
I KNEW IT WAS L! LIKE WHEN HE HAD NO QUALMS ABOUT PUTTING THAT DEATH ROW INMATE ON TV WHEN HE FIRST CHALLENGED ME...
THAT GUY DOESN'T KNOW WHERE TO STOP, EITHER!!
SO... WHERE DO I GET TO EAT MY APPLES?
NO-WHERE, RYUK... OBVIOUSLY
OH, YEAH... YOU CAN'T TALK TO ME IN THE HOUSE.
SO TELL ME TOMORROW, WHEN WE'RE OUTSIDE.
OKAY!
GOT THAT ONE RIGHT, TOO.
FROM THE NUMBER OF CAMERAS AND HOW THEY'RE PLACED, I'D SAY HE EXPECTS TO NAIL ME PRETTY FAST.
BUT NOW THAT RYUK HAS TOLD ME WHERE THE CAMERAS ARE, AND BECAUSE I HAVE EVERYTHING IN PLACE,
I CAN ACT LIKE...
...A MODEL STUDENT, PREPARING FOR HIS ENTRANCE EXAMS...
Krackle
BARBECUE
WHILE USING THE DEATH NOTE TO KILL CRIMINALS WHO'RE ON THE NEWS RIGHT NOW!!
KRUNCH

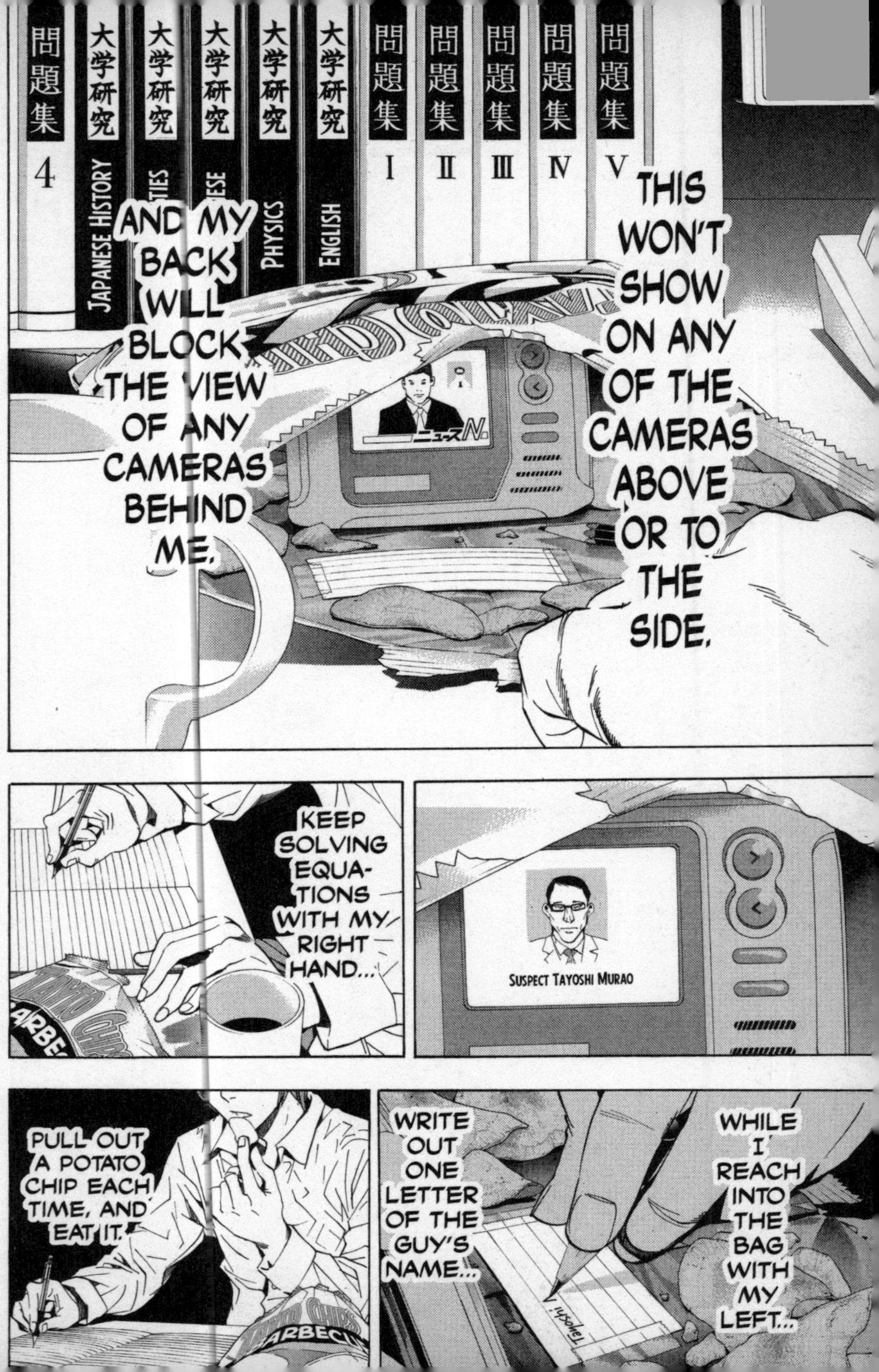
THIS WON'T SHOW ON ANY OF THE CAMERAS ABOVE OR TO THE SIDE.
AND MY BACK WILL BLOCK THE VIEW OF ANY CAMERAS BEHIND ME.
SUSPECT TAYOSHI MURAO
KEEP SOLVING EQUATIONS WITH MY RIGHT HAND...
WHILE I REACH INTO THE BAG WITH MY LEFT...
WRITE OUT ONE LETTER OF THE GUY'S NAME...
PULL OUT A POTATO CHIP EACH TIME, AND EAT IT.

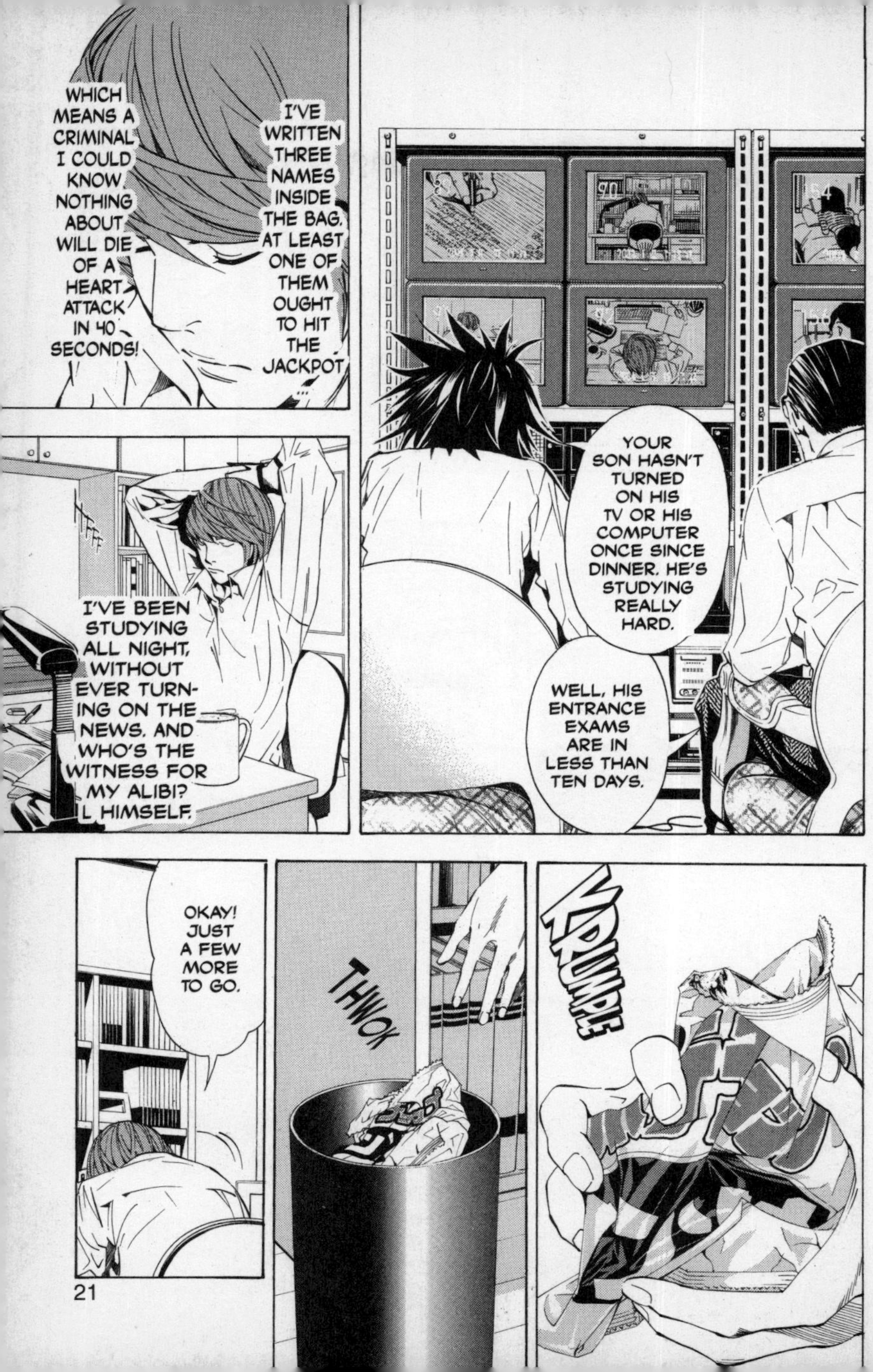
YOUR SON HASN'T TURNED ON HIS TV OR HIS COMPUTER ONCE SINCE DINNER. HE'S STUDYING REALLY HARD.
WELL, HIS ENTRANCE EXAMS ARE IN LESS THAN TEN DAYS.
I'VE WRITTEN THREE NAMES INSIDE THE BAG. AT LEAST ONE OF THEM OUGHT TO HIT THE JACKPOT...
WHICH MEANS A CRIMINAL I COULD KNOW NOTHING ABOUT WILL DIE OF A HEART ATTACK IN 40 SECONDS!
HFFF
I'VE BEEN STUDYING ALL NIGHT, WITHOUT EVER TURNING ON THE NEWS. AND WHO'S THE WITNESS FOR MY ALIBI? L HIMSELF.
KRUMPLE
THWOK
OKAY! JUST A FEW MORE TO GO.

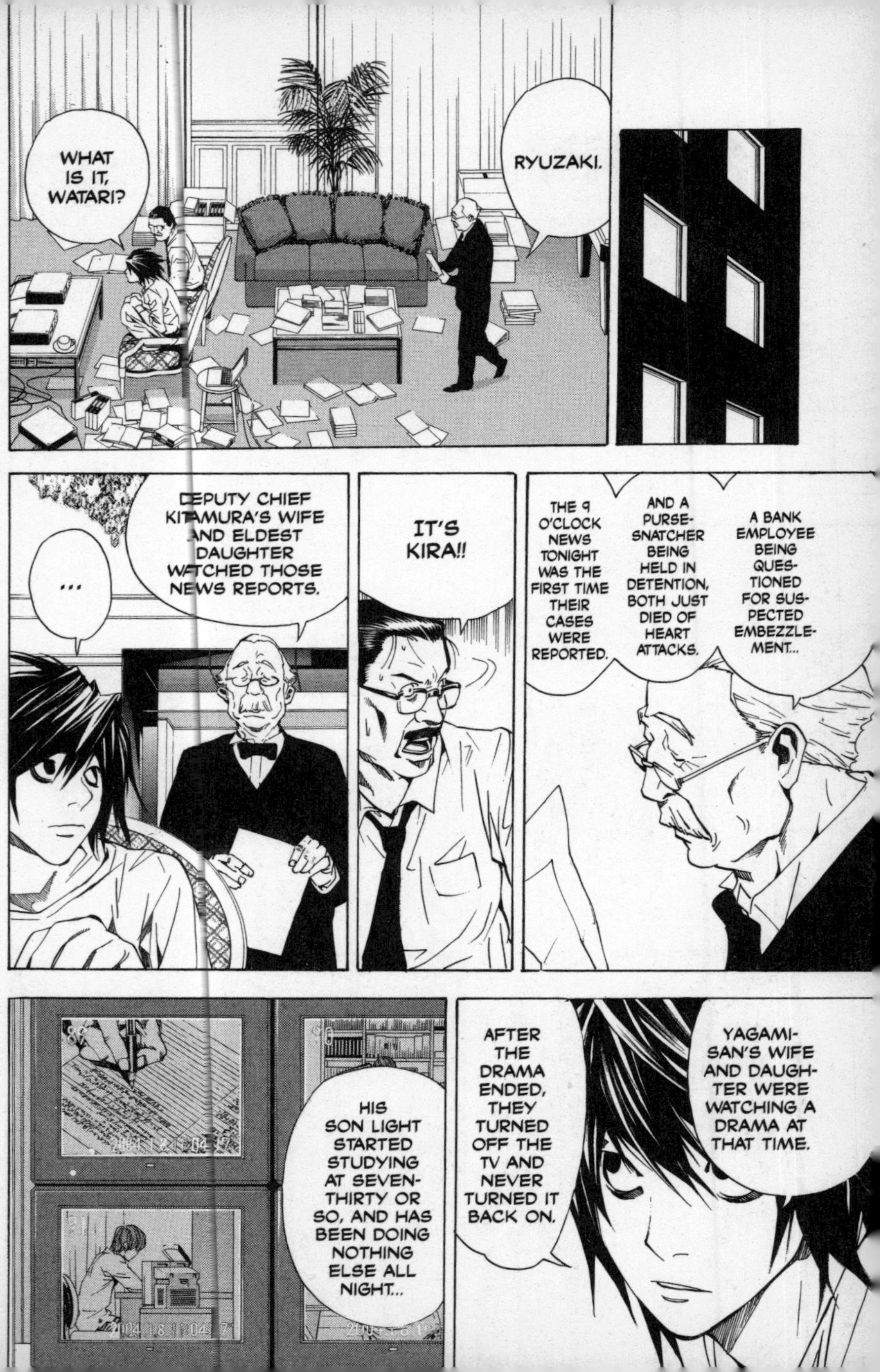
RYUZAKI.
WHAT IS IT, WATARI?
A BANK EMPLOYEE BEING QUESTIONED FOR SUSPECTED EMBEZZLEMENT...
AND A PURSE-SNATCHER BEING HELD IN DETENTION, BOTH JUST DIED OF HEART ATTACKS.
THE 9 O'CLOCK NEWS TONIGHT WAS THE FIRST TIME THEIR CASES WERE REPORTED.
IT'S KIRA!!
DEPUTY CHIEF KITAMURA'S WIFE AND ELDEST DAUGHTER WATCHED THOSE NEWS REPORTS.
...
YAGAMI-SAN'S WIFE AND DAUGHTER WERE WATCHING A DRAMA AT THAT TIME.
AFTER THE DRAMA ENDED, THEY TURNED OFF THE TV AND NEVER TURNED IT BACK ON.
HIS SON LIGHT STARTED STUDYING AT SEVEN-THIRTY OR SO, AND HAS BEEN DOING NOTHING ELSE ALL NIGHT...

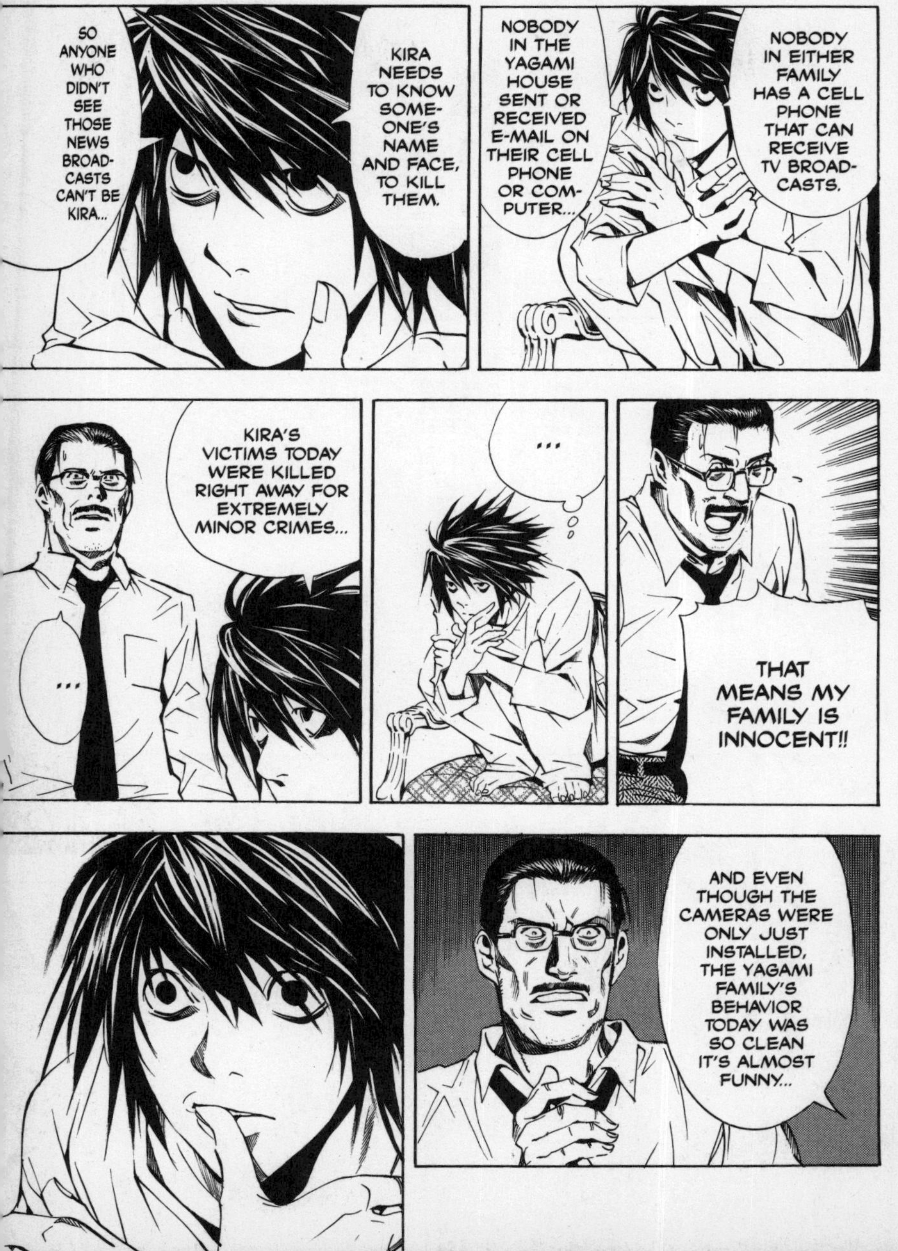
NOBODY IN EITHER FAMILY HAS A CELL PHONE THAT CAN RECEIVE TV BROADCASTS.
NOBODY IN THE YAGAMI HOUSE SENT OR RECEIVED E-MAIL ON THEIR CELL PHONE OR COMPUTER...
KIRA NEEDS TO KNOW SOMEONE'S NAME AND FACE, TO KILL THEM.
SO ANYONE WHO DIDN'T SEE THOSE NEWS BROADCASTS CAN'T BE KIRA...
THAT MEANS MY FAMILY IS INNOCENT!!
...
KIRA'S VICTIMS TODAY WERE KILLED RIGHT AWAY FOR EXTREMELY MINOR CRIMES...
...
AND EVEN THOUGH THE CAMERAS WERE ONLY JUST INSTALLED, THE YAGAMI FAMILY'S BEHAVIOR TODAY WAS SO CLEAN IT'S ALMOST FUNNY...

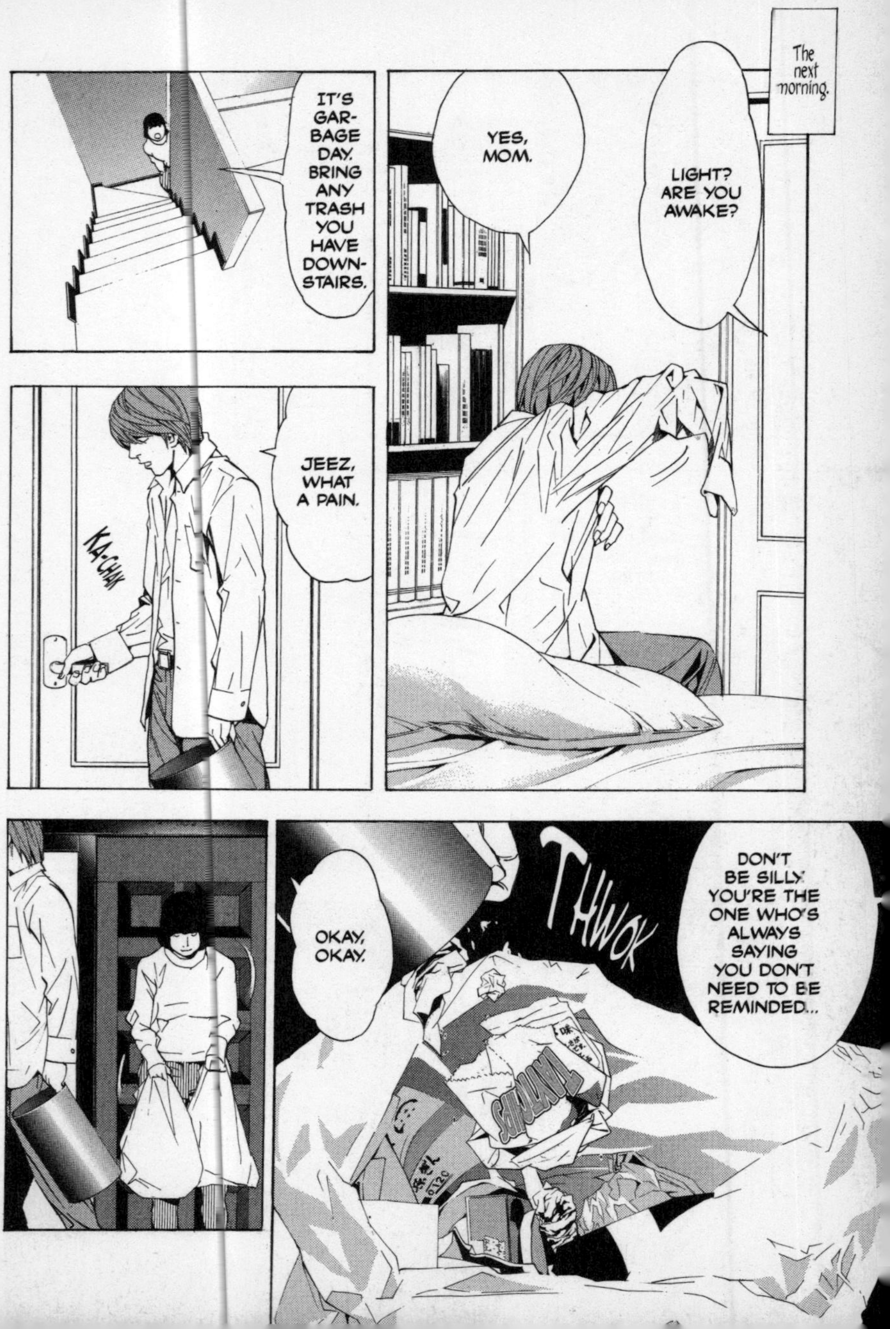
The next morning.
LIGHT? ARE YOU AWAKE?
YES, MOM.
IT'S GARBAGE DAY. BRING ANY TRASH YOU HAVE DOWNSTAIRS.
JEEZ, WHAT A PAIN.
KA-CHAK
DON'T BE SILLY. YOU'RE THE ONE WHO'S ALWAYS SAYING YOU DON'T NEED TO BE REMINDED...
THWOK
OKAY, OKAY.

READ THIS WAY

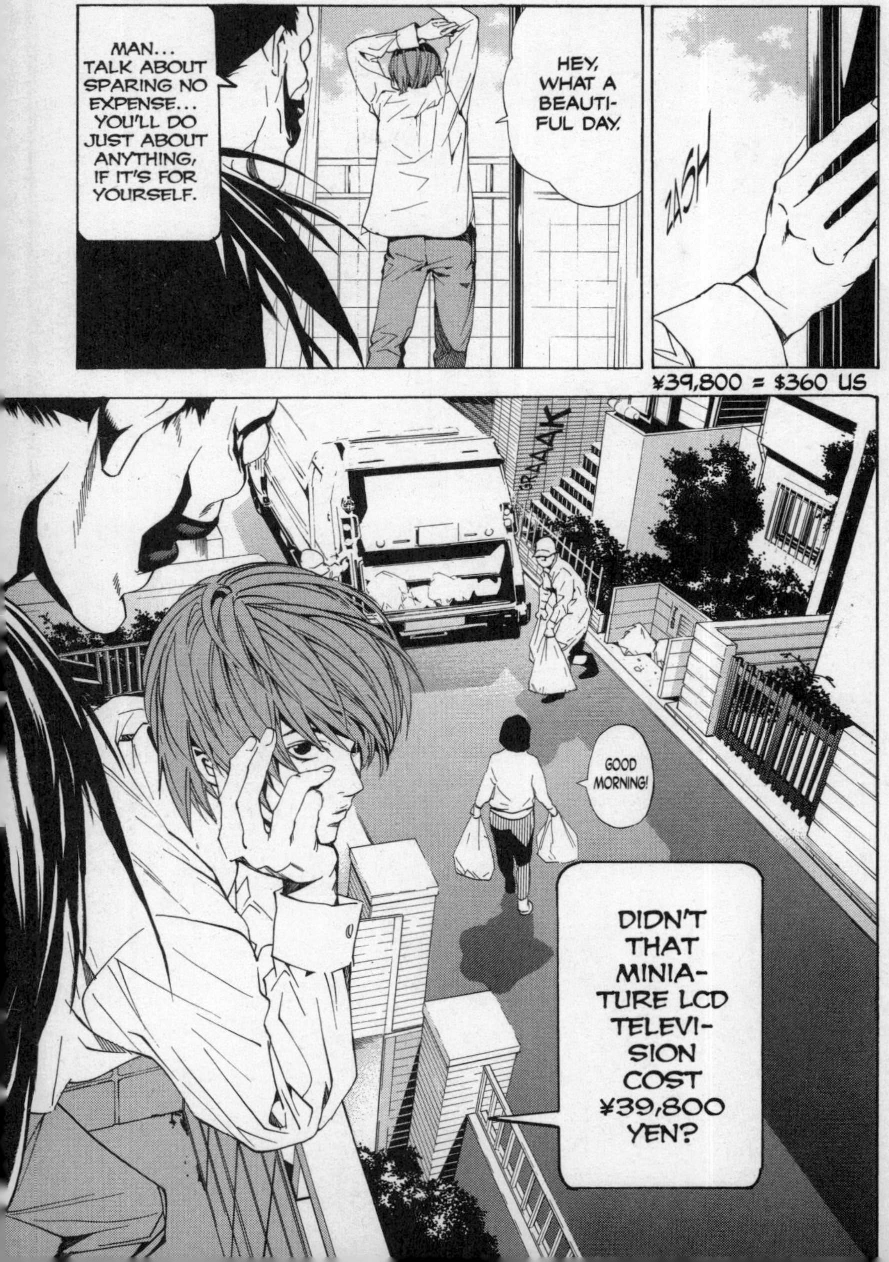

ZASH
HEY, WHAT A BEAUTIFUL DAY.
MAN... TALK ABOUT SPARING NO EXPENSE... YOU'LL DO JUST ABOUT ANYTHING, IF IT'S FOR YOURSELF.
¥39,800 = $360 US
GRAAAK
GOOD MORNING!
DIDN'T THAT MINIATURE LCD TELEVISION COST ¥39,800 YEN?

DEATH NOTE
How to use it
XI

- Even after the individual's name, the time of death, and death condition on the DEATH NOTE were filled out, the time and condition of death can be altered as many times as you want, as long as it is changed within 6 minutes and 40 seconds from the time it was filled in. But, of course, this is only possible before the victim dies.

デスノートに名前、死の時刻、死の状況を書いた後でも、6分40秒以内であれば、死の時刻、死の状況は何度でも変更できる。しかし、もちろん6分40秒以内であっても、変更が可能なのは死んでしまう前である。

- Whenever you want to change anything written on the DEATH NOTE within 6 minutes and 40 seconds after you wrote, you must first rule out the characters you want to erase with two straight lines.

デスノートに書いた内容を6分40秒以内で変更する場合、まず直したい部分の文字の上に二本の棒線を引く。

- As you see above, the time and condition of death can be changed, but once the victim's name has been written, the individual's death can never be avoided.

時間や死の状況は上記のように変更可能であるが、名前を書かれた人間の死は、どんな手段をもっても取り消せない。

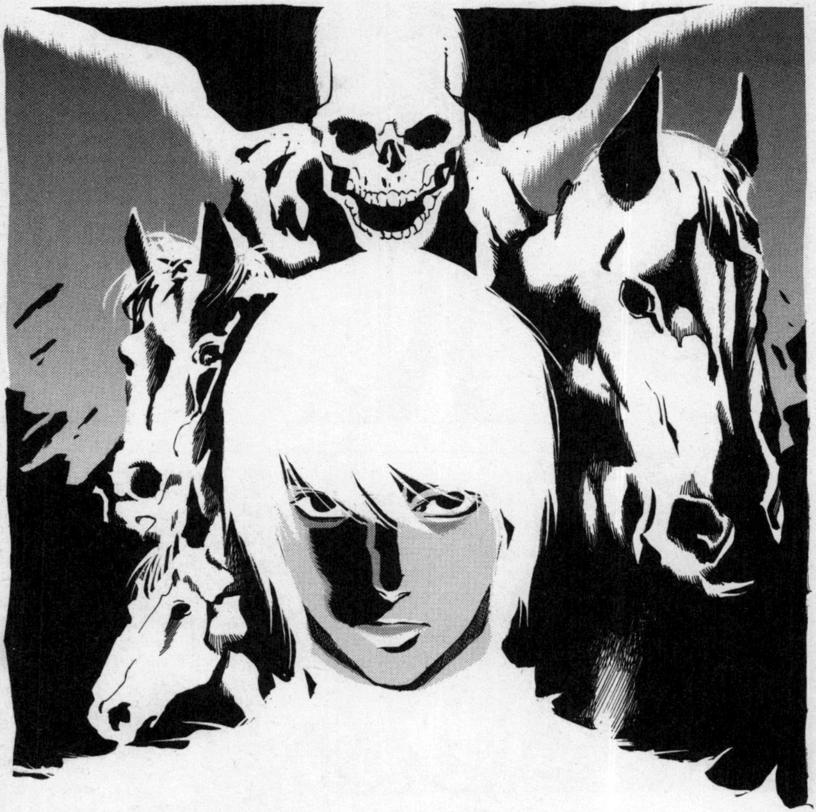

chapter 18 Gaze

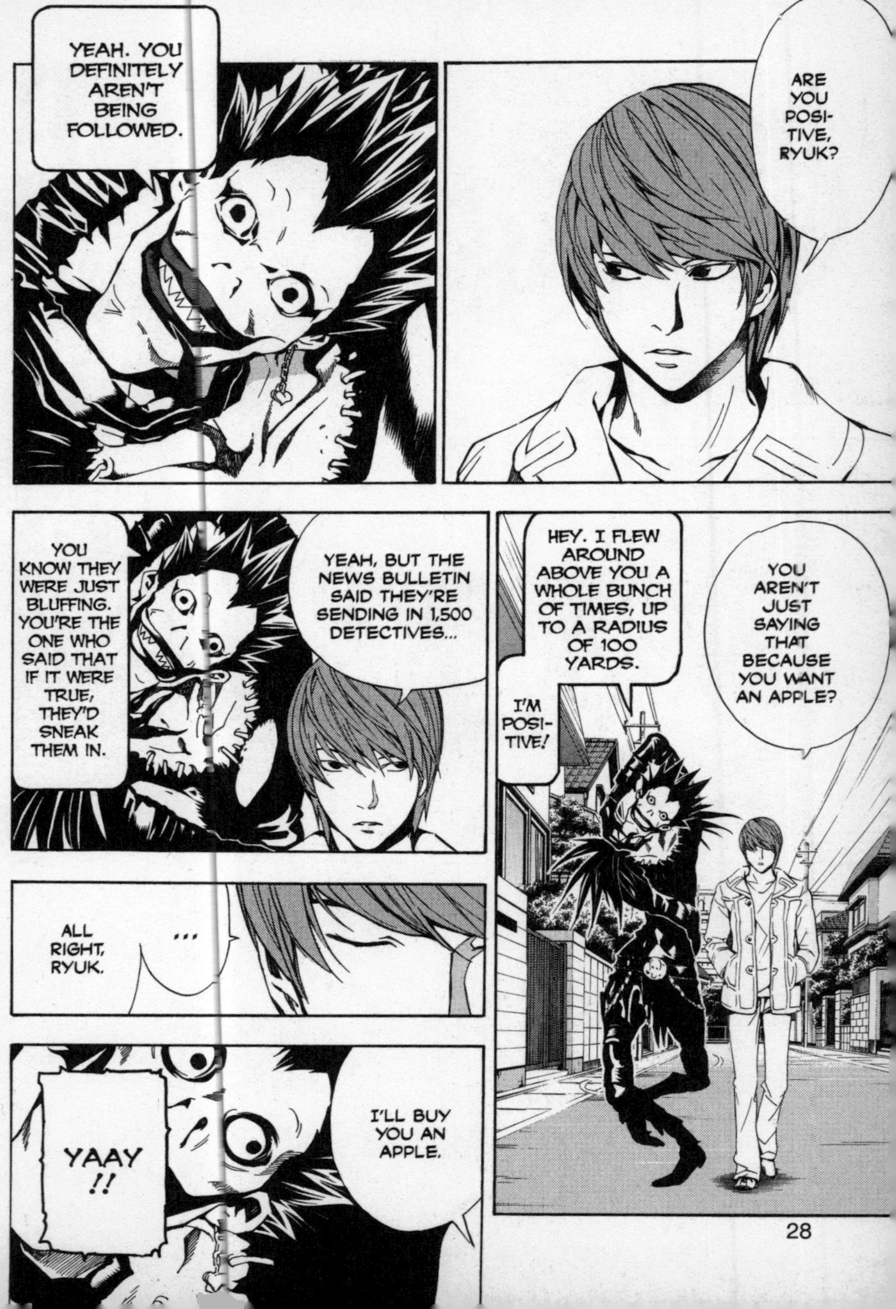

ARE YOU POSITIVE, RYUK?
YEAH. YOU DEFINITELY AREN'T BEING FOLLOWED.
YOU AREN'T JUST SAYING THAT BECAUSE YOU WANT AN APPLE?
HEY. I FLEW AROUND ABOVE YOU A WHOLE BUNCH OF TIMES, UP TO A RADIUS OF 100 YARDS.
I'M POSITIVE!
YEAH, BUT THE NEWS BULLETIN SAID THEY'RE SENDING IN 1,500 DETECTIVES...
YOU KNOW THEY WERE JUST BLUFFING. YOU'RE THE ONE WHO SAID THAT IF IT WERE TRUE, THEY'D SNEAK THEM IN.
...
ALL RIGHT, RYUK.
I'LL BUY YOU AN APPLE.
YAAY!!

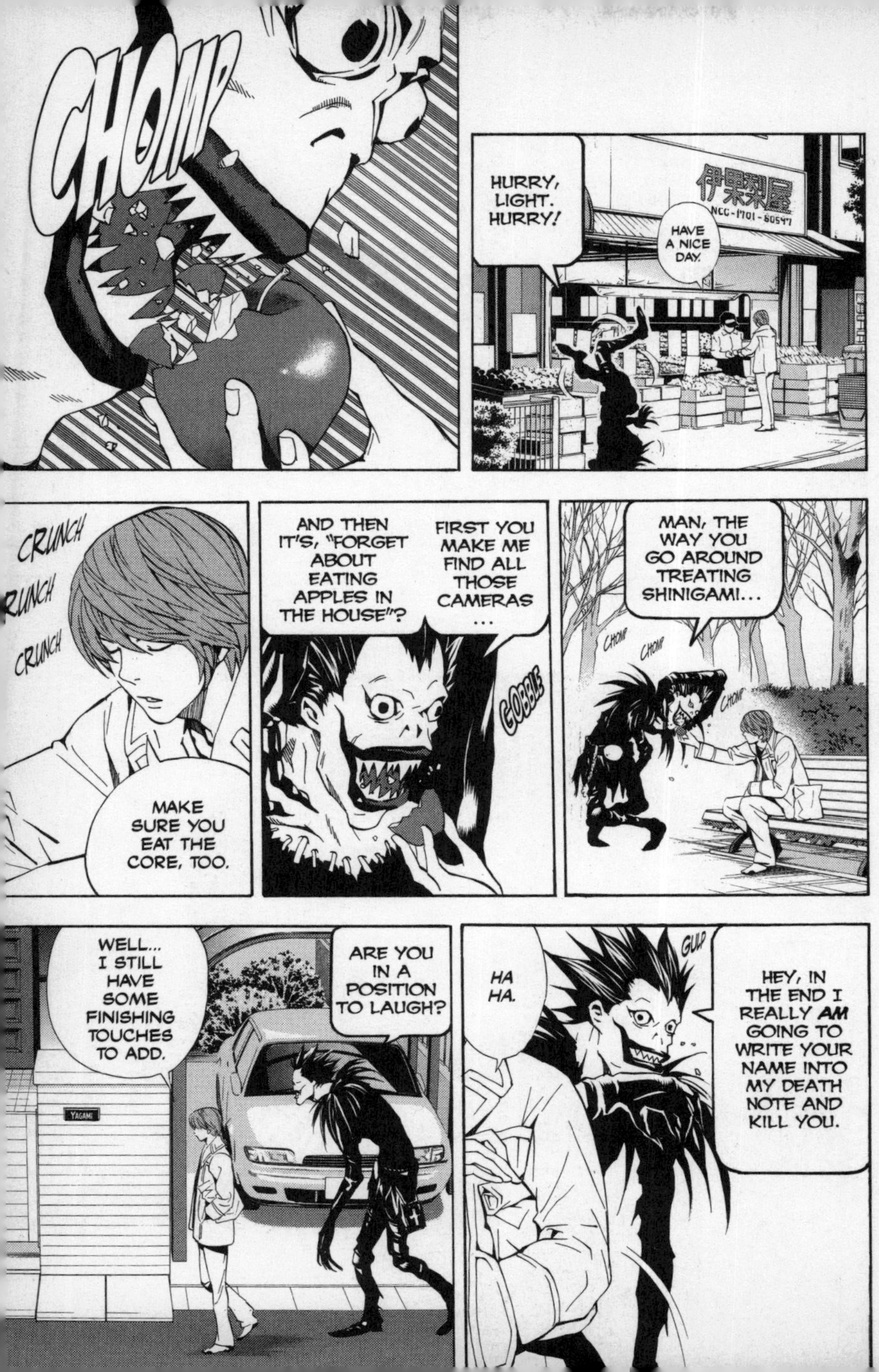

HURRY, LIGHT. HURRY!
伊果梨屋
HAVE A NICE DAY.
CHOMP
MAN, THE WAY YOU GO AROUND TREATING SHINIGAMI...
CHOMP
CHOMP
CHOMP
FIRST YOU MAKE ME FIND ALL THOSE CAMERAS ...
AND THEN IT'S, "FORGET ABOUT EATING APPLES IN THE HOUSE"?
GOBBLE
CRUNCH
CRUNCH
CRUNCH
MAKE SURE YOU EAT THE CORE, TOO.
GULP
HEY, IN THE END I REALLY ***AM*** GOING TO WRITE YOUR NAME INTO MY DEATH NOTE AND KILL YOU.
HA HA.
ARE YOU IN A POSITION TO LAUGH?
WELL... I STILL HAVE SOME FINISHING TOUCHES TO ADD.
YAGAMI

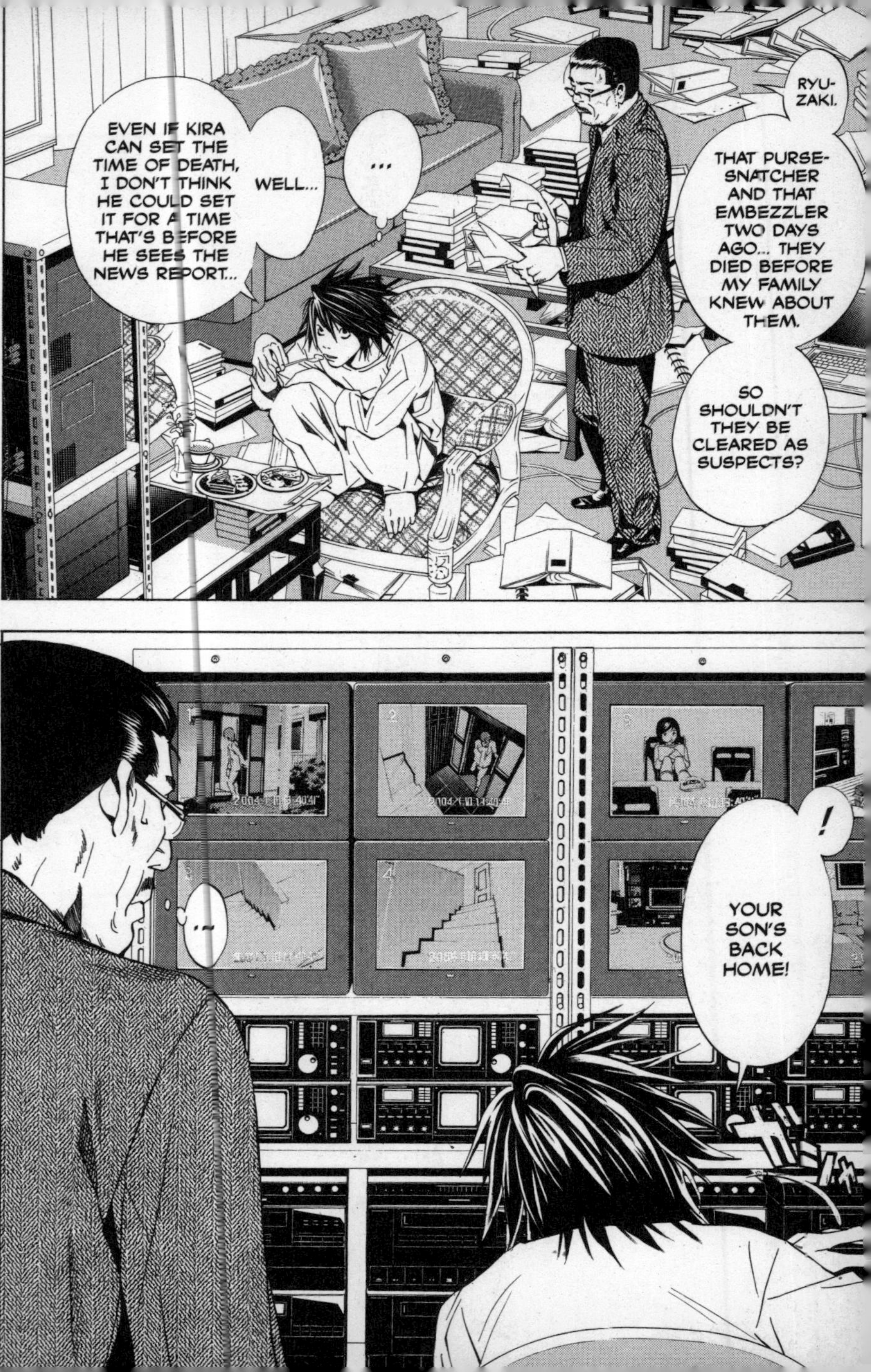
RYU-ZAKI.
THAT PURSE-SNATCHER AND THAT EMBEZZLER TWO DAYS AGO... THEY DIED BEFORE MY FAMILY KNEW ABOUT THEM.
SO SHOULDN'T THEY BE CLEARED AS SUSPECTS?
...
WELL...
EVEN IF KIRA CAN SET THE TIME OF DEATH, I DON'T THINK HE COULD SET IT FOR A TIME THAT'S BEFORE HE SEES THE NEWS REPORT...
!
YOUR SON'S BACK HOME!
...

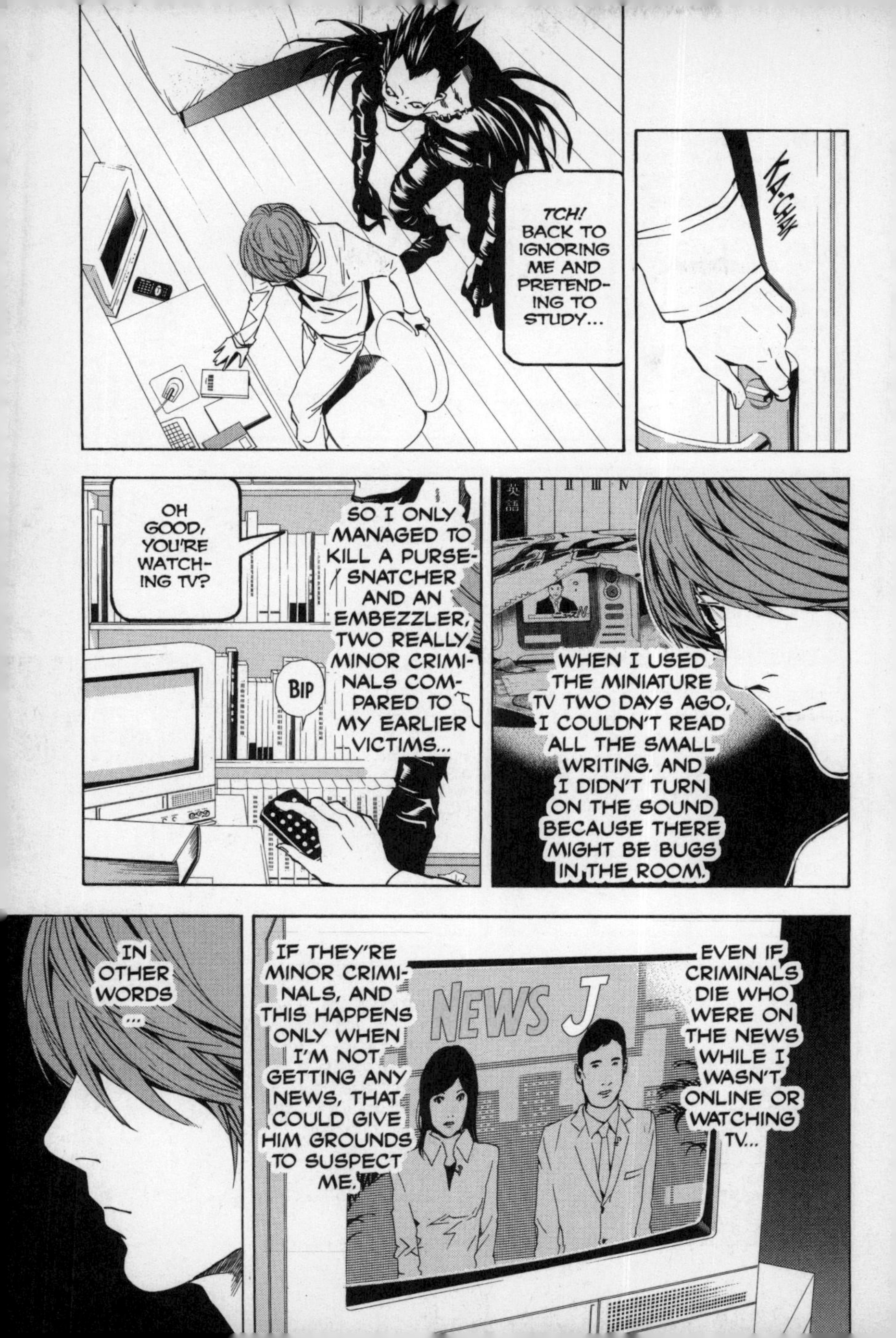
KA-CHAK
TCH! BACK TO IGNORING ME AND PRETENDING TO STUDY...
WHEN I USED THE MINIATURE TV TWO DAYS AGO, I COULDN'T READ ALL THE SMALL WRITING. AND I DIDN'T TURN ON THE SOUND BECAUSE THERE MIGHT BE BUGS IN THE ROOM.
SO I ONLY MANAGED TO KILL A PURSE-SNATCHER AND AN EMBEZZLER, TWO REALLY MINOR CRIMINALS COMPARED TO MY EARLIER VICTIMS...
OH GOOD, YOU'RE WATCHING TV?
BIP
EVEN IF CRIMINALS DIE WHO WERE ON THE NEWS WHILE I WASN'T ONLINE OR WATCHING TV...
NEWS J
IF THEY'RE MINOR CRIMINALS, AND THIS HAPPENS ONLY WHEN I'M NOT GETTING ANY NEWS, THAT COULD GIVE HIM GROUNDS TO SUSPECT ME.
IN OTHER WORDS...

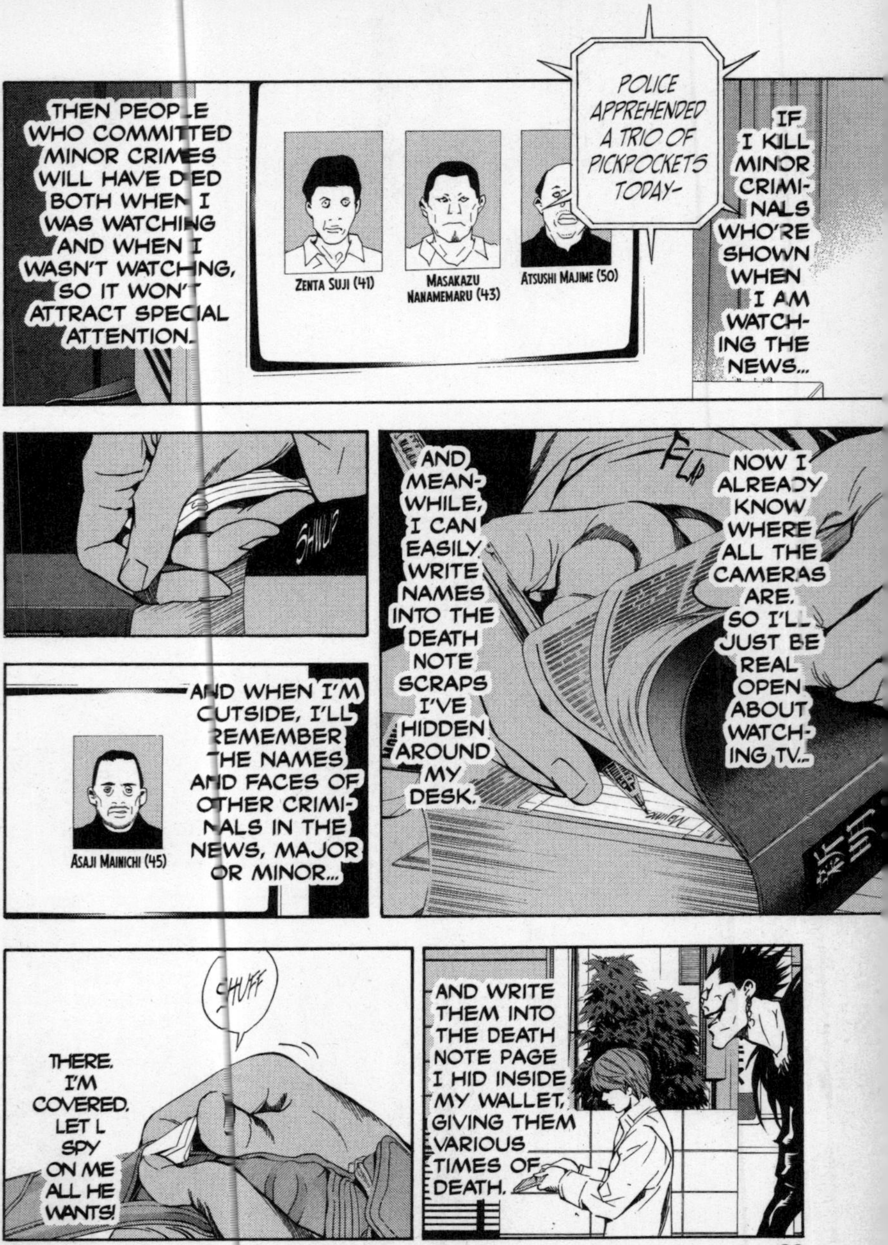
IF I KILL MINOR CRIMINALS WHO'RE SHOWN WHEN I AM WATCHING THE NEWS...
POLICE APPREHENDED A TRIO OF PICKPOCKETS TODAY-
ZENTA SUJI (41)
MASAKAZU NANAMEMARU (43)
ATSUSHI MAJIME (50)
THEN PEOPLE WHO COMMITTED MINOR CRIMES WILL HAVE DIED BOTH WHEN I WAS WATCHING AND WHEN I WASN'T WATCHING, SO IT WON'T ATTRACT SPECIAL ATTENTION...
NOW I ALREADY KNOW WHERE ALL THE CAMERAS ARE. SO I'LL JUST BE REAL OPEN ABOUT WATCHING TV...
FLAP
AND MEANWHILE, I CAN EASILY WRITE NAMES INTO THE DEATH NOTE SCRAPS I'VE HIDDEN AROUND MY DESK.
SHWUP
AND WHEN I'M OUTSIDE, I'LL REMEMBER THE NAMES AND FACES OF OTHER CRIMINALS IN THE NEWS, MAJOR OR MINOR...
ASAJI MAINICHI (45)
AND WRITE THEM INTO THE DEATH NOTE PAGE I HID INSIDE MY WALLET, GIVING THEM VARIOUS TIMES OF DEATH.
SHUFF
THERE. I'M COVERED. LET L SPY ON ME ALL HE WANTS!

READ THIS WAY

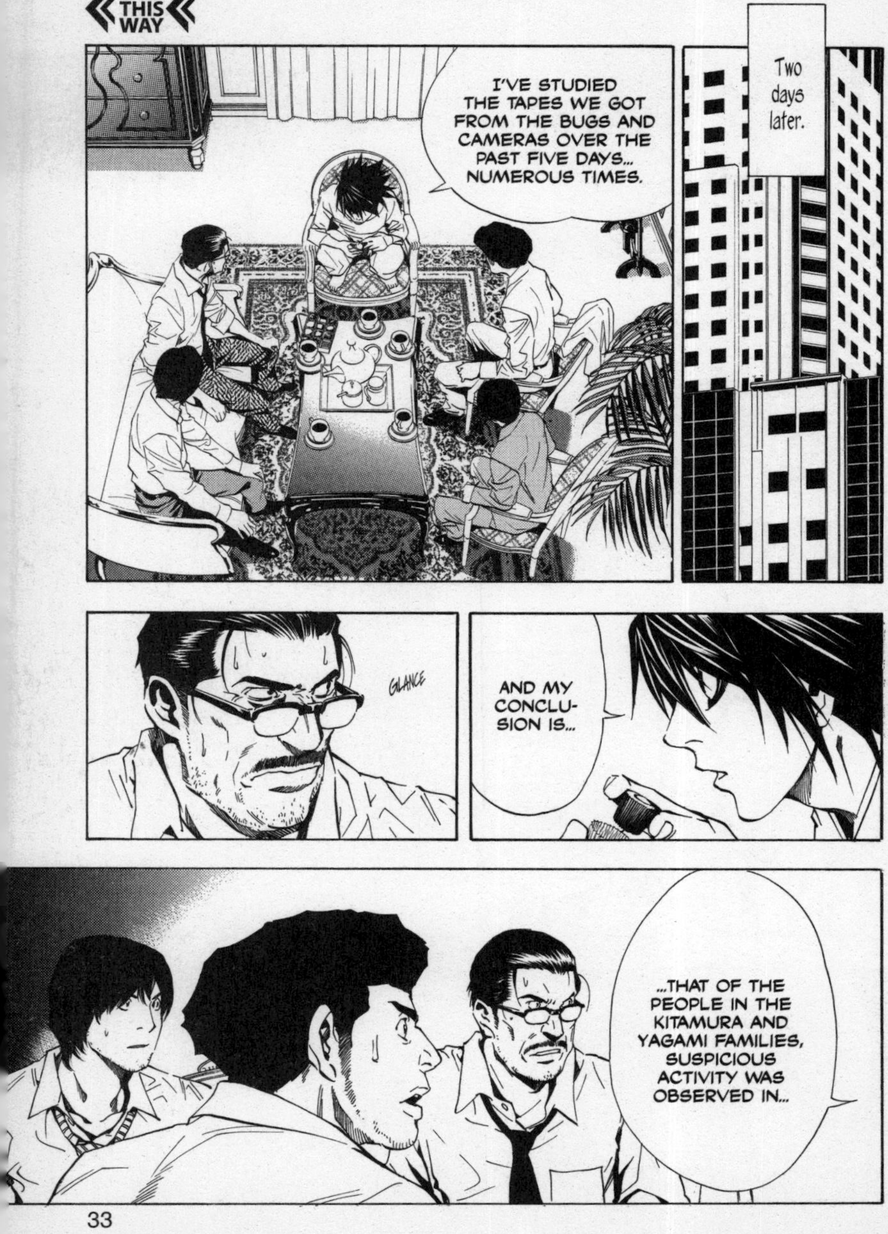

Two days later.
I'VE STUDIED THE TAPES WE GOT FROM THE BUGS AND CAMERAS OVER THE PAST FIVE DAYS... NUMEROUS TIMES.
AND MY CONCLUSION IS...
GLANCE
...THAT OF THE PEOPLE IN THE KITAMURA AND YAGAMI FAMILIES, SUSPICIOUS ACTIVITY WAS OBSERVED IN...

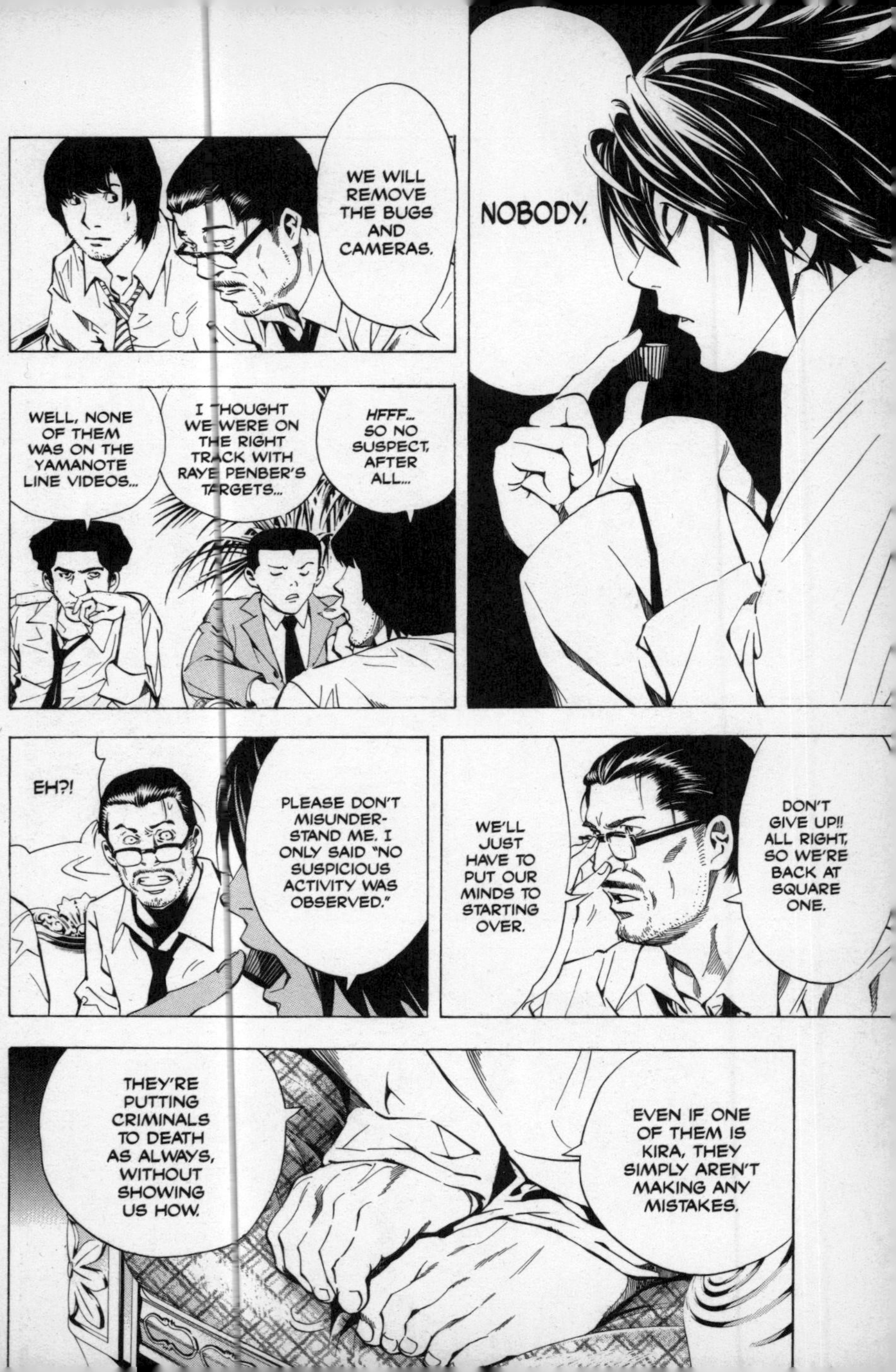
NOBODY.
WE WILL REMOVE THE BUGS AND CAMERAS.
HFFF... SO NO SUSPECT, AFTER ALL...
I THOUGHT WE WERE ON THE RIGHT TRACK WITH RAYE PENBER'S TARGETS...
WELL, NONE OF THEM WAS ON THE YAMANOTE LINE VIDEOS...
DON'T GIVE UP!! ALL RIGHT, SO WE'RE BACK AT SQUARE ONE.
WE'LL JUST HAVE TO PUT OUR MINDS TO STARTING OVER.
PLEASE DON'T MISUNDER-STAND ME. I ONLY SAID "NO SUSPICIOUS ACTIVITY WAS OBSERVED."
EH?!
EVEN IF ONE OF THEM IS KIRA, THEY SIMPLY AREN'T MAKING ANY MISTAKES.
THEY'RE PUTTING CRIMINALS TO DEATH AS ALWAYS, WITHOUT SHOWING US HOW.

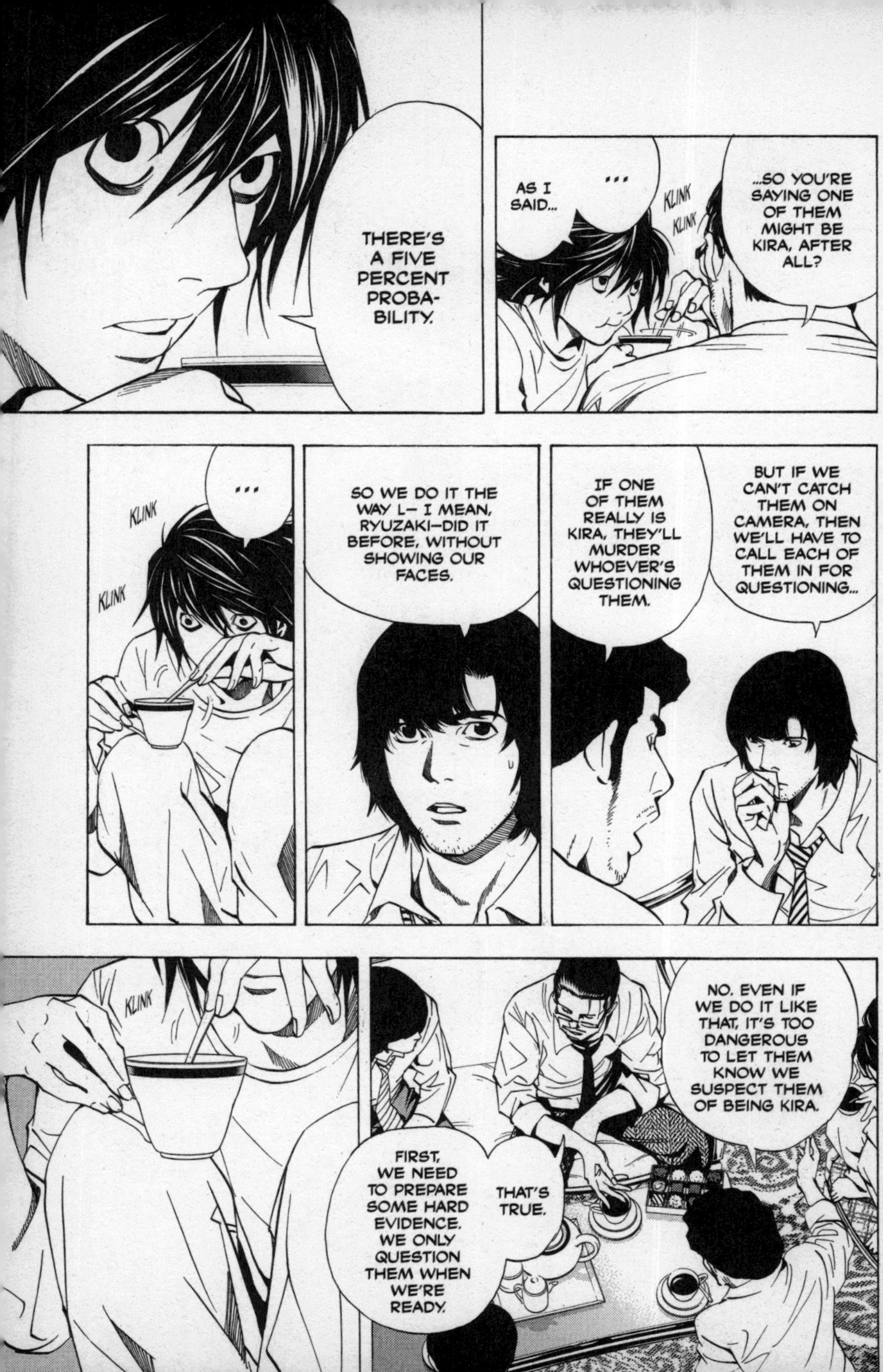
...SO YOU'RE SAYING ONE OF THEM MIGHT BE KIRA, AFTER ALL?
KLINK
KLINK
...
AS I SAID...
THERE'S A FIVE PERCENT PROBA-BILITY.
BUT IF WE CAN'T CATCH THEM ON CAMERA, THEN WE'LL HAVE TO CALL EACH OF THEM IN FOR QUESTIONING...
IF ONE OF THEM REALLY IS KIRA, THEY'LL MURDER WHOEVER'S QUESTIONING THEM.
SO WE DO IT THE WAY L— I MEAN, RYUZAKI—DID IT BEFORE, WITHOUT SHOWING OUR FACES.
...
KLINK
KLINK
NO. EVEN IF WE DO IT LIKE THAT, IT'S TOO DANGEROUS TO LET THEM KNOW WE SUSPECT THEM OF BEING KIRA.
THAT'S TRUE.
FIRST, WE NEED TO PREPARE SOME HARD EVIDENCE. WE ONLY QUESTION THEM WHEN WE'RE READY.
KLINK

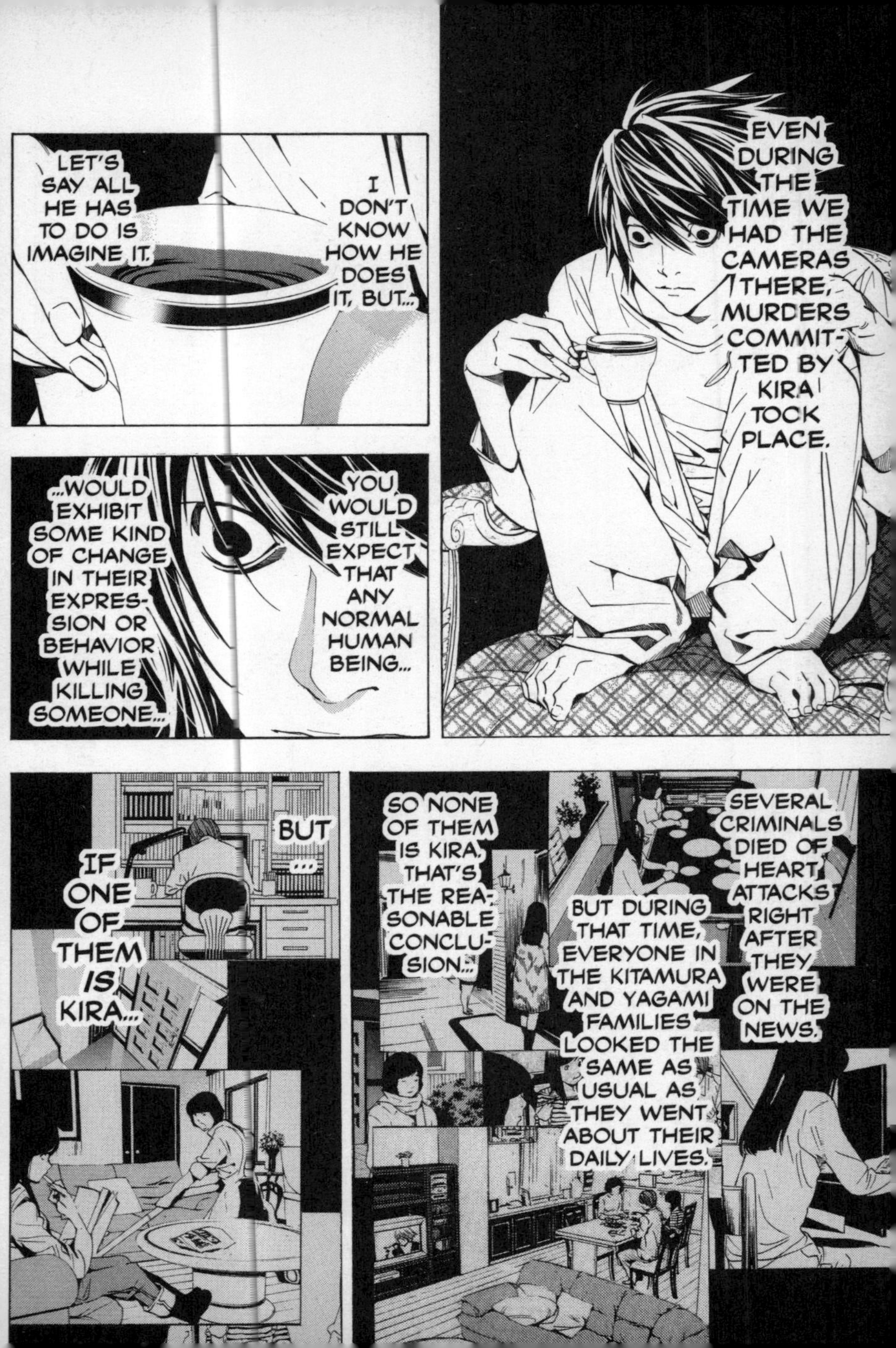
EVEN DURING THE TIME WE HAD THE CAMERAS THERE, MURDERS COMMITTED BY KIRA TOCK PLACE.
I DON'T KNOW HOW HE DOES IT, BUT...
LET'S SAY ALL HE HAS TO DO IS IMAGINE IT.
YOU WOULD STILL EXPECT THAT ANY NORMAL HUMAN BEING...
...WOULD EXHIBIT SOME KIND OF CHANGE IN THEIR EXPRESSION OR BEHAVIOR WHILE KILLING SOMEONE...
SEVERAL CRIMINALS DIED OF HEART ATTACKS RIGHT AFTER THEY WERE ON THE NEWS.
BUT DURING THAT TIME, EVERYONE IN THE KITAMURA AND YAGAMI FAMILIES LOOKED THE SAME AS USUAL AS THEY WENT ABOUT THEIR DAILY LIVES.
SO NONE OF THEM IS KIRA, THAT'S THE REASONABLE CONCLUSION...
BUT...
IF ONE OF THEM IS KIRA...

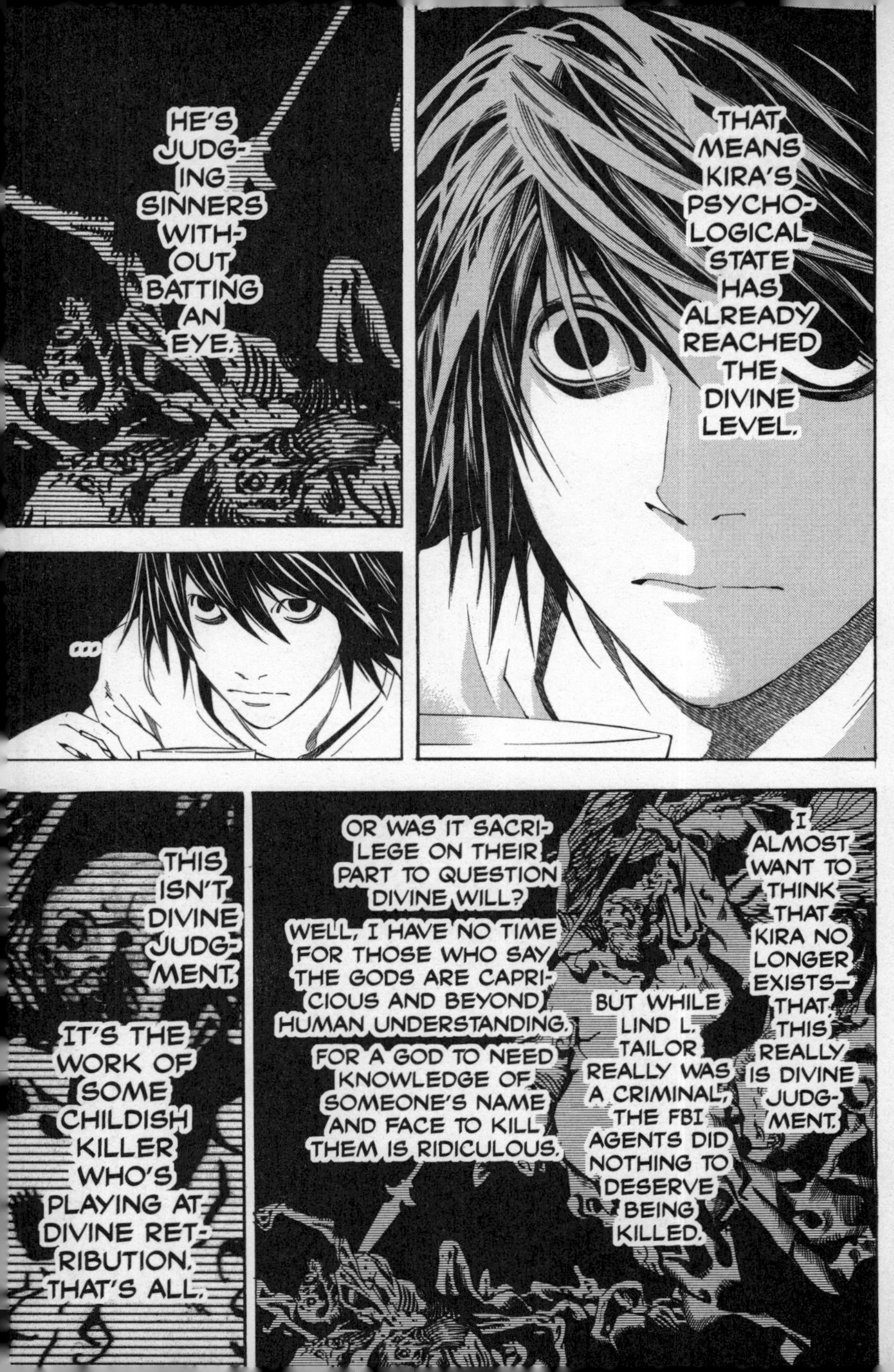
THAT MEANS KIRA'S PSYCHOLOGICAL STATE HAS ALREADY REACHED THE DIVINE LEVEL.
HE'S JUDGING SINNERS WITHOUT BATTING AN EYE.
...
I ALMOST WANT TO THINK THAT KIRA NO LONGER EXISTS—THAT THIS REALLY IS DIVINE JUDGMENT.
BUT WHILE LIND L. TAILOR REALLY WAS A CRIMINAL, THE FBI AGENTS DID NOTHING TO DESERVE BEING KILLED.
OR WAS IT SACRILEGE ON THEIR PART TO QUESTION DIVINE WILL?
WELL, I HAVE NO TIME FOR THOSE WHO SAY THE GODS ARE CAPRICIOUS AND BEYOND HUMAN UNDERSTANDING.
FOR A GOD TO NEED KNOWLEDGE OF SOMEONE'S NAME AND FACE TO KILL THEM IS RIDICULOUS.
THIS ISN'T DIVINE JUDGMENT.
IT'S THE WORK OF SOME CHILDISH KILLER WHO'S PLAYING AT DIVINE RETRIBUTION. THAT'S ALL.

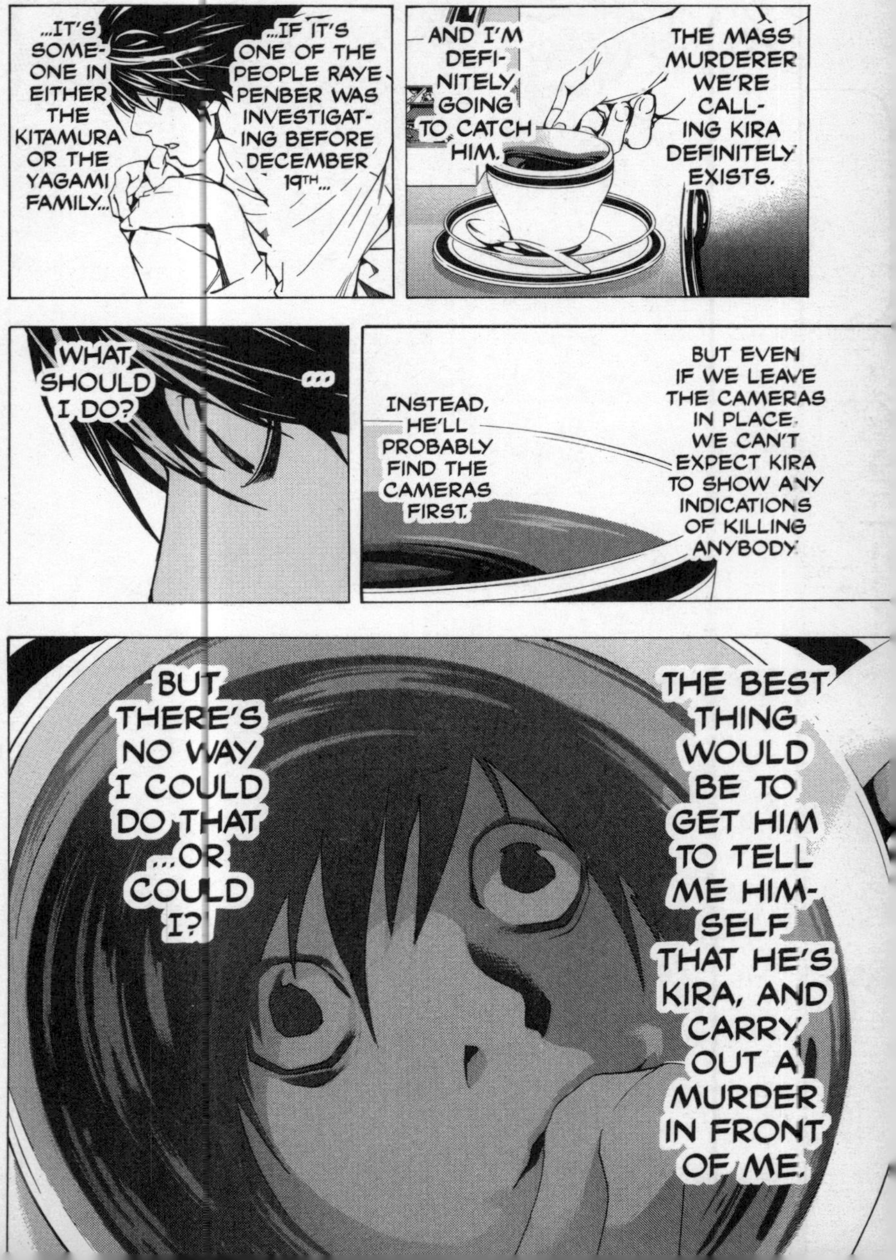
THE MASS MURDERER WE'RE CALLING KIRA DEFINITELY EXISTS.
AND I'M DEFINITELY GOING TO CATCH HIM.
...IF IT'S ONE OF THE PEOPLE RAYE PENBER WAS INVESTIGATING BEFORE DECEMBER 19TH...
...IT'S SOMEONE IN EITHER THE KITAMURA OR THE YAGAMI FAMILY...
BUT EVEN IF WE LEAVE THE CAMERAS IN PLACE, WE CAN'T EXPECT KIRA TO SHOW ANY INDICATIONS OF KILLING ANYBODY.
INSTEAD, HE'LL PROBABLY FIND THE CAMERAS FIRST.
...
WHAT SHOULD I DO?
THE BEST THING WOULD BE TO GET HIM TO TELL ME HIMSELF THAT HE'S KIRA, AND CARRY OUT A MURDER IN FRONT OF ME.
BUT THERE'S NO WAY I COULD DO THAT ...OR COULD I?

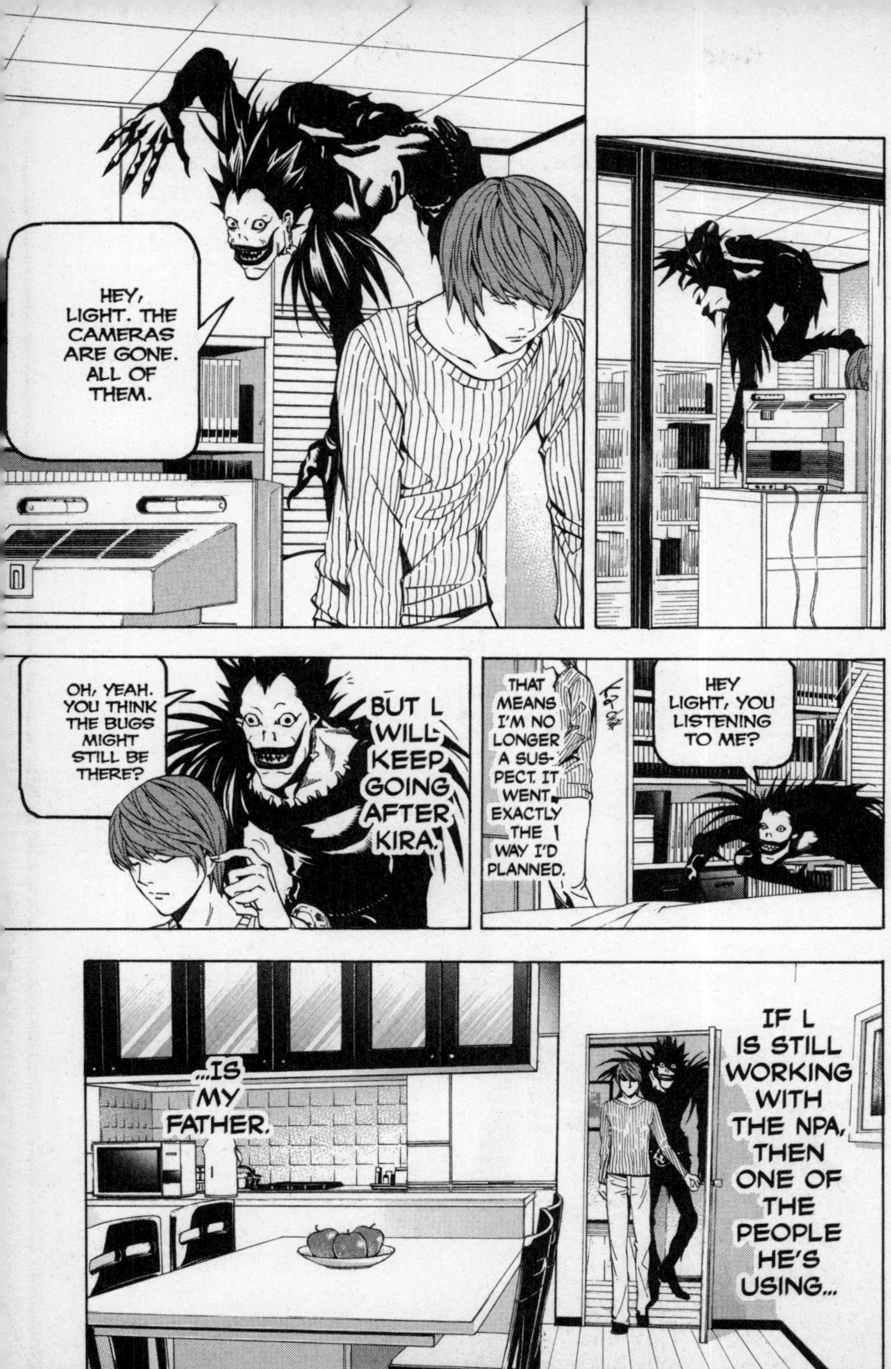
HEY, LIGHT. THE CAMERAS ARE GONE. ALL OF THEM.
HEY LIGHT, YOU LISTENING TO ME?
THAT MEANS I'M NO LONGER A SUSPECT. IT WENT EXACTLY THE WAY I'D PLANNED.
BUT L WILL KEEP GOING AFTER KIRA.
OH, YEAH. YOU THINK THE BUGS MIGHT STILL BE THERE?
IF L IS STILL WORKING WITH THE NPA, THEN ONE OF THE PEOPLE HE'S USING...
...IS MY FATHER.

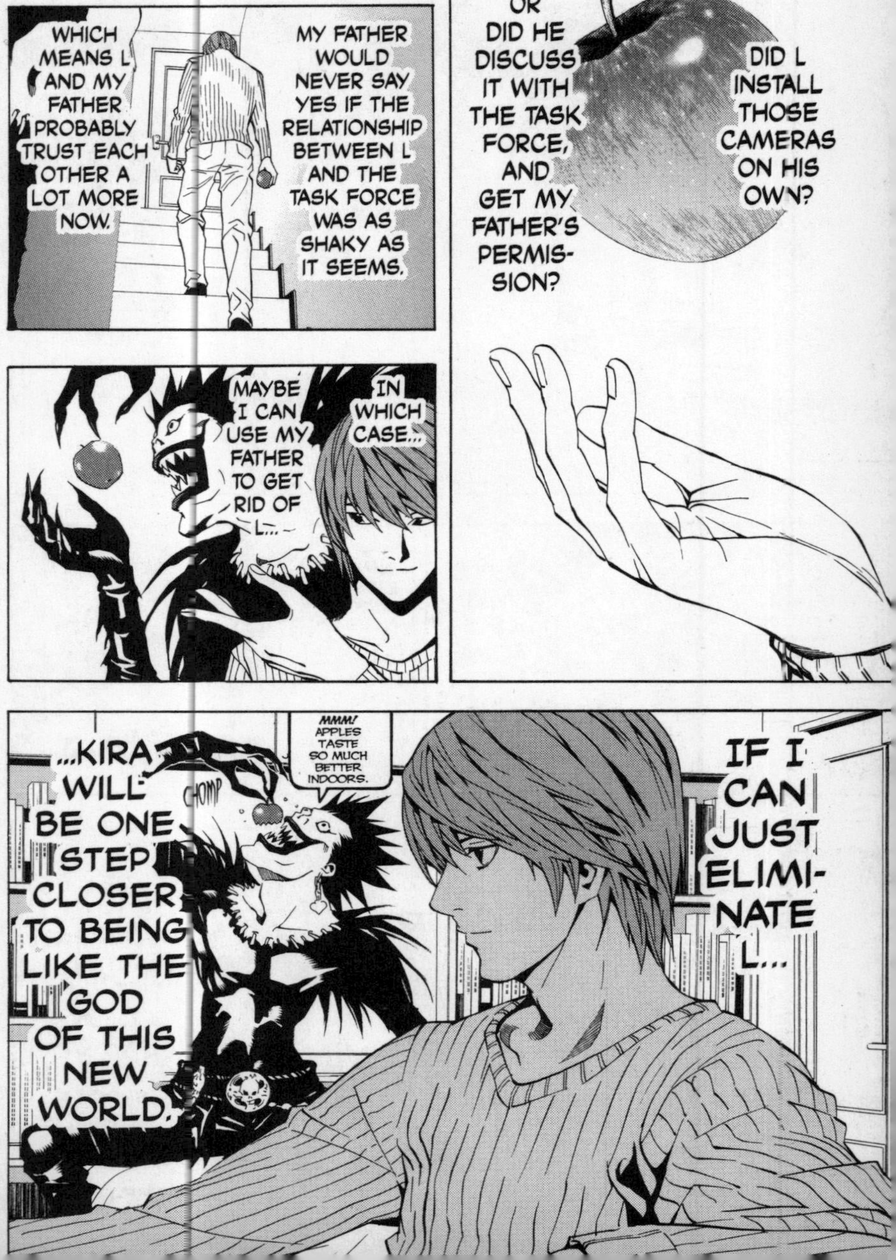
DID L INSTALL THOSE CAMERAS ON HIS OWN?
OR DID HE DISCUSS IT WITH THE TASK FORCE, AND GET MY FATHER'S PERMIS-SION?
MY FATHER WOULD NEVER SAY YES IF THE RELATIONSHIP BETWEEN L AND THE TASK FORCE WAS AS SHAKY AS IT SEEMS.
WHICH MEANS L AND MY FATHER PROBABLY TRUST EACH OTHER A LOT MORE NOW.
IN WHICH CASE...
MAYBE I CAN USE MY FATHER TO GET RID OF L...
IF I CAN JUST ELIMI-NATE L...
MMM! APPLES TASTE SO MUCH BETTER INDOORS.
CHOMP
...KIRA WILL BE ONE STEP CLOSER TO BEING LIKE THE GOD OF THIS NEW WORLD.

READ THIS WAY

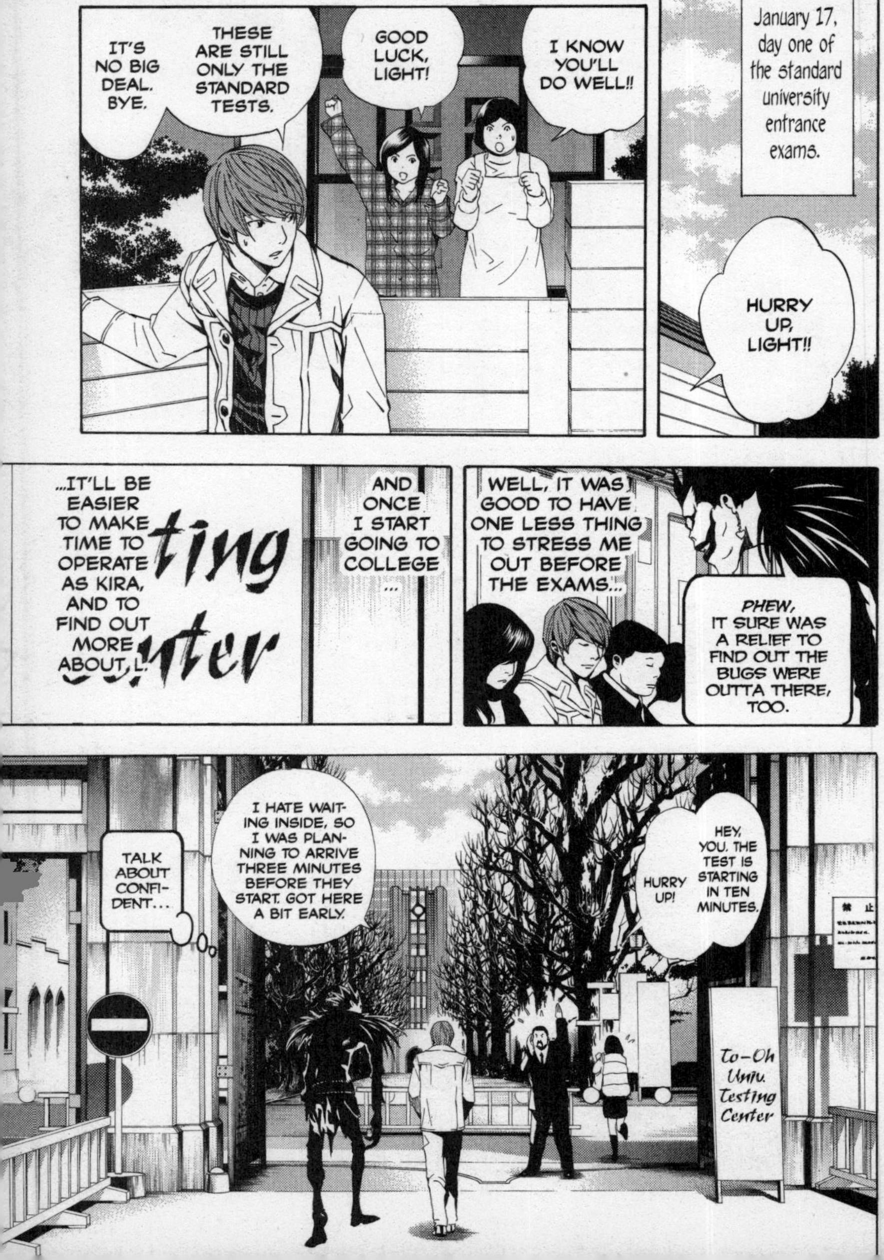
January 17, day one of the standard university entrance exams.
HURRY UP, LIGHT!!
I KNOW YOU'LL DO WELL!!
GOOD LUCK, LIGHT!
THESE ARE STILL ONLY THE STANDARD TESTS.
IT'S NO BIG DEAL. BYE.
PHEW, IT SURE WAS A RELIEF TO FIND OUT THE BUGS WERE OUTTA THERE, TOO.
WELL, IT WAS GOOD TO HAVE ONE LESS THING TO STRESS ME OUT BEFORE THE EXAMS...
AND ONCE I START GOING TO COLLEGE...
...IT'LL BE EASIER TO MAKE TIME TO OPERATE AS KIRA, AND TO FIND OUT MORE ABOUT L.
HEY, YOU. THE TEST IS STARTING IN TEN MINUTES.
HURRY UP!
To-Oh Univ. Testing Center
I HATE WAITING INSIDE, SO I WAS PLANNING TO ARRIVE THREE MINUTES BEFORE THEY START. GOT HERE A BIT EARLY.
TALK ABOUT CONFIDENT...

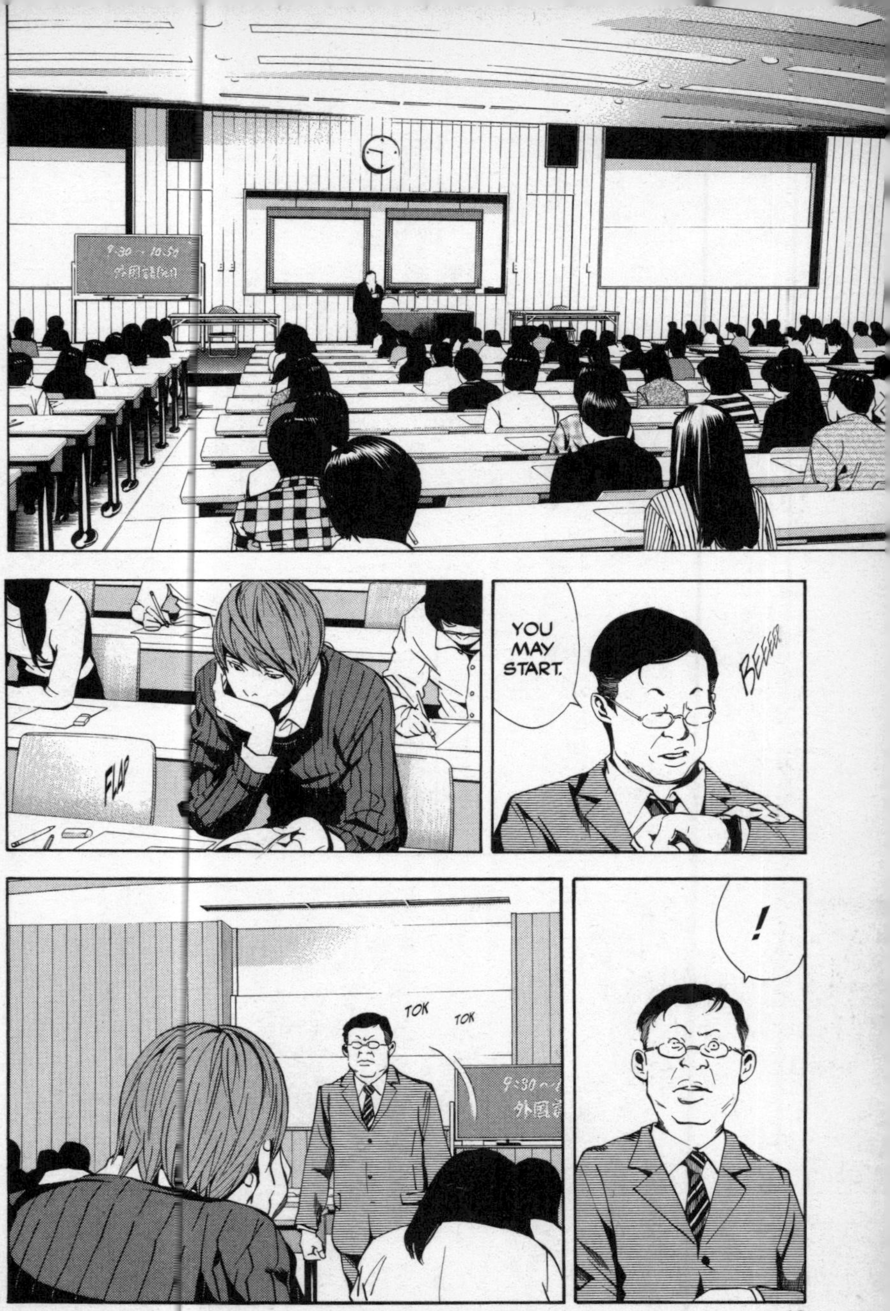
YOU MAY START.
BEEEP
FLAP
!
TOK
TOK

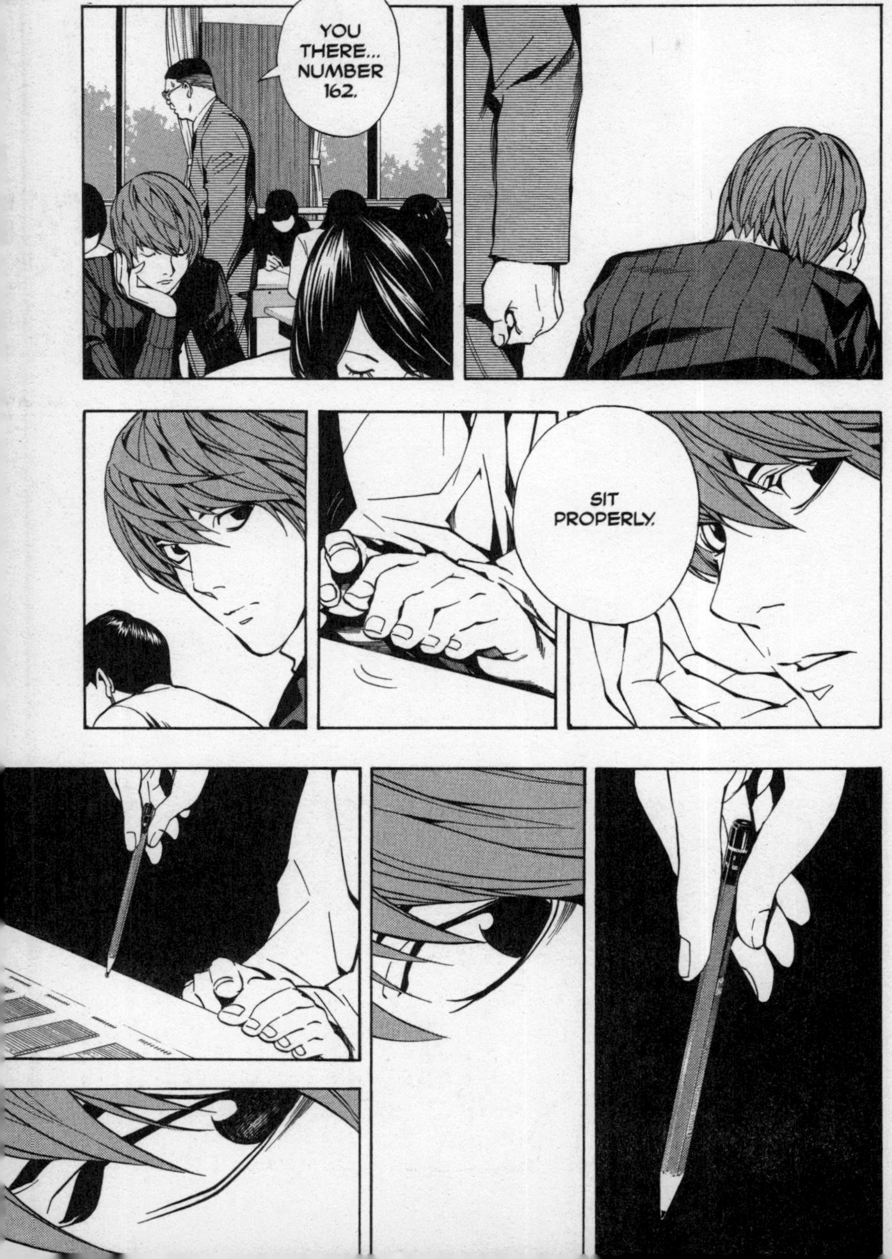
YOU THERE... NUMBER 162.
SIT PROPERLY.

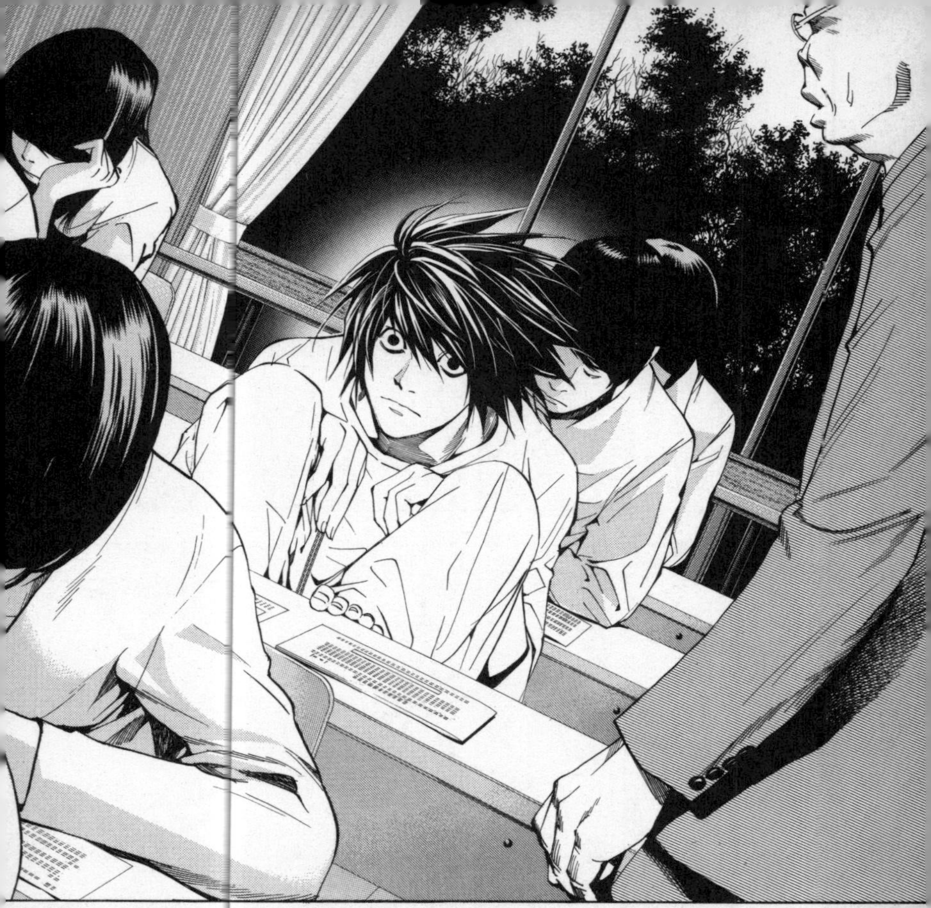
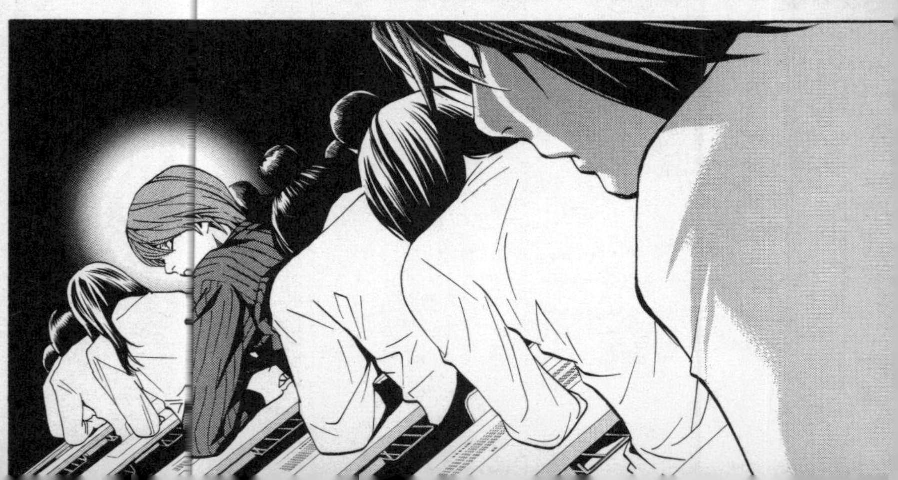

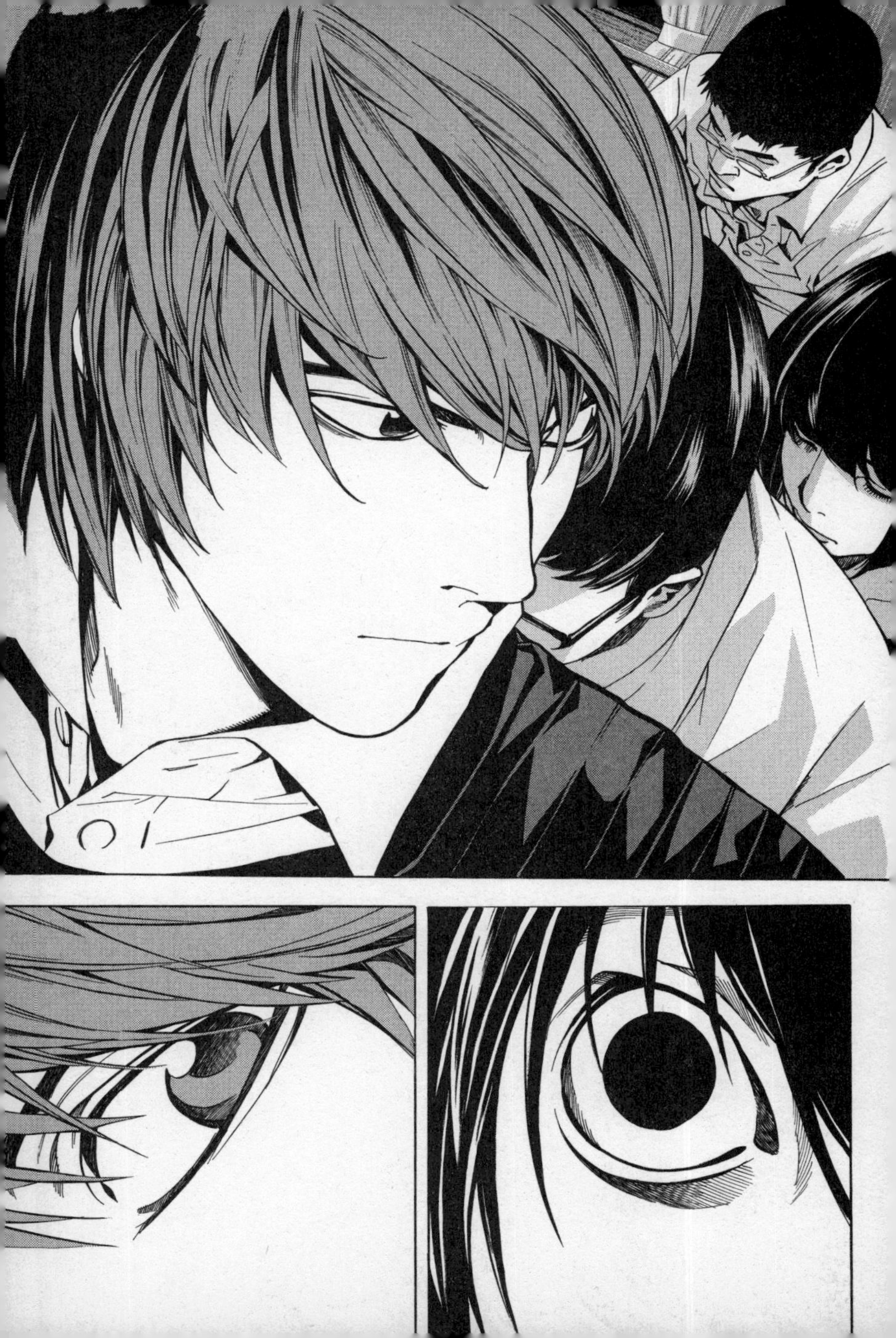

chapter 19 Humiliation

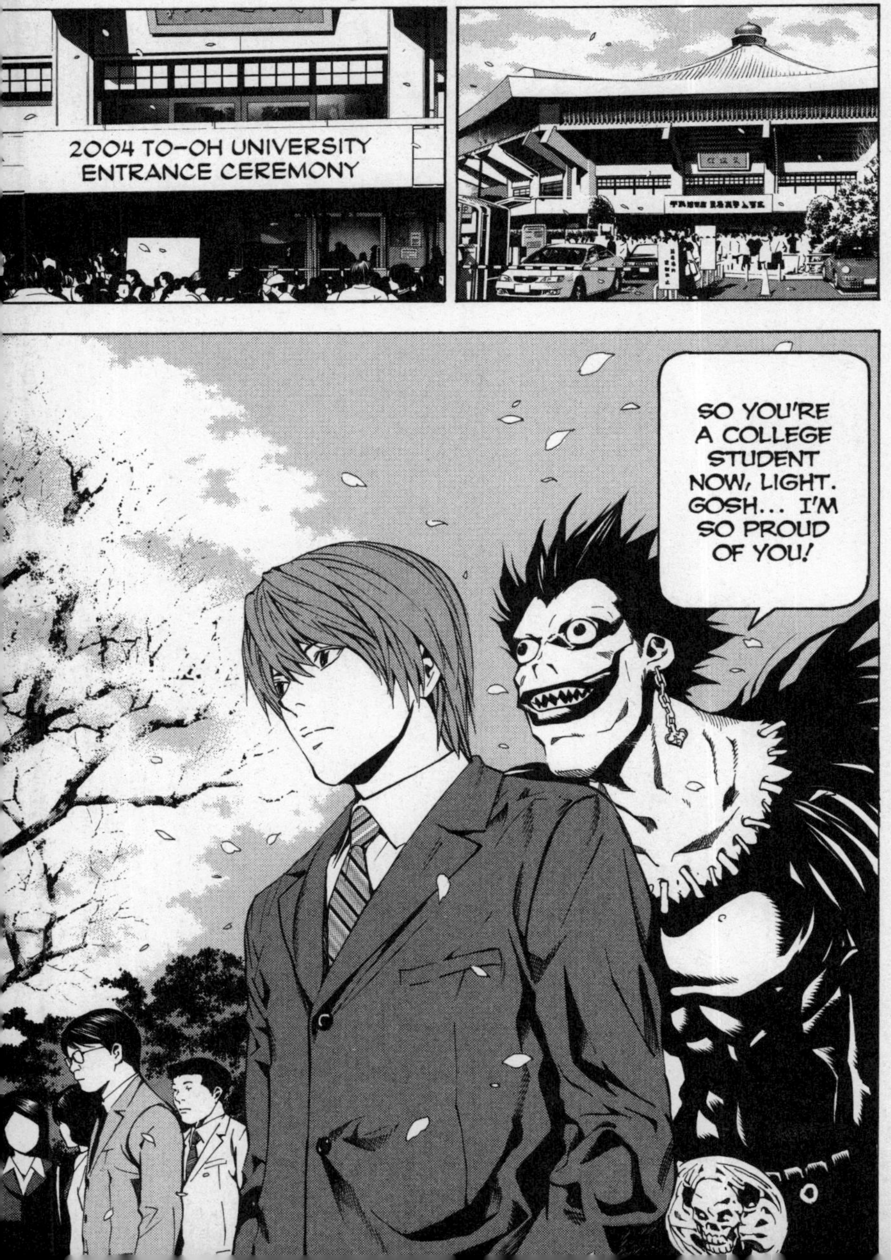
2004 TO-OH UNIVERSITY ENTRANCE CEREMONY
SO YOU'RE A COLLEGE STUDENT NOW, LIGHT. GOSH... I'M SO PROUD OF YOU!

chapter 19 Humiliation

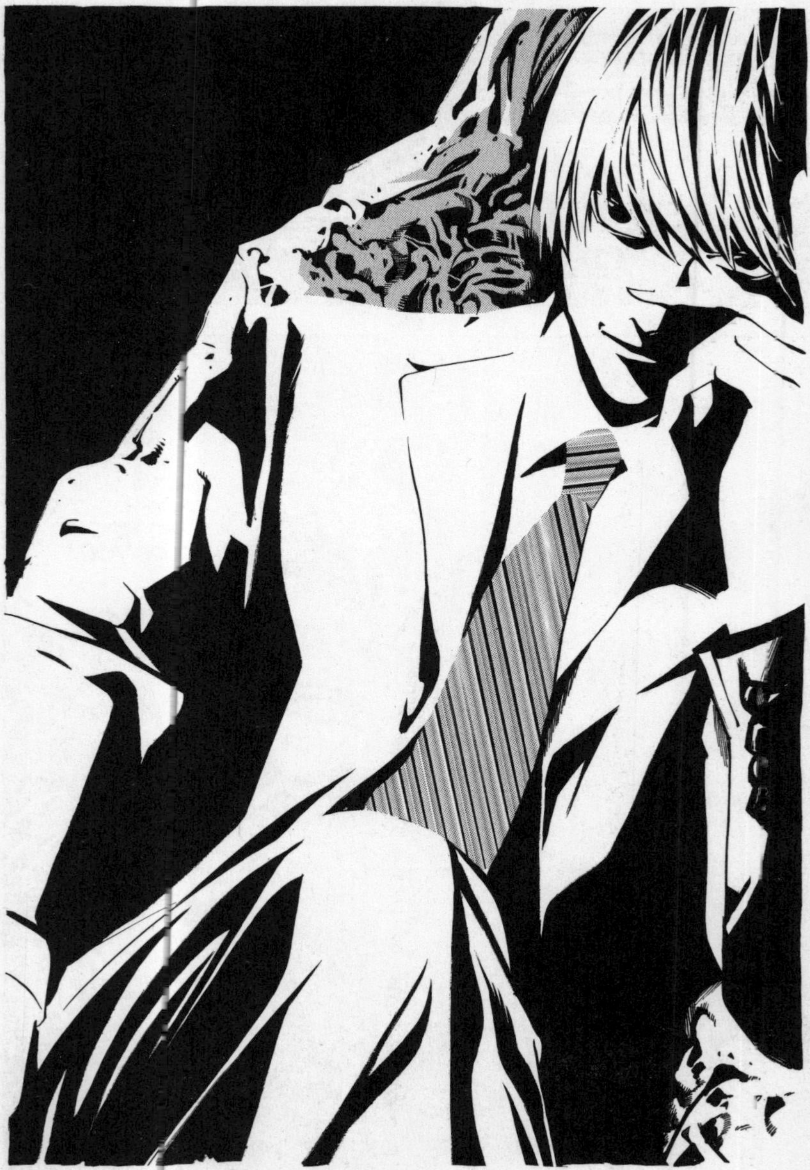

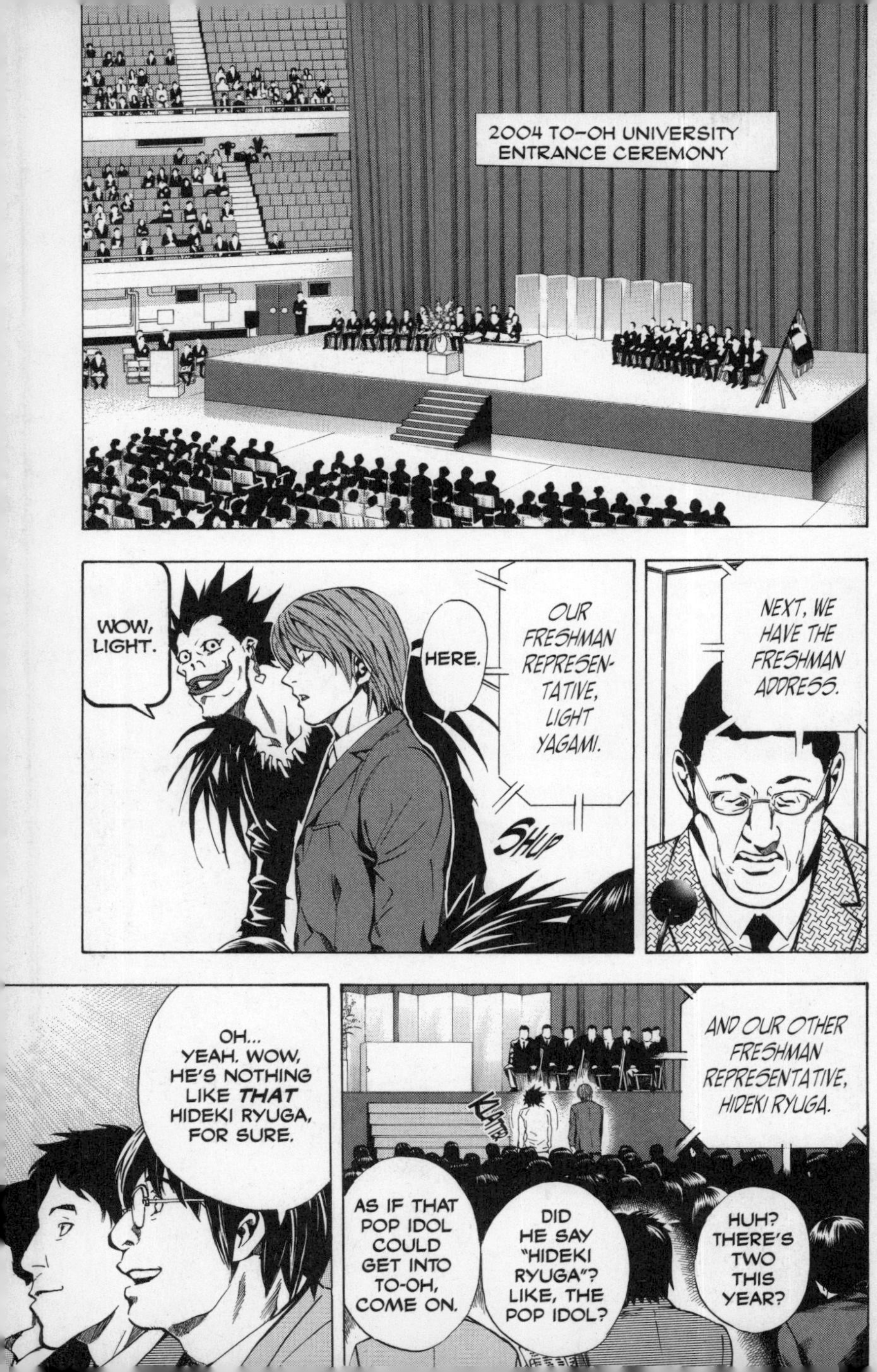

2004 TO-OH UNIVERSITY ENTRANCE CEREMONY
NEXT, WE HAVE THE FRESHMAN ADDRESS.
OUR FRESHMAN REPRESENTATIVE, LIGHT YAGAMI.
HERE.
SHUP
WOW, LIGHT.
AND OUR OTHER FRESHMAN REPRESENTATIVE, HIDEKI RYUGA.
HUH? THERE'S TWO THIS YEAR?
DID HE SAY "HIDEKI RYUGA"? LIKE, THE POP IDOL?
AS IF THAT POP IDOL COULD GET INTO TO-OH, COME ON.
OH... YEAH. WOW, HE'S NOTHING LIKE *THAT* HIDEKI RYUGA, FOR SURE.

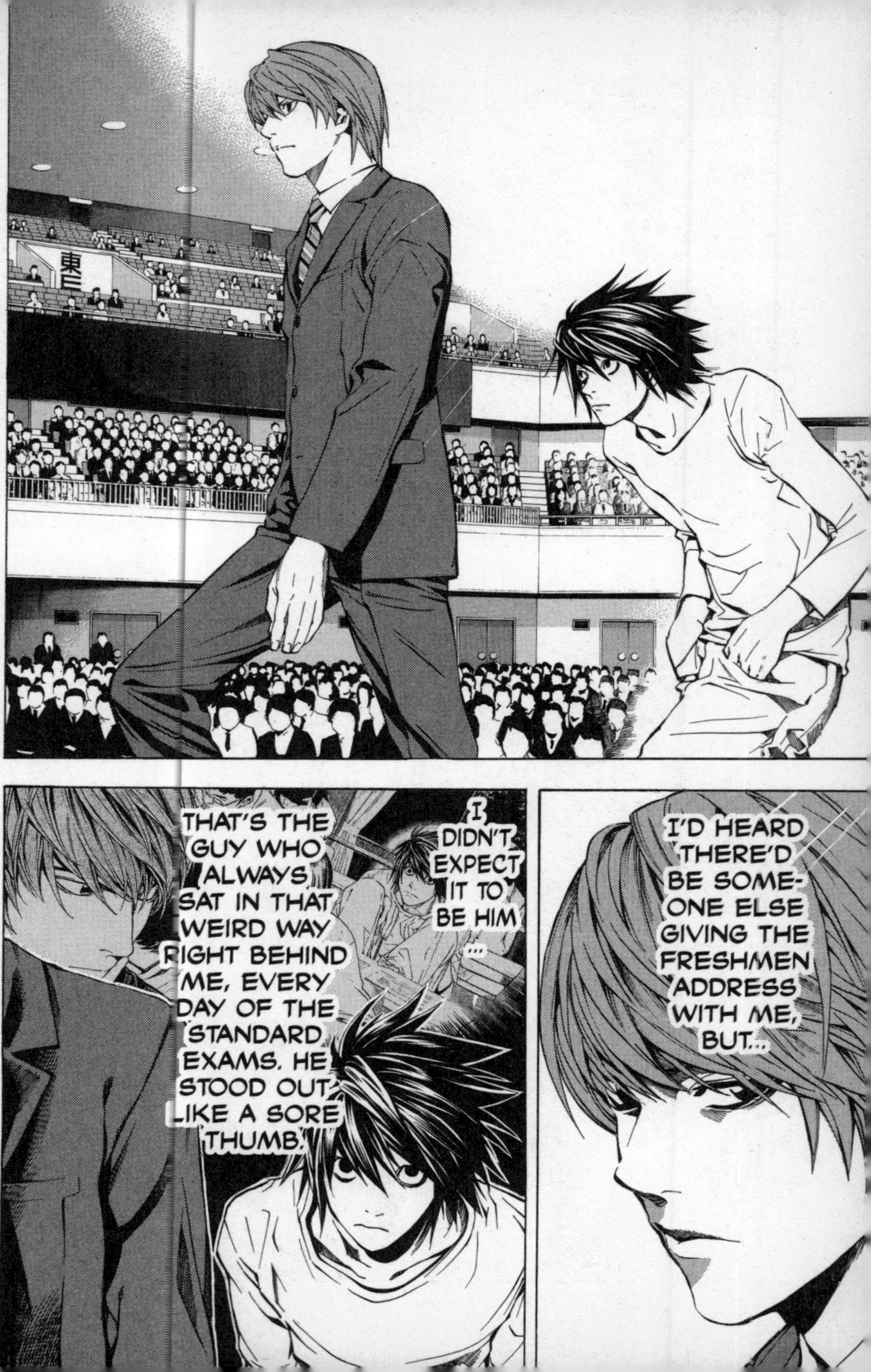
I'D HEARD THERE'D BE SOME-ONE ELSE GIVING THE FRESHMEN ADDRESS WITH ME, BUT...
I DIDN'T EXPECT IT TO BE HIM...
THAT'S THE GUY WHO ALWAYS SAT IN THAT WEIRD WAY RIGHT BEHIND ME, EVERY DAY OF THE STANDARD EXAMS. HE STOOD OUT LIKE A SORE THUMB.

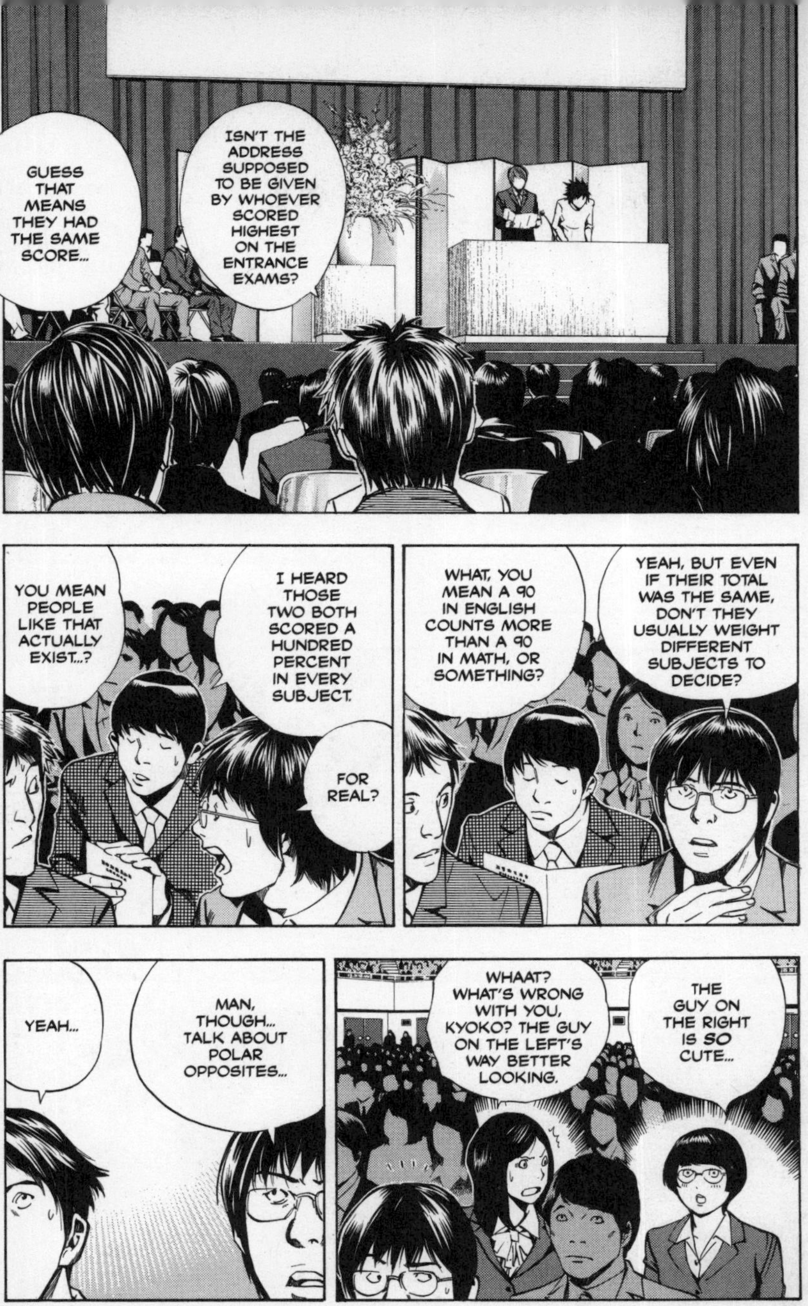
ISN'T THE ADDRESS SUPPOSED TO BE GIVEN BY WHOEVER SCORED HIGHEST ON THE ENTRANCE EXAMS?
GUESS THAT MEANS THEY HAD THE SAME SCORE...
YEAH, BUT EVEN IF THEIR TOTAL WAS THE SAME, DON'T THEY USUALLY WEIGHT DIFFERENT SUBJECTS TO DECIDE?
WHAT, YOU MEAN A 90 IN ENGLISH COUNTS MORE THAN A 90 IN MATH, OR SOMETHING?
I HEARD THOSE TWO BOTH SCORED A HUNDRED PERCENT IN EVERY SUBJECT.
FOR REAL?
YOU MEAN PEOPLE LIKE THAT ACTUALLY EXIST...?
THE GUY ON THE RIGHT IS SO CUTE...
WHAAT? WHAT'S WRONG WITH YOU, KYOKO? THE GUY ON THE LEFT'S WAY BETTER LOOKING.
MAN, THOUGH... TALK ABOUT POLAR OPPOSITES...
YEAH...

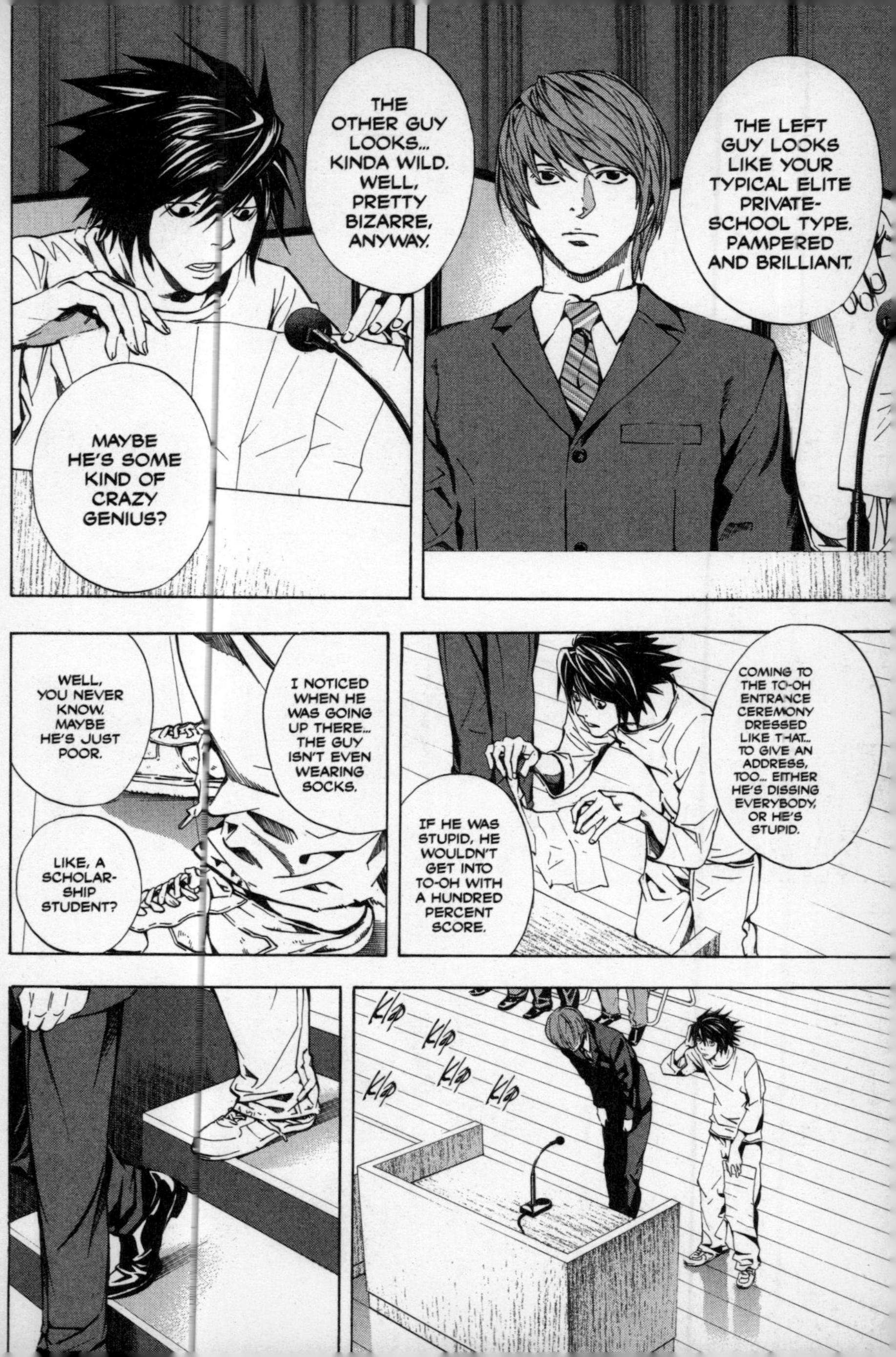
THE LEFT GUY LOOKS LIKE YOUR TYPICAL ELITE PRIVATE-SCHOOL TYPE. PAMPERED AND BRILLIANT.
THE OTHER GUY LOOKS... KINDA WILD. WELL, PRETTY BIZARRE, ANYWAY.
MAYBE HE'S SOME KIND OF CRAZY GENIUS?
COMING TO THE TO-OH ENTRANCE CEREMONY DRESSED LIKE THAT... TO GIVE AN ADDRESS, TOO... EITHER HE'S DISSING EVERYBODY, OR HE'S STUPID.
IF HE WAS STUPID, HE WOULDN'T GET INTO TO-OH WITH A HUNDRED PERCENT SCORE.
I NOTICED WHEN HE WAS GOING UP THERE... THE GUY ISN'T EVEN WEARING SOCKS.
WELL, YOU NEVER KNOW. MAYBE HE'S JUST POOR.
LIKE, A SCHOLARSHIP STUDENT?
KLAP
KLAP
KLAP
KLAP
KLAP
KLAP

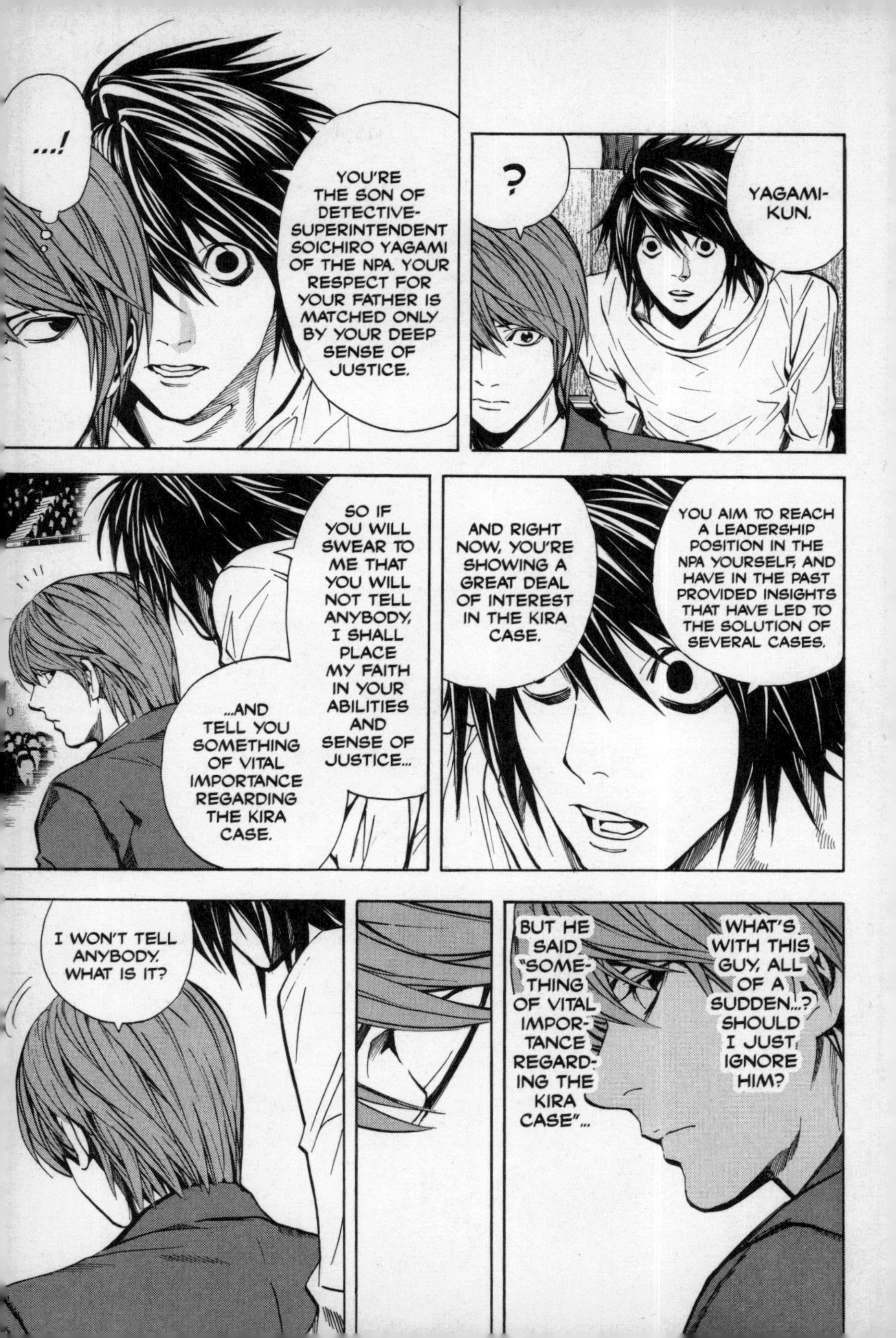
YAGAMI-KUN.
?
YOU'RE THE SON OF DETECTIVE-SUPERINTENDENT SOICHIRO YAGAMI OF THE NPA. YOUR RESPECT FOR YOUR FATHER IS MATCHED ONLY BY YOUR DEEP SENSE OF JUSTICE.
...!
YOU AIM TO REACH A LEADERSHIP POSITION IN THE NPA YOURSELF, AND HAVE IN THE PAST PROVIDED INSIGHTS THAT HAVE LED TO THE SOLUTION OF SEVERAL CASES.
AND RIGHT NOW, YOU'RE SHOWING A GREAT DEAL OF INTEREST IN THE KIRA CASE.
SO IF YOU WILL SWEAR TO ME THAT YOU WILL NOT TELL ANYBODY, I SHALL PLACE MY FAITH IN YOUR ABILITIES AND SENSE OF JUSTICE...
...AND TELL YOU SOMETHING OF VITAL IMPORTANCE REGARDING THE KIRA CASE.
WHAT'S WITH THIS GUY, ALL OF A SUDDEN...? SHOULD I JUST IGNORE HIM?
BUT HE SAID "SOMETHING OF VITAL IMPORTANCE REGARDING THE KIRA CASE"...
I WON'T TELL ANYBODY. WHAT IS IT?

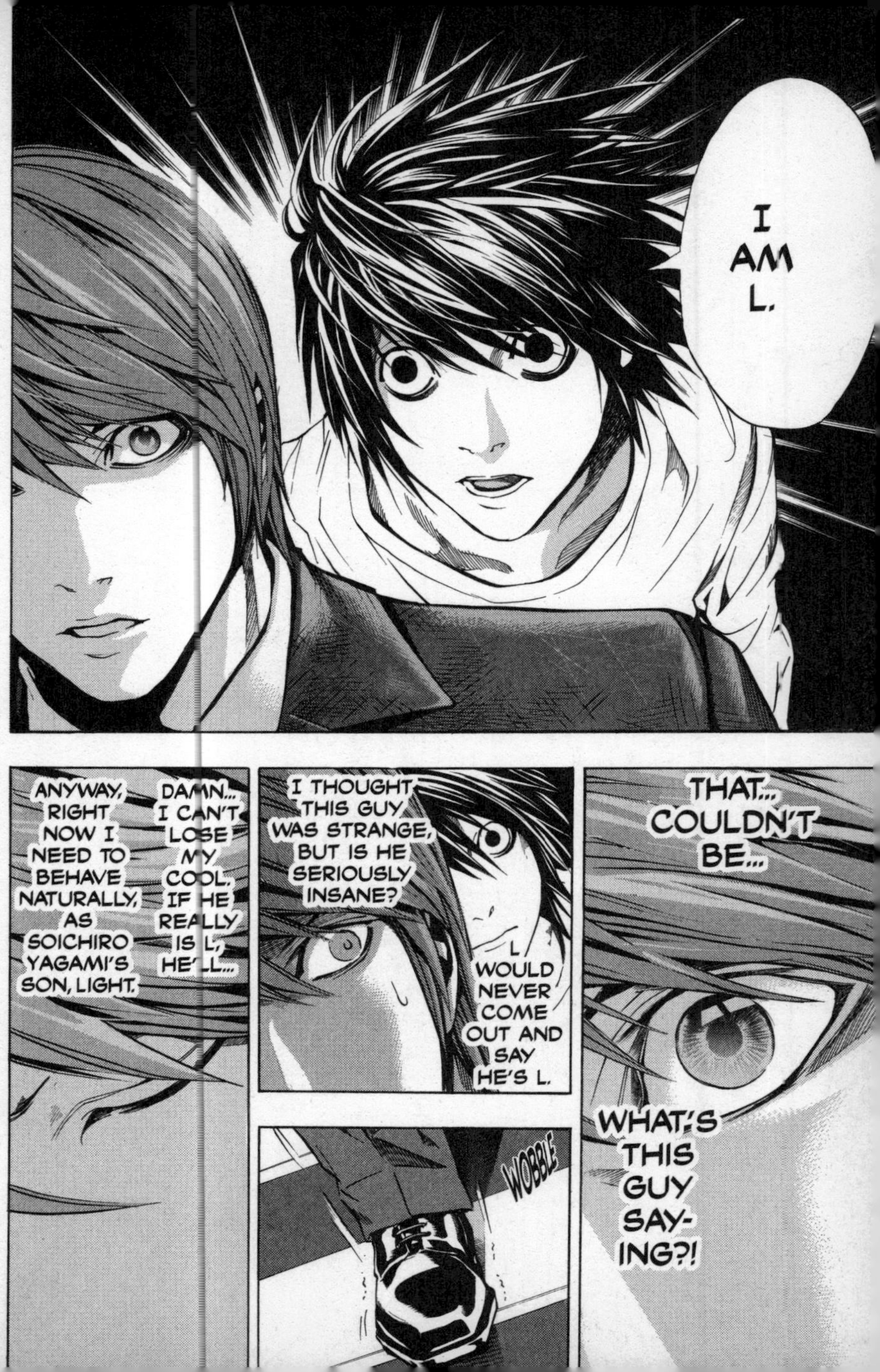
I AM L.
THAT... COULDN'T BE...
WHAT'S THIS GUY SAYING?!
I THOUGHT THIS GUY WAS STRANGE, BUT IS HE SERIOUSLY INSANE?
L WOULD NEVER COME OUT AND SAY HE'S L.
WOBBLE
DAMN... I CAN'T LOSE MY COOL. IF HE REALLY IS L, HE'LL...
ANYWAY, RIGHT NOW I NEED TO BEHAVE NATURALLY, AS SOICHIRO YAGAMI'S SON, LIGHT.

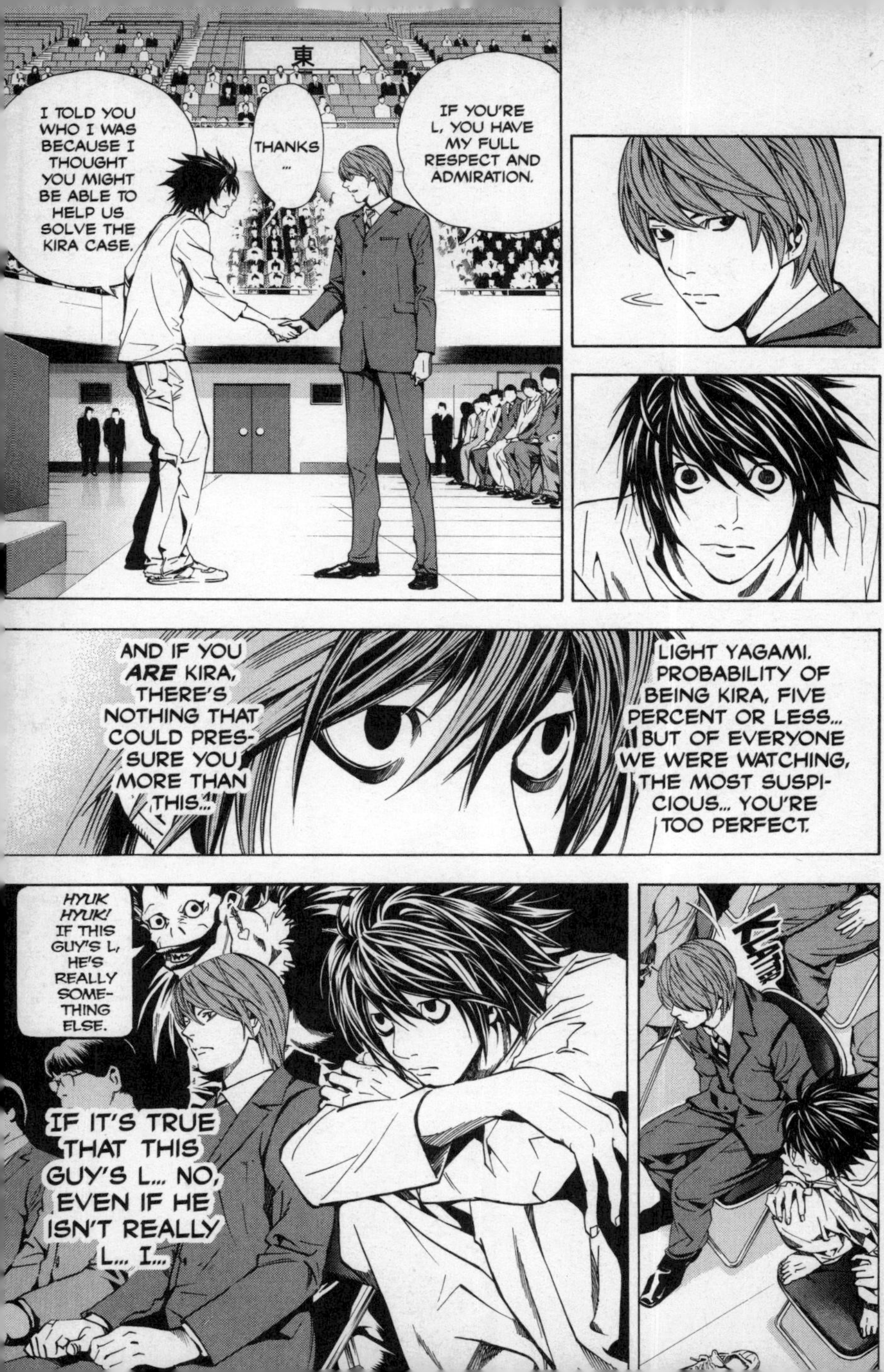
IF YOU'RE L, YOU HAVE MY FULL RESPECT AND ADMIRATION.
THANKS ...
I TOLD YOU WHO I WAS BECAUSE I THOUGHT YOU MIGHT BE ABLE TO HELP US SOLVE THE KIRA CASE.
LIGHT YAGAMI. PROBABILITY OF BEING KIRA, FIVE PERCENT OR LESS... BUT OF EVERYONE WE WERE WATCHING, THE MOST SUSPICIOUS... YOU'RE TOO PERFECT.
AND IF YOU *ARE* KIRA, THERE'S NOTHING THAT COULD PRESSURE YOU MORE THAN THIS...!
KLATTR
HYUK HYUK! IF THIS GUY'S L, HE'S REALLY SOMETHING ELSE.
IF IT'S TRUE THAT THIS GUY'S L... NO, EVEN IF HE ISN'T REALLY L... I...

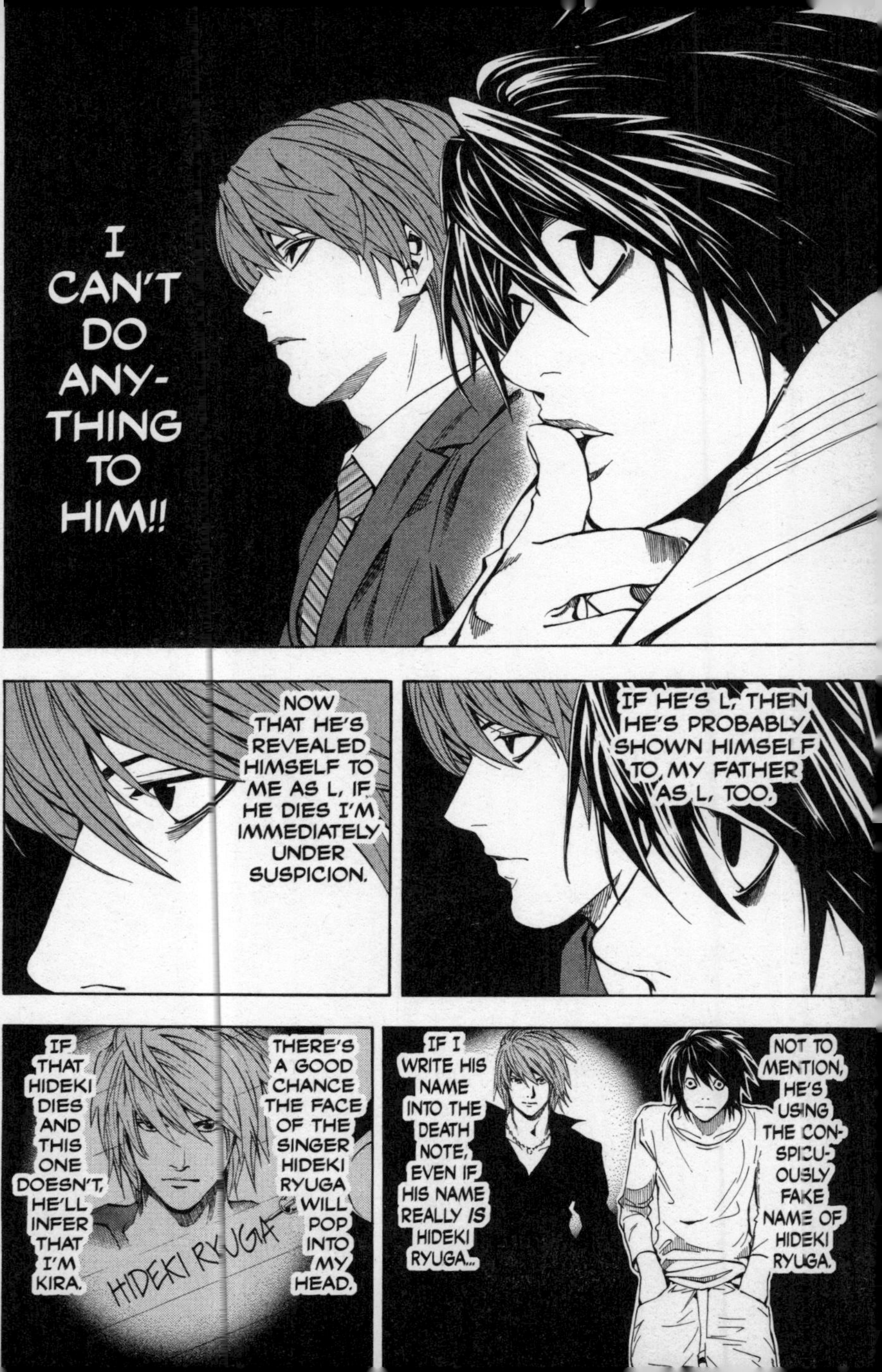
I CAN'T DO ANYTHING TO HIM!!
IF HE'S L, THEN HE'S PROBABLY SHOWN HIMSELF TO MY FATHER AS L, TOO.
NOW THAT HE'S REVEALED HIMSELF TO ME AS L, IF HE DIES I'M IMMEDIATELY UNDER SUSPICION.
NOT TO MENTION, HE'S USING THE CONSPICUOUSLY FAKE NAME OF HIDEKI RYUGA.
IF I WRITE HIS NAME INTO THE DEATH NOTE, EVEN IF HIS NAME REALLY *IS* HIDEKI RYUGA...
THERE'S A GOOD CHANCE THE FACE OF THE SINGER HIDEKI RYUGA WILL POP INTO MY HEAD.
HIDEKI RYUGA
IF THAT HIDEKI DIES AND THIS ONE DOESN'T, HE'LL INFER THAT I'M KIRA.

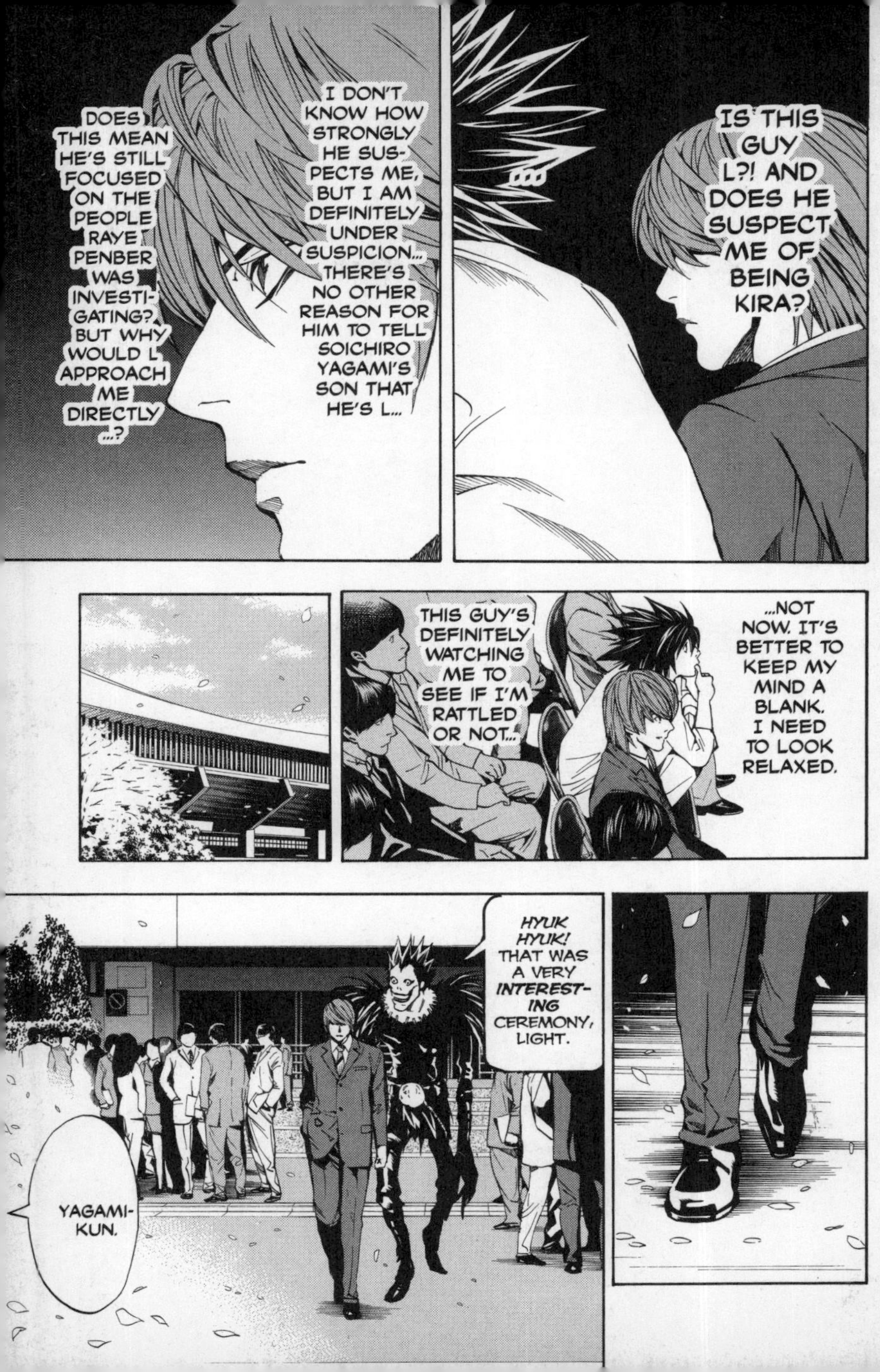
IS THIS GUY L?! AND DOES HE SUSPECT ME OF BEING KIRA?
...
I DON'T KNOW HOW STRONGLY HE SUS-PECTS ME, BUT I AM DEFINITELY UNDER SUSPICION... THERE'S NO OTHER REASON FOR HIM TO TELL SOICHIRO YAGAMI'S SON THAT HE'S L...
DOES THIS MEAN HE'S STILL FOCUSED ON THE PEOPLE RAYE PENBER WAS INVESTI-GATING? BUT WHY WOULD L APPROACH ME DIRECTLY ...?
...NOT NOW. IT'S BETTER TO KEEP MY MIND A BLANK. I NEED TO LOOK RELAXED.
THIS GUY'S DEFINITELY WATCHING ME TO SEE IF I'M RATTLED OR NOT...
HYUK HYUK! THAT WAS A VERY ***INTEREST-ING*** CEREMONY, LIGHT.
YAGAMI-KUN.

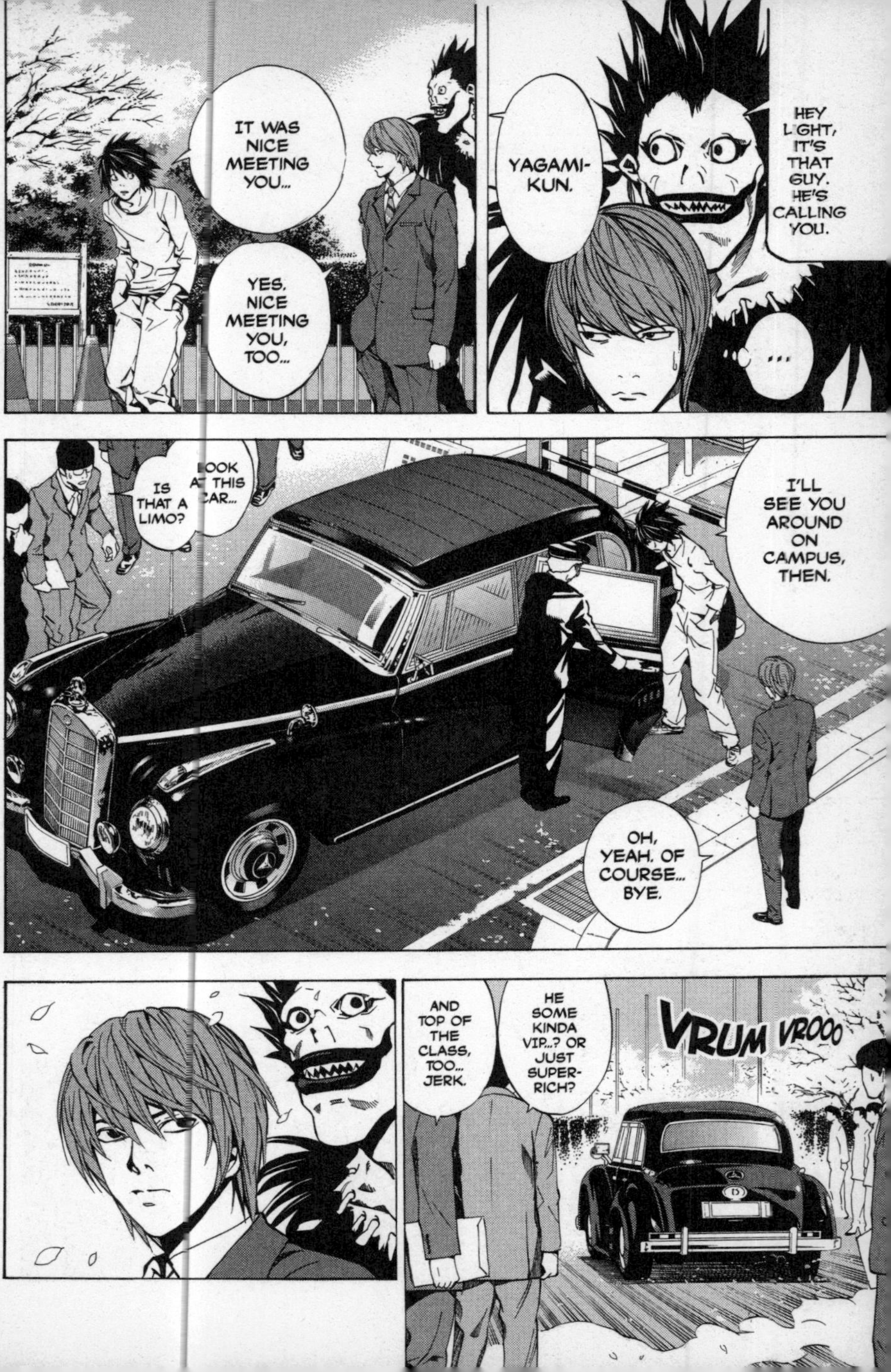

YAGAMI-KUN.
HEY LIGHT, IT'S THAT GUY. HE'S CALLING YOU.
...
IT WAS NICE MEETING YOU...
YES. NICE MEETING YOU, TOO...
I'LL SEE YOU AROUND ON CAMPUS, THEN.
OH, YEAH. OF COURSE... BYE.
LOOK AT THIS CAR...
IS THAT A LIMO?
VRUM VROOO
HE SOME KINDA VIP...? OR JUST SUPER-RICH?
AND TOP OF THE CLASS, TOO... JERK.

KA-TUNK KA-TUNK

SHWOO

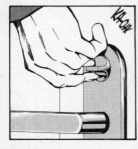

KA-CHAK

HOW'D IT GO, TODAI FRESHMAN REPRESEN- TATIVE?

KREE

?

TOK

TOK

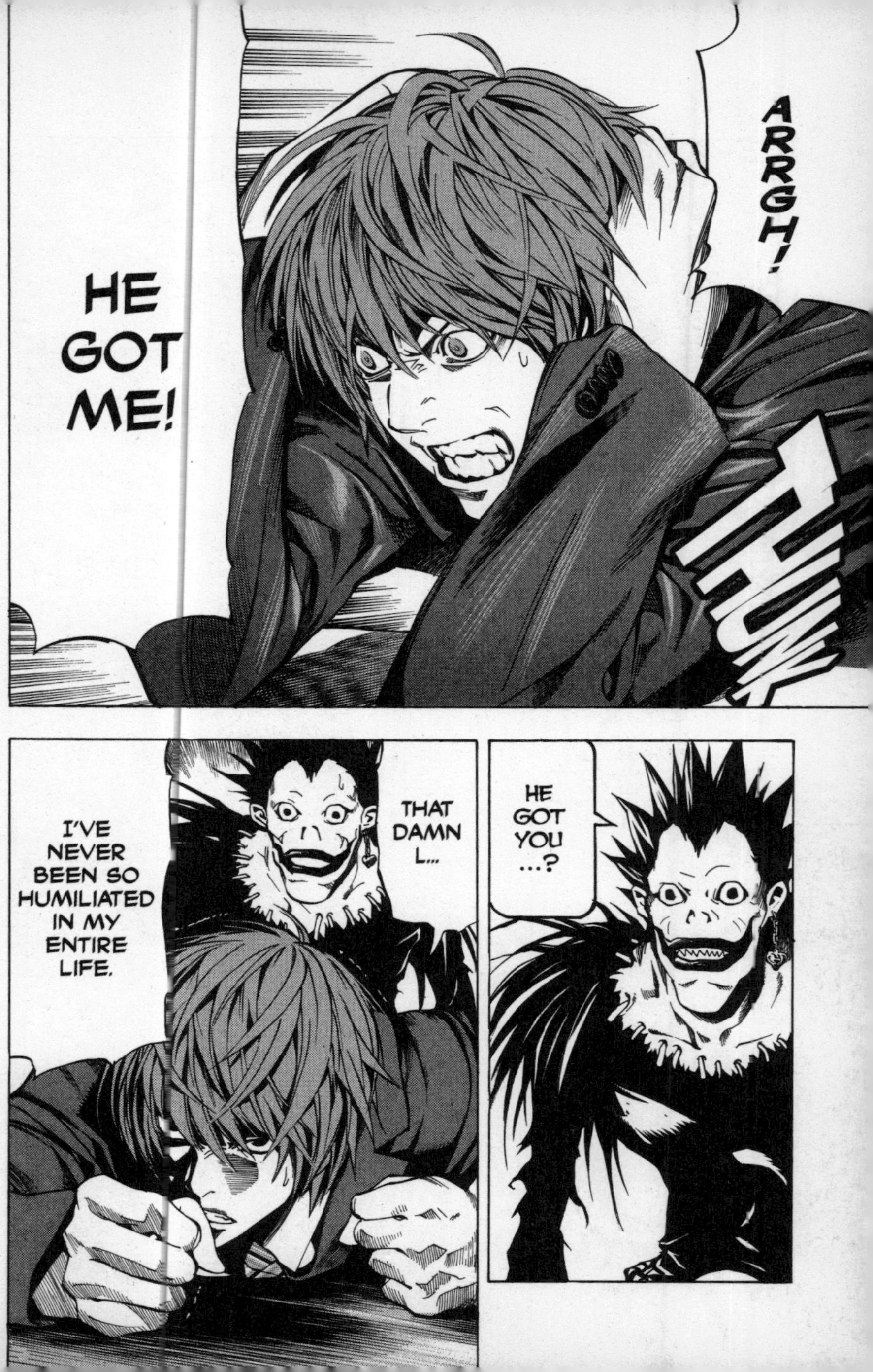
ARRGH!
THUNK
HE GOT ME!
HE GOT YOU ...?
THAT DAMN L...
I'VE NEVER BEEN SO HUMILIATED IN MY ENTIRE LIFE.

READ THIS WAY

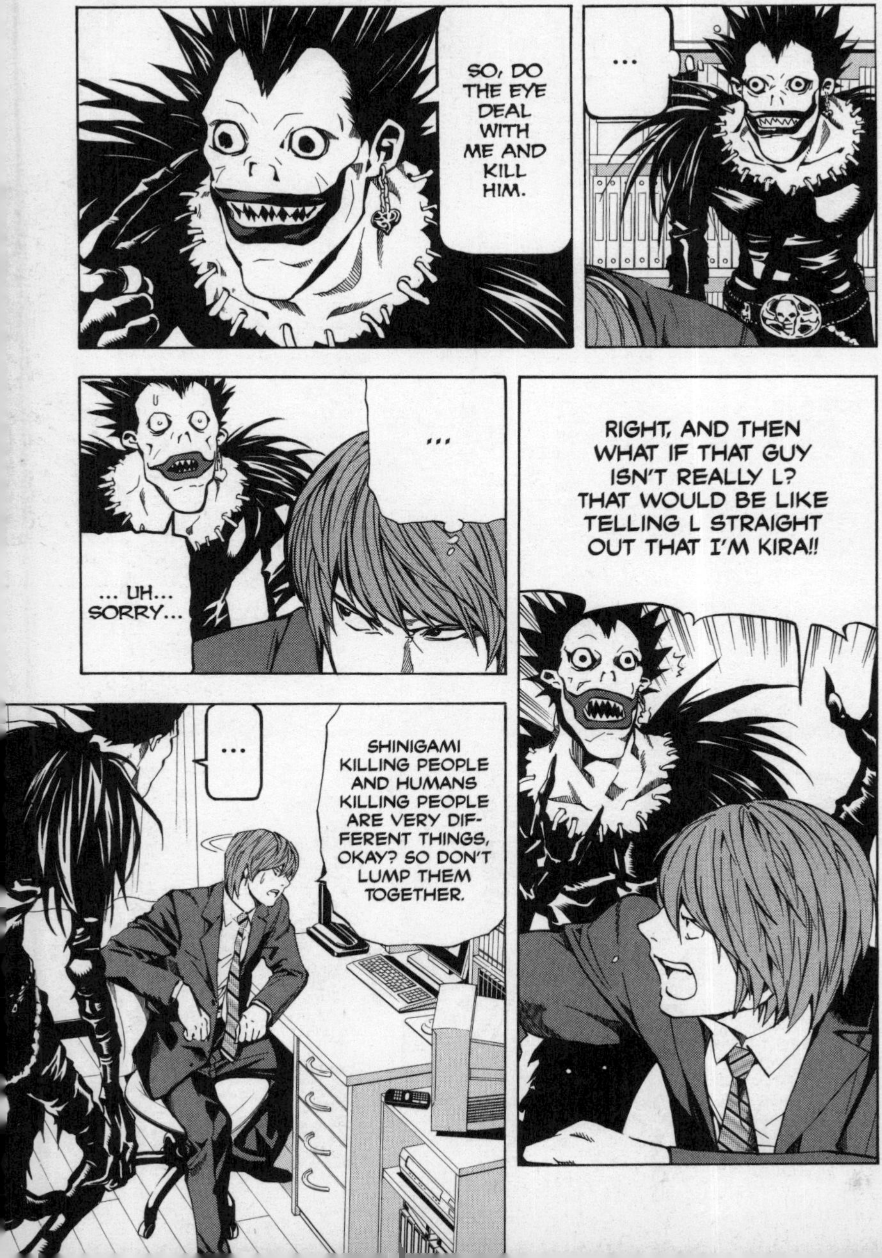
...
SO, DO THE EYE DEAL WITH ME AND KILL HIM.
RIGHT, AND THEN WHAT IF THAT GUY ISN'T REALLY L? THAT WOULD BE LIKE TELLING L STRAIGHT OUT THAT I'M KIRA!!
...
... UH... SORRY...
SHINIGAMI KILLING PEOPLE AND HUMANS KILLING PEOPLE ARE VERY DIF-FERENT THINGS, OKAY? SO DON'T LUMP THEM TOGETHER.
...

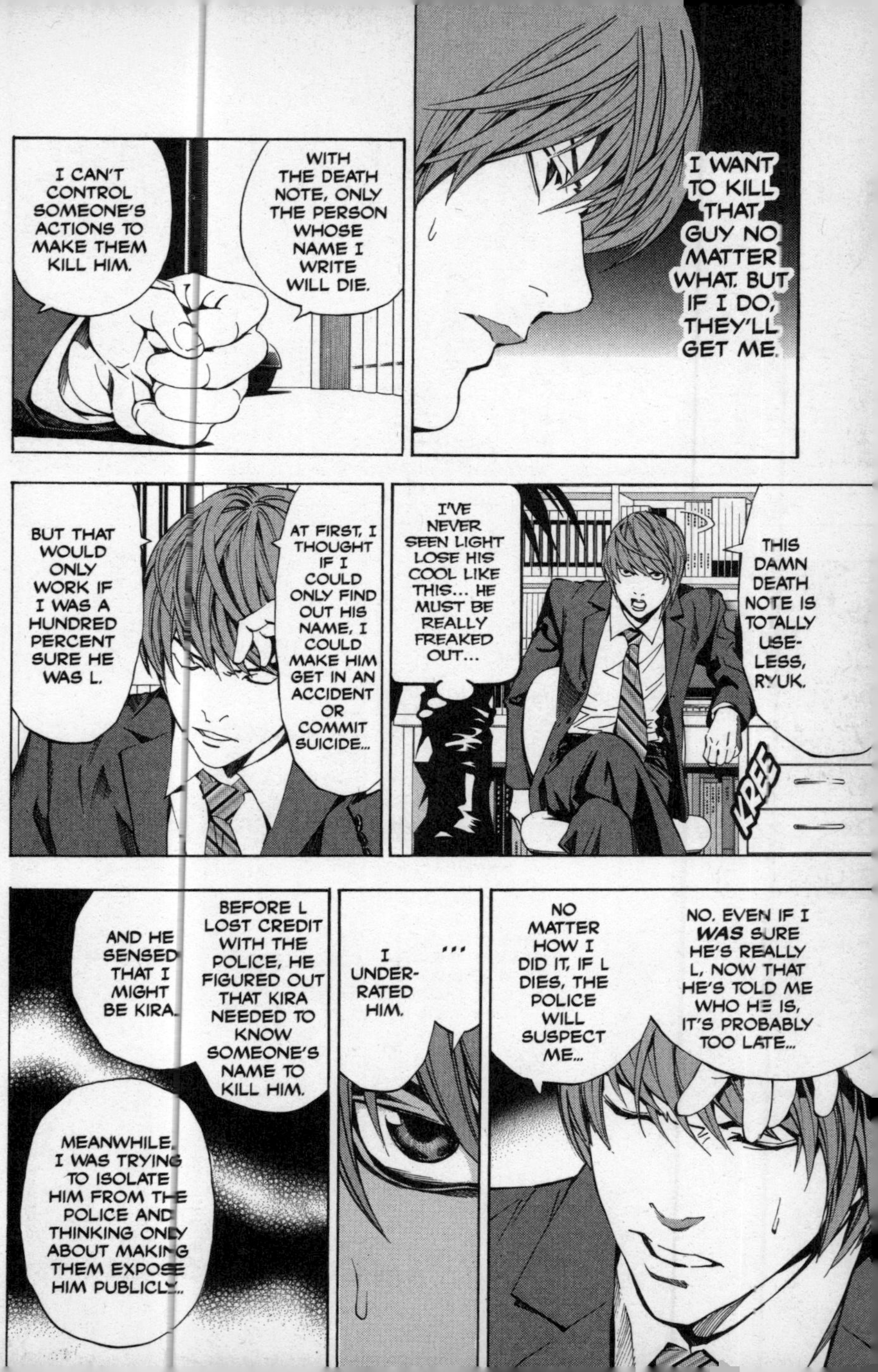

I WANT TO KILL THAT GUY NO MATTER WHAT. BUT IF I DO, THEY'LL GET ME.
WITH THE DEATH NOTE, ONLY THE PERSON WHOSE NAME I WRITE WILL DIE.
I CAN'T CONTROL SOMEONE'S ACTIONS TO MAKE THEM KILL HIM.
THIS DAMN DEATH NOTE IS TOTALLY USELESS, RYUK.
KREE
I'VE NEVER SEEN LIGHT LOSE HIS COOL LIKE THIS... HE MUST BE REALLY FREAKED OUT...
AT FIRST, I THOUGHT IF I COULD ONLY FIND OUT HIS NAME, I COULD MAKE HIM GET IN AN ACCIDENT OR COMMIT SUICIDE...
BUT THAT WOULD ONLY WORK IF I WAS A HUNDRED PERCENT SURE HE WAS L.
NO. EVEN IF I *WAS* SURE HE'S REALLY L, NOW THAT HE'S TOLD ME WHO HE IS, IT'S PROBABLY TOO LATE...
NO MATTER HOW I DID IT, IF L DIES, THE POLICE WILL SUSPECT ME...
...
I UNDERRATED HIM.
BEFORE L LOST CREDIT WITH THE POLICE, HE FIGURED OUT THAT KIRA NEEDED TO KNOW SOMEONE'S NAME TO KILL HIM.
AND HE SENSED THAT I MIGHT BE KIRA.
MEANWHILE, I WAS TRYING TO ISOLATE HIM FROM THE POLICE AND THINKING ONLY ABOUT MAKING THEM EXPOSE HIM PUBLICLY...

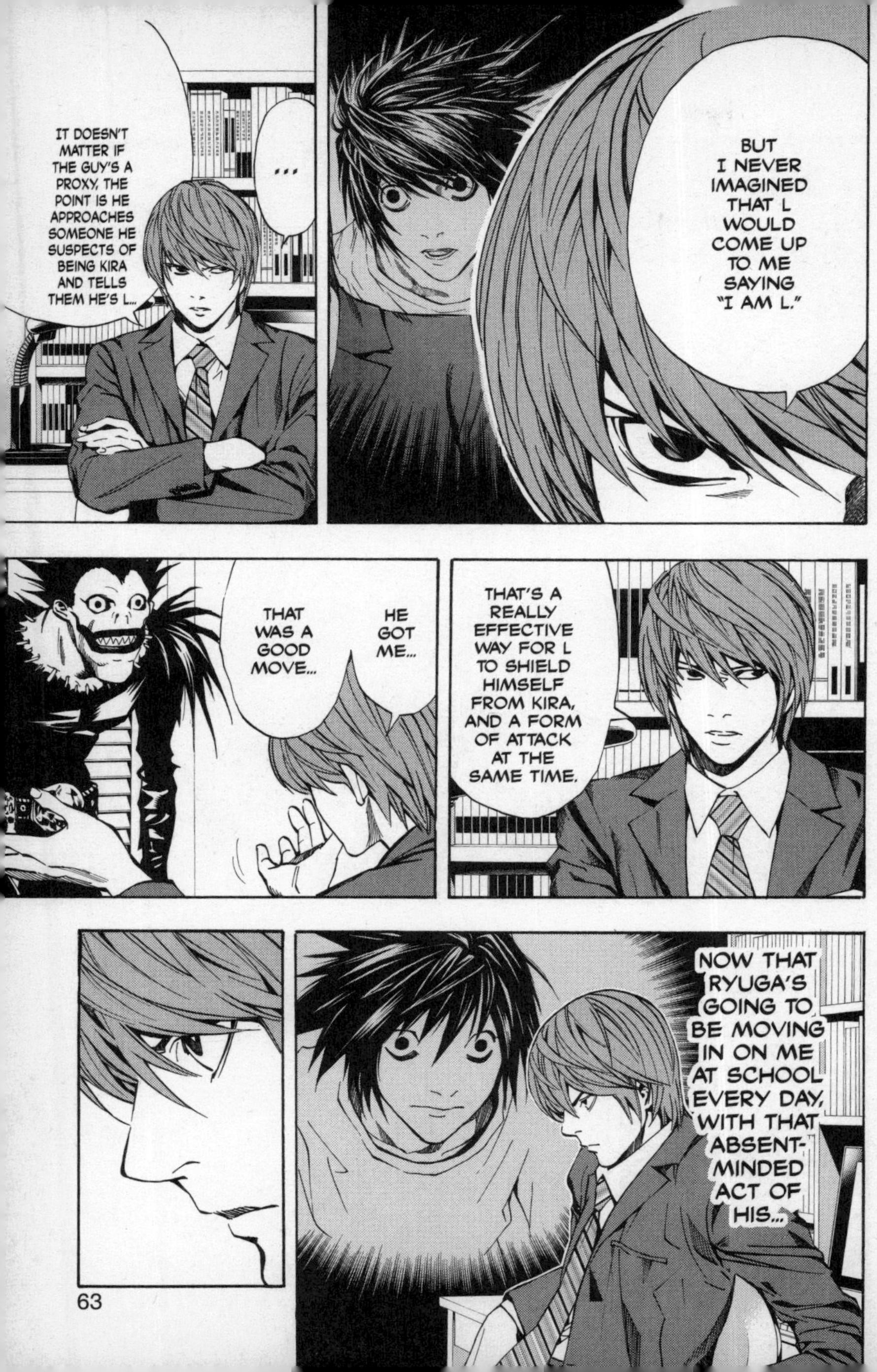
BUT I NEVER IMAGINED THAT L WOULD COME UP TO ME SAYING "I AM L."
...
IT DOESN'T MATTER IF THE GUY'S A PROXY, THE POINT IS HE APPROACHES SOMEONE HE SUSPECTS OF BEING KIRA AND TELLS THEM HE'S L...
THAT'S A REALLY EFFECTIVE WAY FOR L TO SHIELD HIMSELF FROM KIRA, AND A FORM OF ATTACK AT THE SAME TIME.
HE GOT ME...
THAT WAS A GOOD MOVE...
NOW THAT RYUGA'S GOING TO BE MOVING IN ON ME AT SCHOOL EVERY DAY, WITH THAT ABSENT-MINDED ACT OF HIS...

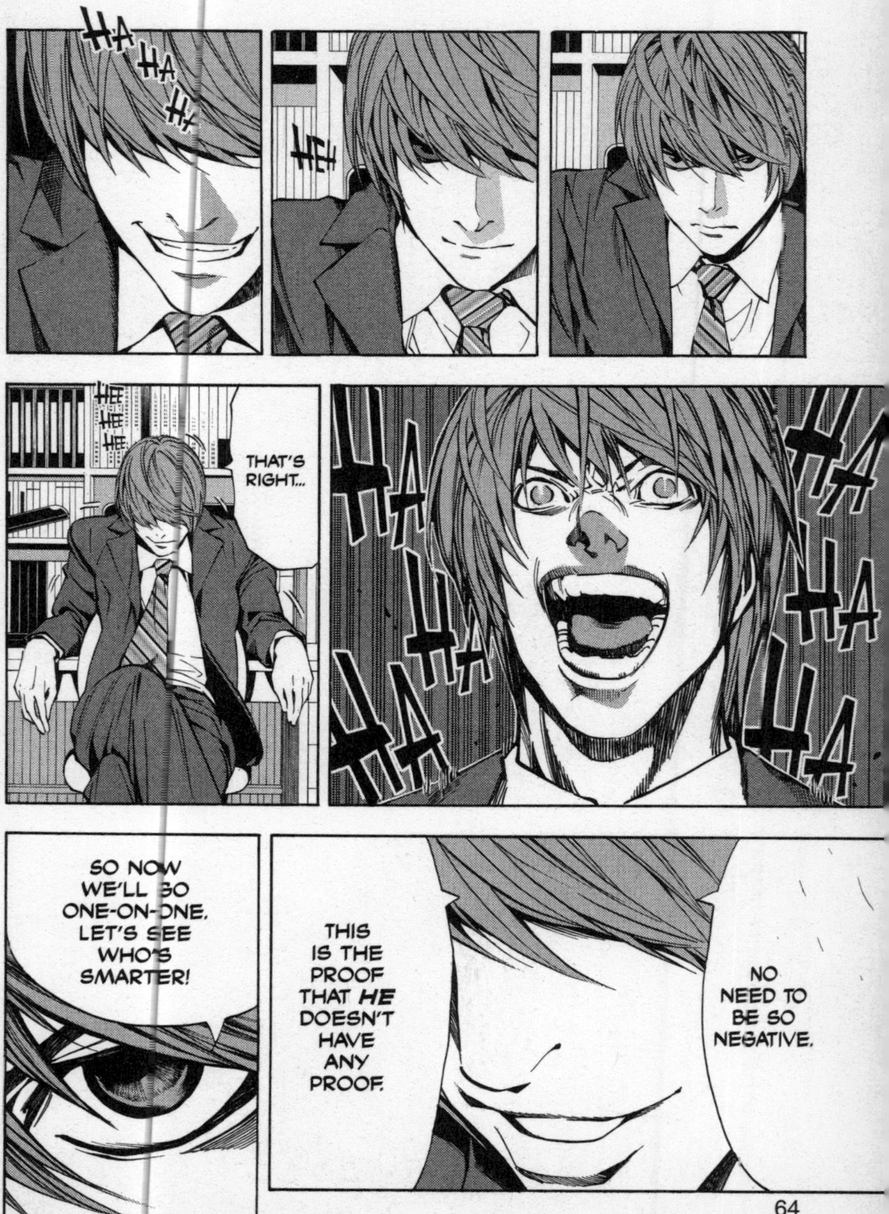
HEH
HA HA HA
HA HA HA HA HA HA HA HA HA
THAT'S RIGHT...
HEE HEE HEE
NO NEED TO BE SO NEGATIVE.
THIS IS THE PROOF THAT ***HE*** DOESN'T HAVE ANY PROOF.
SO NOW WE'LL GO ONE-ON-ONE. LET'S SEE WHO'S SMARTER!

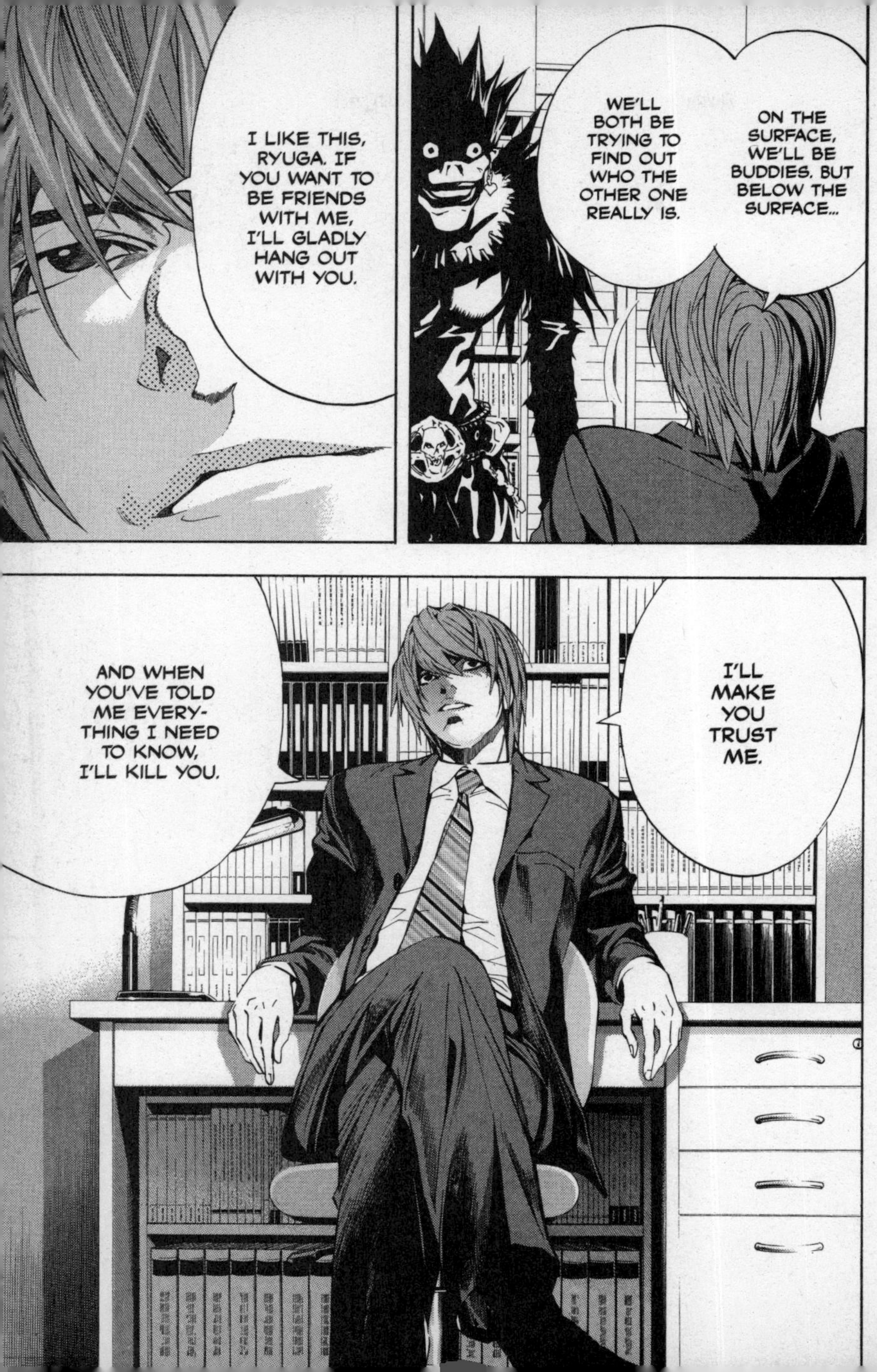
ON THE SURFACE, WE'LL BE BUDDIES. BUT BELOW THE SURFACE...
WE'LL BOTH BE TRYING TO FIND OUT WHO THE OTHER ONE REALLY IS.
I LIKE THIS, RYUGA. IF YOU WANT TO BE FRIENDS WITH ME, I'LL GLADLY HANG OUT WITH YOU.
I'LL MAKE YOU TRUST ME.
AND WHEN YOU'VE TOLD ME EVERY-THING I NEED TO KNOW, I'LL KILL YOU.

DEATH NOTE
How to use it
XII

○ If you lose the DEATH NOTE or have it stolen, you will lose its ownership unless you retrieve it within 490 days.

デスノートを紛失および盗まれた場合、
４９０日以内に再び手にしないと、所有権を失う。

○ If you have traded the eye power of a god of death, you will lose the eye power as well as the memory of the DEATH NOTE, once you lose its ownership.
At the same time, the remaining half of your life will not be restored.

死神の目の取引をした者は、所有権を失うと
ノートの記憶と共に目の能力を失う。
その際、半分になった余命は元には戻らない。

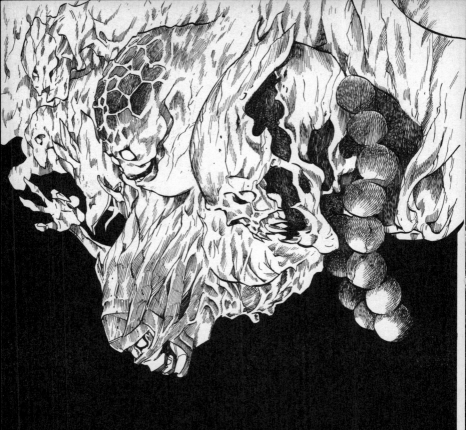

chapter 20 First Move

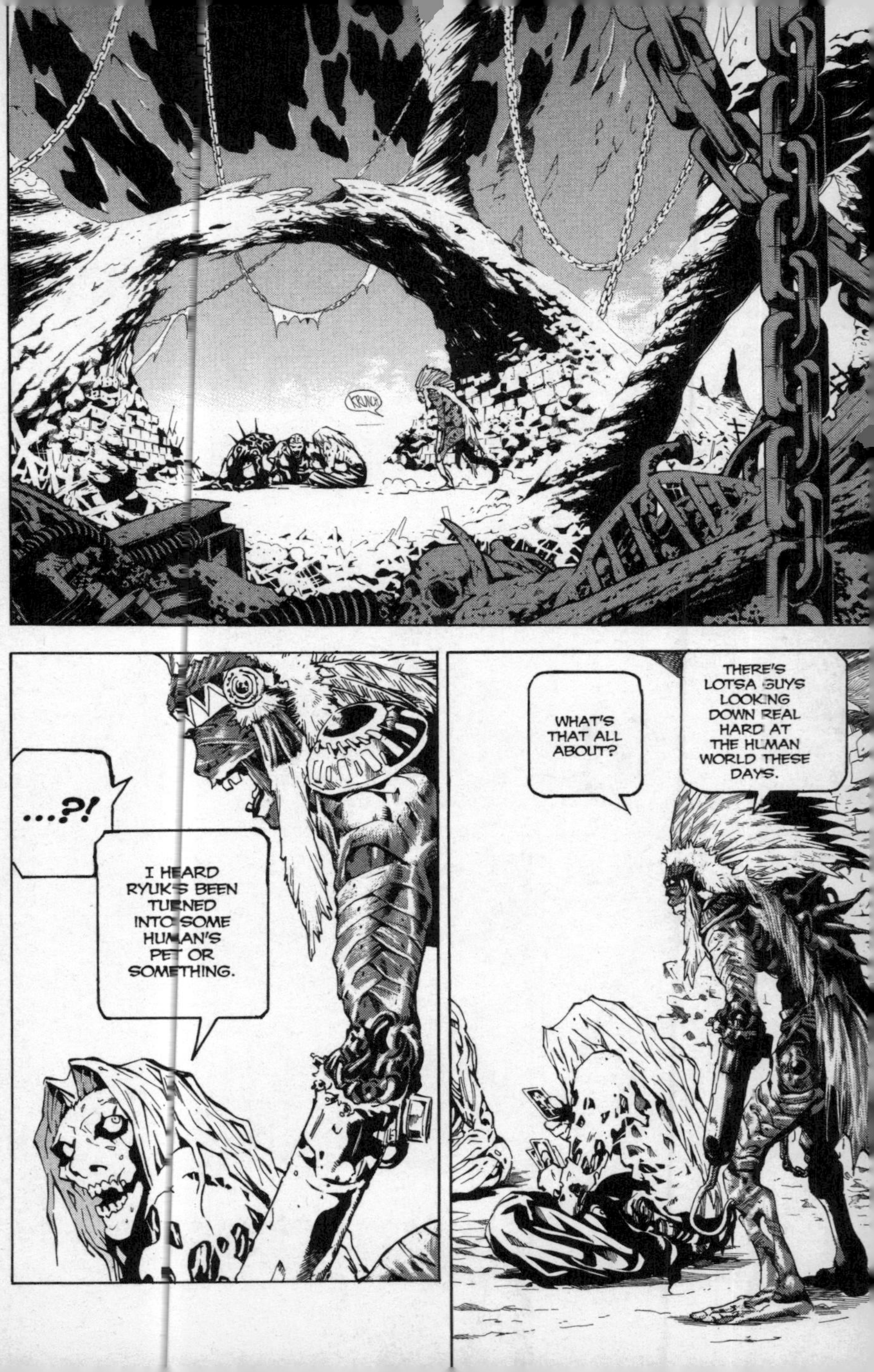
KRUNCH
THERE'S LOTSA GUYS LOOKING DOWN REAL HARD AT THE HUMAN WORLD THESE DAYS.
WHAT'S THAT ALL ABOUT?
...?!
I HEARD RYUK'S BEEN TURNED INTO SOME HUMAN'S PET OR SOMETHING.

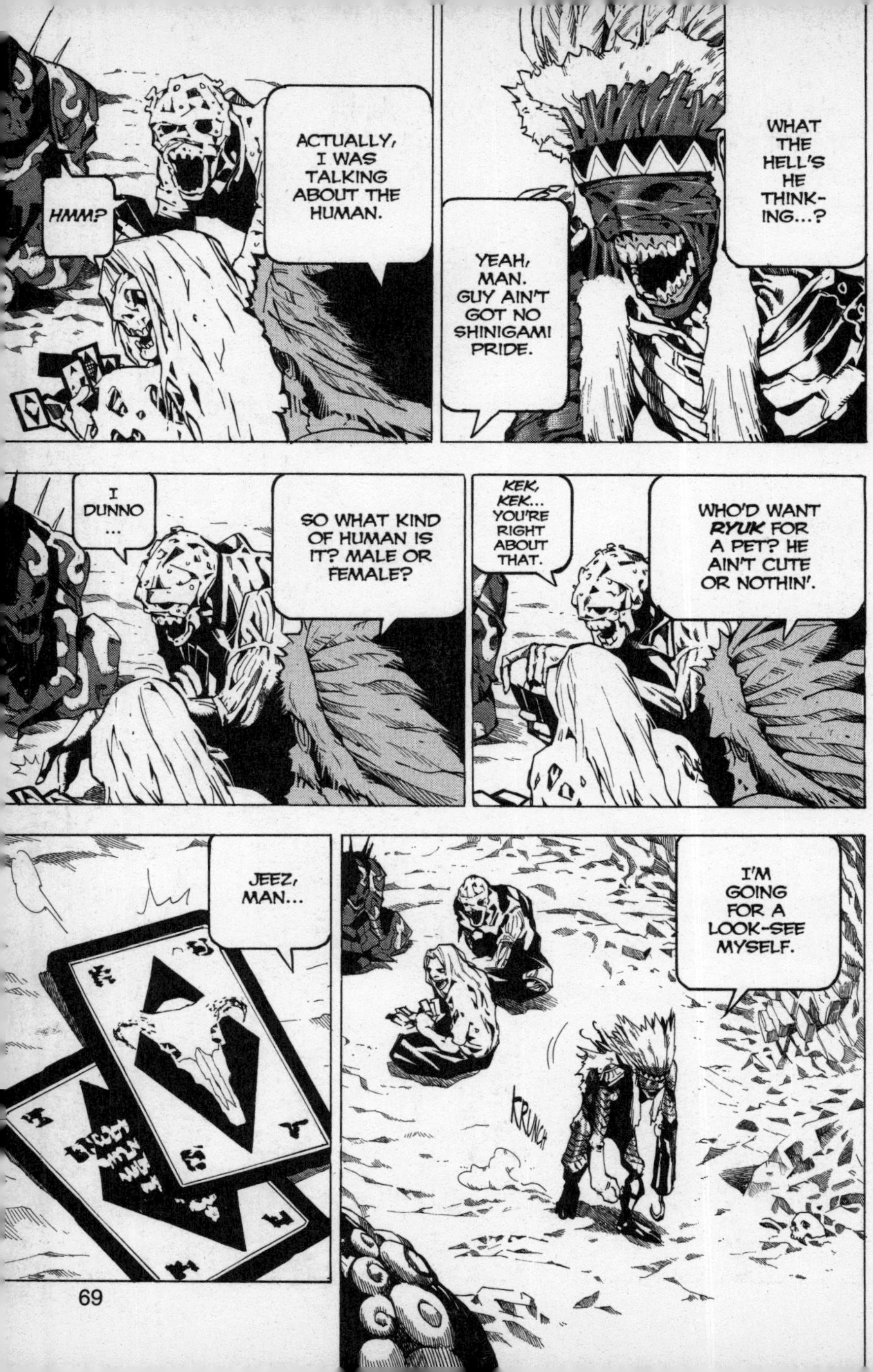
WHAT THE HELL'S HE THINKING...?
YEAH, MAN. GUY AIN'T GOT NO SHINIGAMI PRIDE.
ACTUALLY, I WAS TALKING ABOUT THE HUMAN.
HMM?
WHO'D WANT *RYUK* FOR A PET? HE AIN'T CUTE OR NOTHIN'.
KEK, KEK... YOU'RE RIGHT ABOUT THAT.
SO WHAT KIND OF HUMAN IS IT? MALE OR FEMALE?
I DUNNO ...
I'M GOING FOR A LOOK-SEE MYSELF.
KRUNCH
JEEZ, MAN...

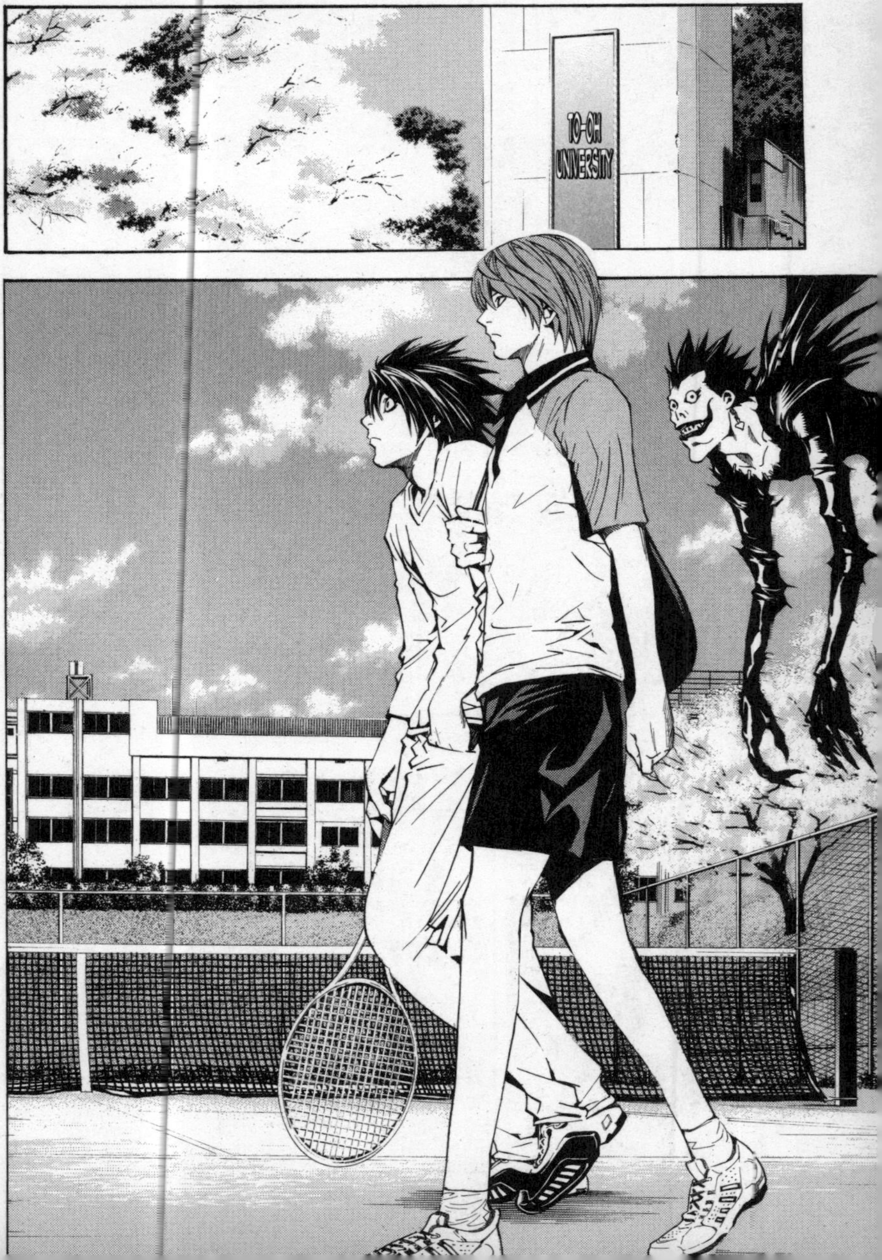
TO-OH UNIVERSITY

READ THIS WAY

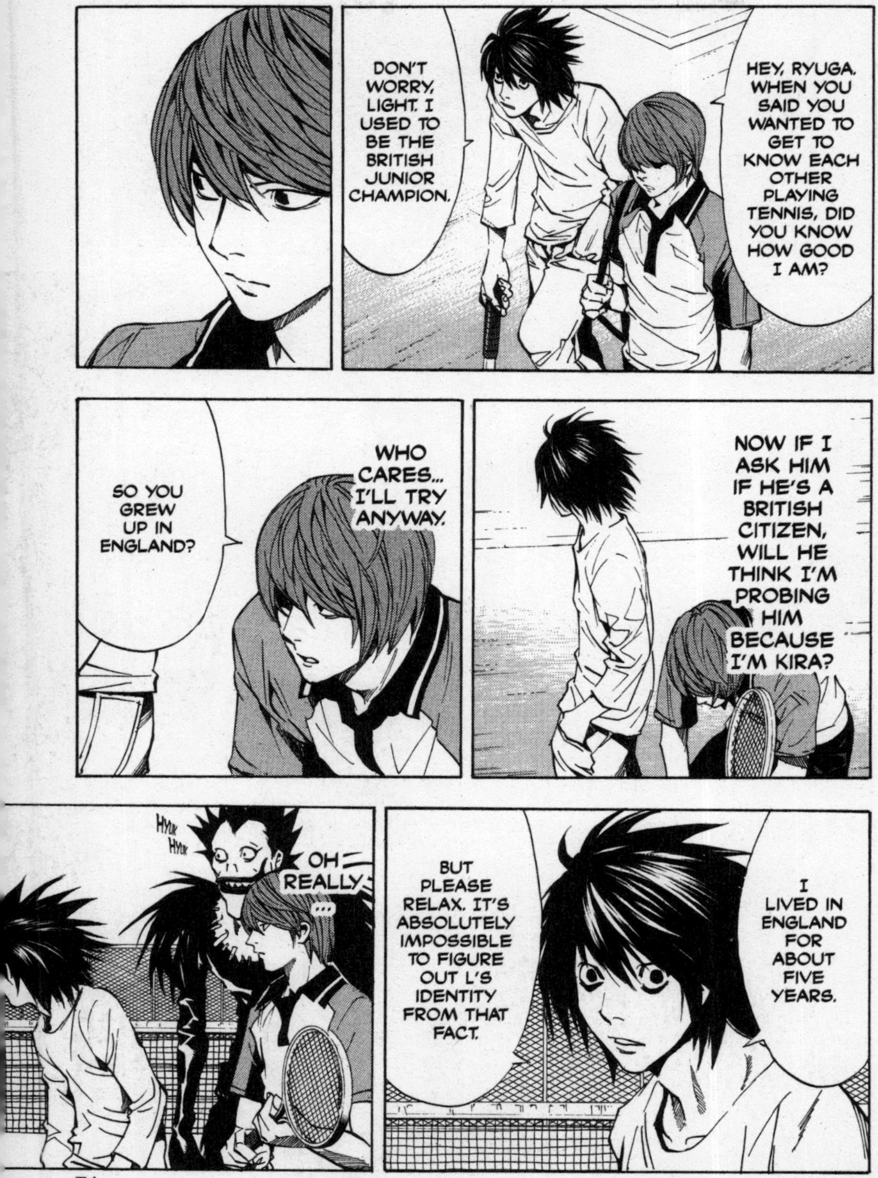
HEY, RYUGA. WHEN YOU SAID YOU WANTED TO GET TO KNOW EACH OTHER PLAYING TENNIS, DID YOU KNOW HOW GOOD I AM?
DON'T WORRY, LIGHT. I USED TO BE THE BRITISH JUNIOR CHAMPION.
NOW IF I ASK HIM IF HE'S A BRITISH CITIZEN, WILL HE THINK I'M PROBING HIM BECAUSE I'M KIRA?
WHO CARES... I'LL TRY ANYWAY.
SO YOU GREW UP IN ENGLAND?
I LIVED IN ENGLAND FOR ABOUT FIVE YEARS.
BUT PLEASE RELAX. IT'S ABSOLUTELY IMPOSSIBLE TO FIGURE OUT L'S IDENTITY FROM THAT FACT.
OH REALLY
...
HYUK HYUK

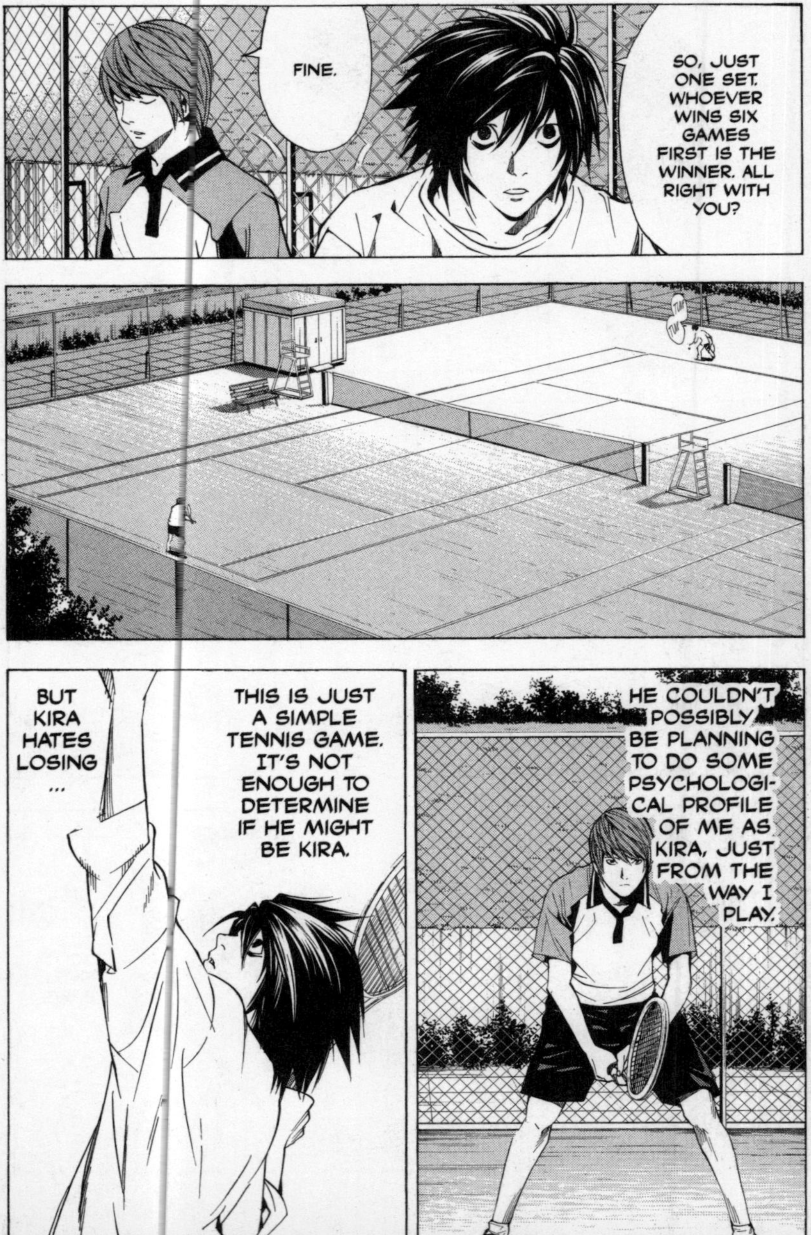
SO, JUST ONE SET. WHOEVER WINS SIX GAMES FIRST IS THE WINNER. ALL RIGHT WITH YOU?
FINE.
HE COULDN'T POSSIBLY BE PLANNING TO DO SOME PSYCHOLOGICAL PROFILE OF ME AS KIRA, JUST FROM THE WAY I PLAY.
THIS IS JUST A SIMPLE TENNIS GAME. IT'S NOT ENOUGH TO DETERMINE IF HE MIGHT BE KIRA.
BUT KIRA HATES LOSING ...

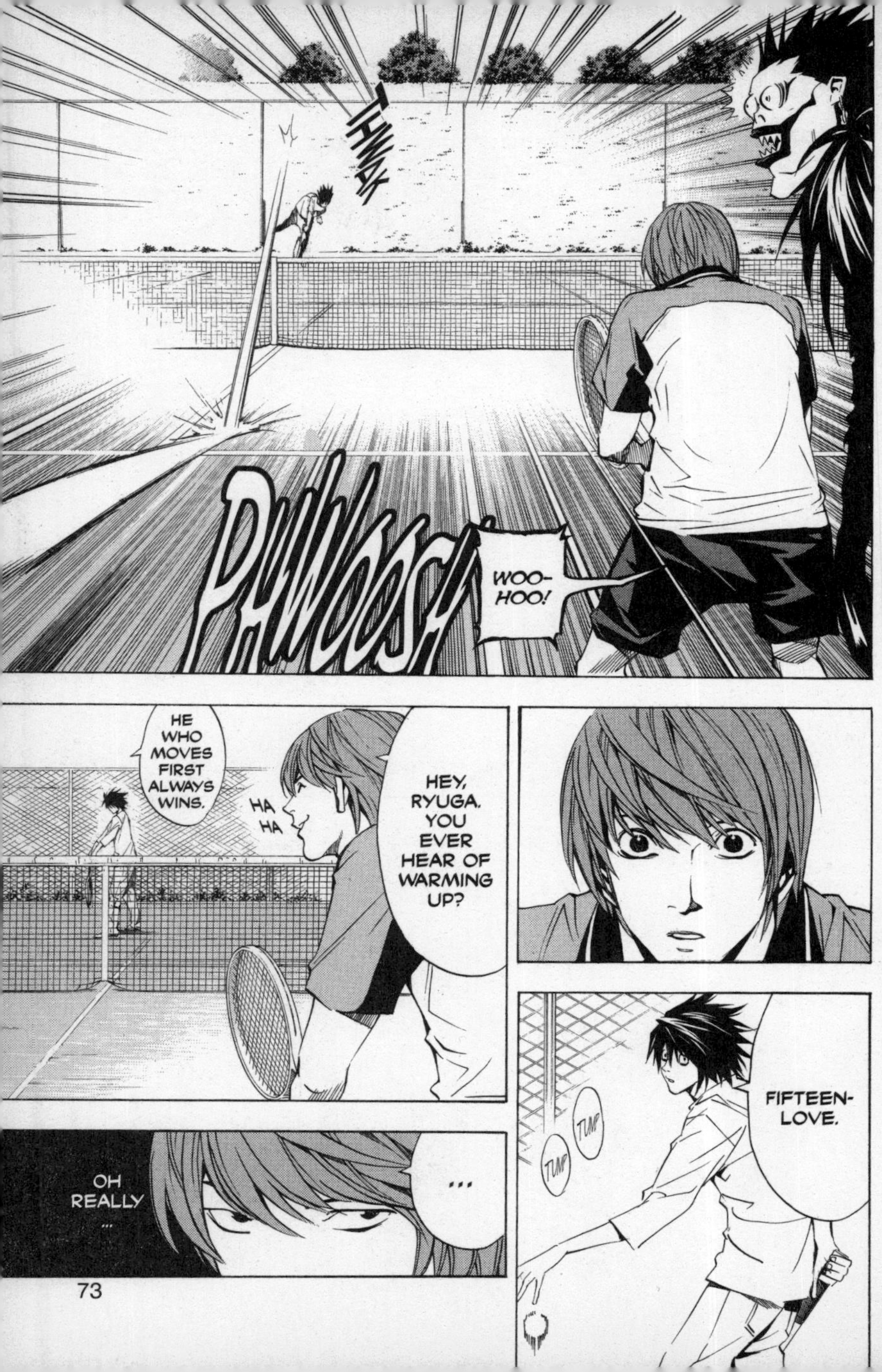
THWACK
PWOOSH
WOO-HOO!
HEY, RYUGA. YOU EVER HEAR OF WARMING UP?
HA HA
HE WHO MOVES FIRST ALWAYS WINS.
FIFTEEN-LOVE.
TUMP
TUMP
...
OH REALLY ...

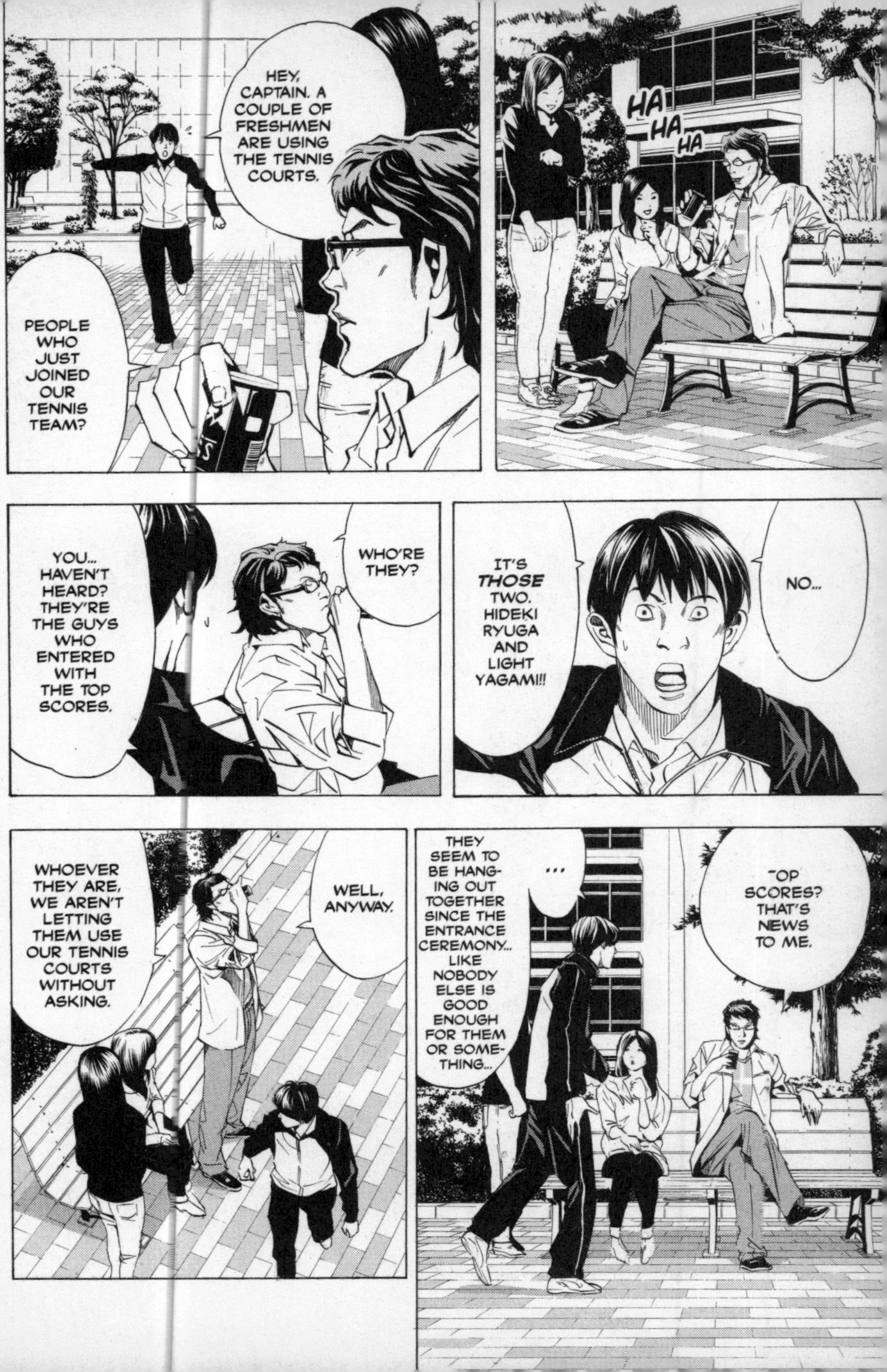
HA HA HA
HEY, CAPTAIN. A COUPLE OF FRESHMEN ARE USING THE TENNIS COURTS.
PEOPLE WHO JUST JOINED OUR TENNIS TEAM?
NO...
IT'S *THOSE* TWO. HIDEKI RYUGA AND LIGHT YAGAMI!!!
WHO'RE THEY?
YOU... HAVEN'T HEARD? THEY'RE THE GUYS WHO ENTERED WITH THE TOP SCORES.
TOP SCORES? THAT'S NEWS TO ME.
...
THEY SEEM TO BE HANGING OUT TOGETHER SINCE THE ENTRANCE CEREMONY... LIKE NOBODY ELSE IS GOOD ENOUGH FOR THEM OR SOMETHING...
WELL, ANYWAY.
WHOEVER THEY ARE, WE AREN'T LETTING THEM USE OUR TENNIS COURTS WITHOUT ASKING.

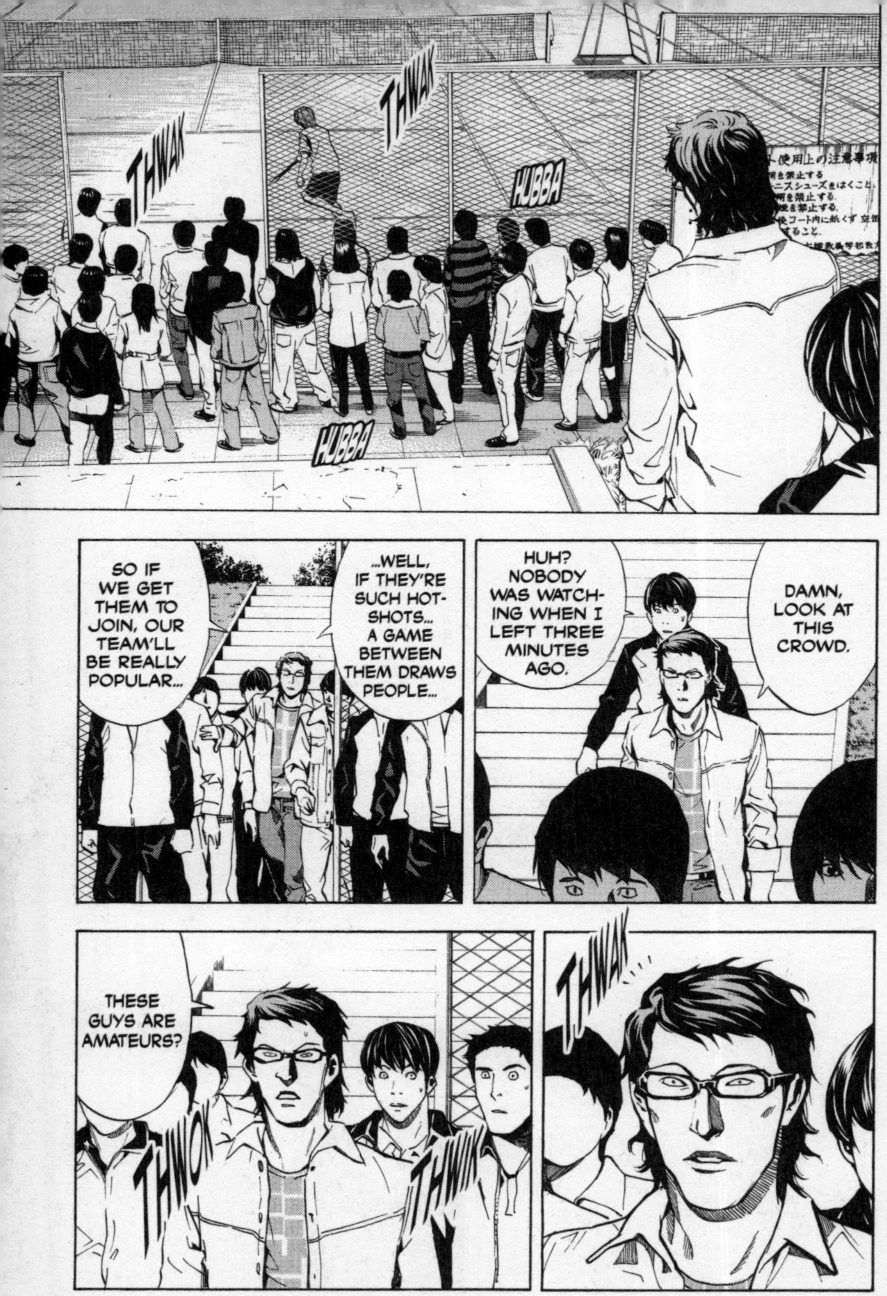
HUBBA
THWAK
THWAK
HUBBA
DAMN, LOOK AT THIS CROWD.
HUH? NOBODY WAS WATCHING WHEN I LEFT THREE MINUTES AGO.
...WELL, IF THEY'RE SUCH HOT-SHOTS... A GAME BETWEEN THEM DRAWS PEOPLE...
SO IF WE GET THEM TO JOIN, OUR TEAM'LL BE REALLY POPULAR...
THWAK
THESE GUYS ARE AMATEURS?
THWAK
THWOK

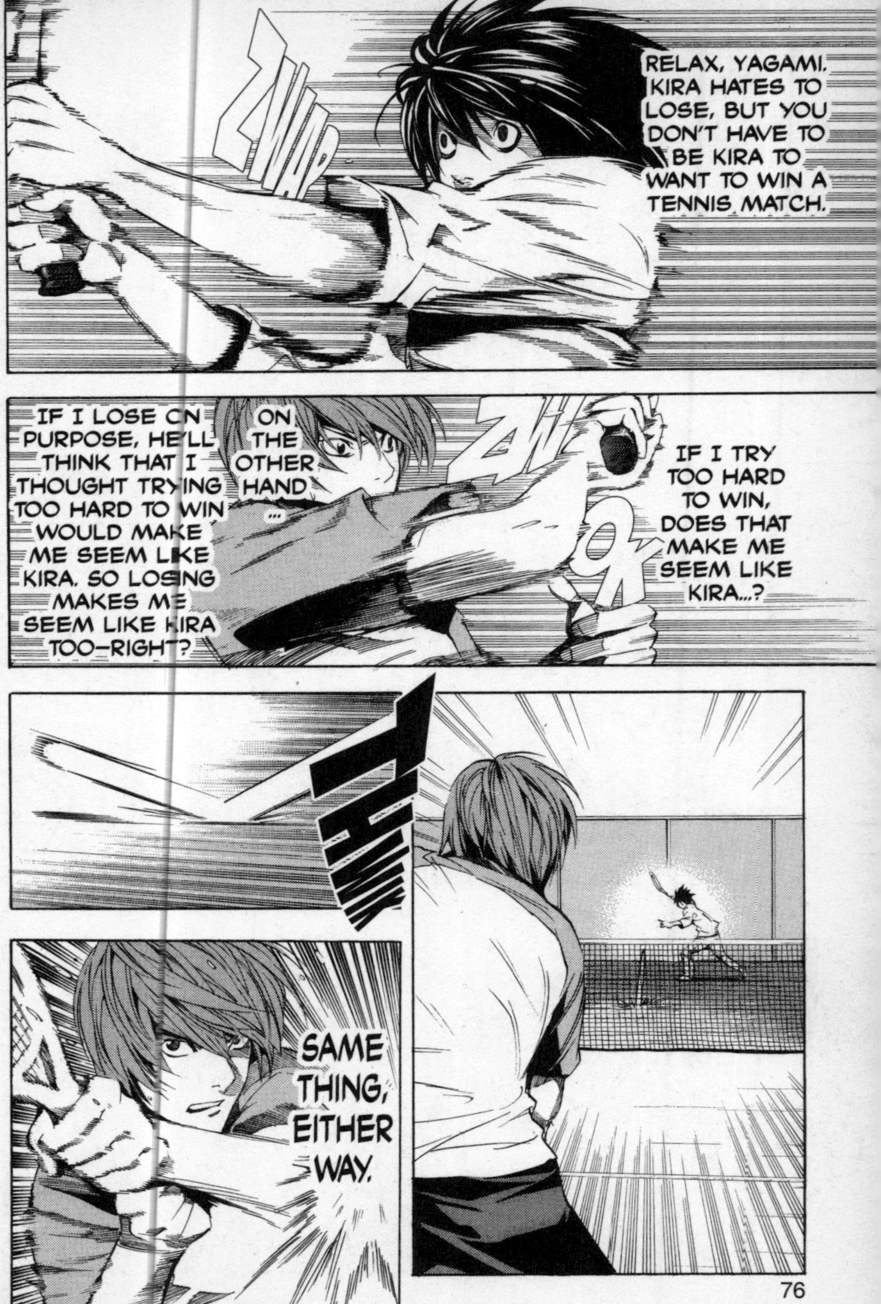
RELAX, YAGAMI. KIRA HATES TO LOSE, BUT YOU DON'T HAVE TO BE KIRA TO WANT TO WIN A TENNIS MATCH.
IF I TRY TOO HARD TO WIN, DOES THAT MAKE ME SEEM LIKE KIRA...?
ON THE OTHER HAND...
IF I LOSE ON PURPOSE, HE'LL THINK THAT I THOUGHT TRYING TOO HARD TO WIN WOULD MAKE ME SEEM LIKE KIRA. SO LOSING MAKES ME SEEM LIKE KIRA TOO—RIGHT?
SAME THING, EITHER WAY.

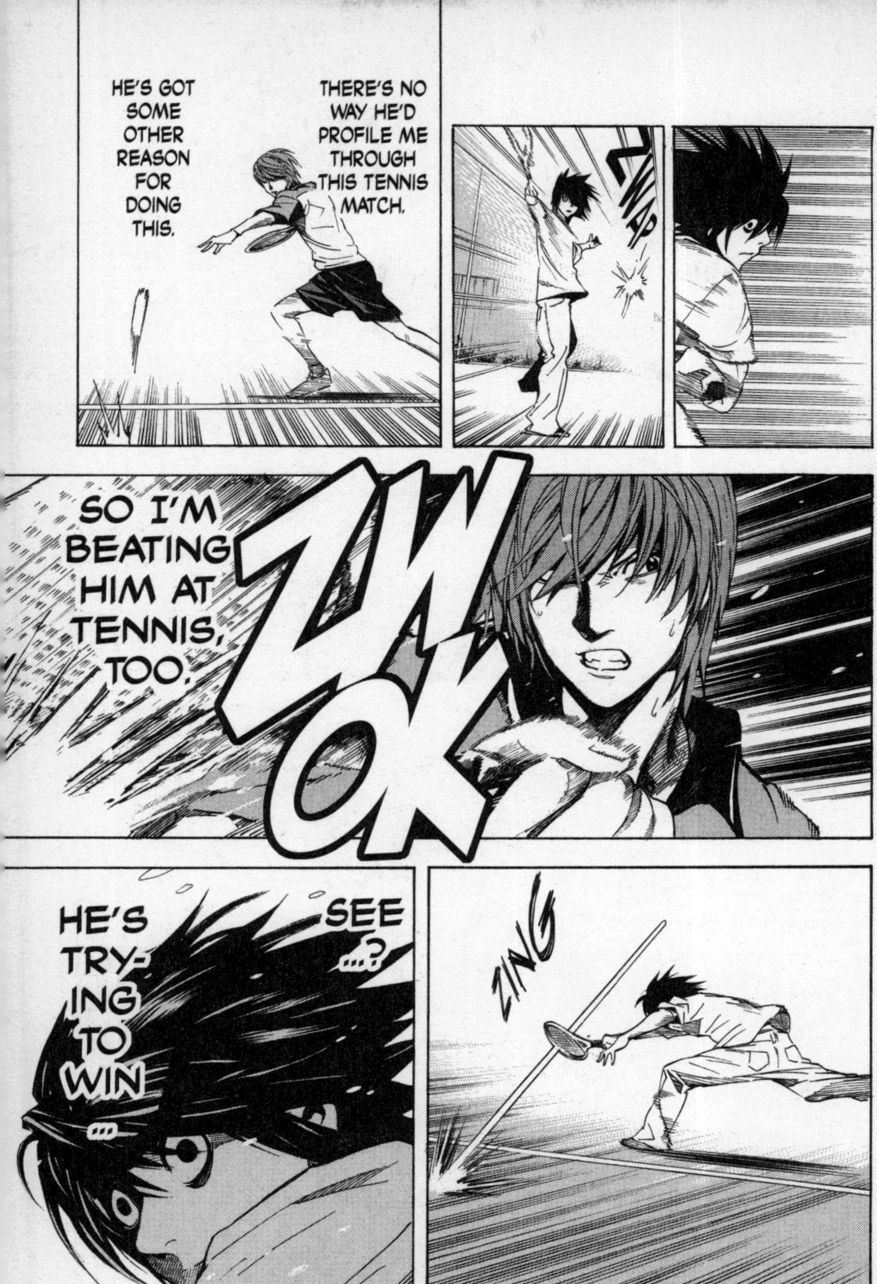
ZWAP
THERE'S NO WAY HE'D PROFILE ME THROUGH THIS TENNIS MATCH.
HE'S GOT SOME OTHER REASON FOR DOING THIS.
ZWOK
SO I'M BEATING HIM AT TENNIS, TOO.
ZING
SEE ...?
HE'S TRY-ING TO WIN ...

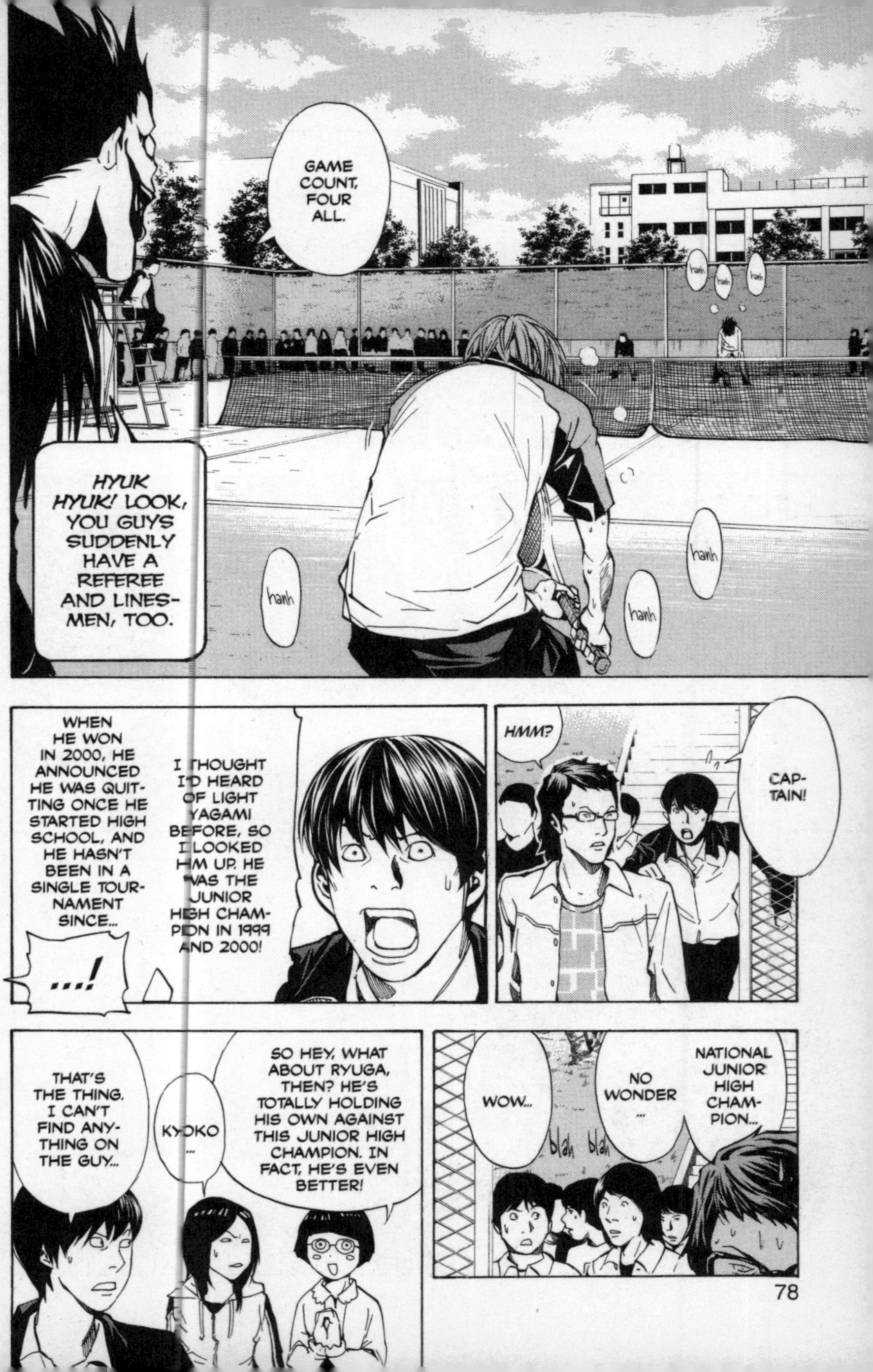

hanh
hanh
hanh
GAME COUNT, FOUR ALL.
hanh
hanh
HYUK HYUK! LOOK, YOU GUYS SUDDENLY HAVE A REFEREE AND LINES-MEN, TOO.
hanh
CAP-TAIN!
HMM?
I THOUGHT I'D HEARD OF LIGHT YAGAMI BEFORE, SO I LOOKED HIM UP. HE WAS THE JUNIOR HIGH CHAMP-PION IN 1999 AND 2000!
WHEN HE WON IN 2000, HE ANNOUNCED HE WAS QUIT-TING ONCE HE STARTED HIGH SCHOOL, AND HE HASN'T BEEN IN A SINGLE TOUR-NAMENT SINCE...
...!
NATIONAL JUNIOR HIGH CHAM-PION...
NO WONDER...
WOW...
blah blah
SO HEY, WHAT ABOUT RYUGA, THEN? HE'S TOTALLY HOLDING HIS OWN AGAINST THIS JUNIOR HIGH CHAMPION. IN FACT, HE'S EVEN BETTER!
KYOKO...
THAT'S THE THING. I CAN'T FIND ANY-THING ON THE GUY...

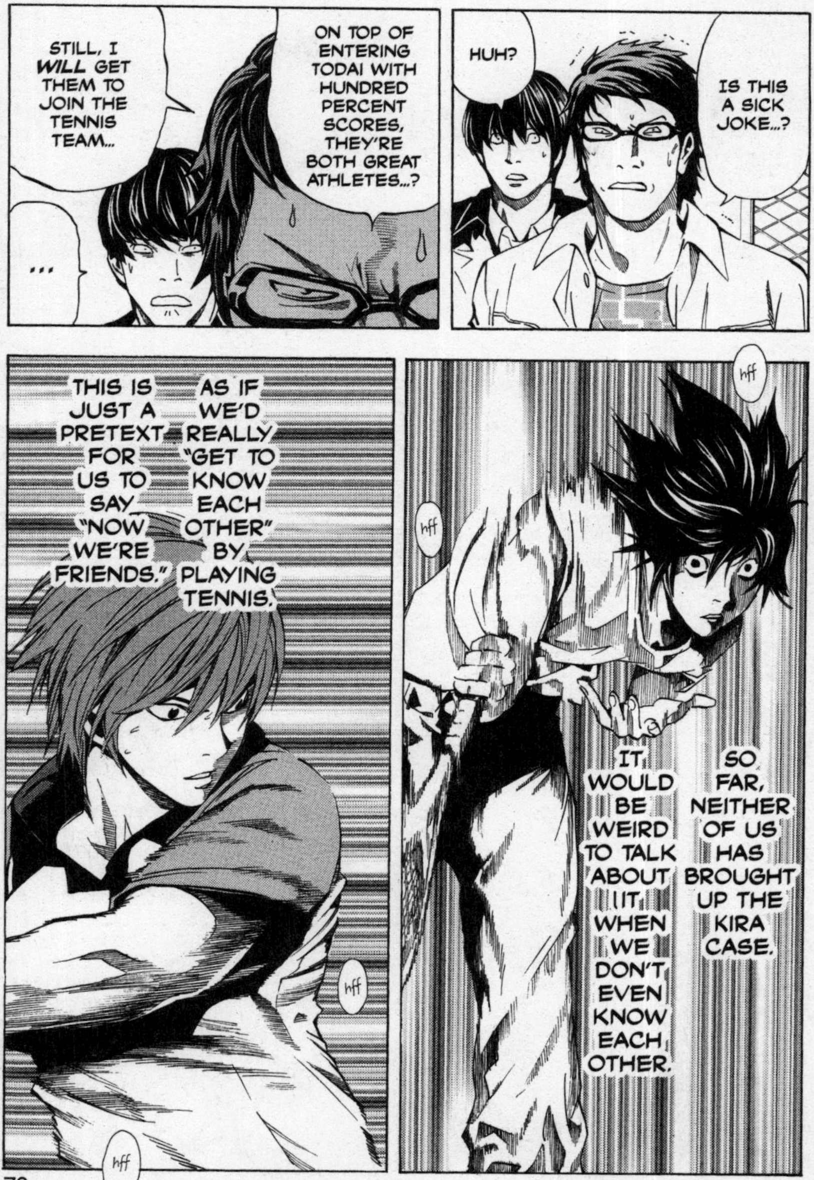
IS THIS A SICK JOKE...?
HUH?
ON TOP OF ENTERING TODAI WITH HUNDRED PERCENT SCORES, THEY'RE BOTH GREAT ATHLETES...?
STILL, I WILL GET THEM TO JOIN THE TENNIS TEAM...
...
hff
SO FAR, NEITHER OF US HAS BROUGHT UP THE KIRA CASE.
IT WOULD BE WEIRD TO TALK ABOUT IT WHEN WE DON'T EVEN KNOW EACH OTHER.
hff
AS IF WE'D REALLY "GET TO KNOW EACH OTHER" BY PLAYING TENNIS.
THIS IS JUST A PRETEXT FOR US TO SAY "NOW WE'RE FRIENDS."
hff
hff

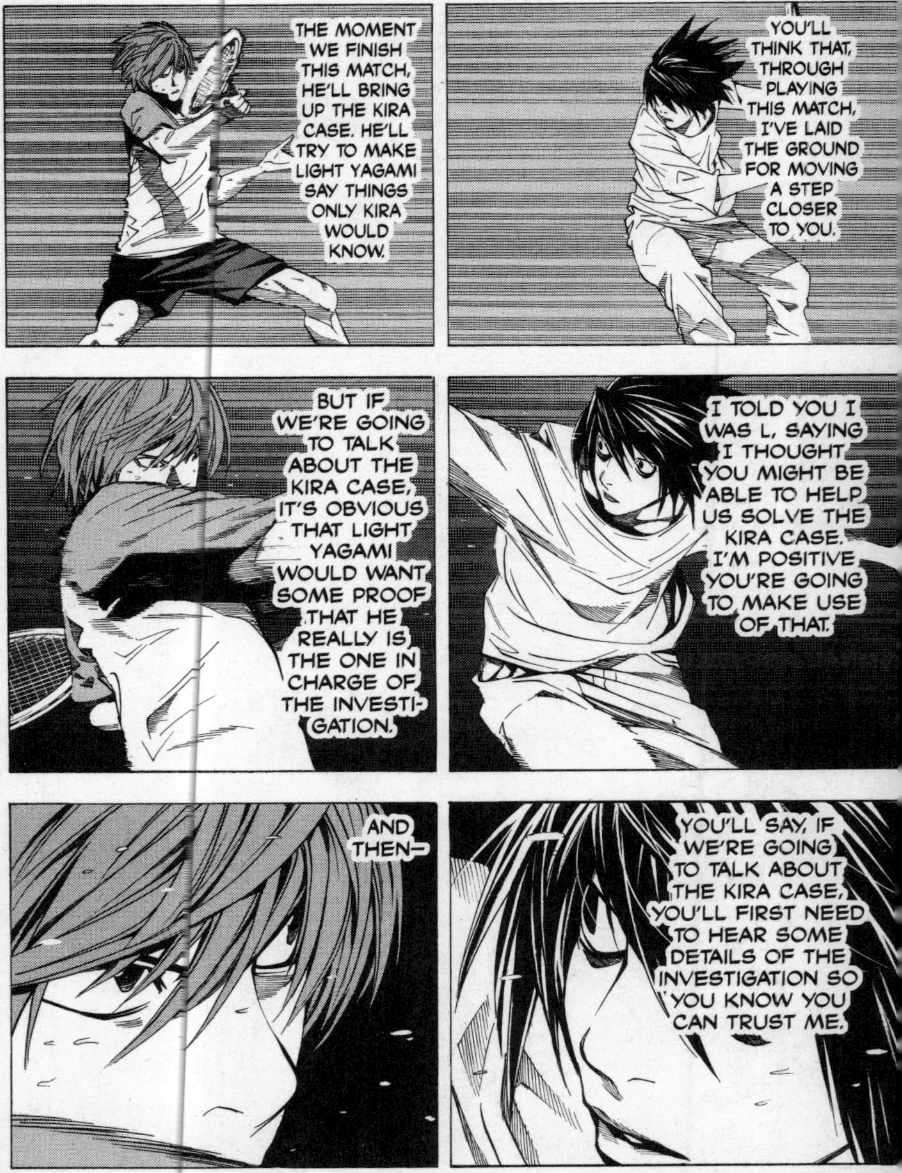
YOU'LL THINK THAT, THROUGH PLAYING THIS MATCH, I'VE LAID THE GROUND FOR MOVING A STEP CLOSER TO YOU.
THE MOMENT WE FINISH THIS MATCH, HE'LL BRING UP THE KIRA CASE. HE'LL TRY TO MAKE LIGHT YAGAMI SAY THINGS ONLY KIRA WOULD KNOW.
I TOLD YOU I WAS L, SAYING I THOUGHT YOU MIGHT BE ABLE TO HELP US SOLVE THE KIRA CASE. I'M POSITIVE YOU'RE GOING TO MAKE USE OF THAT.
BUT IF WE'RE GOING TO TALK ABOUT THE KIRA CASE, IT'S OBVIOUS THAT LIGHT YAGAMI WOULD WANT SOME PROOF THAT HE REALLY IS THE ONE IN CHARGE OF THE INVESTI-GATION.
YOU'LL SAY, IF WE'RE GOING TO TALK ABOUT THE KIRA CASE, YOU'LL FIRST NEED TO HEAR SOME DETAILS OF THE INVESTIGATION SO YOU KNOW YOU CAN TRUST ME.
AND THEN—

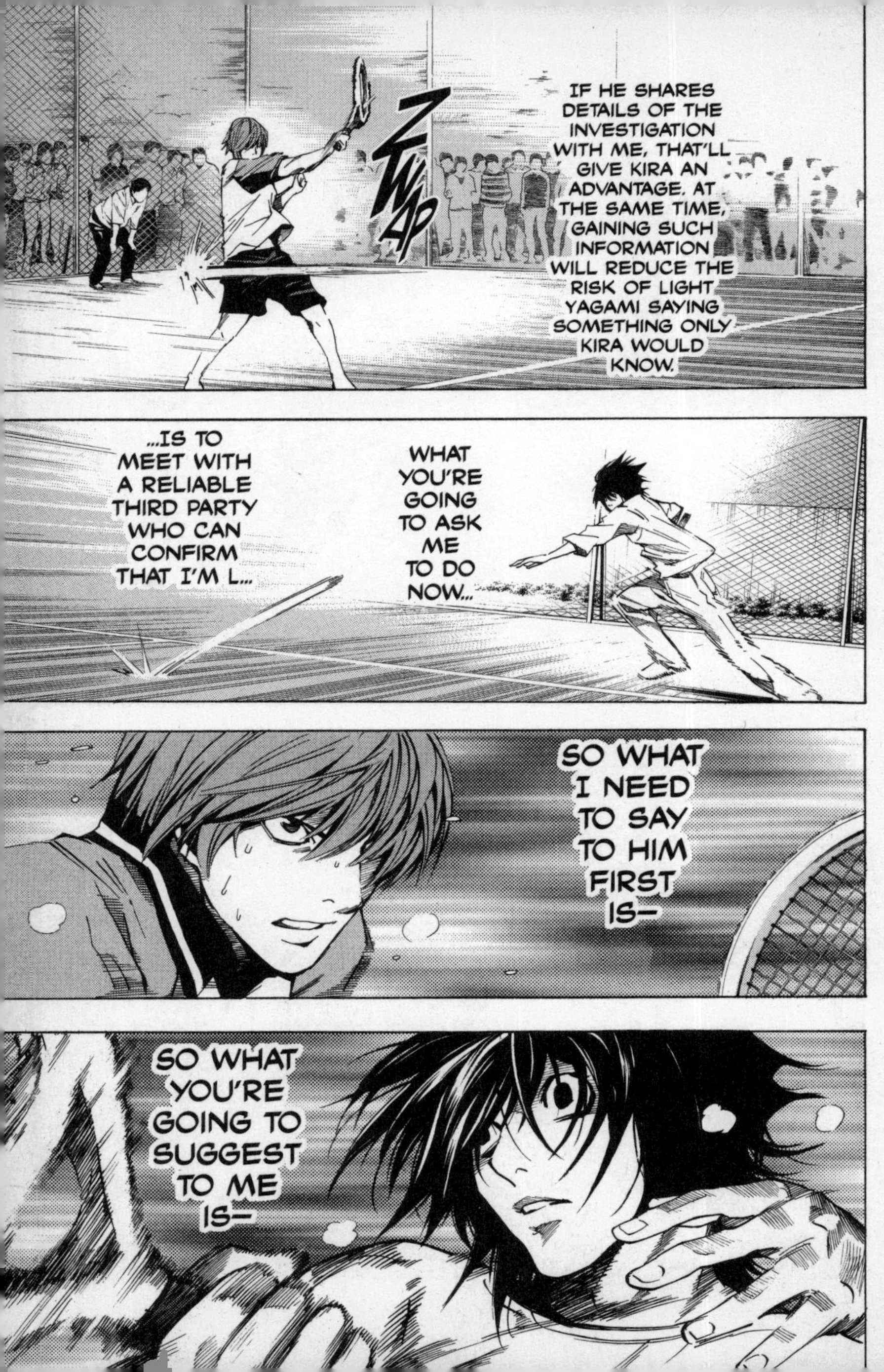
IF HE SHARES DETAILS OF THE INVESTIGATION WITH ME, THAT'LL GIVE KIRA AN ADVANTAGE. AT THE SAME TIME, GAINING SUCH INFORMATION WILL REDUCE THE RISK OF LIGHT YAGAMI SAYING SOMETHING ONLY KIRA WOULD KNOW.
ZWAP
WHAT YOU'RE GOING TO ASK ME TO DO NOW...
...IS TO MEET WITH A RELIABLE THIRD PARTY WHO CAN CONFIRM THAT I'M L...
SO WHAT I NEED TO SAY TO HIM FIRST IS—
SO WHAT YOU'RE GOING TO SUGGEST TO ME IS—

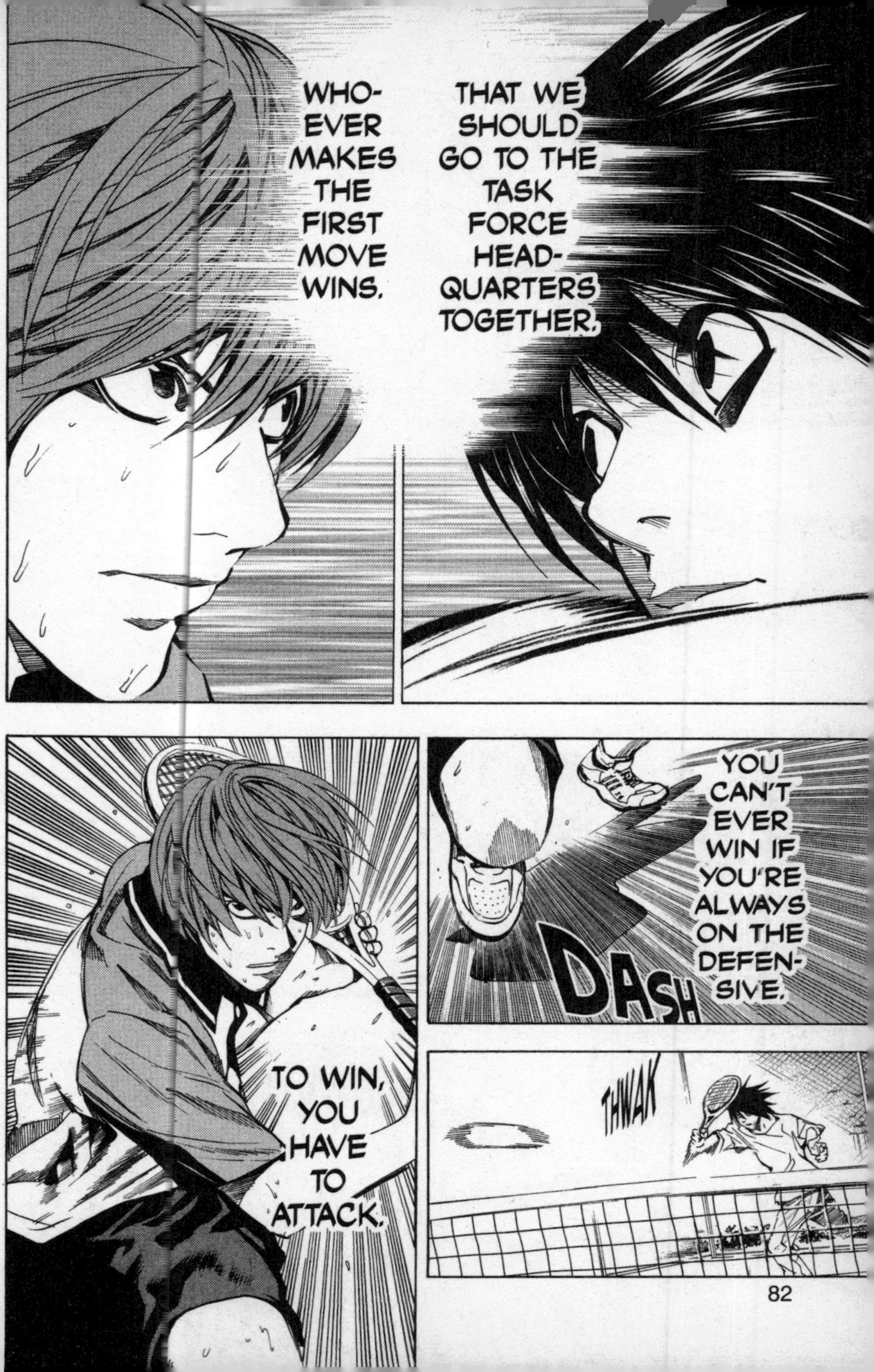
THAT WE SHOULD GO TO THE TASK FORCE HEAD-QUARTERS TOGETHER.
WHO-EVER MAKES THE FIRST MOVE WINS.
YOU CAN'T EVER WIN IF YOU'RE ALWAYS ON THE DEFEN-SIVE.
DASH
THWAK
TO WIN, YOU HAVE TO ATTACK.

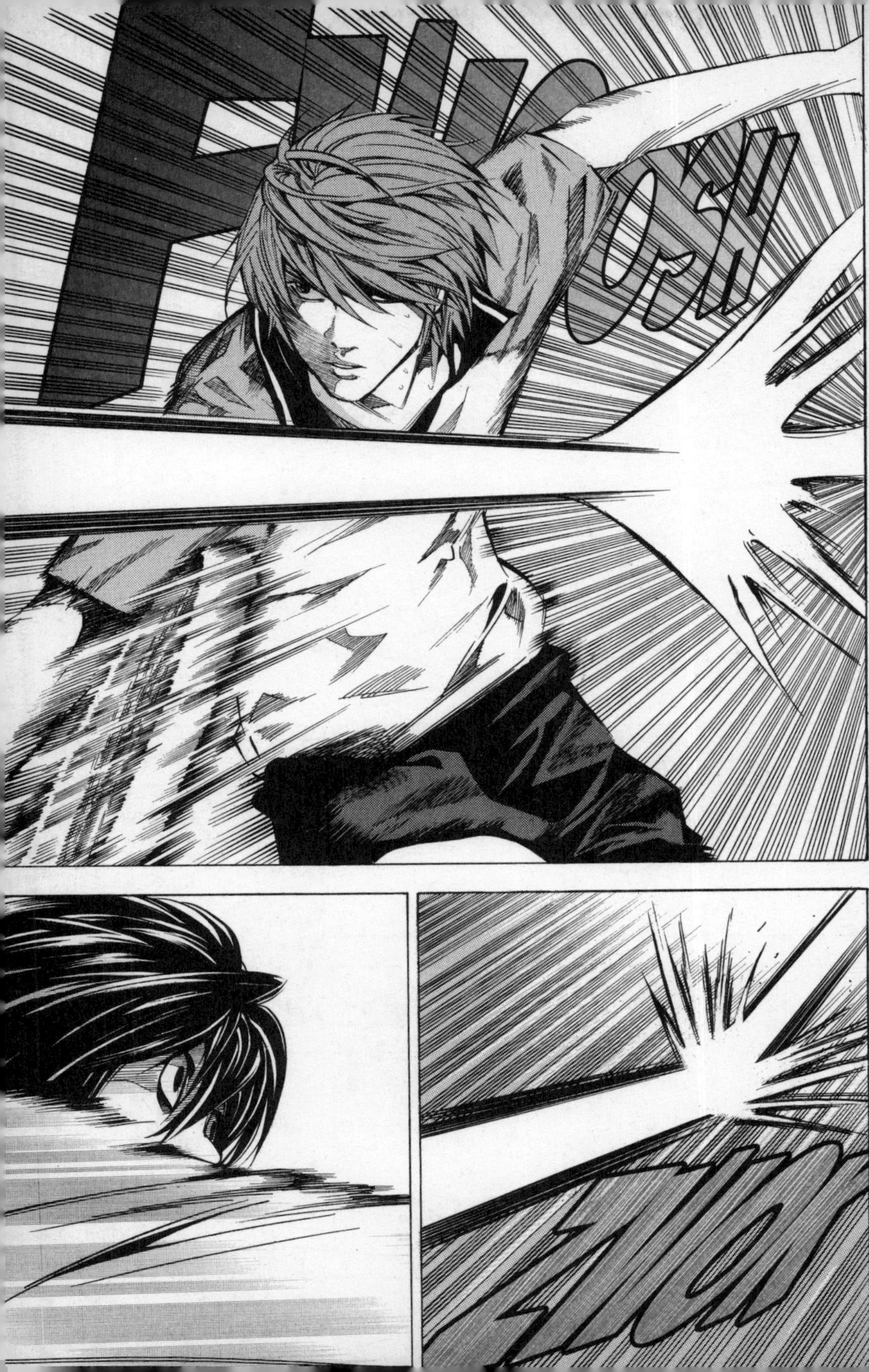

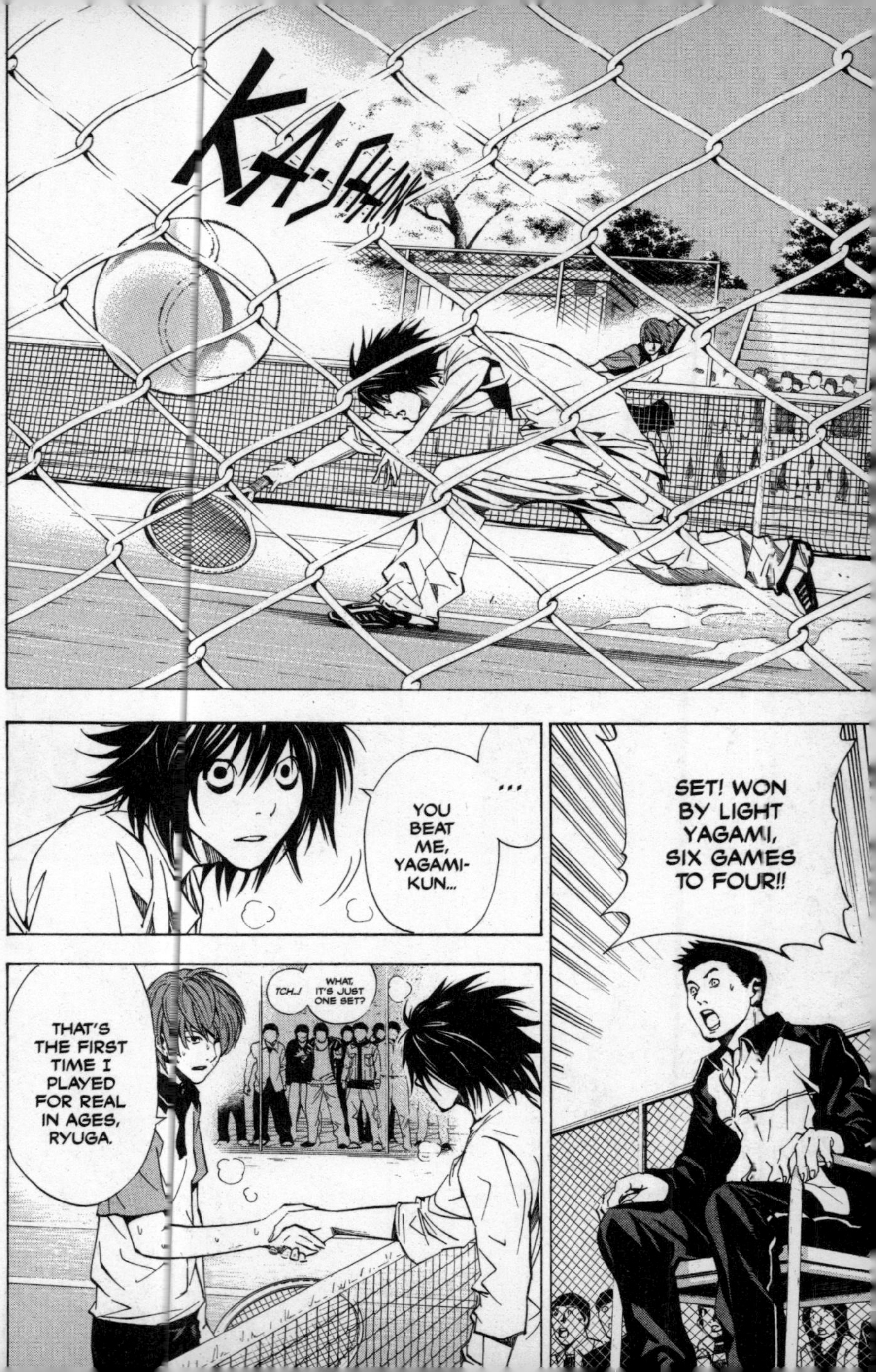
KA-SHANK
SET! WON BY LIGHT YAGAMI, SIX GAMES TO FOUR!!
...
YOU BEAT ME, YAGAMI-KUN...
WHAT, IT'S JUST ONE SET?
TCH..!
THAT'S THE FIRST TIME I PLAYED FOR REAL IN AGES, RYUGA.

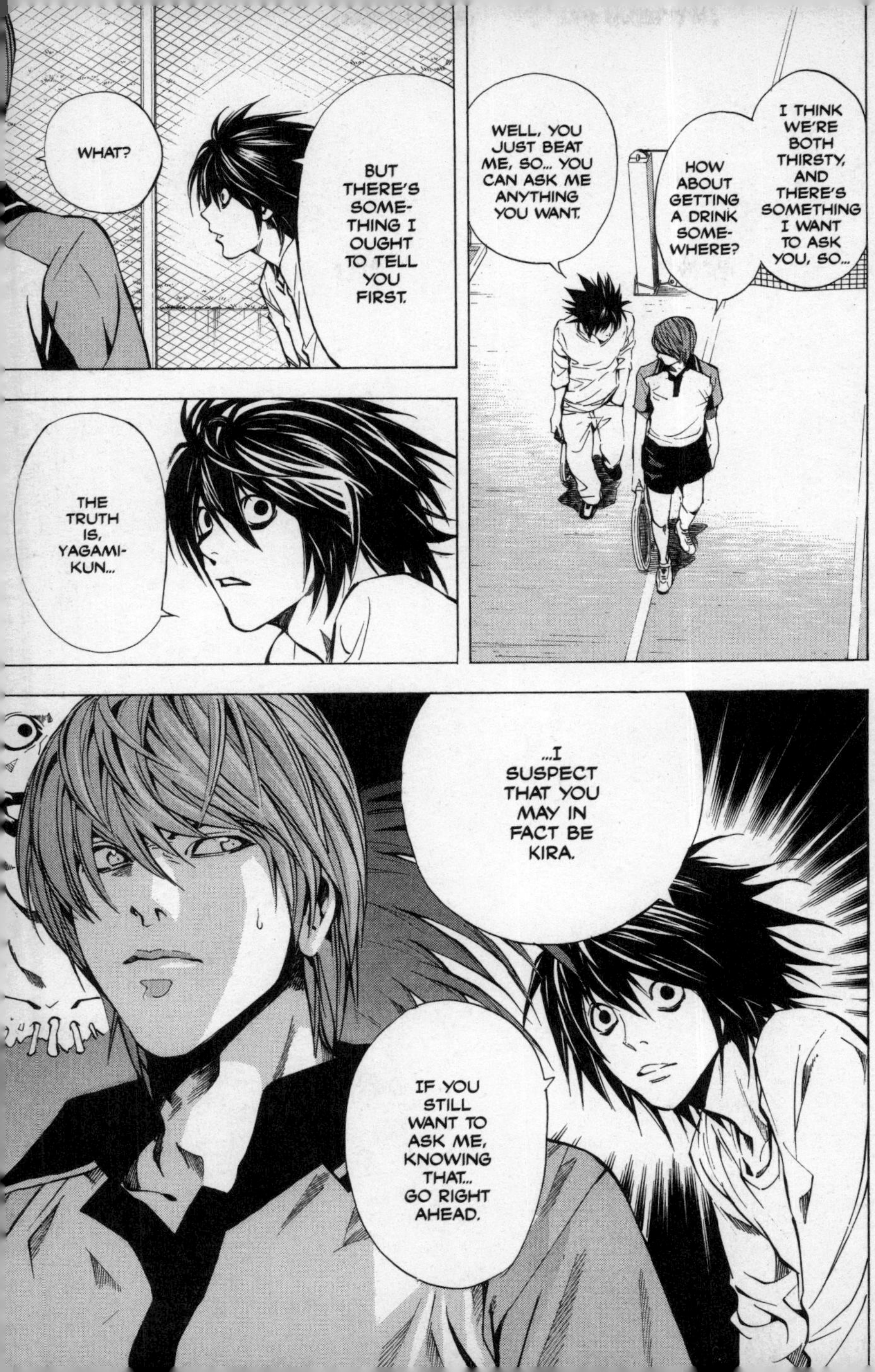

I THINK WE'RE BOTH THIRSTY, AND THERE'S SOMETHING I WANT TO ASK YOU, SO...
HOW ABOUT GETTING A DRINK SOMEWHERE?
WELL, YOU JUST BEAT ME, SO... YOU CAN ASK ME ANYTHING YOU WANT.
BUT THERE'S SOMETHING I OUGHT TO TELL YOU FIRST.
WHAT?
THE TRUTH IS, YAGAMI-KUN...
...I SUSPECT THAT YOU MAY IN FACT BE KIRA.
IF YOU STILL WANT TO ASK ME, KNOWING THAT... GO RIGHT AHEAD.

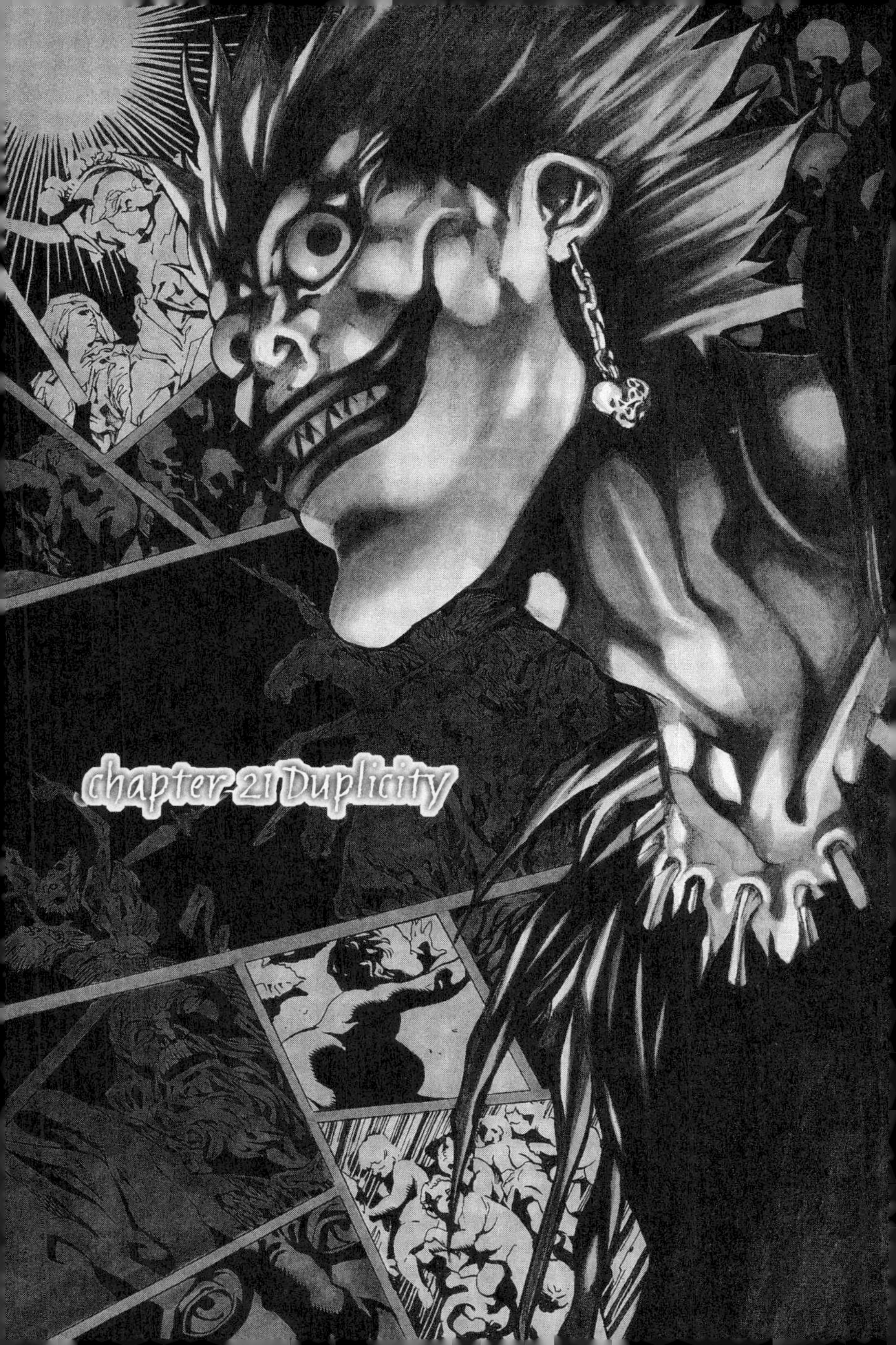
chapter 21 Duplicity

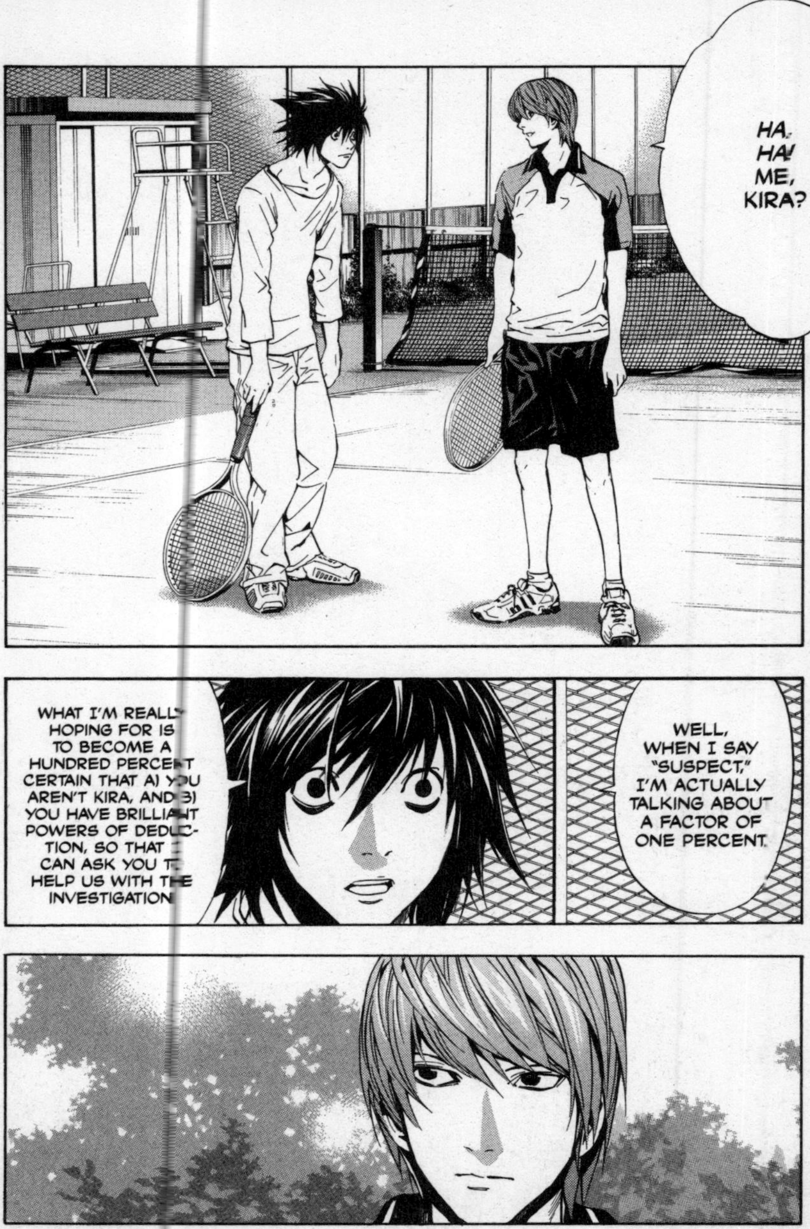
HA. HA! ME, KIRA?
WELL, WHEN I SAY "SUSPECT," I'M ACTUALLY TALKING ABOUT A FACTOR OF ONE PERCENT.
WHAT I'M REALLY HOPING FOR IS TO BECOME A HUNDRED PERCENT CERTAIN THAT A) YOU AREN'T KIRA, AND B) YOU HAVE BRILLIANT POWERS OF DEDUCTION, SO THAT I CAN ASK YOU TO HELP US WITH THE INVESTIGATION.

READ THIS WAY

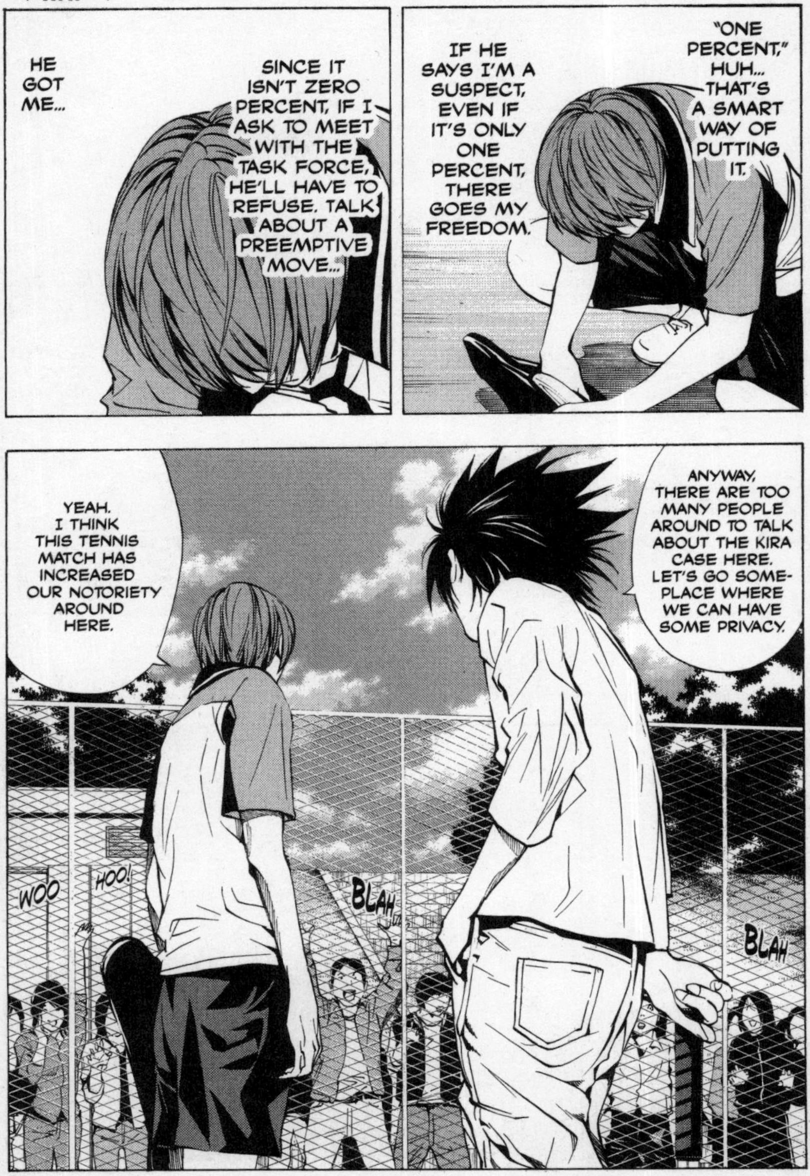
"ONE PERCENT," HUH... THAT'S A SMART WAY OF PUTTING IT.
IF HE SAYS I'M A SUSPECT, EVEN IF IT'S ONLY ONE PERCENT, THERE GOES MY FREEDOM.
SINCE IT ISN'T ZERO PERCENT, IF I ASK TO MEET WITH THE TASK FORCE, HE'LL HAVE TO REFUSE. TALK ABOUT A PREEMPTIVE MOVE...
HE GOT ME...
ANYWAY, THERE ARE TOO MANY PEOPLE AROUND TO TALK ABOUT THE KIRA CASE HERE. LET'S GO SOME-PLACE WHERE WE CAN HAVE SOME PRIVACY.
YEAH. I THINK THIS TENNIS MATCH HAS INCREASED OUR NOTORIETY AROUND HERE.
BLAH
BLAH
HOO!
WOO

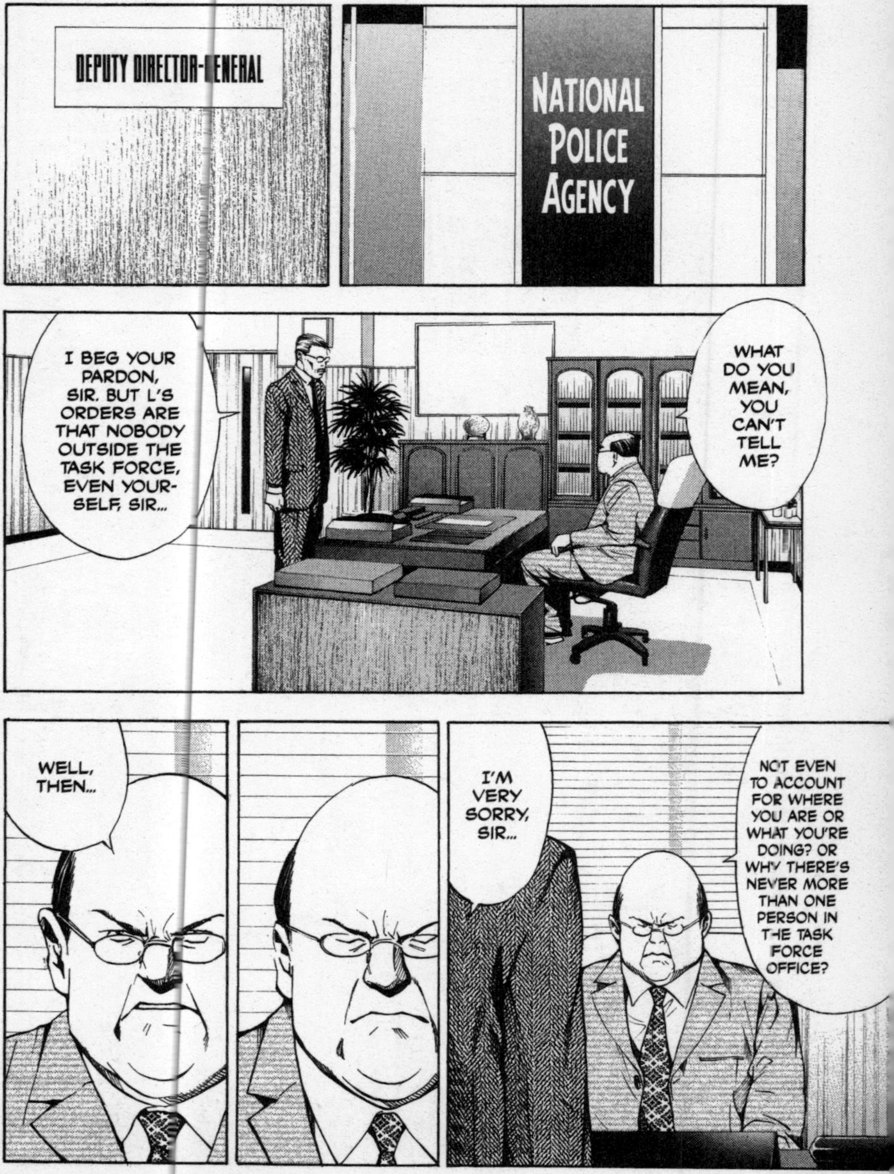
NATIONAL POLICE AGENCY
DEPUTY DIRECTOR-GENERAL
WHAT DO YOU MEAN, YOU CAN'T TELL ME?
I BEG YOUR PARDON, SIR. BUT L'S ORDERS ARE THAT NOBODY OUTSIDE THE TASK FORCE, EVEN YOURSELF, SIR...
NOT EVEN TO ACCOUNT FOR WHERE YOU ARE OR WHAT YOU'RE DOING? OR WHY THERE'S NEVER MORE THAN ONE PERSON IN THE TASK FORCE OFFICE?
I'M VERY SORRY, SIR...
WELL, THEN...

READ THIS WAY

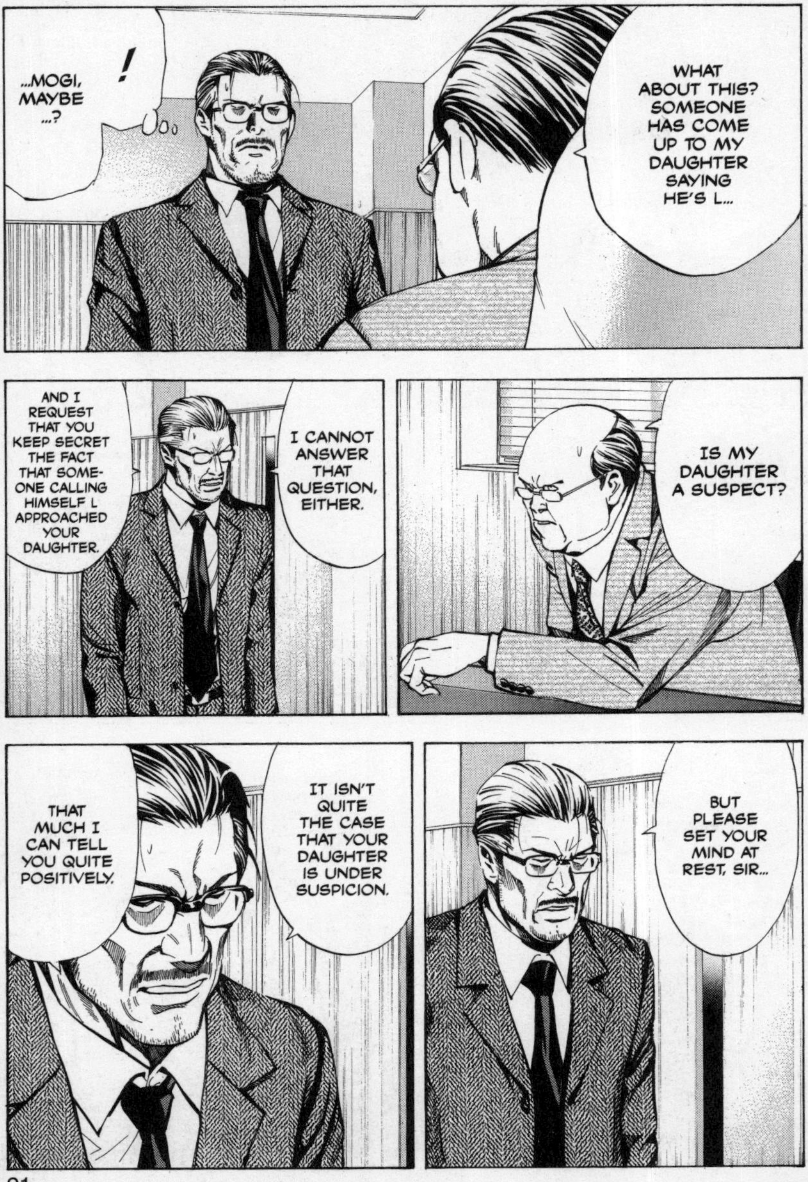
WHAT ABOUT THIS? SOMEONE HAS COME UP TO MY DAUGHTER SAYING HE'S L...
!
...MOGI, MAYBE ...?
IS MY DAUGHTER A SUSPECT?
I CANNOT ANSWER THAT QUESTION, EITHER.
AND I REQUEST THAT YOU KEEP SECRET THE FACT THAT SOME-ONE CALLING HIMSELF L APPROACHED YOUR DAUGHTER.
BUT PLEASE SET YOUR MIND AT REST, SIR...
IT ISN'T QUITE THE CASE THAT YOUR DAUGHTER IS UNDER SUSPICION.
THAT MUCH I CAN TELL YOU QUITE POSITIVELY.

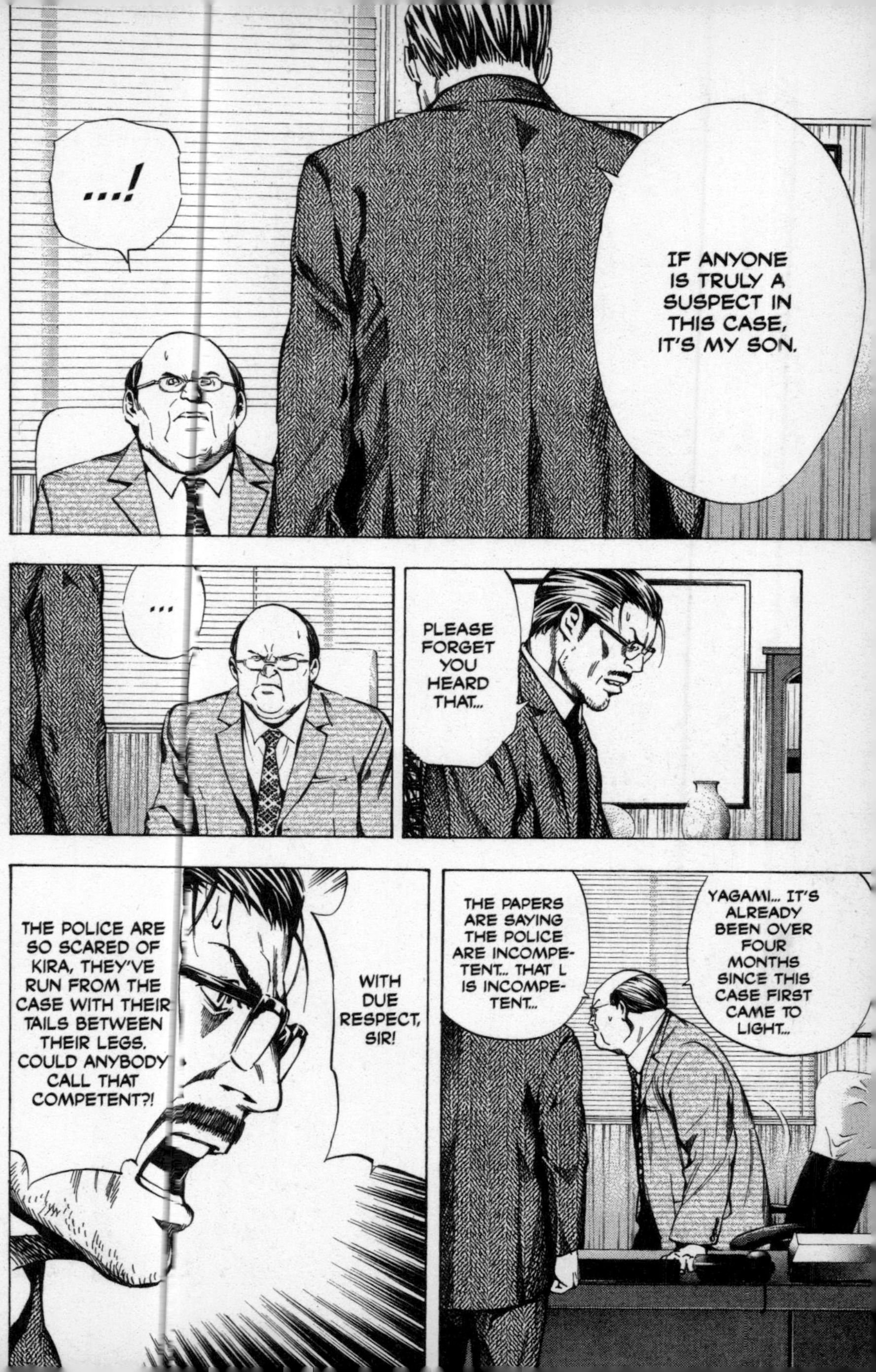
IF ANYONE IS TRULY A SUSPECT IN THIS CASE, IT'S MY SON.
...!
PLEASE FORGET YOU HEARD THAT...
...
YAGAMI... IT'S ALREADY BEEN OVER FOUR MONTHS SINCE THIS CASE FIRST CAME TO LIGHT...
THE PAPERS ARE SAYING THE POLICE ARE INCOMPETENT... THAT L IS INCOMPETENT...
WITH DUE RESPECT, SIR!
THE POLICE ARE SO SCARED OF KIRA, THEY'VE RUN FROM THE CASE WITH THEIR TAILS BETWEEN THEIR LEGS. COULD ANYBODY CALL THAT COMPETENT?!

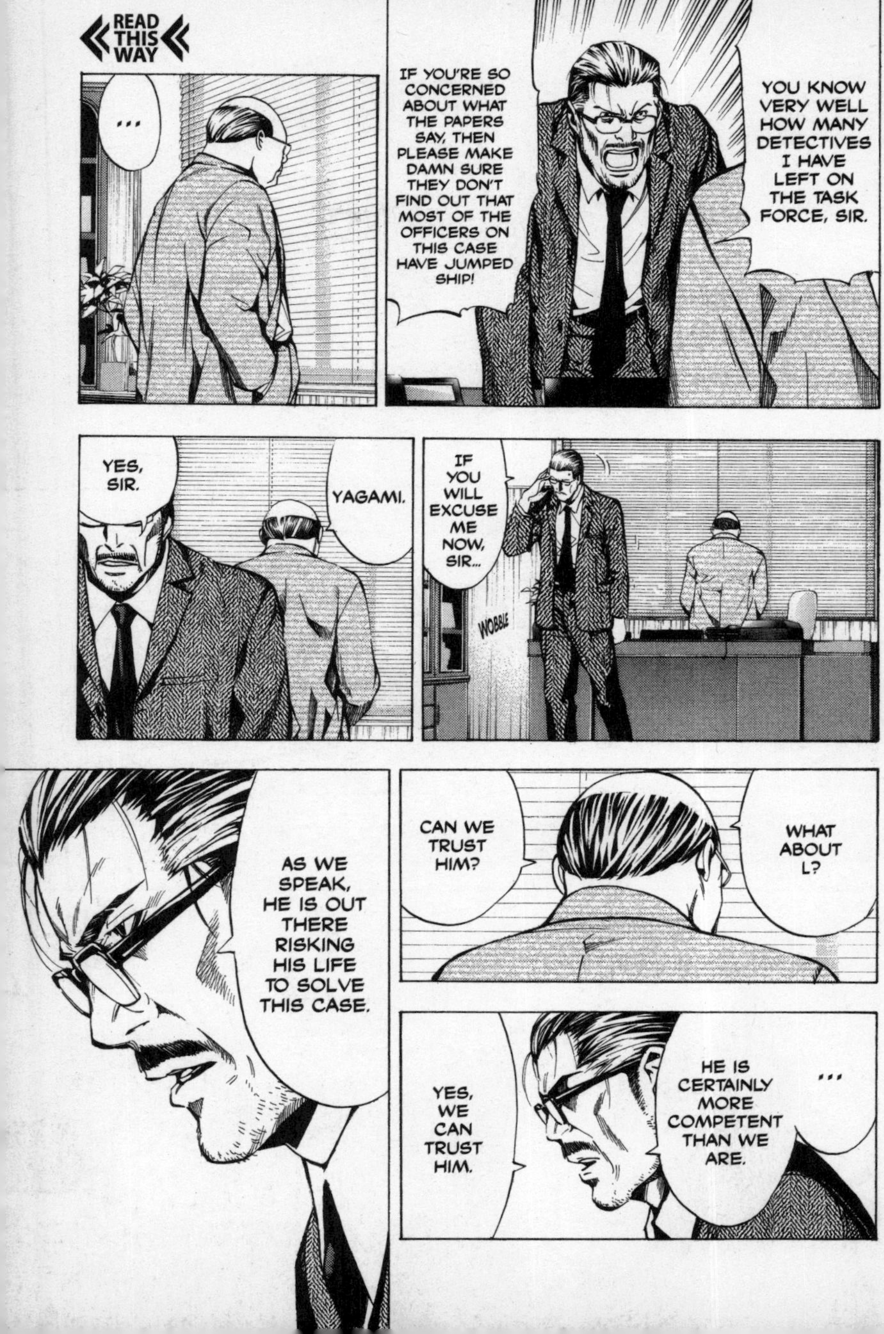
READ THIS WAY
YOU KNOW VERY WELL HOW MANY DETECTIVES I HAVE LEFT ON THE TASK FORCE, SIR.
IF YOU'RE SO CONCERNED ABOUT WHAT THE PAPERS SAY, THEN PLEASE MAKE DAMN SURE THEY DON'T FIND OUT THAT MOST OF THE OFFICERS ON THIS CASE HAVE JUMPED SHIP!
...
IF YOU WILL EXCUSE ME NOW, SIR...
WOBBLE
YAGAMI.
YES, SIR.
WHAT ABOUT L?
CAN WE TRUST HIM?
...
HE IS CERTAINLY MORE COMPETENT THAN WE ARE.
YES, WE CAN TRUST HIM.
AS WE SPEAK, HE IS OUT THERE RISKING HIS LIFE TO SOLVE THIS CASE.

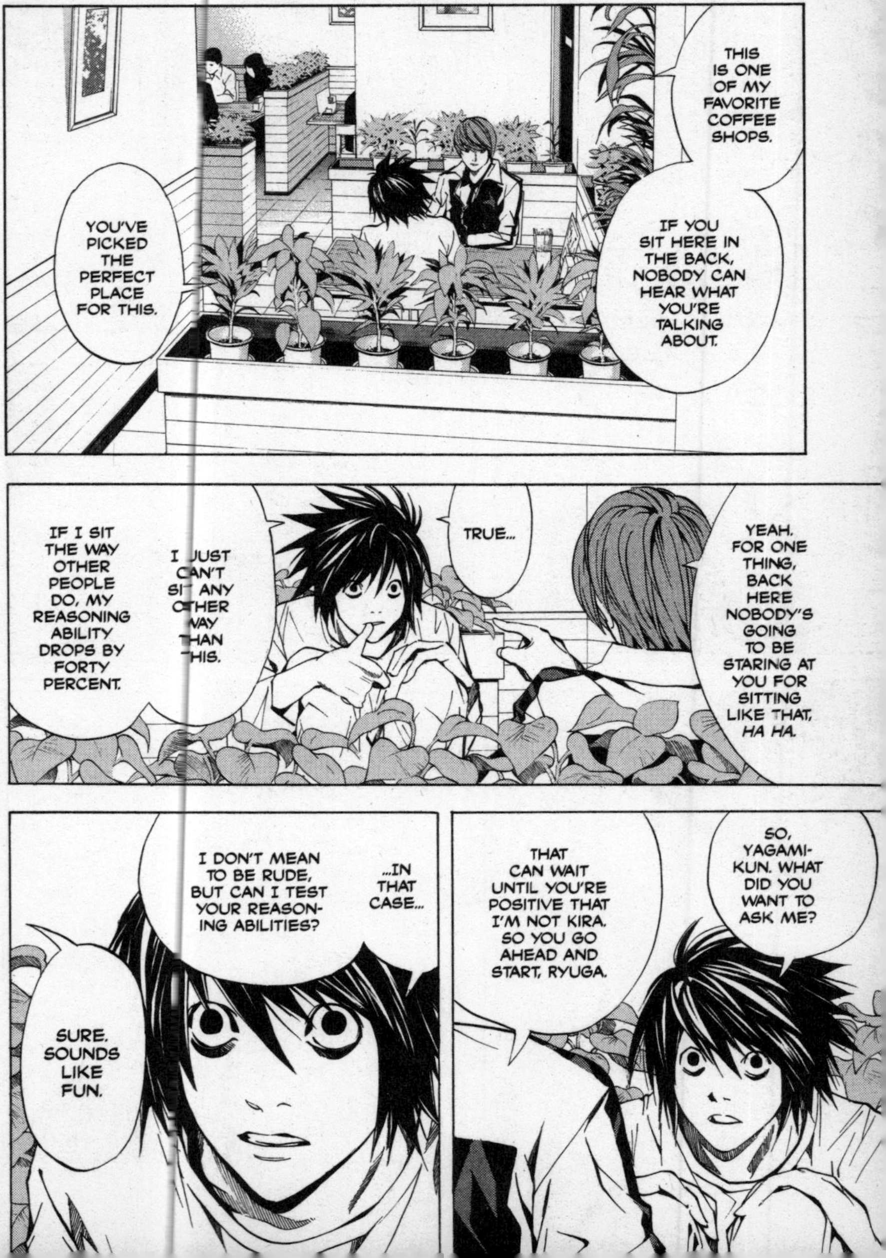
THIS IS ONE OF MY FAVORITE COFFEE SHOPS.
IF YOU SIT HERE IN THE BACK, NOBODY CAN HEAR WHAT YOU'RE TALKING ABOUT.
YOU'VE PICKED THE PERFECT PLACE FOR THIS.
YEAH. FOR ONE THING, BACK HERE NOBODY'S GOING TO BE STARING AT YOU FOR SITTING LIKE THAT, *HA HA*.
TRUE...
I JUST CAN'T SIT ANY OTHER WAY THAN THIS.
IF I SIT THE WAY OTHER PEOPLE DO, MY REASONING ABILITY DROPS BY FORTY PERCENT.
SO, YAGAMI-KUN. WHAT DID YOU WANT TO ASK ME?
THAT CAN WAIT UNTIL YOU'RE POSITIVE THAT I'M NOT KIRA. SO YOU GO AHEAD AND START, RYUGA.
...IN THAT CASE...
I DON'T MEAN TO BE RUDE, BUT CAN I TEST YOUR REASONING ABILITIES?
SURE. SOUNDS LIKE FUN.

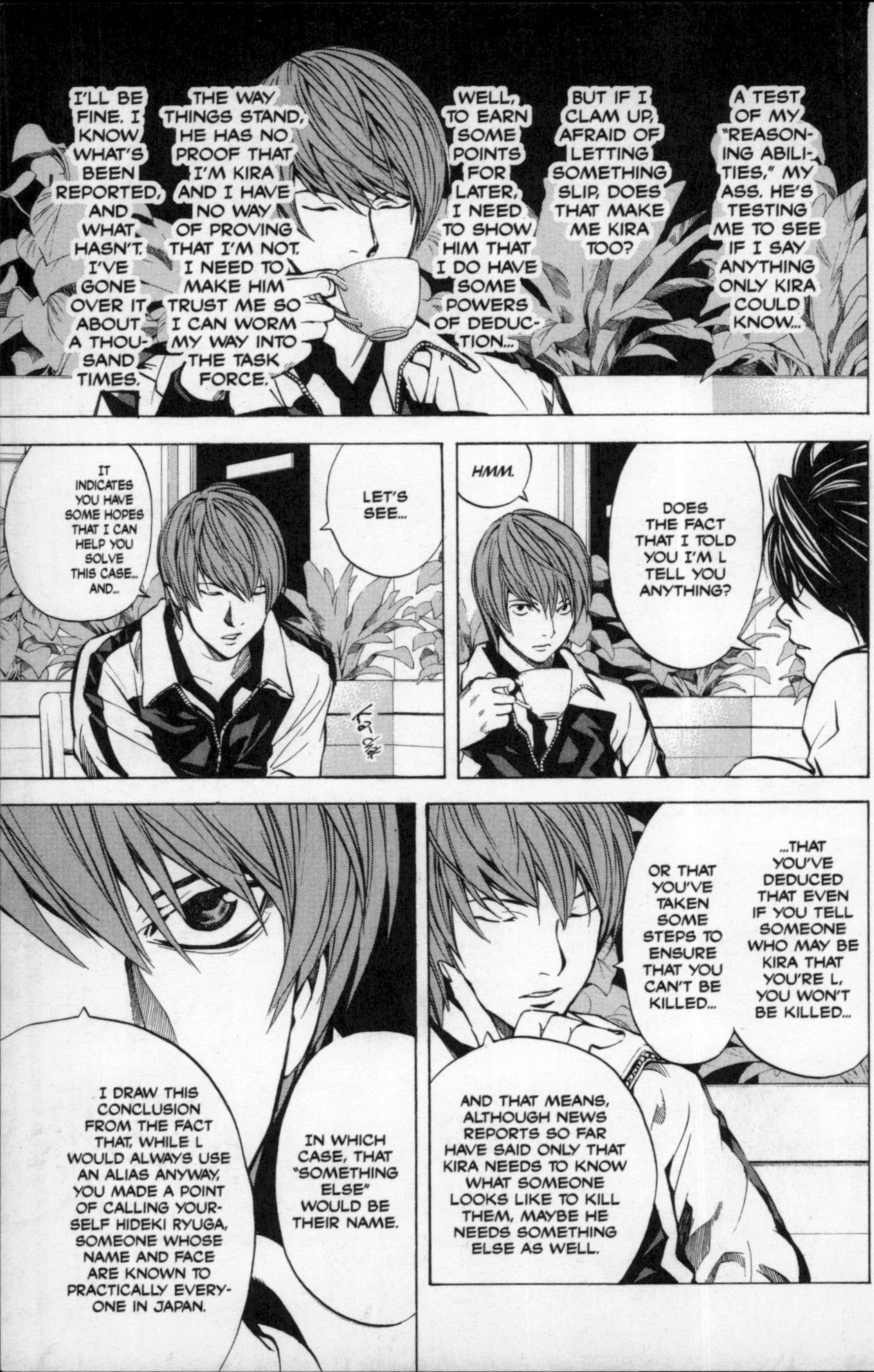
A TEST OF MY "REASONING ABILITIES," MY ASS. HE'S TESTING ME TO SEE IF I SAY ANYTHING ONLY KIRA COULD KNOW...
BUT IF I CLAM UP, AFRAID OF LETTING SOMETHING SLIP, DOES THAT MAKE ME KIRA TOO?
WELL, TO EARN SOME POINTS FOR LATER, I NEED TO SHOW HIM THAT I DO HAVE SOME POWERS OF DEDUCTION...
THE WAY THINGS STAND, HE HAS NO PROOF THAT I'M KIRA AND I HAVE NO WAY OF PROVING THAT I'M NOT. I NEED TO MAKE HIM TRUST ME SO I CAN WORM MY WAY INTO THE TASK FORCE.
I'LL BE FINE. I KNOW WHAT'S BEEN REPORTED, AND WHAT HASN'T. I'VE GONE OVER IT ABOUT A THOUSAND TIMES.
DOES THE FACT THAT I TOLD YOU I'M L TELL YOU ANYTHING?
HMM.
LET'S SEE...
IT INDICATES YOU HAVE SOME HOPES THAT I CAN HELP YOU SOLVE THIS CASE... AND...
...THAT YOU'VE DEDUCED THAT EVEN IF YOU TELL SOMEONE WHO MAY BE KIRA THAT YOU'RE L, YOU WON'T BE KILLED...
OR THAT YOU'VE TAKEN SOME STEPS TO ENSURE THAT YOU CAN'T BE KILLED...
AND THAT MEANS, ALTHOUGH NEWS REPORTS SO FAR HAVE SAID ONLY THAT KIRA NEEDS TO KNOW WHAT SOMEONE LOOKS LIKE TO KILL THEM, MAYBE HE NEEDS SOMETHING ELSE AS WELL.
IN WHICH CASE, THAT "SOMETHING ELSE" WOULD BE THEIR NAME.
I DRAW THIS CONCLUSION FROM THE FACT THAT, WHILE L WOULD ALWAYS USE AN ALIAS ANYWAY, YOU MADE A POINT OF CALLING YOURSELF HIDEKI RYUGA, SOMEONE WHOSE NAME AND FACE ARE KNOWN TO PRACTICALLY EVERYONE IN JAPAN.

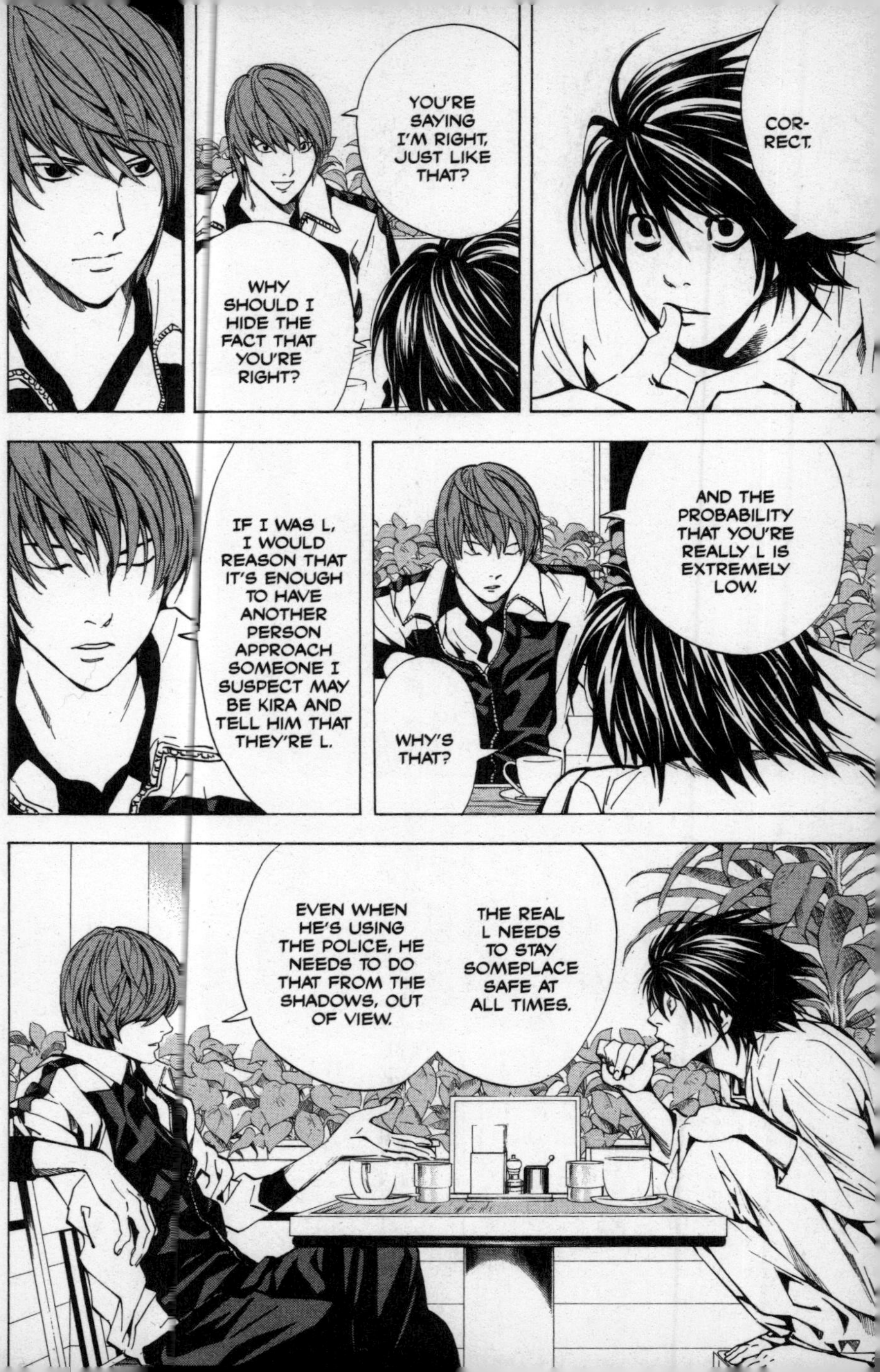
CORRECT.
YOU'RE SAYING I'M RIGHT, JUST LIKE THAT?
WHY SHOULD I HIDE THE FACT THAT YOU'RE RIGHT?
AND THE PROBABILITY THAT YOU'RE REALLY L IS EXTREMELY LOW.
WHY'S THAT?
IF I WAS L, I WOULD REASON THAT IT'S ENOUGH TO HAVE ANOTHER PERSON APPROACH SOMEONE I SUSPECT MAY BE KIRA AND TELL HIM THAT THEY'RE L.
THE REAL L NEEDS TO STAY SOMEPLACE SAFE AT ALL TIMES.
EVEN WHEN HE'S USING THE POLICE, HE NEEDS TO DO THAT FROM THE SHADOWS, OUT OF VIEW.

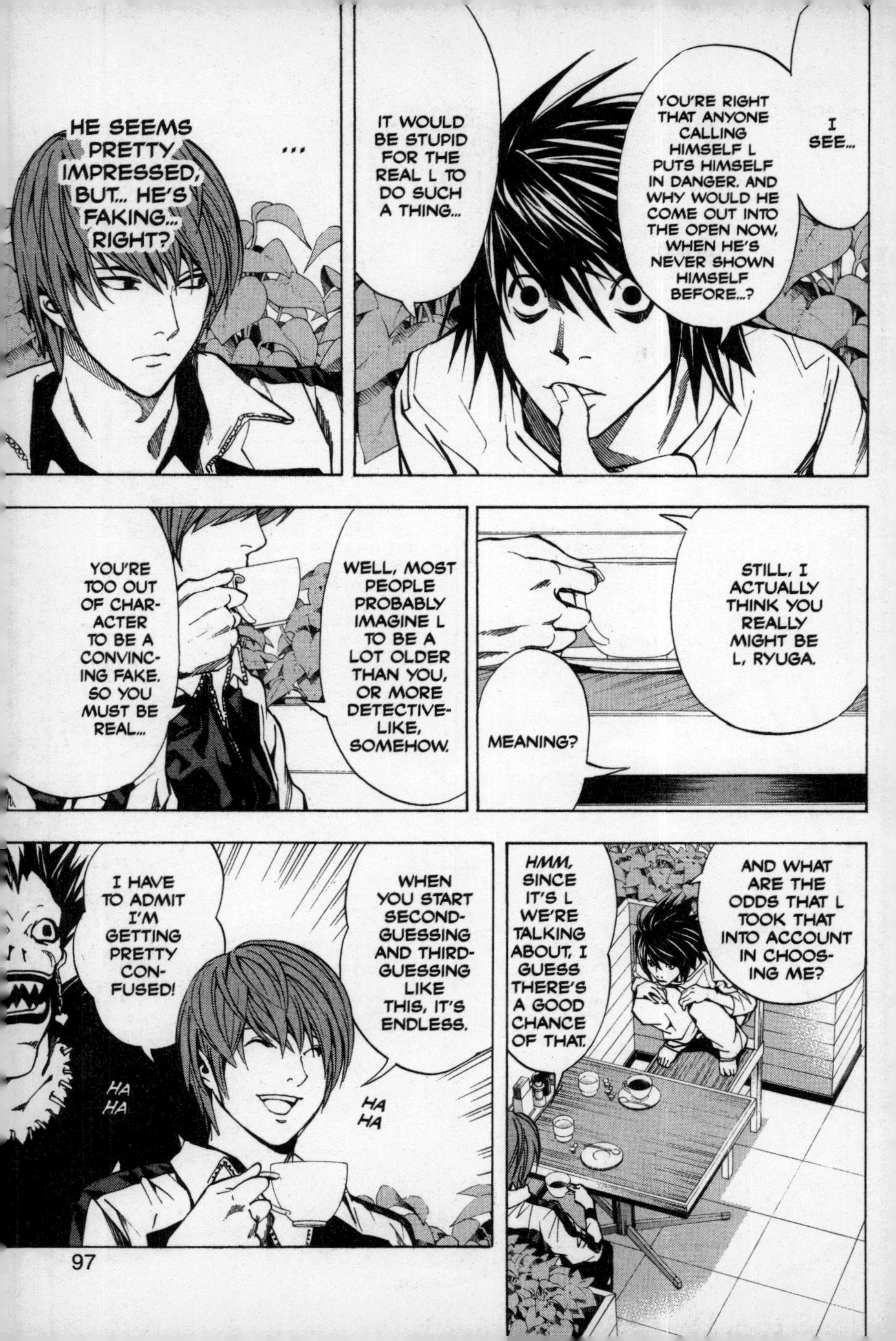
I SEE...
YOU'RE RIGHT THAT ANYONE CALLING HIMSELF L PUTS HIMSELF IN DANGER. AND WHY WOULD HE COME OUT INTO THE OPEN NOW, WHEN HE'S NEVER SHOWN HIMSELF BEFORE...?
IT WOULD BE STUPID FOR THE REAL L TO DO SUCH A THING...
...
HE SEEMS PRETTY IMPRESSED, BUT... HE'S FAKING... RIGHT?
STILL, I ACTUALLY THINK YOU REALLY MIGHT BE L, RYUGA.
MEANING?
WELL, MOST PEOPLE PROBABLY IMAGINE L TO BE A LOT OLDER THAN YOU, OR MORE DETECTIVE-LIKE, SOMEHOW.
YOU'RE TOO OUT OF CHARACTER TO BE A CONVINCING FAKE. SO YOU MUST BE REAL...
AND WHAT ARE THE ODDS THAT L TOOK THAT INTO ACCOUNT IN CHOOSING ME?
HMM, SINCE IT'S L WE'RE TALKING ABOUT, I GUESS THERE'S A GOOD CHANCE OF THAT.
WHEN YOU START SECOND-GUESSING AND THIRD-GUESSING LIKE THIS, IT'S ENDLESS.
HA HA
I HAVE TO ADMIT I'M GETTING PRETTY CONFUSED!
HA HA

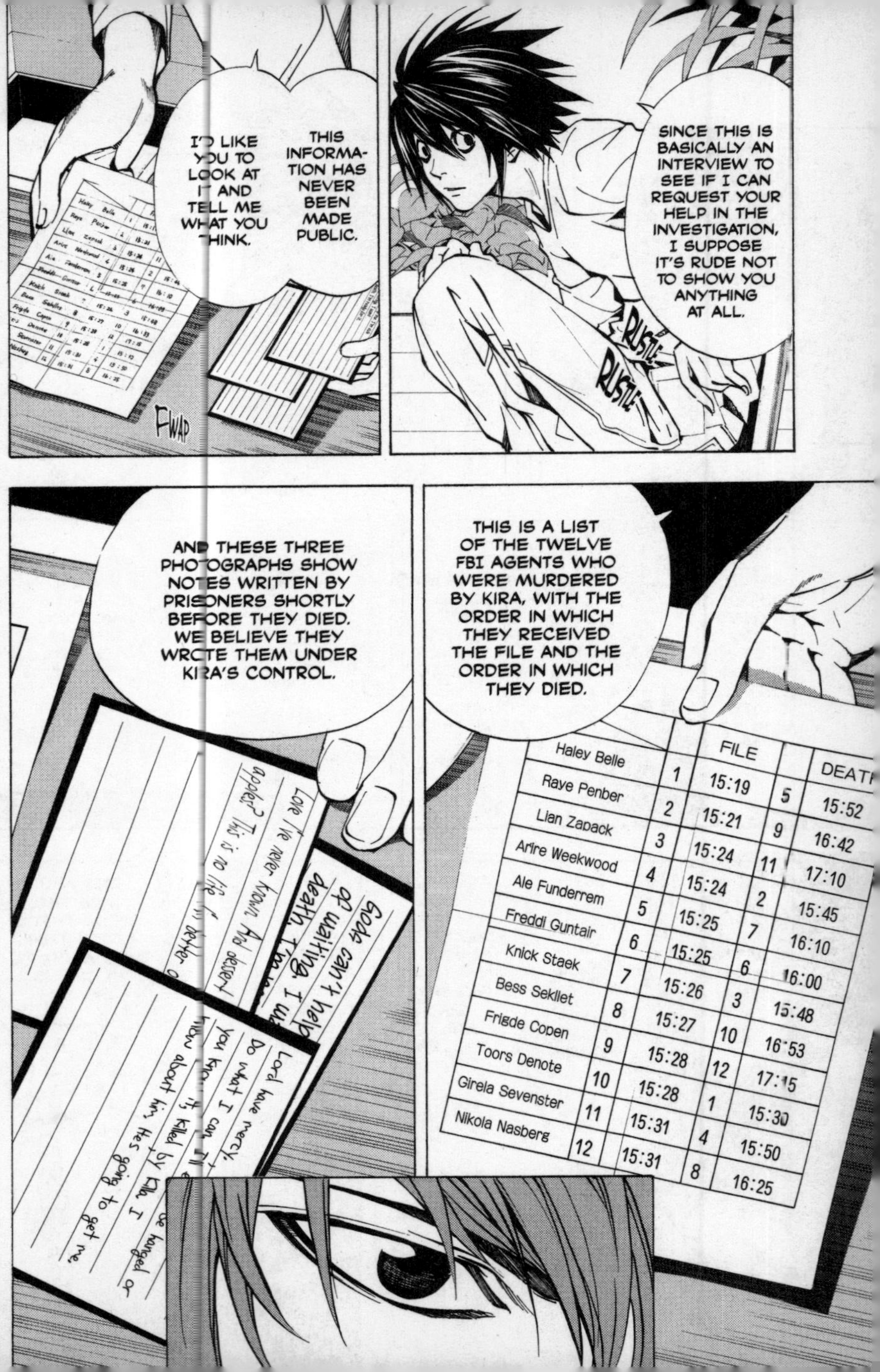
SINCE THIS IS BASICALLY AN INTERVIEW TO SEE IF I CAN REQUEST YOUR HELP IN THE INVESTIGATION, I SUPPOSE IT'S RUDE NOT TO SHOW YOU ANYTHING AT ALL.
RUSTLE
RUSTLE
THIS INFORMATION HAS NEVER BEEN MADE PUBLIC.
I'D LIKE YOU TO LOOK AT IT AND TELL ME WHAT YOU THINK.
FWAP
THIS IS A LIST OF THE TWELVE FBI AGENTS WHO WERE MURDERED BY KIRA, WITH THE ORDER IN WHICH THEY RECEIVED THE FILE AND THE ORDER IN WHICH THEY DIED.
FILE
DEAT
Haley Belle 1 15:19 5 15:52
Raye Penber 2 15:21 9 16:42
Lian Zapack 3 15:24 11 17:10
Arire Weekwood 4 15:24 2 15:45
Ale Funderrem 5 15:25 7 16:10
Freddi Guntair 6 15:25 6 16:00
Knick Staek 7 15:26 3 15:48
Bess Sekllet 8 15:27 10 16:53
Frigde Copen 9 15:28 12 17:15
Toors Denote 10 15:28 1 15:30
Girela Sevenster 11 15:31 4 15:50
Nikola Nasberg 12 15:31 8 16:25
AND THESE THREE PHOTOGRAPHS SHOW NOTES WRITTEN BY PRISONERS SHORTLY BEFORE THEY DIED. WE BELIEVE THEY WROTE THEM UNDER KIRA'S CONTROL.

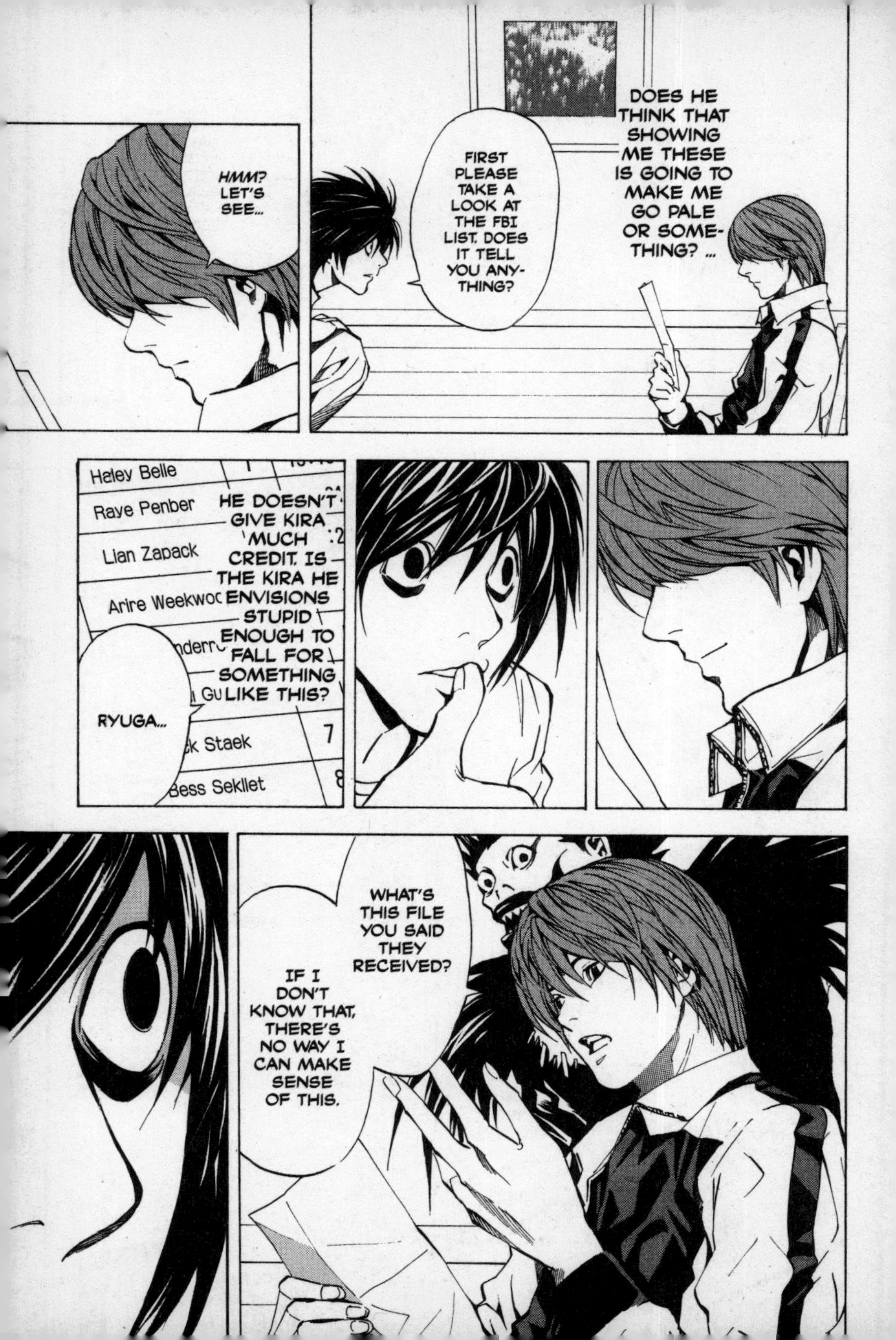

DOES HE THINK THAT SHOWING ME THESE IS GOING TO MAKE ME GO PALE OR SOMETHING? ...
FIRST PLEASE TAKE A LOOK AT THE FBI LIST. DOES IT TELL YOU ANYTHING?
HMM? LET'S SEE...
HE DOESN'T GIVE KIRA MUCH CREDIT. IS THE KIRA HE ENVISIONS STUPID ENOUGH TO FALL FOR SOMETHING LIKE THIS?
Haley Belle
Raye Penber
Lian Zapack
Bess Sekllet
RYUGA...
WHAT'S THIS FILE YOU SAID THEY RECEIVED?
IF I DON'T KNOW THAT, THERE'S NO WAY I CAN MAKE SENSE OF THIS.

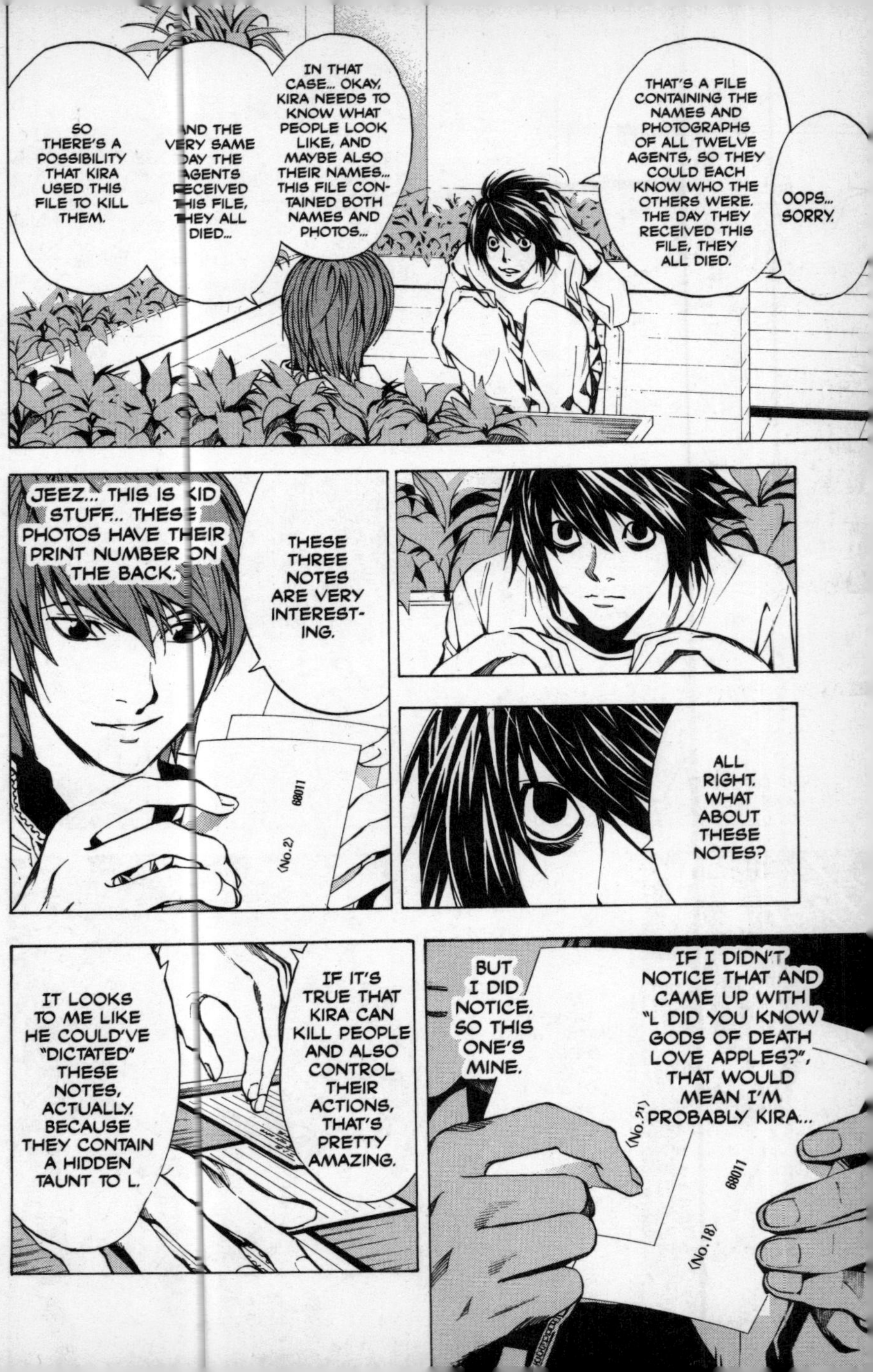
OOPS... SORRY.
THAT'S A FILE CONTAINING THE NAMES AND PHOTOGRAPHS OF ALL TWELVE AGENTS, SO THEY COULD EACH KNOW WHO THE OTHERS WERE. THE DAY THEY RECEIVED THIS FILE, THEY ALL DIED.
IN THAT CASE... OKAY, KIRA NEEDS TO KNOW WHAT PEOPLE LOOK LIKE, AND MAYBE ALSO THEIR NAMES... THIS FILE CONTAINED BOTH NAMES AND PHOTOS...
AND THE VERY SAME DAY THE AGENTS RECEIVED THIS FILE, THEY ALL DIED...
SO THERE'S A POSSIBILITY THAT KIRA USED THIS FILE TO KILL THEM.
ALL RIGHT. WHAT ABOUT THESE NOTES?
THESE THREE NOTES ARE VERY INTERESTING.
JEEZ... THIS IS KID STUFF... THESE PHOTOS HAVE THEIR PRINT NUMBER ON THE BACK.
〈No.2〉 68011
IF I DIDN'T NOTICE THAT AND CAME UP WITH "L DID YOU KNOW GODS OF DEATH LOVE APPLES?", THAT WOULD MEAN I'M PROBABLY KIRA...
BUT I DID NOTICE. SO THIS ONE'S MINE.
〈No.21〉
68011
〈No.18〉
IF IT'S TRUE THAT KIRA CAN KILL PEOPLE AND ALSO CONTROL THEIR ACTIONS, THAT'S PRETTY AMAZING.
IT LOOKS TO ME LIKE HE COULD'VE "DICTATED" THESE NOTES, ACTUALLY. BECAUSE THEY CONTAIN A HIDDEN TAUNT TO L.

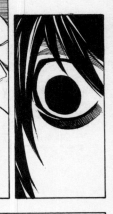

IF YOU TAKE THE FIRST WORD OF EVERY LINE, THEY FORM A SENTENCE, OR RATHER, A QUESTION.
BECAUSE THE ORDER THAT MAKES MOST SENSE WOULD BE, LET'S SEE... "L DO YOU KNOW GODS OF DEATH LOVE APPLES?"
BUT...
THE BACKS OF THE PHOTOS HAVE THEIR PRINT NUMBER ON THEM...
IF YOU PUT THEM IN THAT ORDER—
68011
〈No. 2〉
THE MESSAGE READS "L DO YOU KNOW LOVE APPLES? GODS OF DEATH."
THAT DOESN'T MAKE MUCH SENSE, SO I FIND IT HARD TO BELIEVE KIRA WANTED L TO READ IT LIKE THAT.
INCORRECT.
IN FACT, THERE'S A FOURTH NOTE.
A FOURTH NOTE?!
RUSTLE

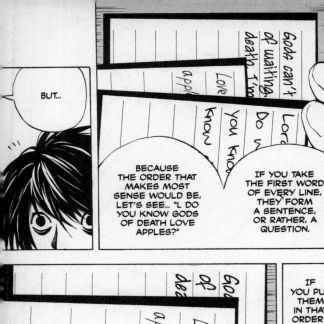

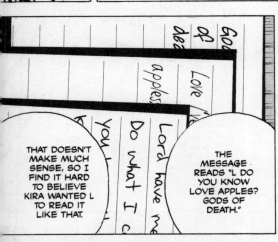

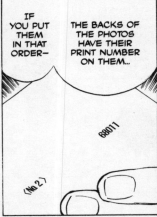

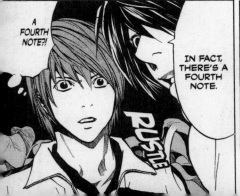

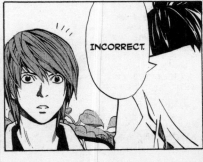

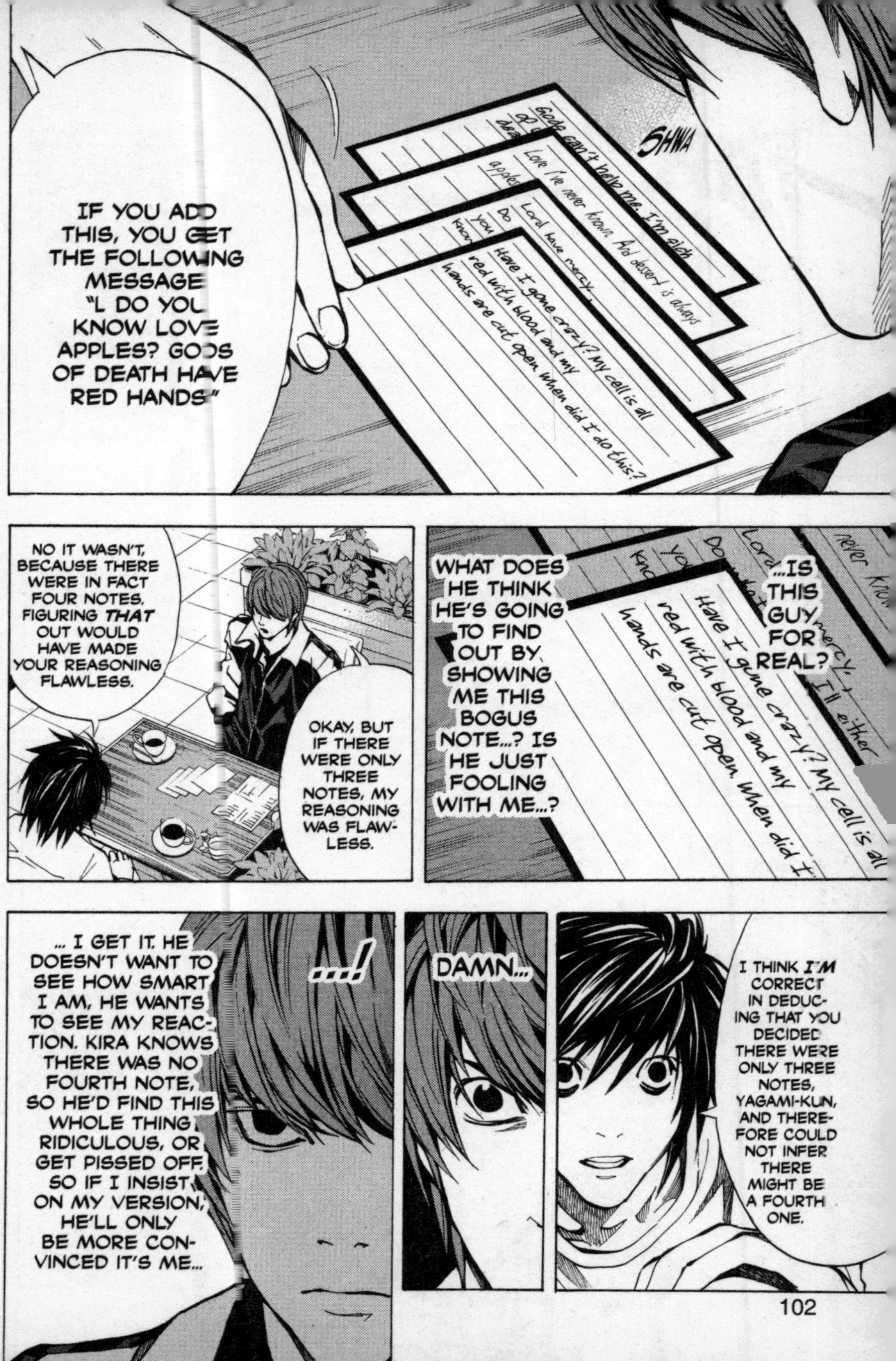

SHWA
Gods can't help me. I'm sick
Love I've never known. And dessert is always
Lord have mercy.
Have I gone crazy? My cell is all red with blood and my hands are cut open. When did I do this?
IF YOU ADD THIS, YOU GET THE FOLLOWING MESSAGE "L DO YOU KNOW LOVE APPLES? GODS OF DEATH HAVE RED HANDS"
Have I gone crazy? My cell is all red with blood and my hands are cut open. When did I
...IS THIS GUY FOR REAL?
WHAT DOES HE THINK HE'S GOING TO FIND OUT BY SHOWING ME THIS BOGUS NOTE...? IS HE JUST FOOLING WITH ME...?
OKAY, BUT IF THERE WERE ONLY THREE NOTES, MY REASONING WAS FLAWLESS.
NO IT WASN'T, BECAUSE THERE WERE IN FACT FOUR NOTES. FIGURING *THAT* OUT WOULD HAVE MADE YOUR REASONING FLAWLESS.
I THINK *I'M* CORRECT IN DEDUCING THAT YOU DECIDED THERE WERE ONLY THREE NOTES, YAGAMI-KUN, AND THEREFORE COULD NOT INFER THERE MIGHT BE A FOURTH ONE.
DAMN...
...!
... I GET IT. HE DOESN'T WANT TO SEE HOW SMART I AM, HE WANTS TO SEE MY REACTION. KIRA KNOWS THERE WAS NO FOURTH NOTE, SO HE'D FIND THIS WHOLE THING RIDICULOUS, OR GET PISSED OFF. SO IF I INSIST ON MY VERSION, HE'LL ONLY BE MORE CONVINCED IT'S ME...

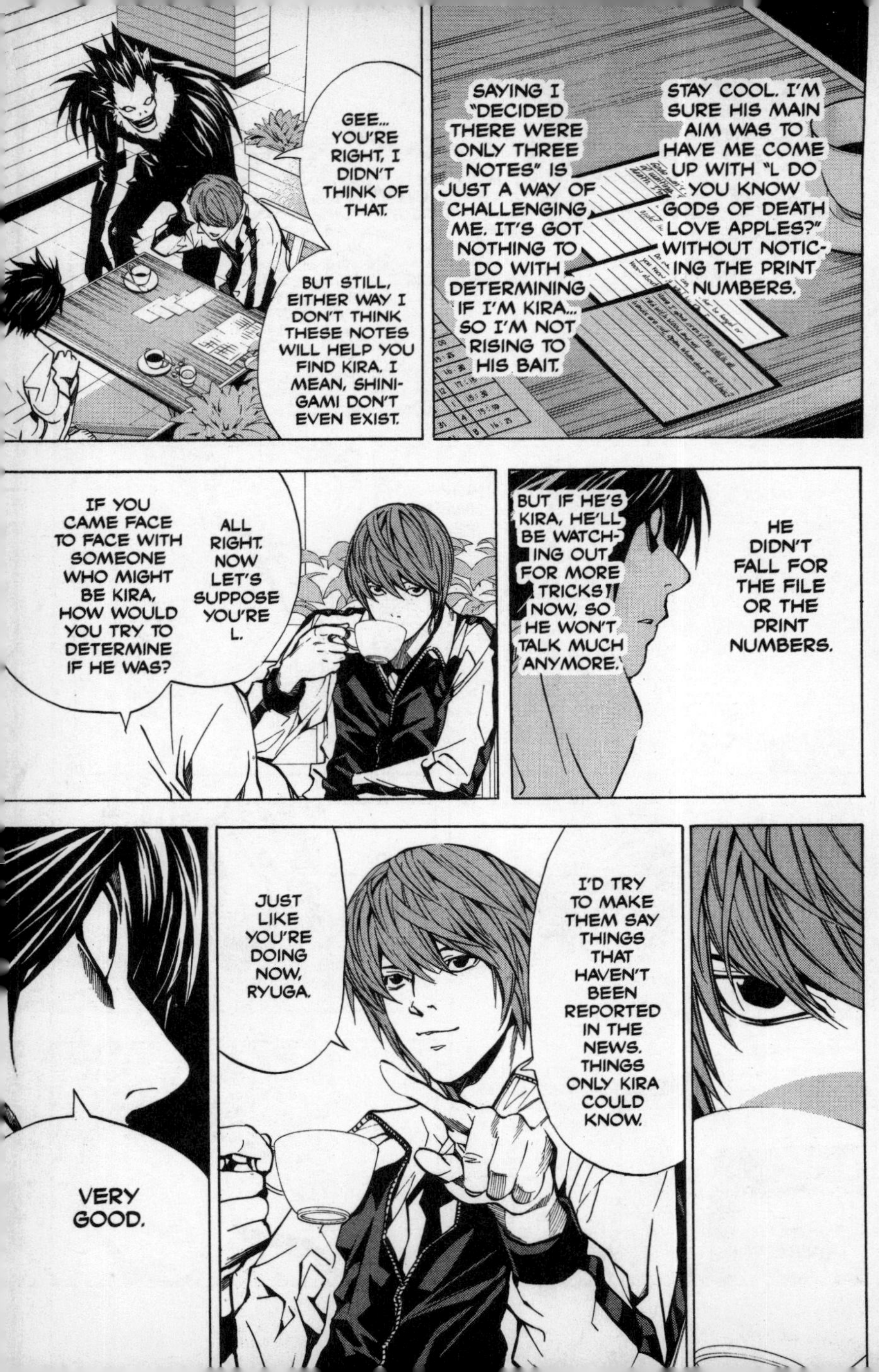
STAY COOL. I'M SURE HIS MAIN AIM WAS TO HAVE ME COME UP WITH "L DO YOU KNOW GODS OF DEATH LOVE APPLES?" WITHOUT NOTICING THE PRINT NUMBERS.
SAYING I "DECIDED THERE WERE ONLY THREE NOTES" IS JUST A WAY OF CHALLENGING ME. IT'S GOT NOTHING TO DO WITH DETERMINING IF I'M KIRA... SO I'M NOT RISING TO HIS BAIT.
GEE... YOU'RE RIGHT, I DIDN'T THINK OF THAT.
BUT STILL, EITHER WAY I DON'T THINK THESE NOTES WILL HELP YOU FIND KIRA. I MEAN, SHINIGAMI DON'T EVEN EXIST.
HE DIDN'T FALL FOR THE FILE OR THE PRINT NUMBERS.
BUT IF HE'S KIRA, HE'LL BE WATCHING OUT FOR MORE TRICKS NOW, SO HE WON'T TALK MUCH ANYMORE.
ALL RIGHT. NOW LET'S SUPPOSE YOU'RE L.
IF YOU CAME FACE TO FACE WITH SOMEONE WHO MIGHT BE KIRA, HOW WOULD YOU TRY TO DETERMINE IF HE WAS?
I'D TRY TO MAKE THEM SAY THINGS THAT HAVEN'T BEEN REPORTED IN THE NEWS. THINGS ONLY KIRA COULD KNOW.
JUST LIKE YOU'RE DOING NOW, RYUGA.
VERY GOOD.

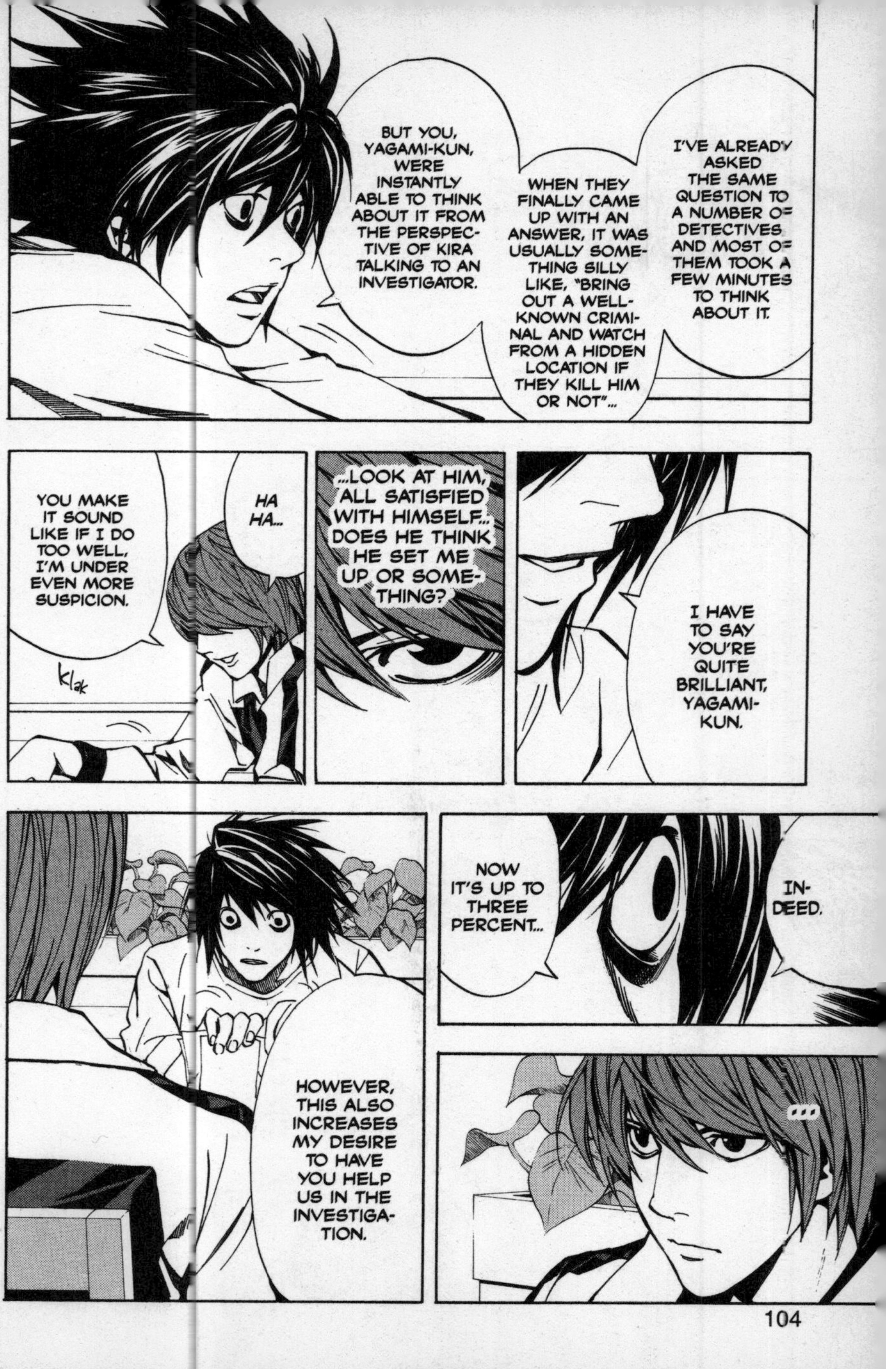
I'VE ALREADY ASKED THE SAME QUESTION TO A NUMBER OF DETECTIVES AND MOST OF THEM TOOK A FEW MINUTES TO THINK ABOUT IT.
WHEN THEY FINALLY CAME UP WITH AN ANSWER, IT WAS USUALLY SOMETHING SILLY LIKE, "BRING OUT A WELL-KNOWN CRIMINAL AND WATCH FROM A HIDDEN LOCATION IF THEY KILL HIM OR NOT"...
BUT YOU, YAGAMI-KUN, WERE INSTANTLY ABLE TO THINK ABOUT IT FROM THE PERSPECTIVE OF KIRA TALKING TO AN INVESTIGATOR.
I HAVE TO SAY YOU'RE QUITE BRILLIANT, YAGAMI-KUN.
...LOOK AT HIM, ALL SATISFIED WITH HIMSELF... DOES HE THINK HE SET ME UP OR SOMETHING?
HA HA...
YOU MAKE IT SOUND LIKE IF I DO TOO WELL, I'M UNDER EVEN MORE SUSPICION.
klak
IN-DEED.
NOW IT'S UP TO THREE PERCENT...
...
HOWEVER, THIS ALSO INCREASES MY DESIRE TO HAVE YOU HELP US IN THE INVESTIGATION.

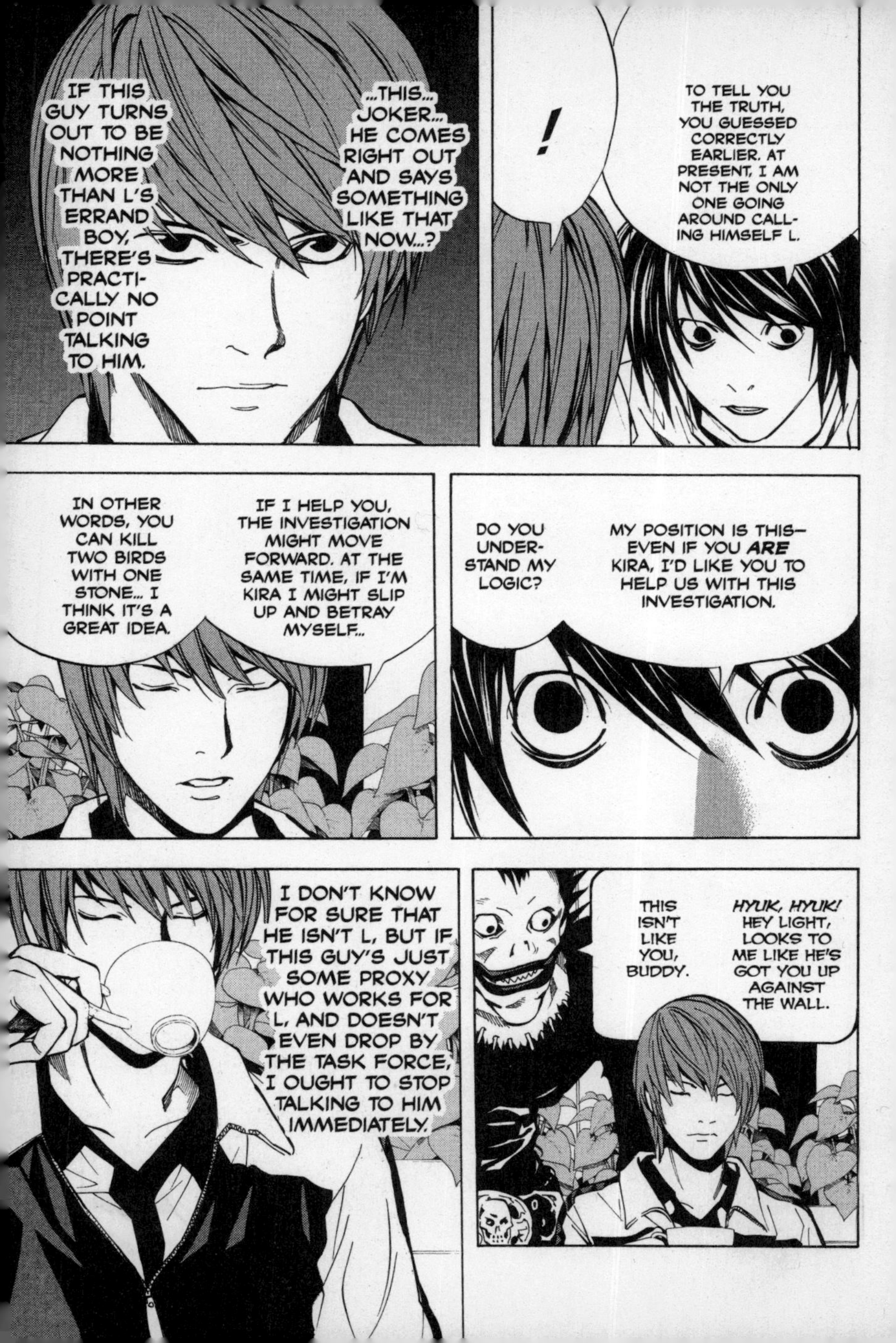

TO TELL YOU THE TRUTH, YOU GUESSED CORRECTLY EARLIER. AT PRESENT, I AM NOT THE ONLY ONE GOING AROUND CALLING HIMSELF L.
!
...THIS... JOKER... HE COMES RIGHT OUT AND SAYS SOMETHING LIKE THAT NOW...?
IF THIS GUY TURNS OUT TO BE NOTHING MORE THAN L'S ERRAND BOY, THERE'S PRACTICALLY NO POINT TALKING TO HIM.
MY POSITION IS THIS—EVEN IF YOU *ARE* KIRA, I'D LIKE YOU TO HELP US WITH THIS INVESTIGATION.
DO YOU UNDERSTAND MY LOGIC?
IF I HELP YOU, THE INVESTIGATION MIGHT MOVE FORWARD. AT THE SAME TIME, IF I'M KIRA I MIGHT SLIP UP AND BETRAY MYSELF...
IN OTHER WORDS, YOU CAN KILL TWO BIRDS WITH ONE STONE... I THINK IT'S A GREAT IDEA.
HYUK, HYUK! HEY LIGHT, LOOKS TO ME LIKE HE'S GOT YOU UP AGAINST THE WALL.
THIS ISN'T LIKE YOU, BUDDY.
I DON'T KNOW FOR SURE THAT HE ISN'T L, BUT IF THIS GUY'S JUST SOME PROXY WHO WORKS FOR L, AND DOESN'T EVEN DROP BY THE TASK FORCE, I OUGHT TO STOP TALKING TO HIM IMMEDIATELY.

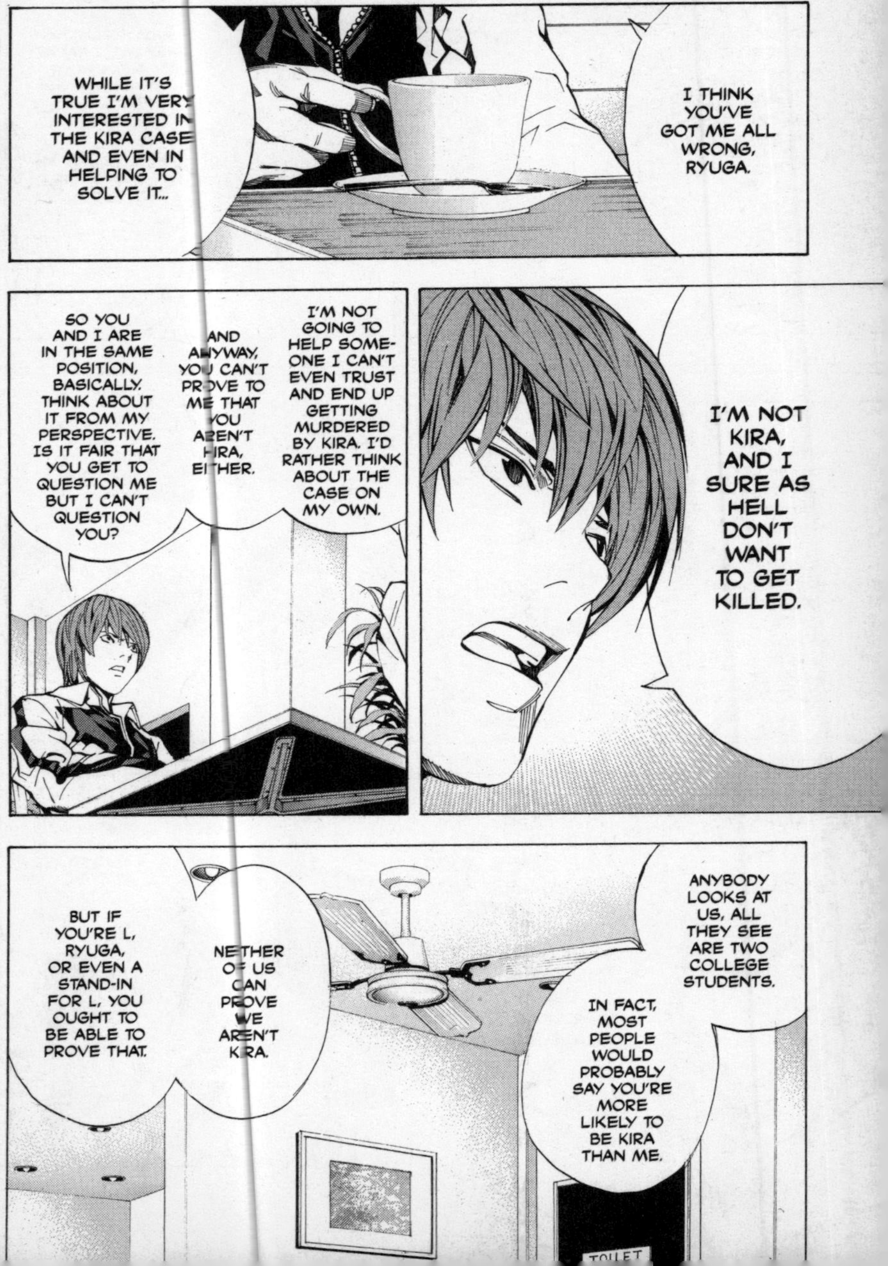
I THINK YOU'VE GOT ME ALL WRONG, RYUGA.
WHILE IT'S TRUE I'M VERY INTERESTED IN THE KIRA CASE AND EVEN IN HELPING TO SOLVE IT...
I'M NOT KIRA, AND I SURE AS HELL DON'T WANT TO GET KILLED.
I'M NOT GOING TO HELP SOMEONE I CAN'T EVEN TRUST AND END UP GETTING MURDERED BY KIRA. I'D RATHER THINK ABOUT THE CASE ON MY OWN.
AND ANYWAY, YOU CAN'T PROVE TO ME THAT YOU AREN'T KIRA, EITHER.
SO YOU AND I ARE IN THE SAME POSITION, BASICALLY. THINK ABOUT IT FROM MY PERSPECTIVE. IS IT FAIR THAT YOU GET TO QUESTION ME BUT I CAN'T QUESTION YOU?
ANYBODY LOOKS AT US, ALL THEY SEE ARE TWO COLLEGE STUDENTS.
IN FACT, MOST PEOPLE WOULD PROBABLY SAY YOU'RE MORE LIKELY TO BE KIRA THAN ME.
NEITHER OF US CAN PROVE WE AREN'T KIRA.
BUT IF YOU'RE L, RYUGA, OR EVEN A STAND-IN FOR L, YOU OUGHT TO BE ABLE TO PROVE THAT.
TOILET

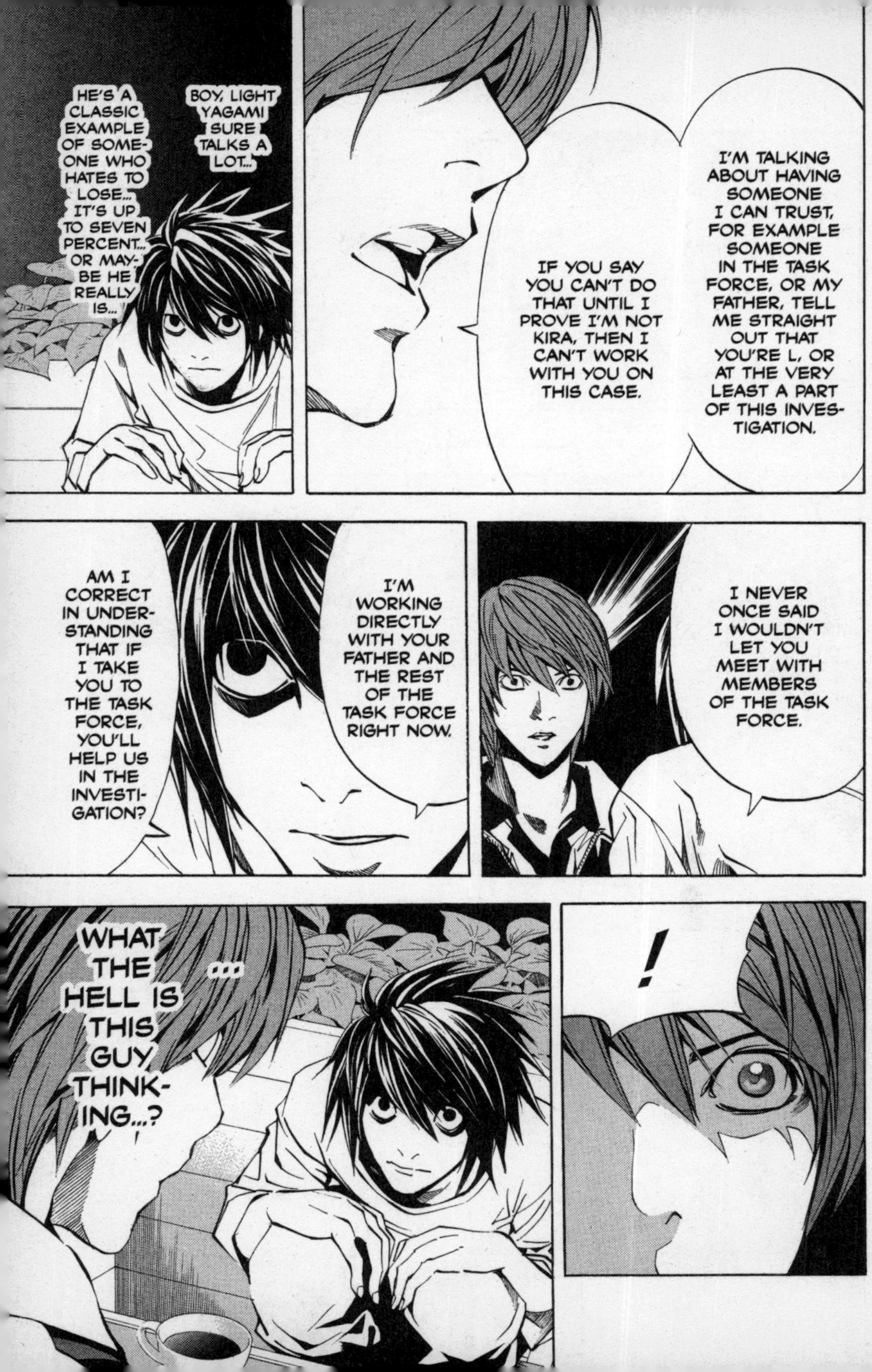
I'M TALKING ABOUT HAVING SOMEONE I CAN TRUST, FOR EXAMPLE SOMEONE IN THE TASK FORCE, OR MY FATHER, TELL ME STRAIGHT OUT THAT YOU'RE L, OR AT THE VERY LEAST A PART OF THIS INVESTIGATION.
IF YOU SAY YOU CAN'T DO THAT UNTIL I PROVE I'M NOT KIRA, THEN I CAN'T WORK WITH YOU ON THIS CASE.
BOY, LIGHT YAGAMI SURE TALKS A LOT...
HE'S A CLASSIC EXAMPLE OF SOMEONE WHO HATES TO LOSE... IT'S UP TO SEVEN PERCENT... OR MAYBE HE REALLY IS...
I NEVER ONCE SAID I WOULDN'T LET YOU MEET WITH MEMBERS OF THE TASK FORCE.
I'M WORKING DIRECTLY WITH YOUR FATHER AND THE REST OF THE TASK FORCE RIGHT NOW.
AM I CORRECT IN UNDERSTANDING THAT IF I TAKE YOU TO THE TASK FORCE, YOU'LL HELP US IN THE INVESTIGATION?
!
...
WHAT THE HELL IS THIS GUY THINKING...?

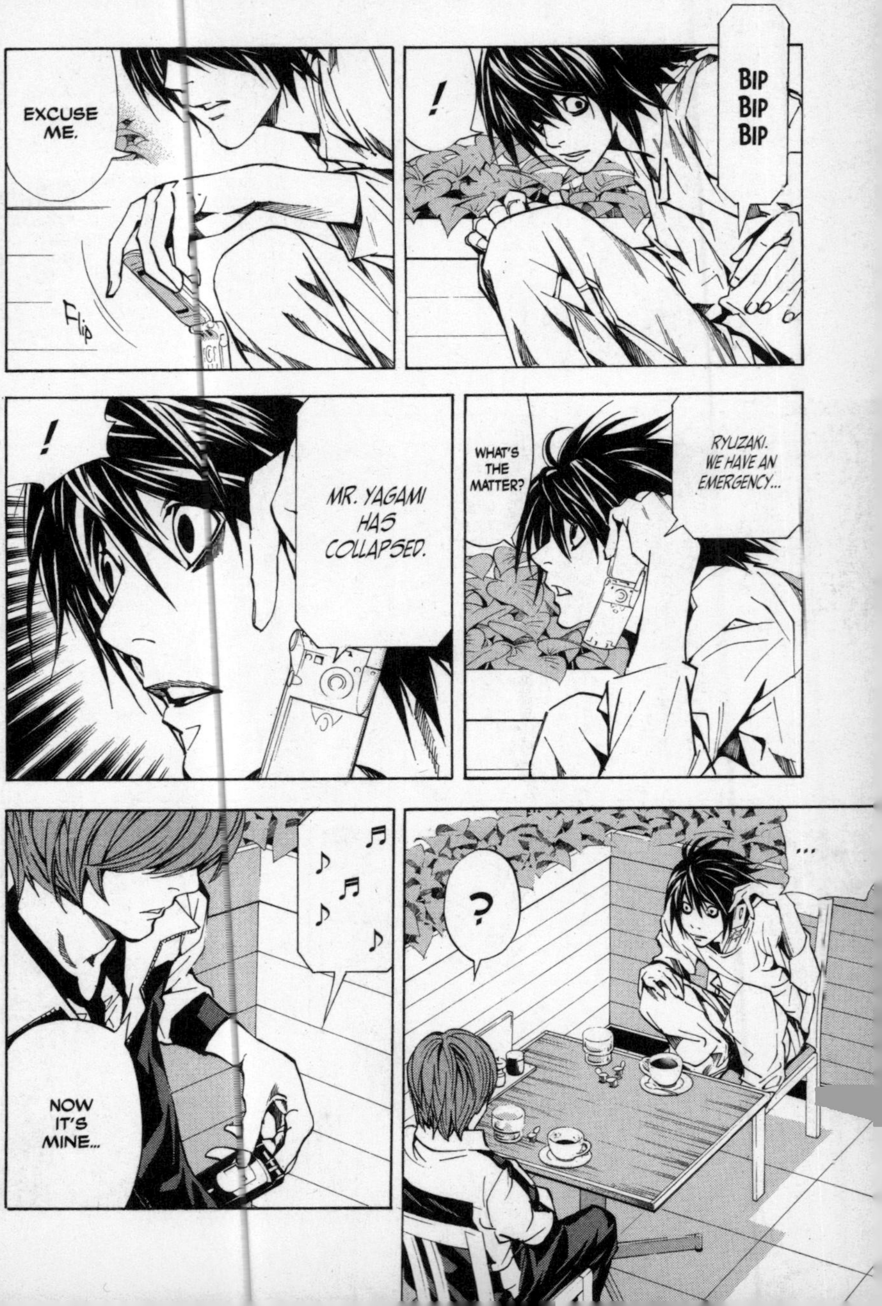
BIP BIP BIP
!
EXCUSE ME.
Flip
RYUZAKI. WE HAVE AN EMERGENCY...
WHAT'S THE MATTER?
MR. YAGAMI HAS COLLAPSED.
!
...
?
♬ ♪ ♬ ♪ ♪
NOW IT'S MINE...

READ THIS WAY

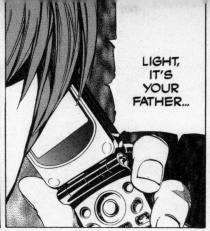

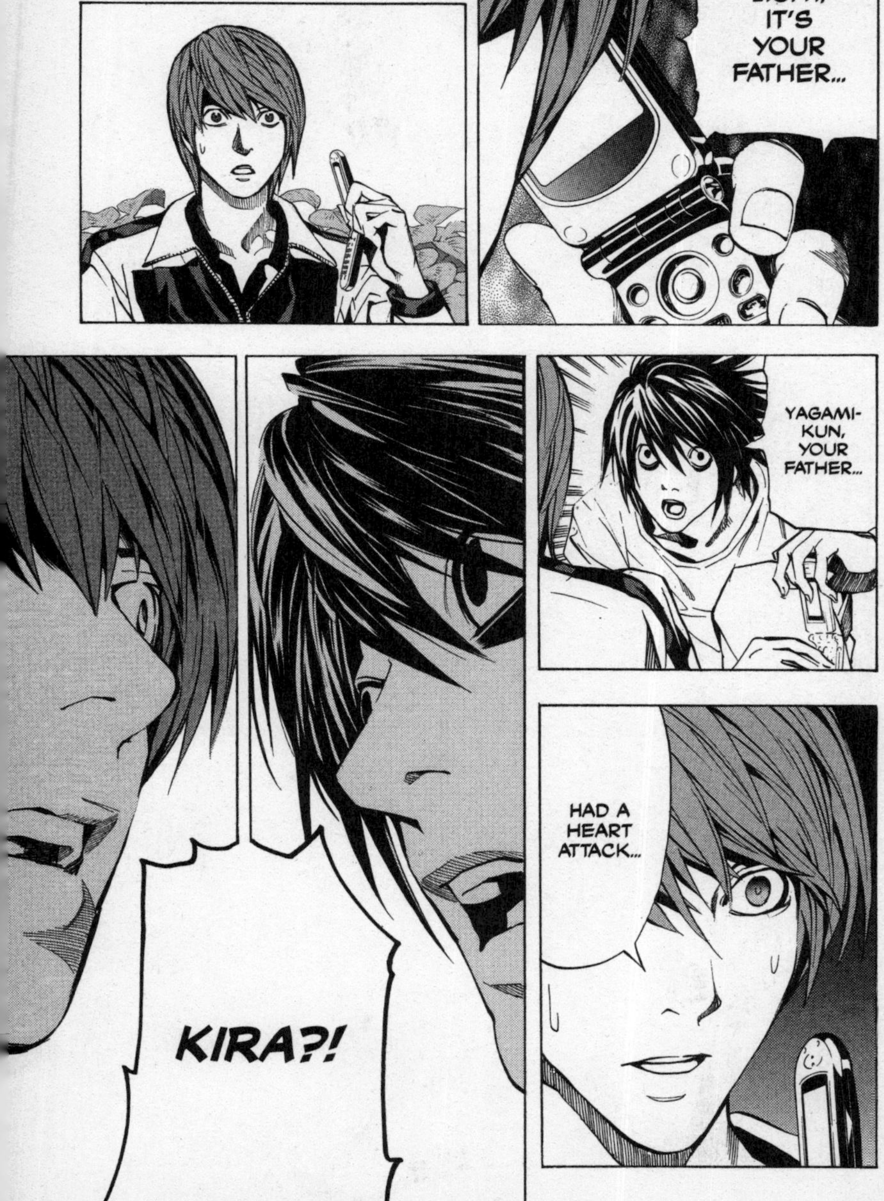
LIGHT, IT'S YOUR FATHER...
YAGAMI-KUN, YOUR FATHER...
HAD A HEART ATTACK...
KIRA?!

DEATH NOTE
How to use it
XIII

○ You may lend the DEATH NOTE to another person while maintaining its ownership.
Subletting it to yet another person is possible, too.

所有権は自分のまま、人にデスノートを貸す事は可能である。
又貸しも構わない。

○ The borrower of the DEATH NOTE will not be followed by a god of death.
The god of death always remains with the owner of the DEATH NOTE.
Also, the borrower cannot trade the eyesight of the god of death.

デスノートを借りた者の方に死神は憑いてこない。
死神は、あくまでも所有者に憑く。
また、借りた者には死神の目の取引はできない。

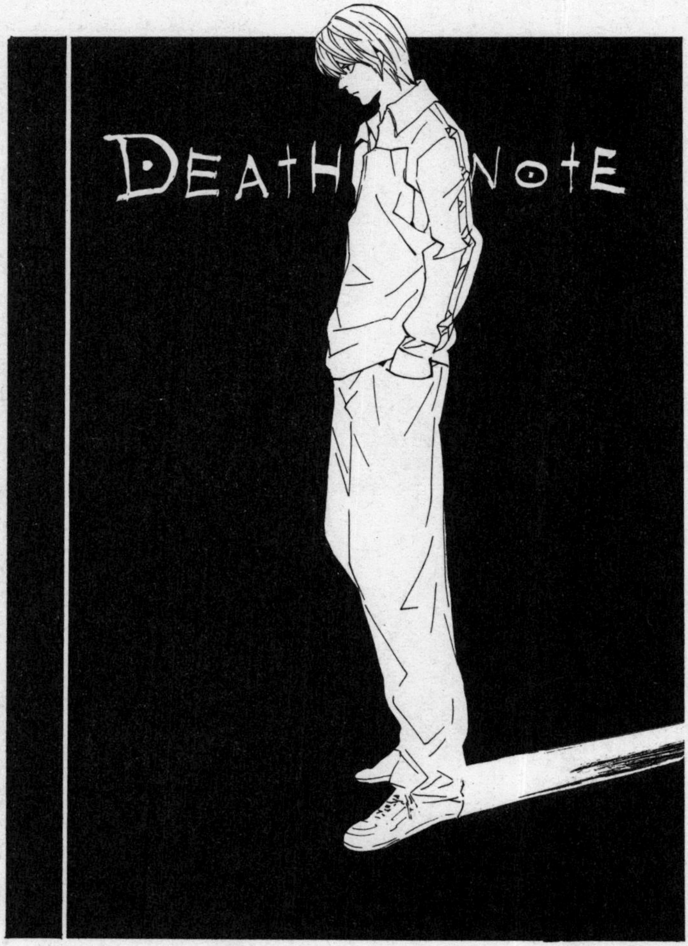
DEATH NOTE

chapter 22 Misfortune

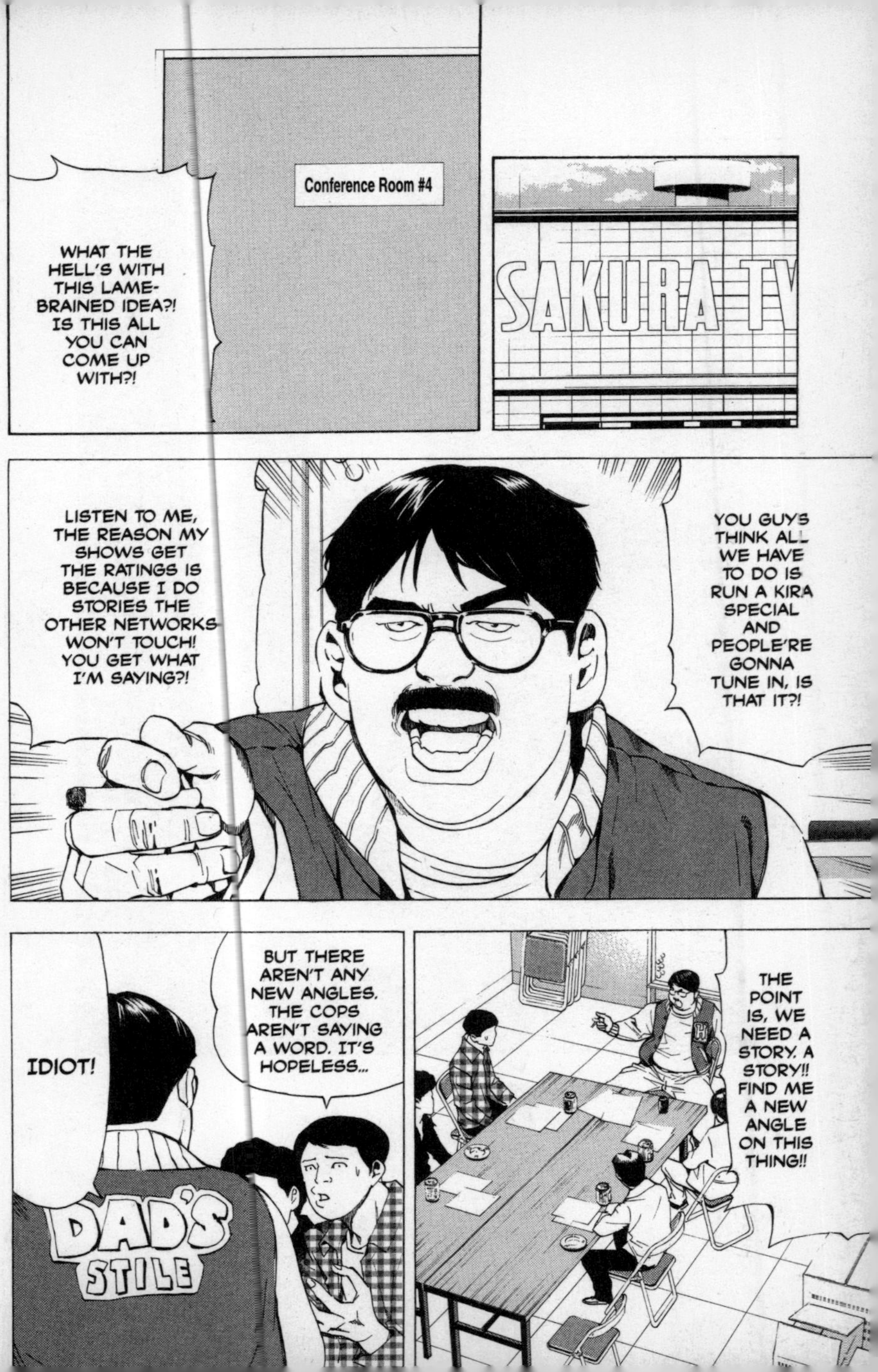
SAKURA TV
Conference Room #4
WHAT THE HELL'S WITH THIS LAME-BRAINED IDEA?! IS THIS ALL YOU CAN COME UP WITH?!
YOU GUYS THINK ALL WE HAVE TO DO IS RUN A KIRA SPECIAL AND PEOPLE'RE GONNA TUNE IN, IS THAT IT?!
LISTEN TO ME, THE REASON MY SHOWS GET THE RATINGS IS BECAUSE I DO STORIES THE OTHER NETWORKS WON'T TOUCH! YOU GET WHAT I'M SAYING?!
THE POINT IS, WE NEED A STORY. A STORY!! FIND ME A NEW ANGLE ON THIS THING!!
BUT THERE AREN'T ANY NEW ANGLES. THE COPS AREN'T SAYING A WORD. IT'S HOPELESS...
IDIOT!
DAD'S STILE

READ THIS WAY

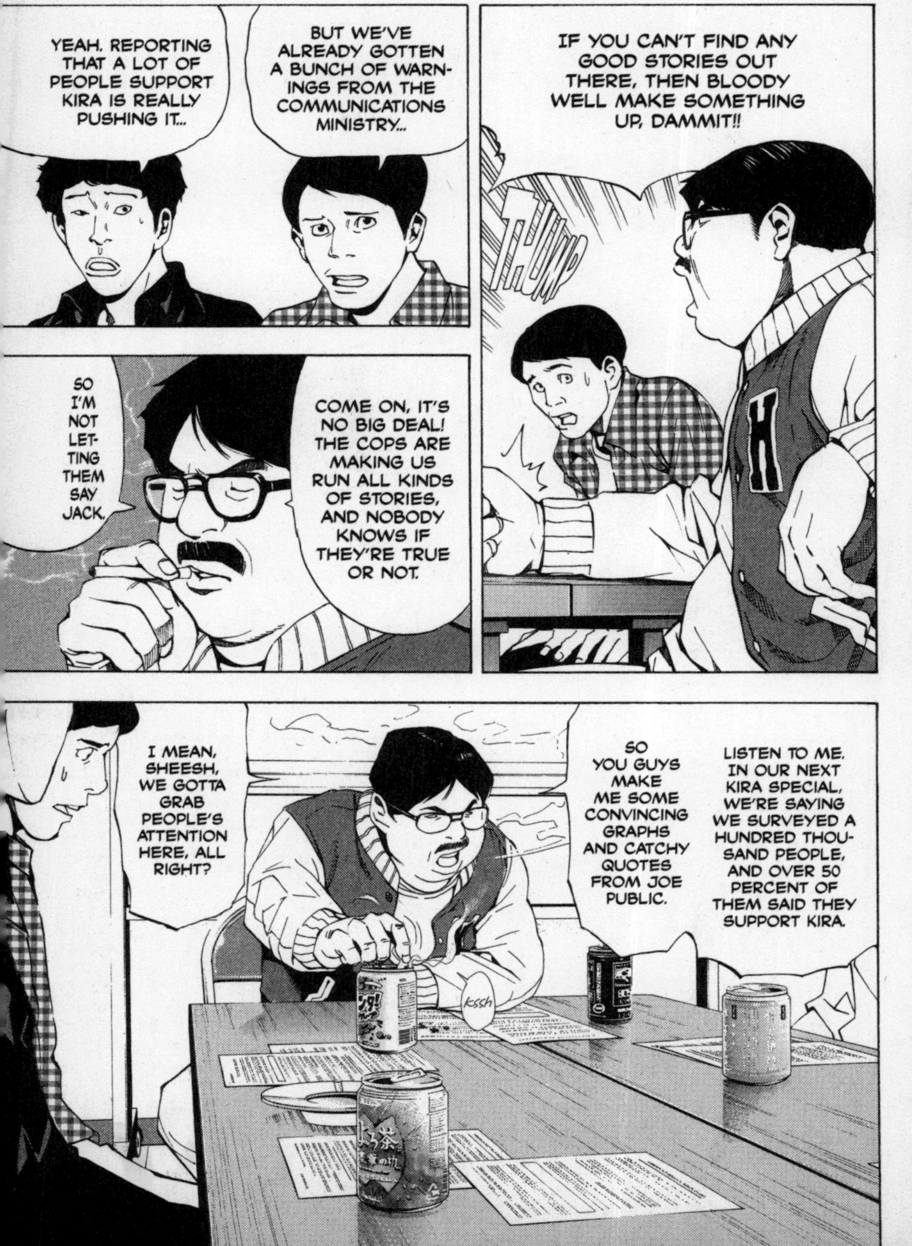
IF YOU CAN'T FIND ANY GOOD STORIES OUT THERE, THEN BLOODY WELL MAKE SOMETHING UP, DAMMIT!!
THUMP
BUT WE'VE ALREADY GOTTEN A BUNCH OF WARN-INGS FROM THE COMMUNICATIONS MINISTRY...
YEAH. REPORTING THAT A LOT OF PEOPLE SUPPORT KIRA IS REALLY PUSHING IT...
COME ON, IT'S NO BIG DEAL! THE COPS ARE MAKING US RUN ALL KINDS OF STORIES, AND NOBODY KNOWS IF THEY'RE TRUE OR NOT.
SO I'M NOT LET-TING THEM SAY JACK.
LISTEN TO ME. IN OUR NEXT KIRA SPECIAL, WE'RE SAYING WE SURVEYED A HUNDRED THOU-SAND PEOPLE, AND OVER 50 PERCENT OF THEM SAID THEY SUPPORT KIRA.
SO YOU GUYS MAKE ME SOME CONVINCING GRAPHS AND CATCHY QUOTES FROM JOE PUBLIC.
I MEAN, SHEESH, WE GOTTA GRAB PEOPLE'S ATTENTION HERE, ALL RIGHT?
kssh

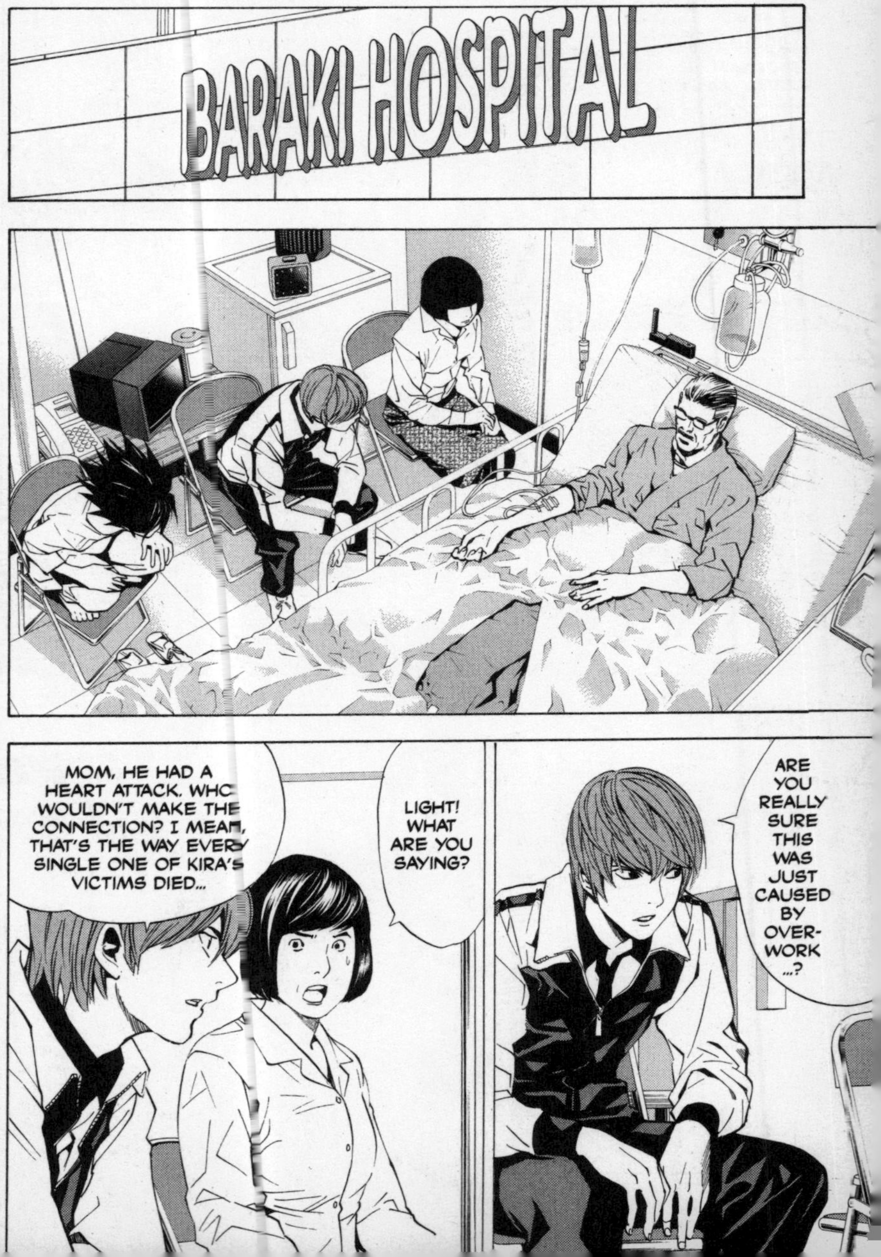
BARAKI HOSPITAL
ARE YOU REALLY SURE THIS WAS JUST CAUSED BY OVER-WORK ...?
LIGHT! WHAT ARE YOU SAYING?
MOM, HE HAD A HEART ATTACK. WHO WOULDN'T MAKE THE CONNECTION? I MEAN, THAT'S THE WAY EVERY SINGLE ONE OF KIRA'S VICTIMS DIED...

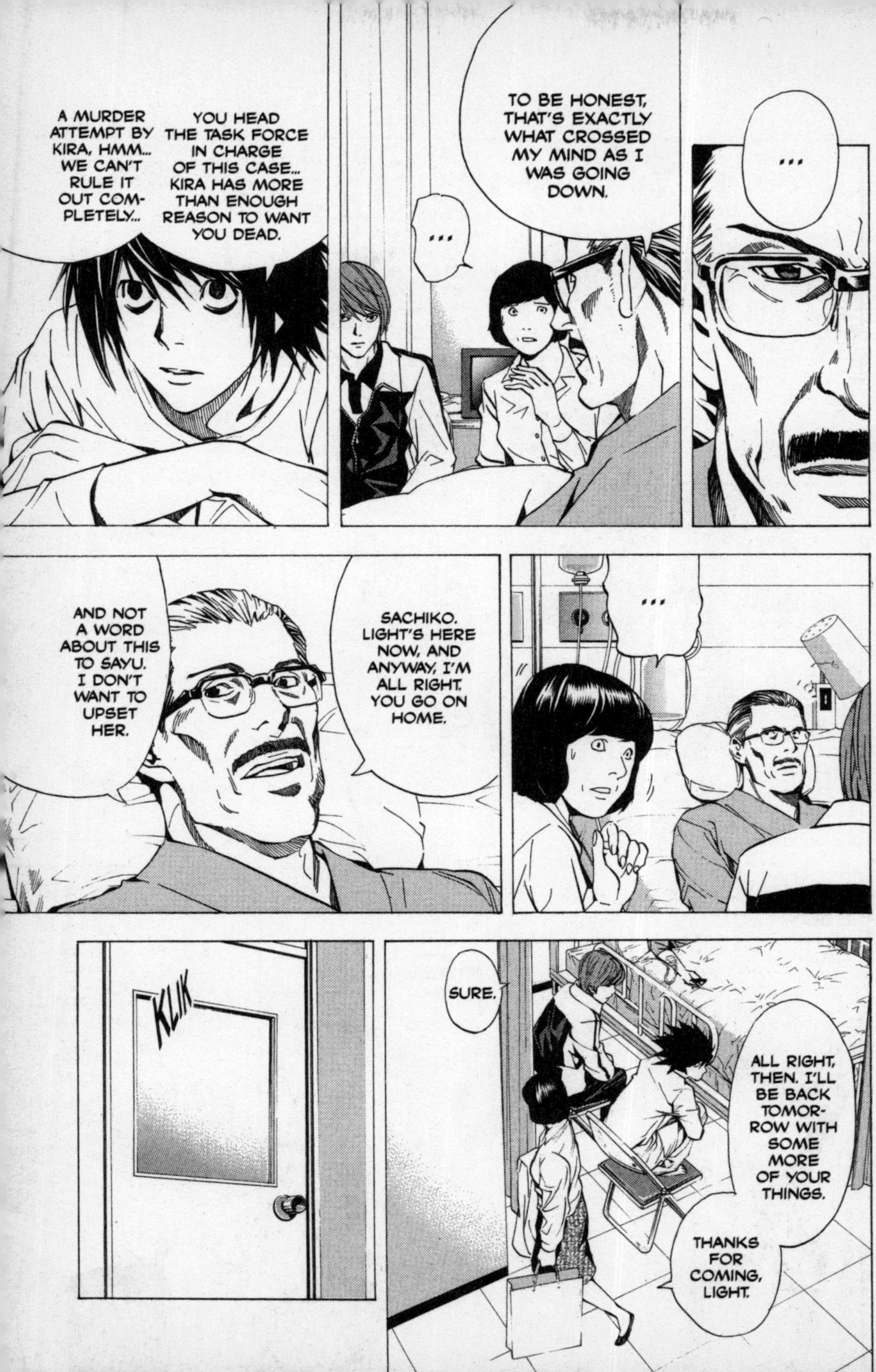
...
TO BE HONEST, THAT'S EXACTLY WHAT CROSSED MY MIND AS I WAS GOING DOWN.
...
YOU HEAD THE TASK FORCE IN CHARGE OF THIS CASE... KIRA HAS MORE THAN ENOUGH REASON TO WANT YOU DEAD.
A MURDER ATTEMPT BY KIRA, HMM... WE CAN'T RULE IT OUT COM-PLETELY...
...
SACHIKO. LIGHT'S HERE NOW, AND ANYWAY, I'M ALL RIGHT. YOU GO ON HOME.
AND NOT A WORD ABOUT THIS TO SAYU. I DON'T WANT TO UPSET HER.
ALL RIGHT, THEN. I'LL BE BACK TOMOR-ROW WITH SOME MORE OF YOUR THINGS.
THANKS FOR COMING, LIGHT.
SURE.
KLIK

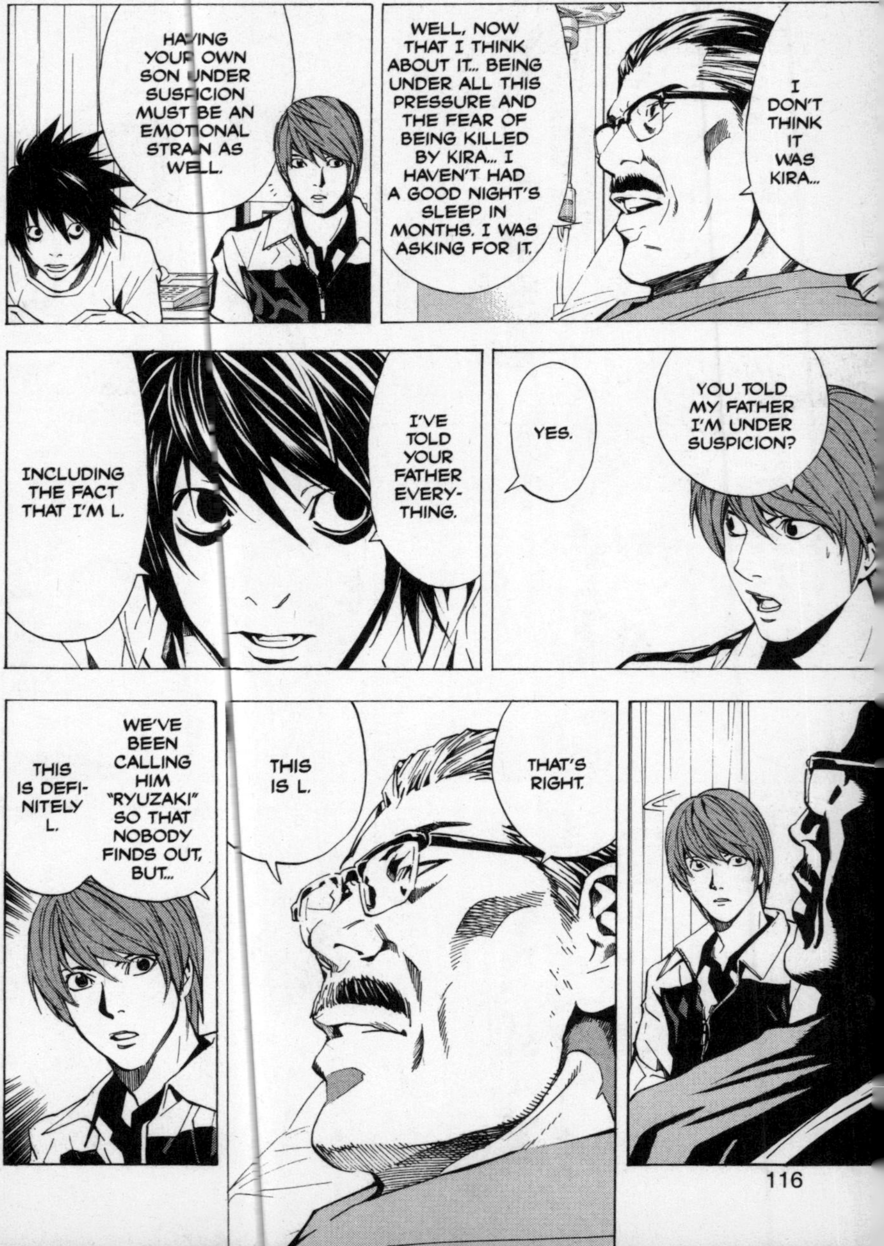
I DON'T THINK IT WAS KIRA...
WELL, NOW THAT I THINK ABOUT IT... BEING UNDER ALL THIS PRESSURE AND THE FEAR OF BEING KILLED BY KIRA... I HAVEN'T HAD A GOOD NIGHT'S SLEEP IN MONTHS. I WAS ASKING FOR IT.
HAVING YOUR OWN SON UNDER SUSPICION MUST BE AN EMOTIONAL STRAIN AS WELL.
YOU TOLD MY FATHER I'M UNDER SUSPICION?
YES.
I'VE TOLD YOUR FATHER EVERY-THING.
INCLUDING THE FACT THAT I'M L.
THAT'S RIGHT.
THIS IS L.
WE'VE BEEN CALLING HIM "RYUZAKI" SO THAT NOBODY FINDS OUT, BUT...
THIS IS DEFI-NITELY L.

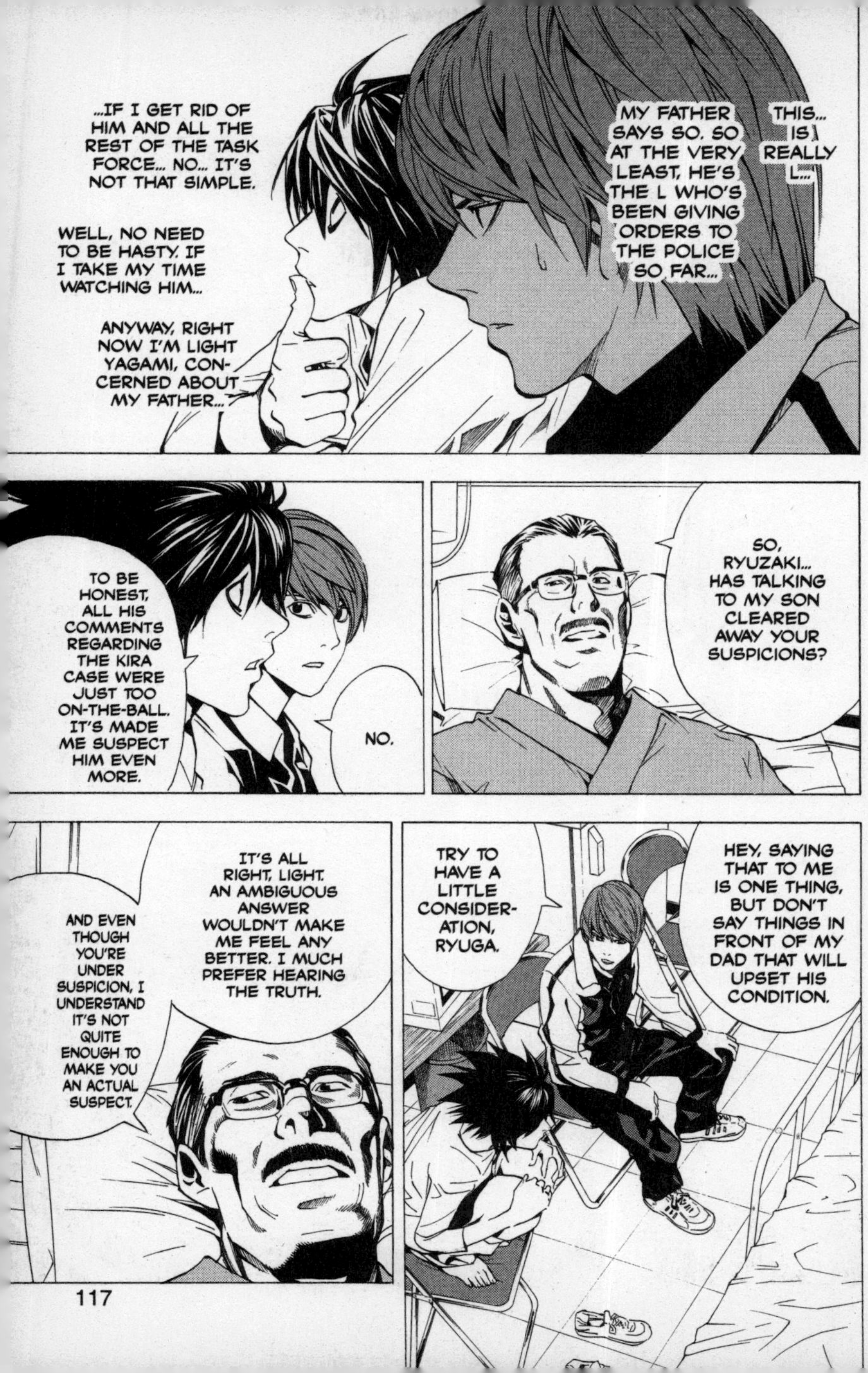
THIS... IS REALLY L...
MY FATHER SAYS SO. SO AT THE VERY LEAST, HE'S THE L WHO'S BEEN GIVING ORDERS TO THE POLICE SO FAR...
...IF I GET RID OF HIM AND ALL THE REST OF THE TASK FORCE... NO... IT'S NOT THAT SIMPLE.
WELL, NO NEED TO BE HASTY. IF I TAKE MY TIME WATCHING HIM...
ANYWAY, RIGHT NOW I'M LIGHT YAGAMI, CONCERNED ABOUT MY FATHER...
SO, RYUZAKI... HAS TALKING TO MY SON CLEARED AWAY YOUR SUSPICIONS?
NO.
TO BE HONEST, ALL HIS COMMENTS REGARDING THE KIRA CASE WERE JUST TOO ON-THE-BALL. IT'S MADE ME SUSPECT HIM EVEN MORE.
HEY, SAYING THAT TO ME IS ONE THING, BUT DON'T SAY THINGS IN FRONT OF MY DAD THAT WILL UPSET HIS CONDITION.
TRY TO HAVE A LITTLE CONSIDERATION, RYUGA.
IT'S ALL RIGHT, LIGHT. AN AMBIGUOUS ANSWER WOULDN'T MAKE ME FEEL ANY BETTER. I MUCH PREFER HEARING THE TRUTH.
AND EVEN THOUGH YOU'RE UNDER SUSPICION, I UNDERSTAND IT'S NOT QUITE ENOUGH TO MAKE YOU AN ACTUAL SUSPECT.

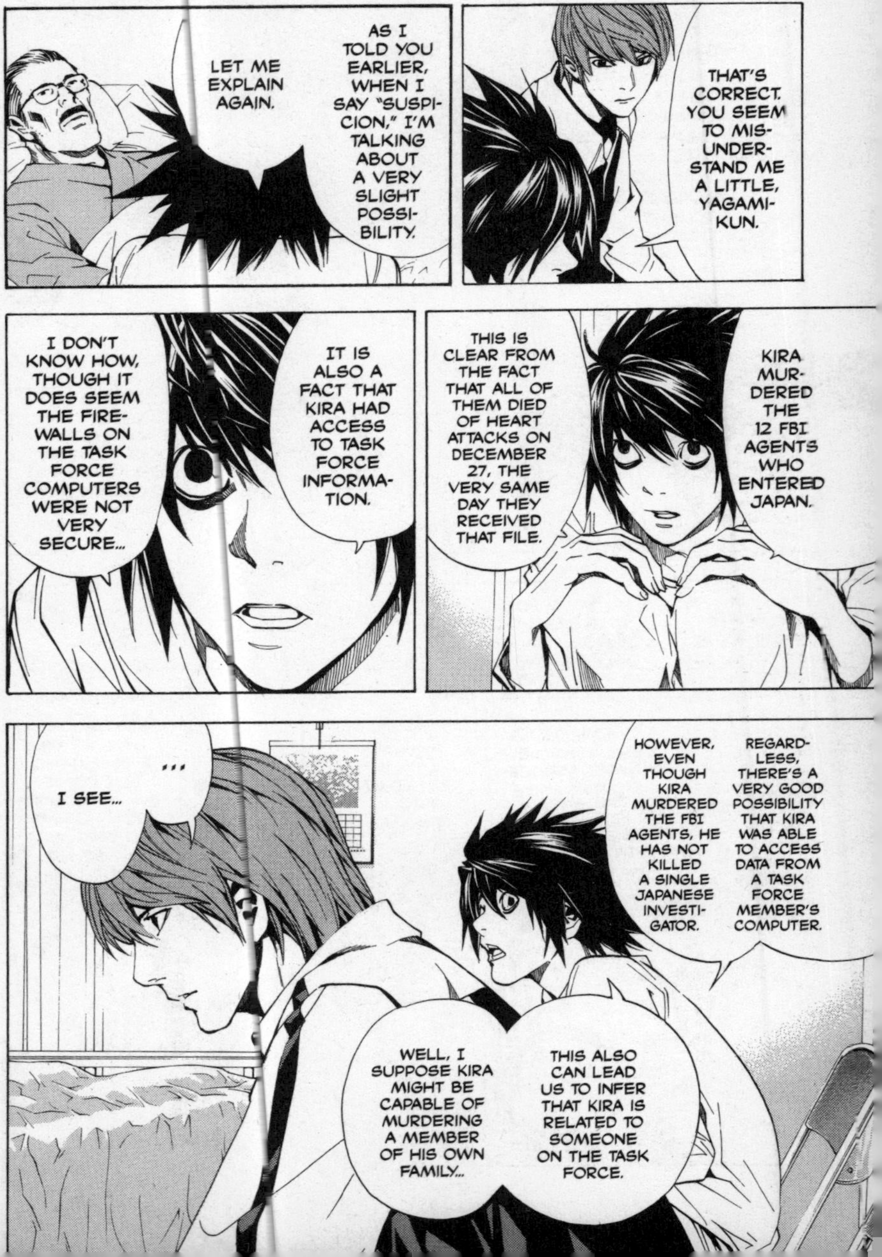
THAT'S CORRECT. YOU SEEM TO MISUNDERSTAND ME A LITTLE, YAGAMI-KUN.
AS I TOLD YOU EARLIER, WHEN I SAY "SUSPICION," I'M TALKING ABOUT A VERY SLIGHT POSSIBILITY.
LET ME EXPLAIN AGAIN.
KIRA MURDERED THE 12 FBI AGENTS WHO ENTERED JAPAN.
THIS IS CLEAR FROM THE FACT THAT ALL OF THEM DIED OF HEART ATTACKS ON DECEMBER 27, THE VERY SAME DAY THEY RECEIVED THAT FILE.
IT IS ALSO A FACT THAT KIRA HAD ACCESS TO TASK FORCE INFORMATION.
I DON'T KNOW HOW, THOUGH IT DOES SEEM THE FIREWALLS ON THE TASK FORCE COMPUTERS WERE NOT VERY SECURE...
REGARDLESS, THERE'S A VERY GOOD POSSIBILITY THAT KIRA WAS ABLE TO ACCESS DATA FROM A TASK FORCE MEMBER'S COMPUTER.
HOWEVER, EVEN THOUGH KIRA MURDERED THE FBI AGENTS, HE HAS NOT KILLED A SINGLE JAPANESE INVESTIGATOR.
THIS ALSO CAN LEAD US TO INFER THAT KIRA IS RELATED TO SOMEONE ON THE TASK FORCE.
WELL, I SUPPOSE KIRA MIGHT BE CAPABLE OF MURDERING A MEMBER OF HIS OWN FAMILY...
...
I SEE...

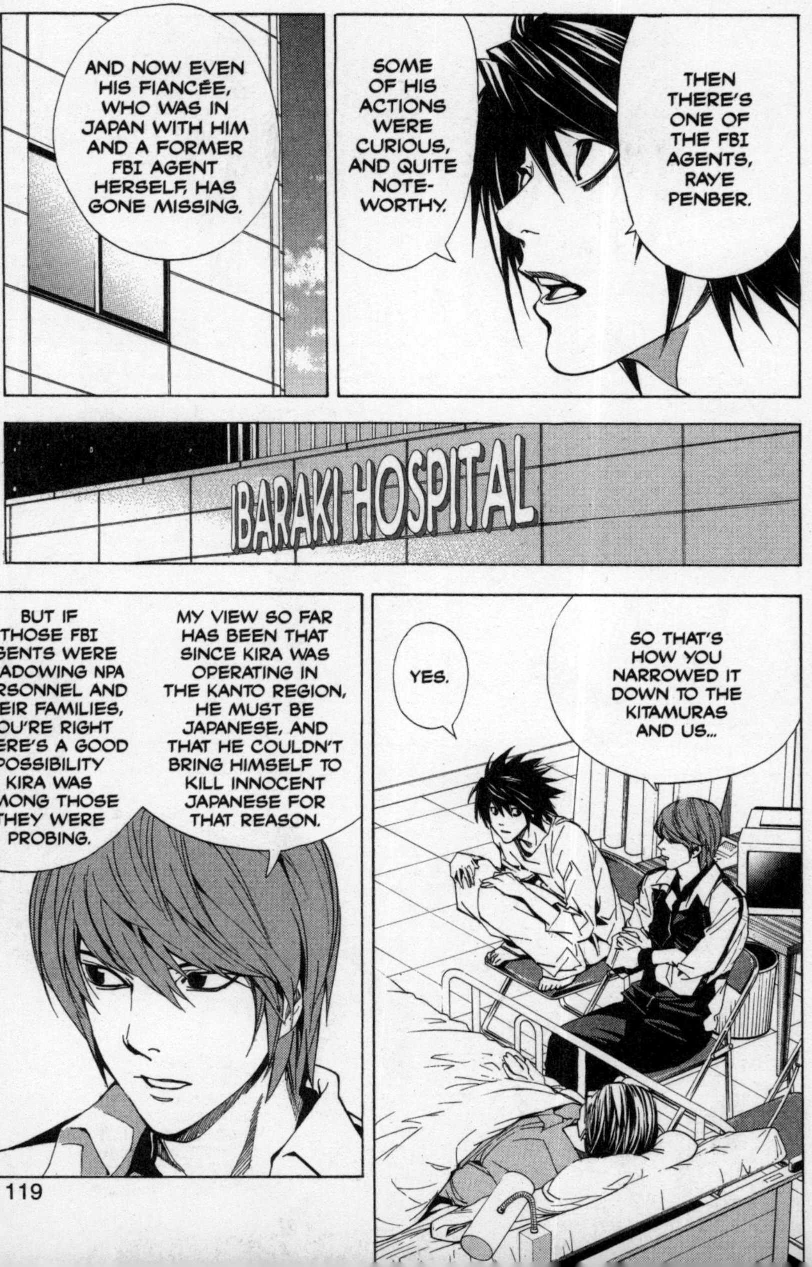
THEN THERE'S ONE OF THE FBI AGENTS, RAYE PENBER.
SOME OF HIS ACTIONS WERE CURIOUS, AND QUITE NOTE-WORTHY.
AND NOW EVEN HIS FIANCÉE, WHO WAS IN JAPAN WITH HIM AND A FORMER FBI AGENT HERSELF, HAS GONE MISSING.
IBARAKI HOSPITAL
SO THAT'S HOW YOU NARROWED IT DOWN TO THE KITAMURAS AND US...
YES.
MY VIEW SO FAR HAS BEEN THAT SINCE KIRA WAS OPERATING IN THE KANTO REGION, HE MUST BE JAPANESE, AND THAT HE COULDN'T BRING HIMSELF TO KILL INNOCENT JAPANESE FOR THAT REASON.
BUT IF THOSE FBI AGENTS WERE SHADOWING NPA PERSONNEL AND THEIR FAMILIES, YOU'RE RIGHT THERE'S A GOOD POSSIBILITY KIRA WAS AMONG THOSE THEY WERE PROBING.

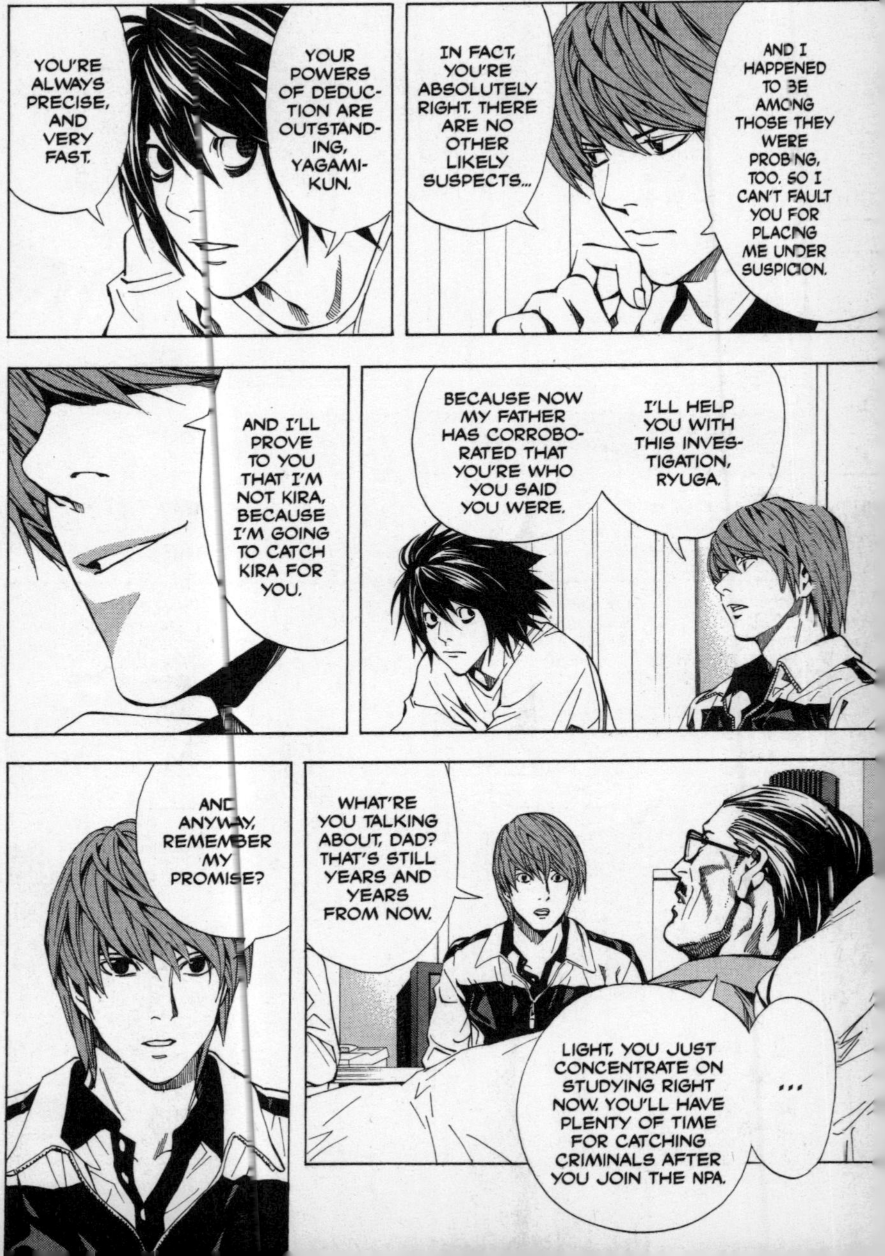
IN FACT, YOU'RE ABSOLUTELY RIGHT. THERE ARE NO OTHER LIKELY SUSPECTS...
AND I HAPPENED TO BE AMONG THOSE THEY WERE PROBING, TOO. SO I CAN'T FAULT YOU FOR PLACING ME UNDER SUSPICION.
YOUR POWERS OF DEDUCTION ARE OUTSTANDING, YAGAMI-KUN.
YOU'RE ALWAYS PRECISE, AND VERY FAST.
I'LL HELP YOU WITH THIS INVESTIGATION, RYUGA.
BECAUSE NOW MY FATHER HAS CORROBORATED THAT YOU'RE WHO YOU SAID YOU WERE.
AND I'LL PROVE TO YOU THAT I'M NOT KIRA, BECAUSE I'M GOING TO CATCH KIRA FOR YOU.
LIGHT, YOU JUST CONCENTRATE ON STUDYING RIGHT NOW. YOU'LL HAVE PLENTY OF TIME FOR CATCHING CRIMINALS AFTER YOU JOIN THE NPA.
WHAT'RE YOU TALKING ABOUT, DAD? THAT'S STILL YEARS AND YEARS FROM NOW.
...
AND ANYWAY, REMEMBER MY PROMISE?

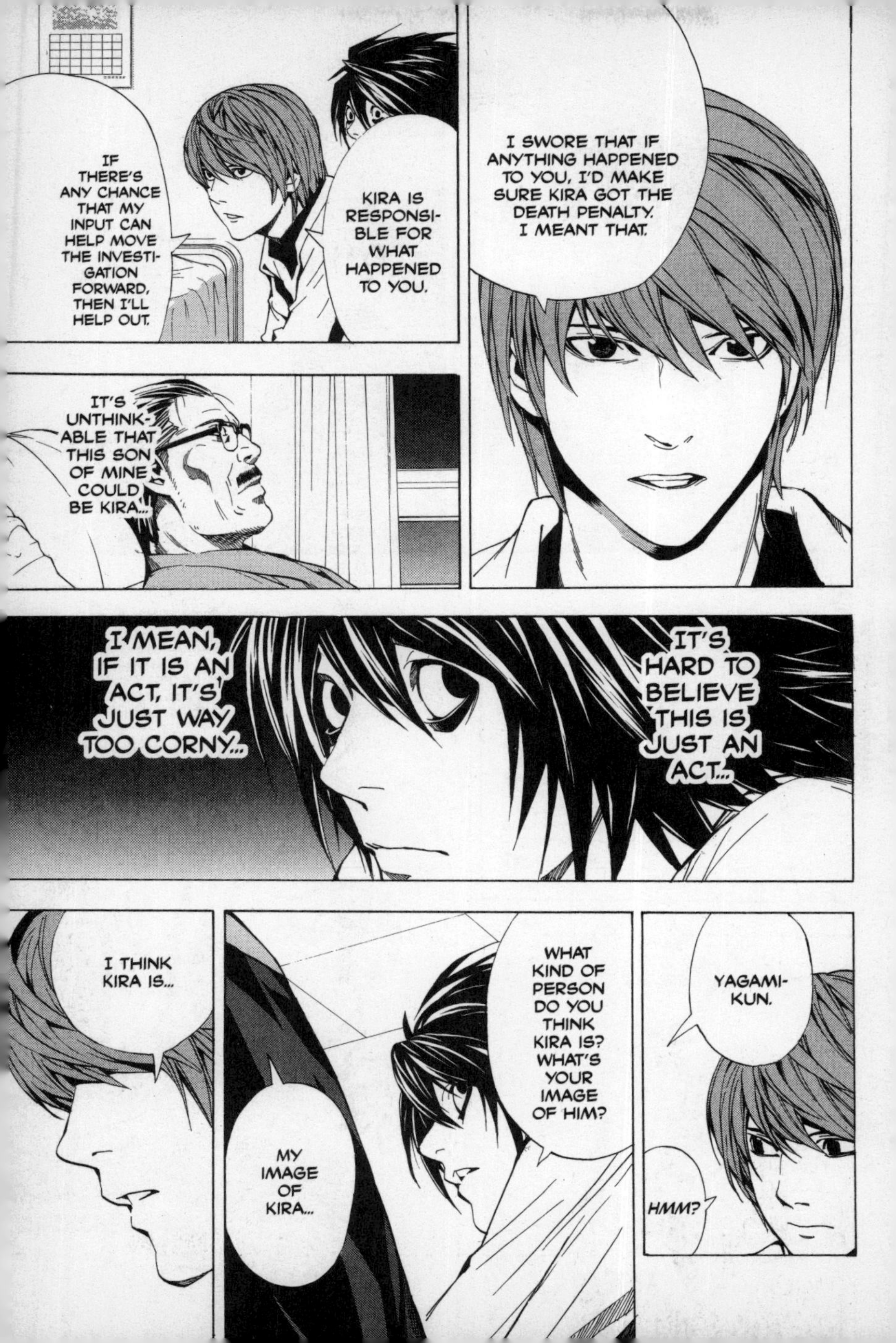
I SWORE THAT IF ANYTHING HAPPENED TO YOU, I'D MAKE SURE KIRA GOT THE DEATH PENALTY. I MEANT THAT.
KIRA IS RESPONSIBLE FOR WHAT HAPPENED TO YOU.
IF THERE'S ANY CHANCE THAT MY INPUT CAN HELP MOVE THE INVESTIGATION FORWARD, THEN I'LL HELP OUT.
IT'S UNTHINKABLE THAT THIS SON OF MINE COULD BE KIRA...
IT'S HARD TO BELIEVE THIS IS JUST AN ACT...
I MEAN, IF IT IS AN ACT, IT'S JUST WAY TOO CORNY...
YAGAMI-KUN.
HMM?
WHAT KIND OF PERSON DO YOU THINK KIRA IS? WHAT'S YOUR IMAGE OF HIM?
MY IMAGE OF KIRA...
I THINK KIRA IS...

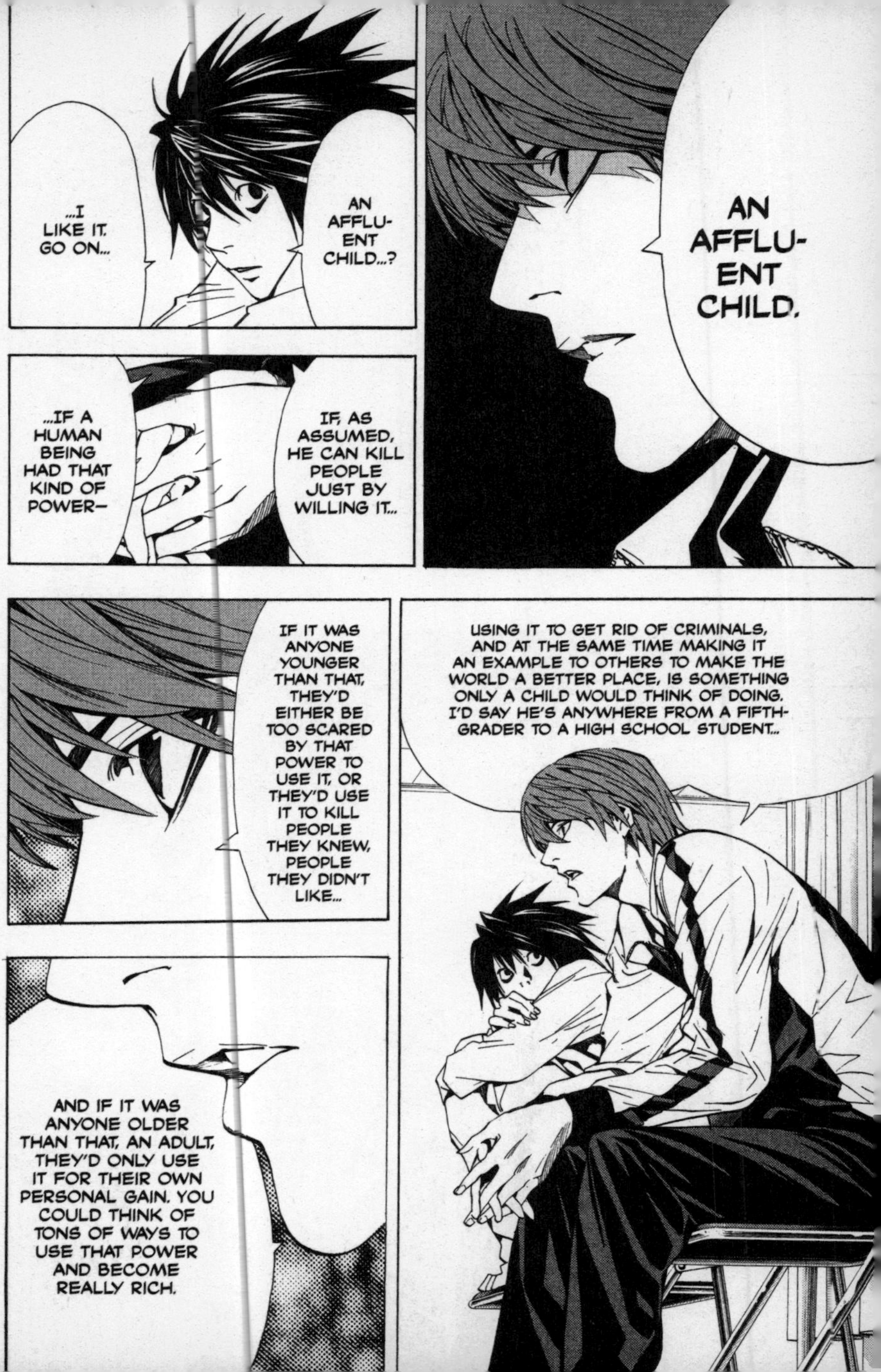
AN AFFLU-ENT CHILD.
AN AFFLU-ENT CHILD...?
...I LIKE IT. GO ON...
IF, AS ASSUMED, HE CAN KILL PEOPLE JUST BY WILLING IT...
...IF A HUMAN BEING HAD THAT KIND OF POWER—
USING IT TO GET RID OF CRIMINALS, AND AT THE SAME TIME MAKING IT AN EXAMPLE TO OTHERS TO MAKE THE WORLD A BETTER PLACE, IS SOMETHING ONLY A CHILD WOULD THINK OF DOING. I'D SAY HE'S ANYWHERE FROM A FIFTH-GRADER TO A HIGH SCHOOL STUDENT...
IF IT WAS ANYONE YOUNGER THAN THAT, THEY'D EITHER BE TOO SCARED BY THAT POWER TO USE IT, OR THEY'D USE IT TO KILL PEOPLE THEY KNEW, PEOPLE THEY DIDN'T LIKE...
AND IF IT WAS ANYONE OLDER THAN THAT, AN ADULT, THEY'D ONLY USE IT FOR THEIR OWN PERSONAL GAIN. YOU COULD THINK OF TONS OF WAYS TO USE THAT POWER AND BECOME REALLY RICH.

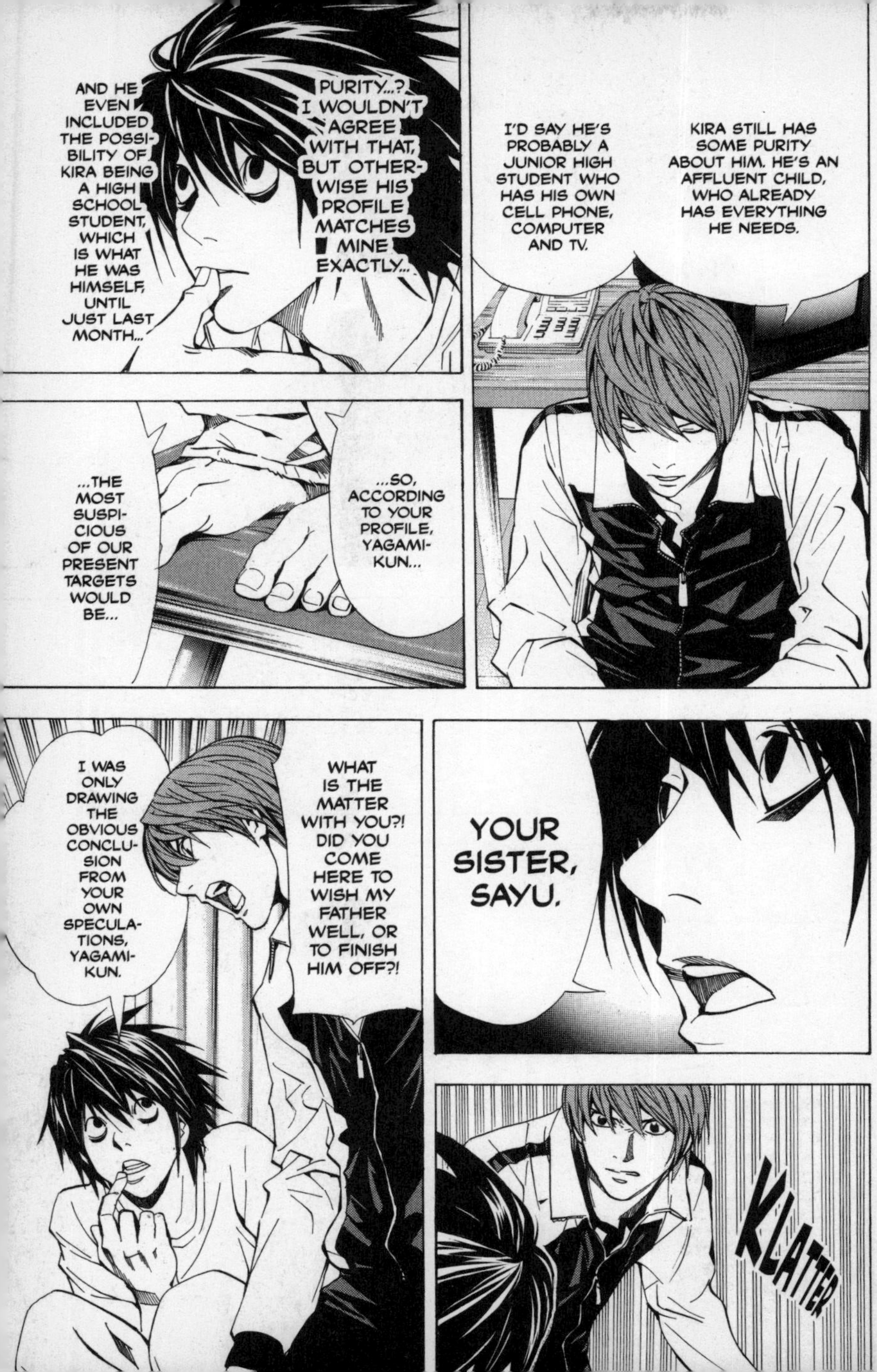
KIRA STILL HAS SOME PURITY ABOUT HIM. HE'S AN AFFLUENT CHILD, WHO ALREADY HAS EVERYTHING HE NEEDS.
I'D SAY HE'S PROBABLY A JUNIOR HIGH STUDENT WHO HAS HIS OWN CELL PHONE, COMPUTER AND TV.
PURITY...? I WOULDN'T AGREE WITH THAT, BUT OTHER-WISE HIS PROFILE MATCHES MINE EXACTLY...
AND HE EVEN INCLUDED THE POSSI-BILITY OF KIRA BEING A HIGH SCHOOL STUDENT, WHICH IS WHAT HE WAS HIMSELF, UNTIL JUST LAST MONTH...
...SO, ACCORDING TO YOUR PROFILE, YAGAMI-KUN...
...THE MOST SUSPI-CIOUS OF OUR PRESENT TARGETS WOULD BE...
YOUR SISTER, SAYU.
KLATTER
WHAT IS THE MATTER WITH YOU?! DID YOU COME HERE TO WISH MY FATHER WELL, OR TO FINISH HIM OFF?!
I WAS ONLY DRAWING THE OBVIOUS CONCLU-SION FROM YOUR OWN SPECULA-TIONS, YAGAMI-KUN.

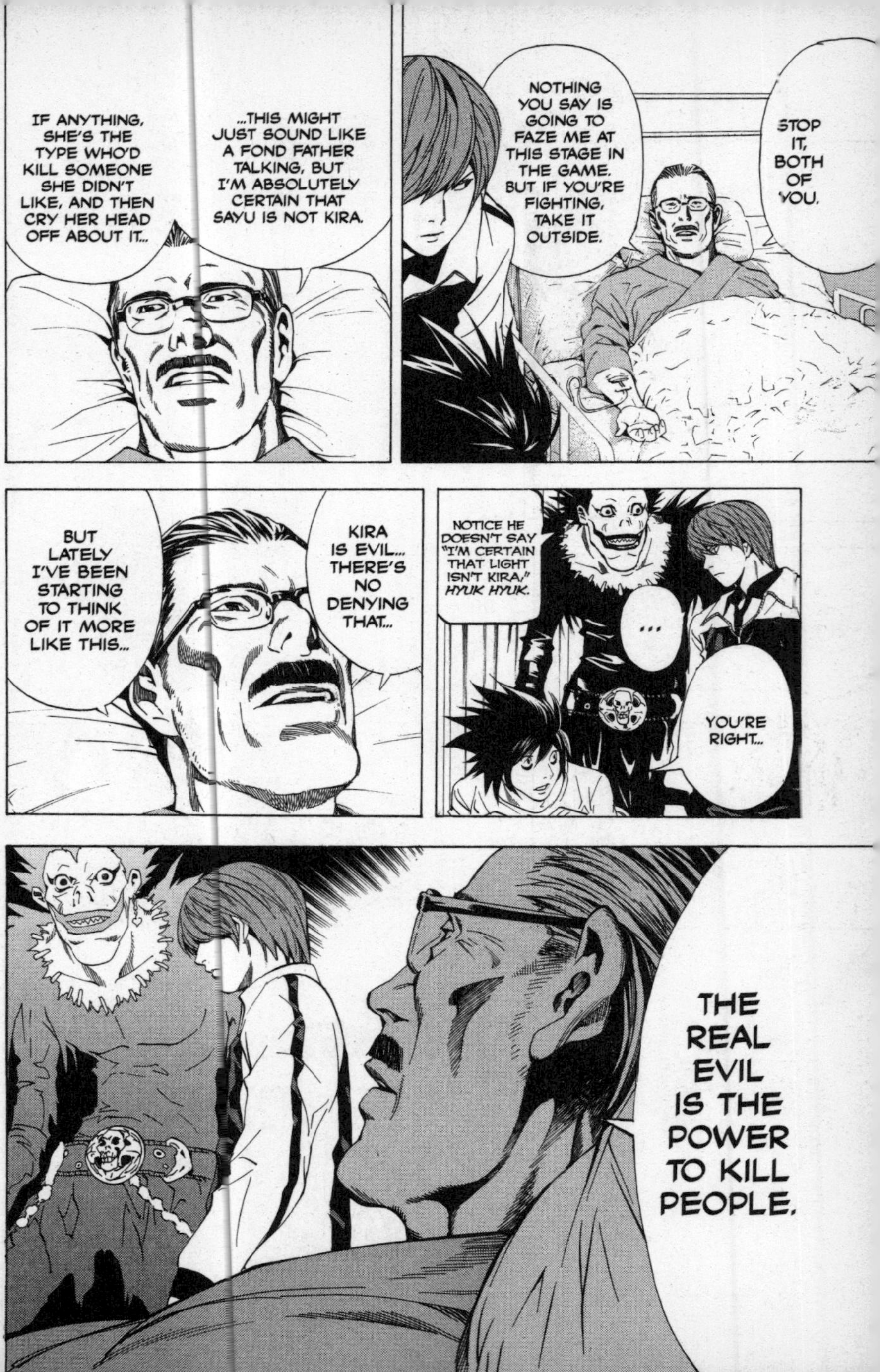
STOP IT, BOTH OF YOU.
NOTHING YOU SAY IS GOING TO FAZE ME AT THIS STAGE IN THE GAME. BUT IF YOU'RE FIGHTING, TAKE IT OUTSIDE.
...THIS MIGHT JUST SOUND LIKE A FOND FATHER TALKING, BUT I'M ABSOLUTELY CERTAIN THAT SAYU IS NOT KIRA.
IF ANYTHING, SHE'S THE TYPE WHO'D KILL SOMEONE SHE DIDN'T LIKE, AND THEN CRY HER HEAD OFF ABOUT IT...
NOTICE HE DOESN'T SAY "I'M CERTAIN THAT LIGHT ISN'T KIRA," *HYUK HYUK*.
...
YOU'RE RIGHT...
KIRA IS EVIL... THERE'S NO DENYING THAT...
BUT LATELY I'VE BEEN STARTING TO THINK OF IT MORE LIKE THIS...
THE REAL EVIL IS THE POWER TO KILL PEOPLE.

READ THIS WAY

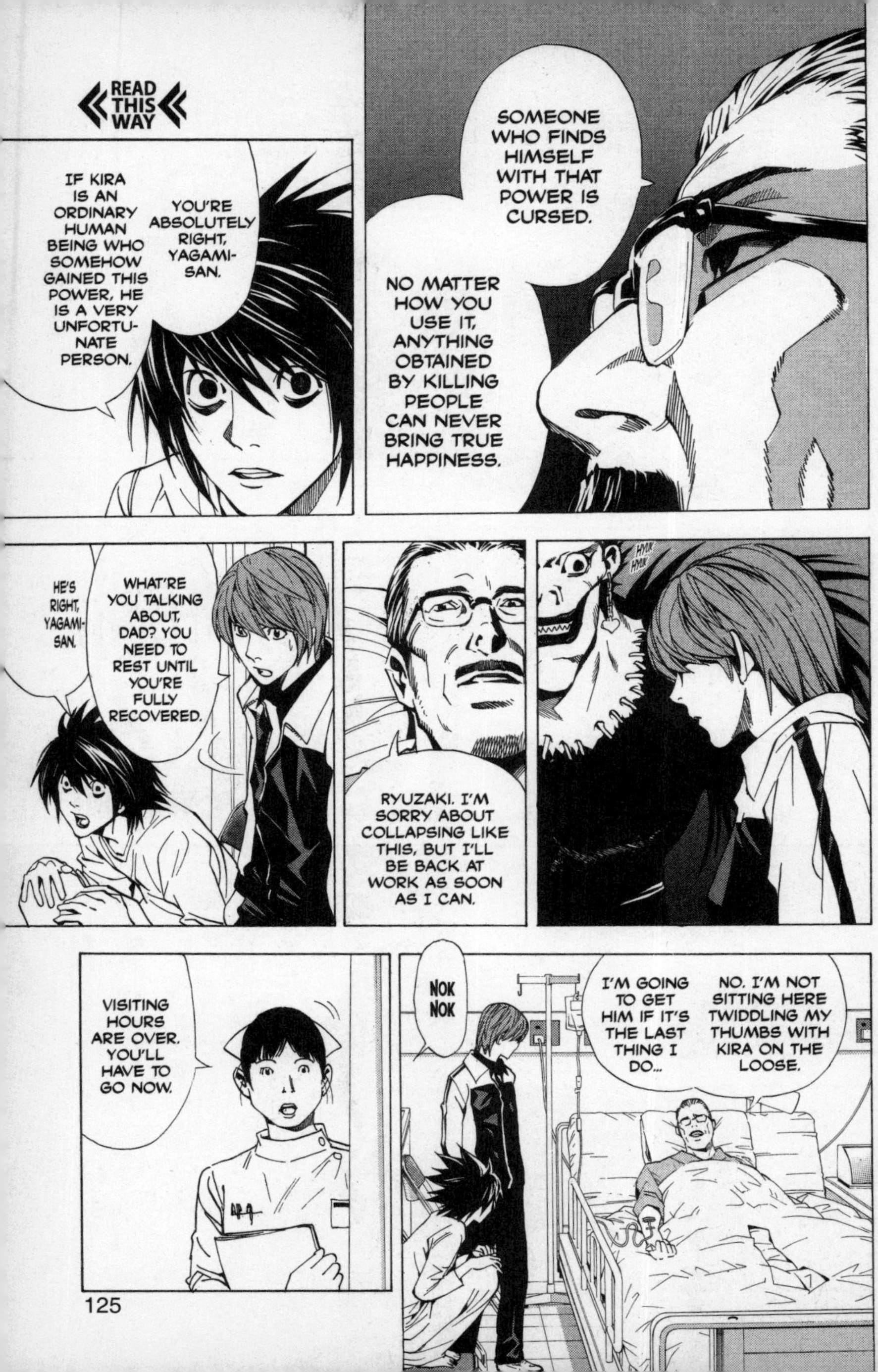
SOMEONE WHO FINDS HIMSELF WITH THAT POWER IS CURSED.
NO MATTER HOW YOU USE IT, ANYTHING OBTAINED BY KILLING PEOPLE CAN NEVER BRING TRUE HAPPINESS.
YOU'RE ABSOLUTELY RIGHT, YAGAMI-SAN.
IF KIRA IS AN ORDINARY HUMAN BEING WHO SOMEHOW GAINED THIS POWER, HE IS A VERY UNFORTU-NATE PERSON.
HYUK HYUK
RYUZAKI. I'M SORRY ABOUT COLLAPSING LIKE THIS, BUT I'LL BE BACK AT WORK AS SOON AS I CAN.
WHAT'RE YOU TALKING ABOUT, DAD? YOU NEED TO REST UNTIL YOU'RE FULLY RECOVERED.
HE'S RIGHT, YAGAMI-SAN.
NO. I'M NOT SITTING HERE TWIDDLING MY THUMBS WITH KIRA ON THE LOOSE.
I'M GOING TO GET HIM IF IT'S THE LAST THING I DO...
NOK NOK
VISITING HOURS ARE OVER. YOU'LL HAVE TO GO NOW.

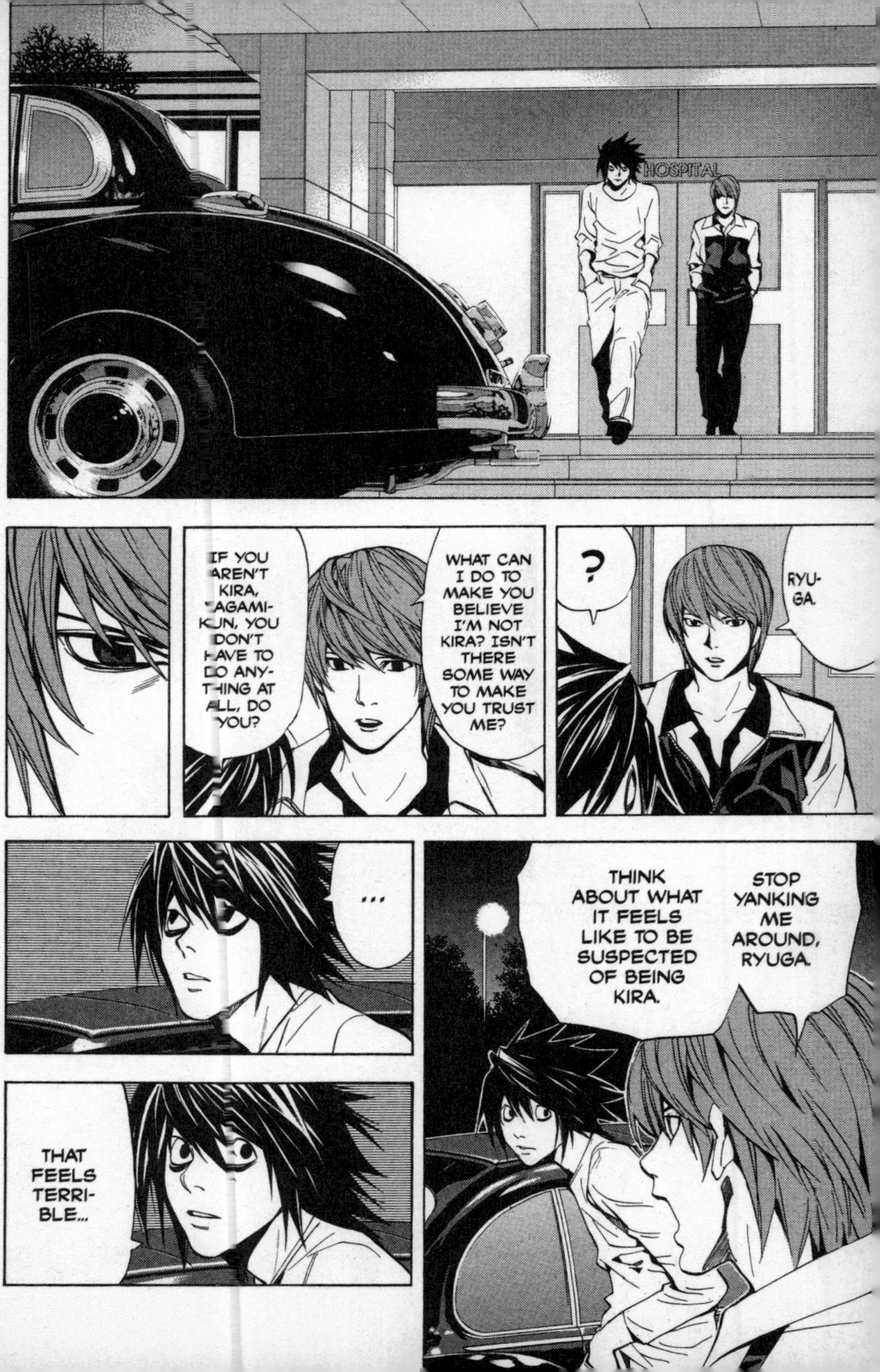
HOSPITAL
RYU-GA.
?
WHAT CAN I DO TO MAKE YOU BELIEVE I'M NOT KIRA? ISN'T THERE SOME WAY TO MAKE YOU TRUST ME?
IF YOU AREN'T KIRA, YAGAMI-KUN, YOU DON'T HAVE TO DO ANY-THING AT ALL, DO YOU?
STOP YANKING ME AROUND, RYUGA.
THINK ABOUT WHAT IT FEELS LIKE TO BE SUSPECTED OF BEING KIRA.
...
THAT FEELS TERRI-BLE...

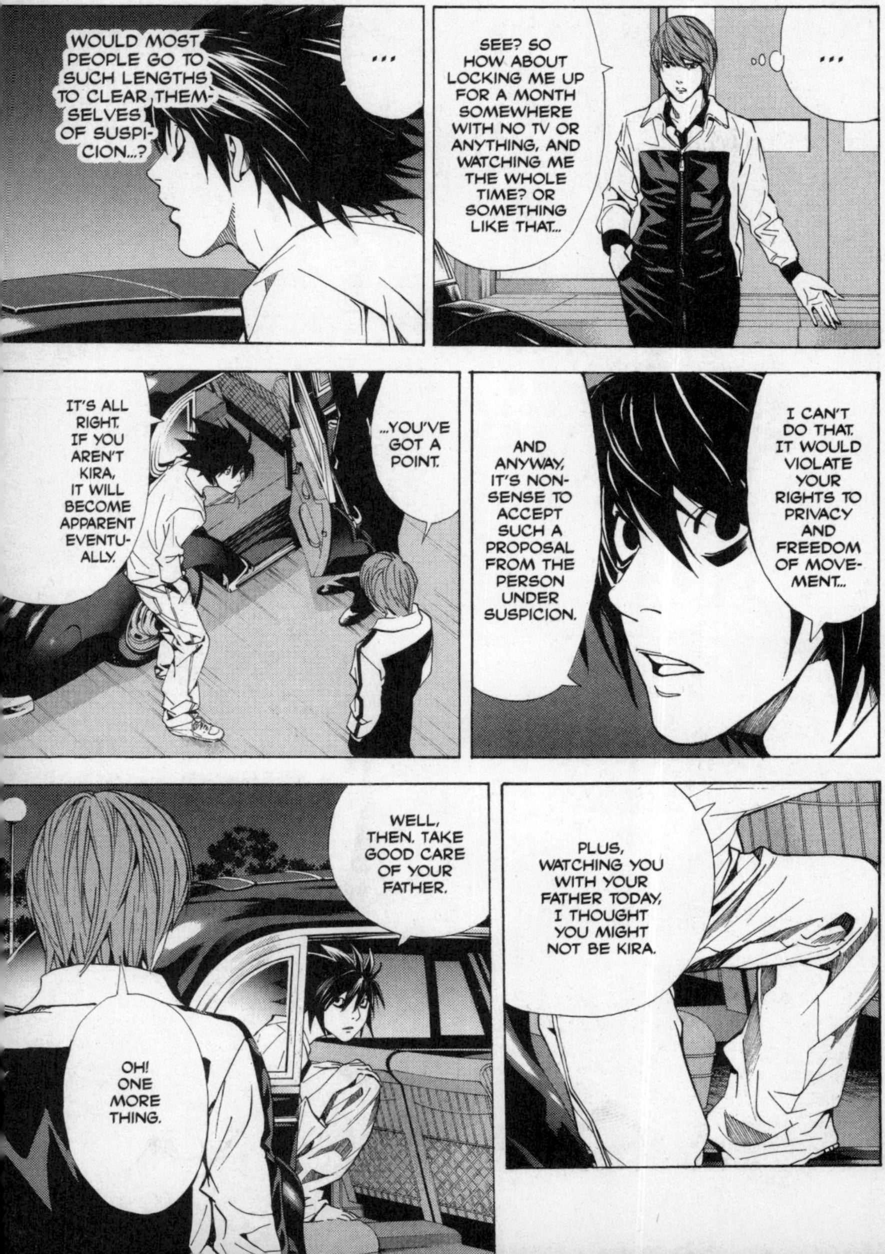
...
SEE? SO HOW ABOUT LOCKING ME UP FOR A MONTH SOMEWHERE WITH NO TV OR ANYTHING, AND WATCHING ME THE WHOLE TIME? OR SOMETHING LIKE THAT...
...
WOULD MOST PEOPLE GO TO SUCH LENGTHS TO CLEAR THEM-SELVES OF SUSPI-CION...?
I CAN'T DO THAT. IT WOULD VIOLATE YOUR RIGHTS TO PRIVACY AND FREEDOM OF MOVE-MENT...
AND ANYWAY, IT'S NON-SENSE TO ACCEPT SUCH A PROPOSAL FROM THE PERSON UNDER SUSPICION.
...YOU'VE GOT A POINT.
IT'S ALL RIGHT. IF YOU AREN'T KIRA, IT WILL BECOME APPARENT EVENTU-ALLY.
PLUS, WATCHING YOU WITH YOUR FATHER TODAY, I THOUGHT YOU MIGHT NOT BE KIRA.
WELL, THEN. TAKE GOOD CARE OF YOUR FATHER.
OH! ONE MORE THING.

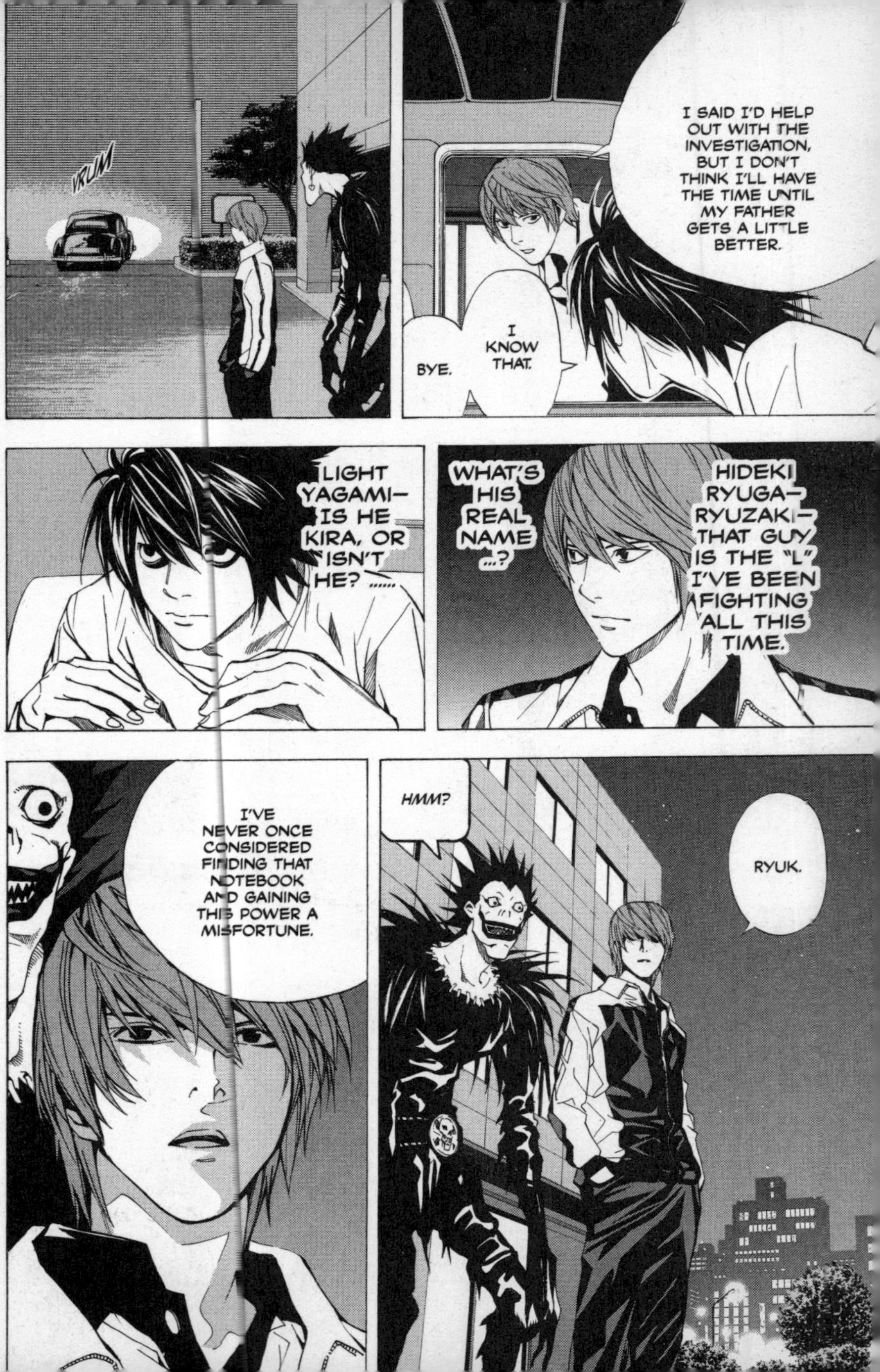
I SAID I'D HELP OUT WITH THE INVESTIGATION, BUT I DON'T THINK I'LL HAVE THE TIME UNTIL MY FATHER GETS A LITTLE BETTER.
I KNOW THAT.
BYE.
VRUM
HIDEKI RYUGA— RYUZAKI— THAT GUY IS THE "L" I'VE BEEN FIGHTING ALL THIS TIME.
WHAT'S HIS REAL NAME ...?
LIGHT YAGAMI— IS HE KIRA, OR ISN'T HE? ......
RYUK.
HMM?
I'VE NEVER ONCE CONSIDERED FINDING THAT NOTEBOOK AND GAINING THIS POWER A MISFORTUNE.

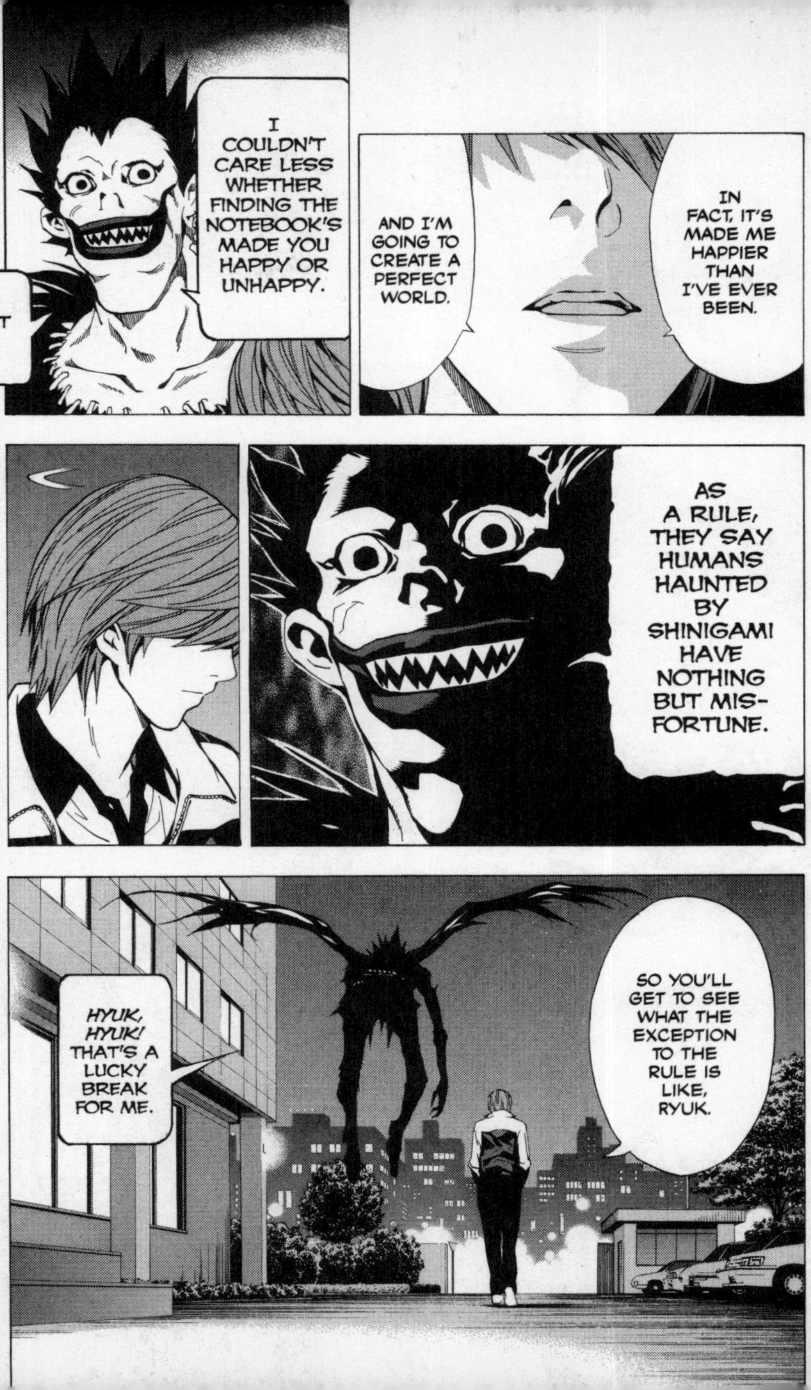
IN FACT, IT'S MADE ME HAPPIER THAN I'VE EVER BEEN.
AND I'M GOING TO CREATE A PERFECT WORLD.
I COULDN'T CARE LESS WHETHER FINDING THE NOTEBOOK'S MADE YOU HAPPY OR UNHAPPY.
BUT ...
AS A RULE, THEY SAY HUMANS HAUNTED BY SHINIGAMI HAVE NOTHING BUT MIS-FORTUNE.
SO YOU'LL GET TO SEE WHAT THE EXCEPTION TO THE RULE IS LIKE, RYUK.
HYUK, HYUK! THAT'S A LUCKY BREAK FOR ME.

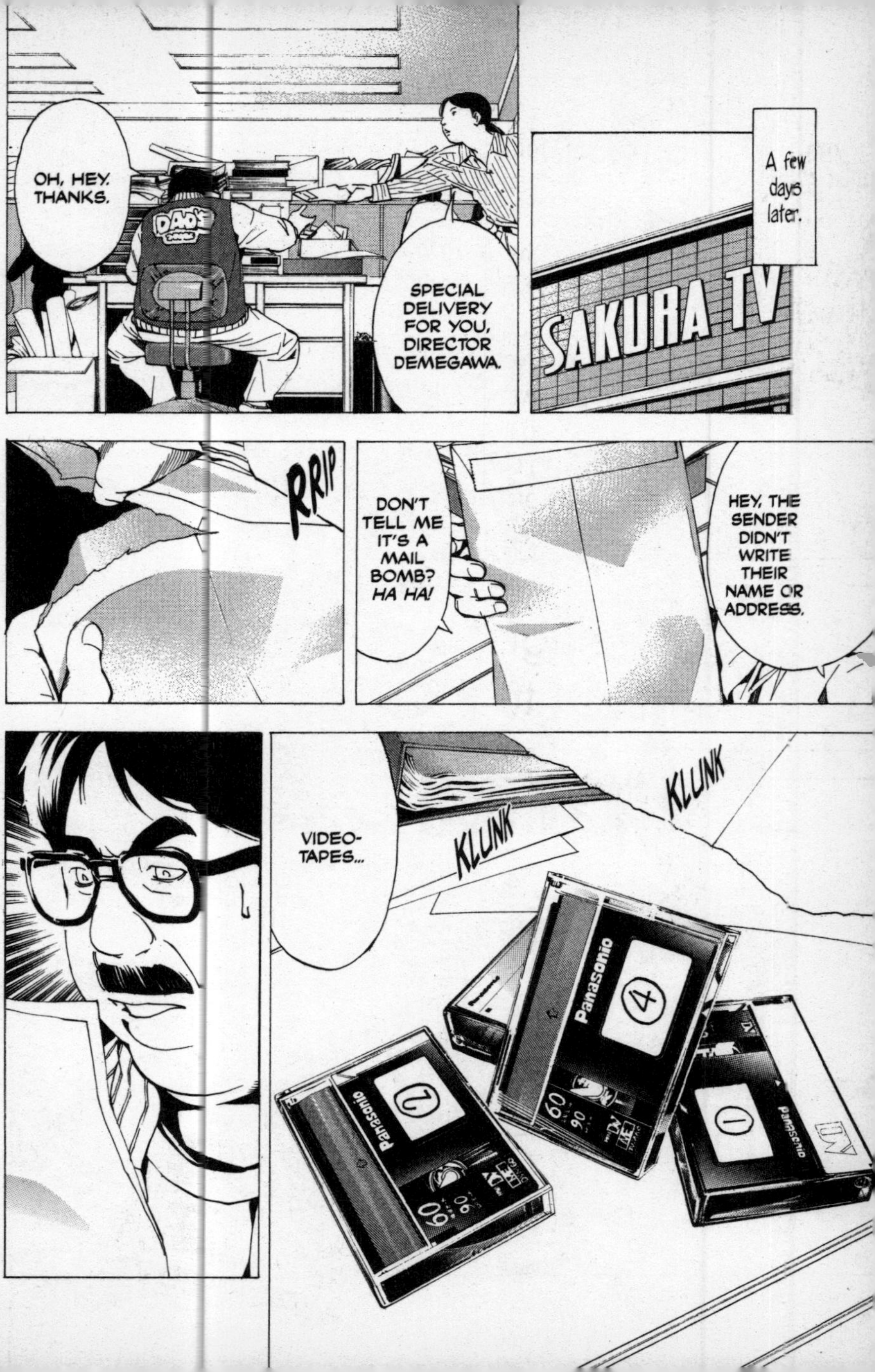
A few days later.
SAKURA TV
SPECIAL DELIVERY FOR YOU, DIRECTOR DEMEGAWA.
OH, HEY. THANKS.
HEY, THE SENDER DIDN'T WRITE THEIR NAME OR ADDRESS.
DON'T TELL ME IT'S A MAIL BOMB? HA HA!
RRIP
KLUNK
KLUNK
VIDEO-TAPES...

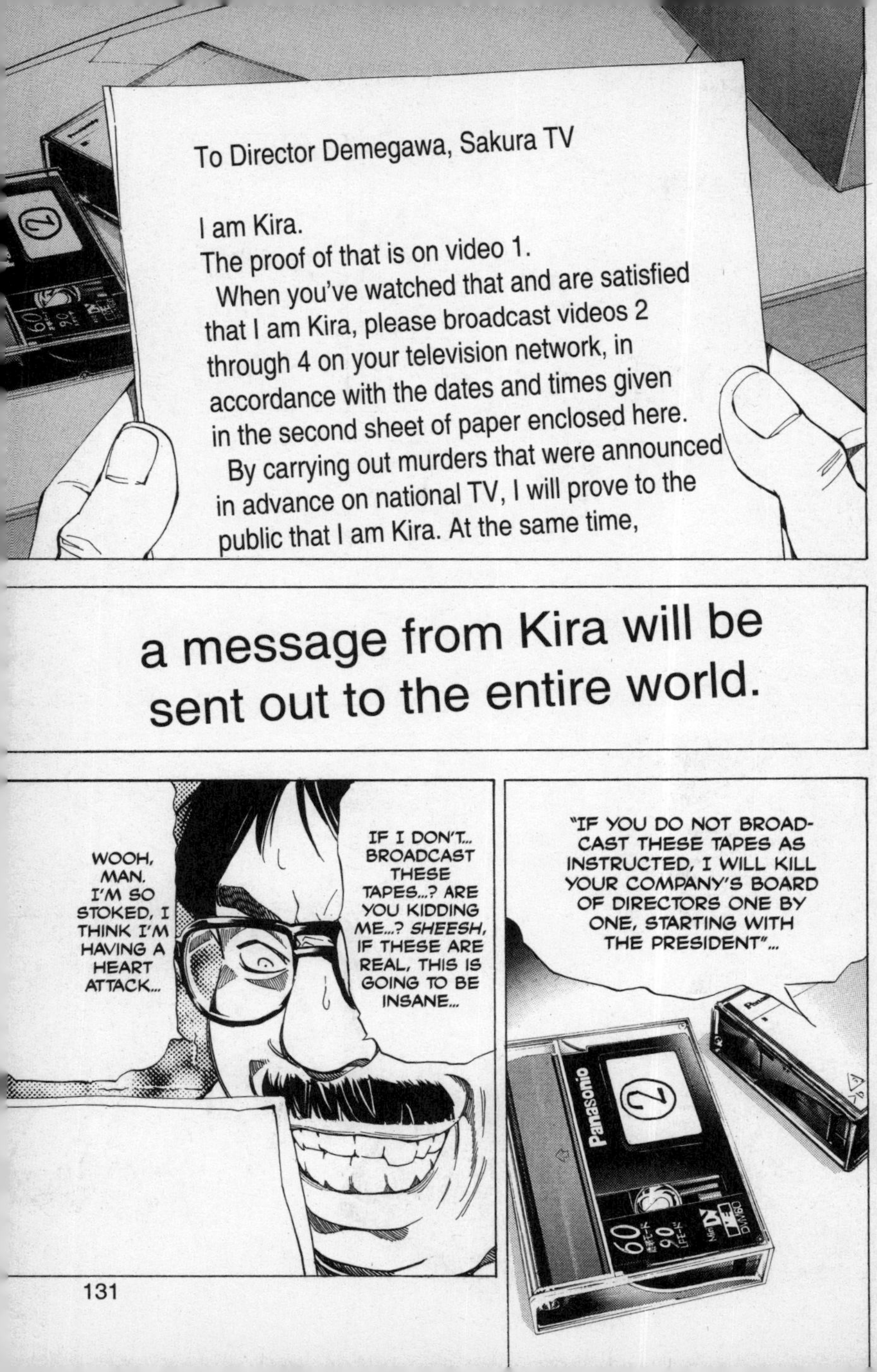
To Director Demegawa, Sakura TV
I am Kira.
The proof of that is on video 1.
When you've watched that and are satisfied that I am Kira, please broadcast videos 2 through 4 on your television network, in accordance with the dates and times given in the second sheet of paper enclosed here.
By carrying out murders that were announced in advance on national TV, I will prove to the public that I am Kira. At the same time,
a message from Kira will be sent out to the entire world.
"IF YOU DO NOT BROADCAST THESE TAPES AS INSTRUCTED, I WILL KILL YOUR COMPANY'S BOARD OF DIRECTORS ONE BY ONE, STARTING WITH THE PRESIDENT"...
Panasonic
IF I DON'T... BROADCAST THESE TAPES...? ARE YOU KIDDING ME...? *SHEESH*, IF THESE ARE REAL, THIS IS GOING TO BE INSANE...
WOOH, MAN. I'M SO STOKED, I THINK I'M HAVING A HEART ATTACK...

chapter 23 Hard Run

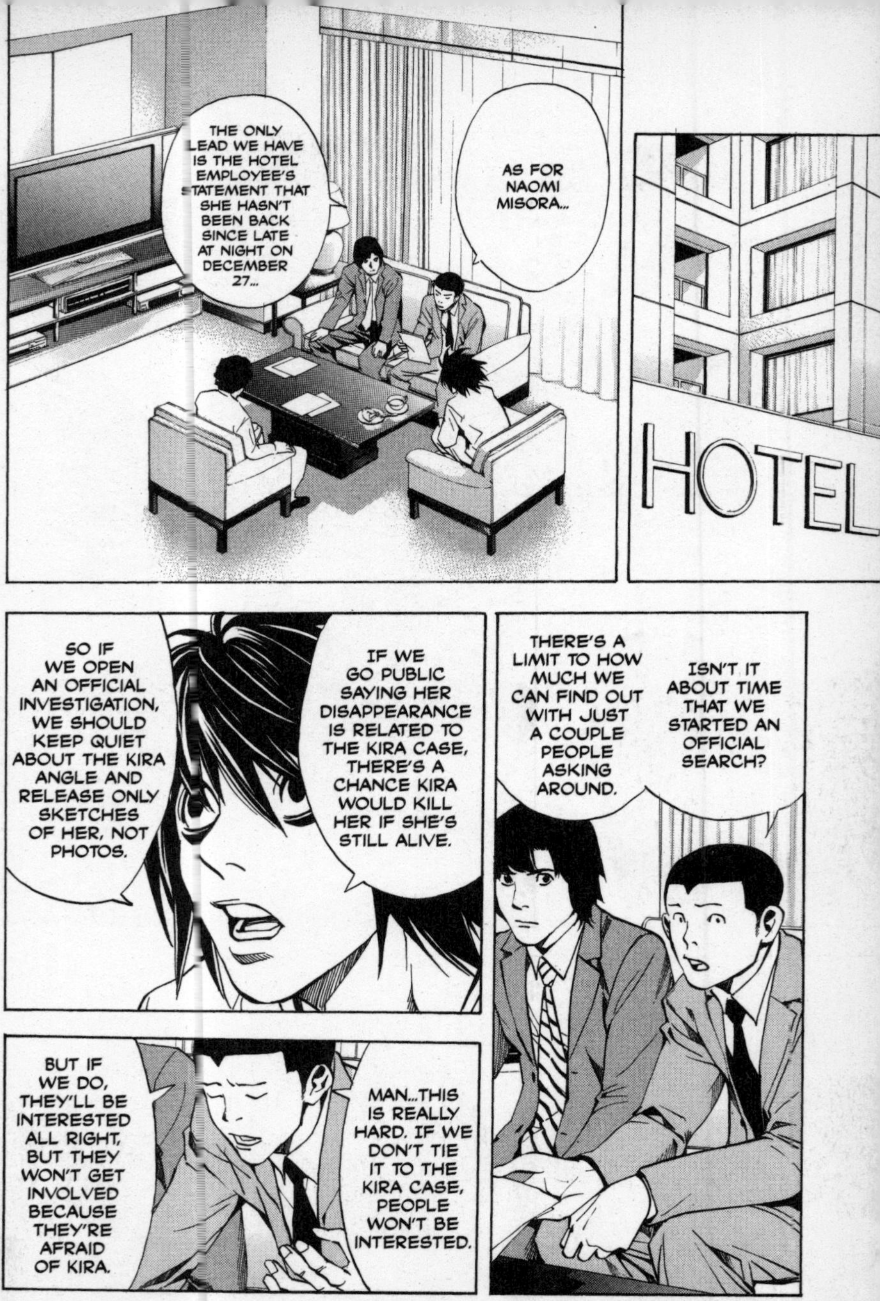
HOTEL
AS FOR NAOMI MISORA...
THE ONLY LEAD WE HAVE IS THE HOTEL EMPLOYEE'S STATEMENT THAT SHE HASN'T BEEN BACK SINCE LATE AT NIGHT ON DECEMBER 27...
ISN'T IT ABOUT TIME THAT WE STARTED AN OFFICIAL SEARCH?
THERE'S A LIMIT TO HOW MUCH WE CAN FIND OUT WITH JUST A COUPLE PEOPLE ASKING AROUND.
IF WE GO PUBLIC SAYING HER DISAPPEARANCE IS RELATED TO THE KIRA CASE, THERE'S A CHANCE KIRA WOULD KILL HER IF SHE'S STILL ALIVE.
SO IF WE OPEN AN OFFICIAL INVESTIGATION, WE SHOULD KEEP QUIET ABOUT THE KIRA ANGLE AND RELEASE ONLY SKETCHES OF HER, NOT PHOTOS.
MAN...THIS IS REALLY HARD. IF WE DON'T TIE IT TO THE KIRA CASE, PEOPLE WON'T BE INTERESTED.
BUT IF WE DO, THEY'LL BE INTERESTED ALL RIGHT, BUT THEY WON'T GET INVOLVED BECAUSE THEY'RE AFRAID OF KIRA.

READ THIS WAY

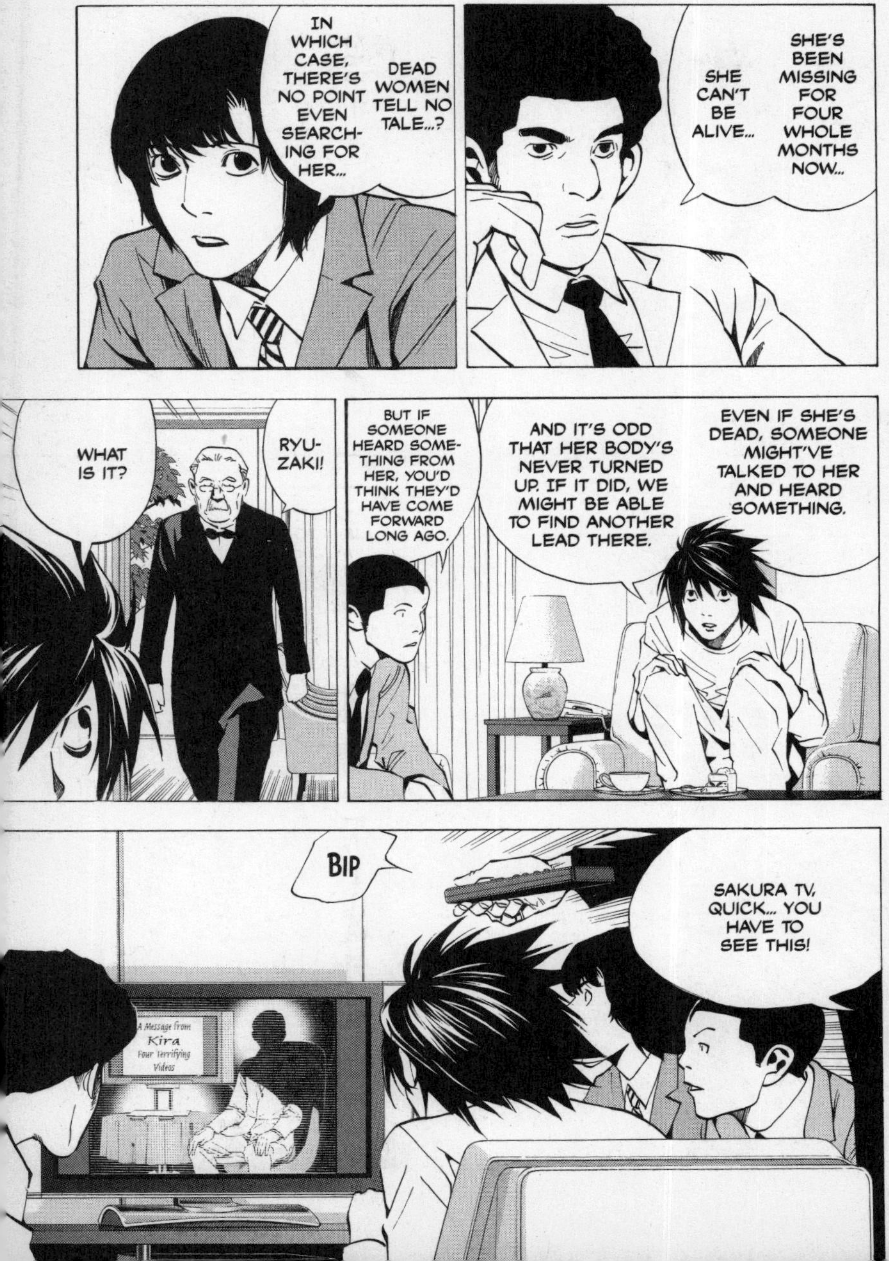
SHE'S BEEN MISSING FOR FOUR WHOLE MONTHS NOW...
SHE CAN'T BE ALIVE...
DEAD WOMEN TELL NO TALE...?
IN WHICH CASE, THERE'S NO POINT EVEN SEARCHING FOR HER...
EVEN IF SHE'S DEAD, SOMEONE MIGHT'VE TALKED TO HER AND HEARD SOMETHING.
AND IT'S ODD THAT HER BODY'S NEVER TURNED UP. IF IT DID, WE MIGHT BE ABLE TO FIND ANOTHER LEAD THERE.
BUT IF SOMEONE HEARD SOMETHING FROM HER, YOU'D THINK THEY'D HAVE COME FORWARD LONG AGO.
RYUZAKI!
WHAT IS IT?
SAKURA TV, QUICK... YOU HAVE TO SEE THIS!
BIP
A Message from Kira Four Terrifying Videos

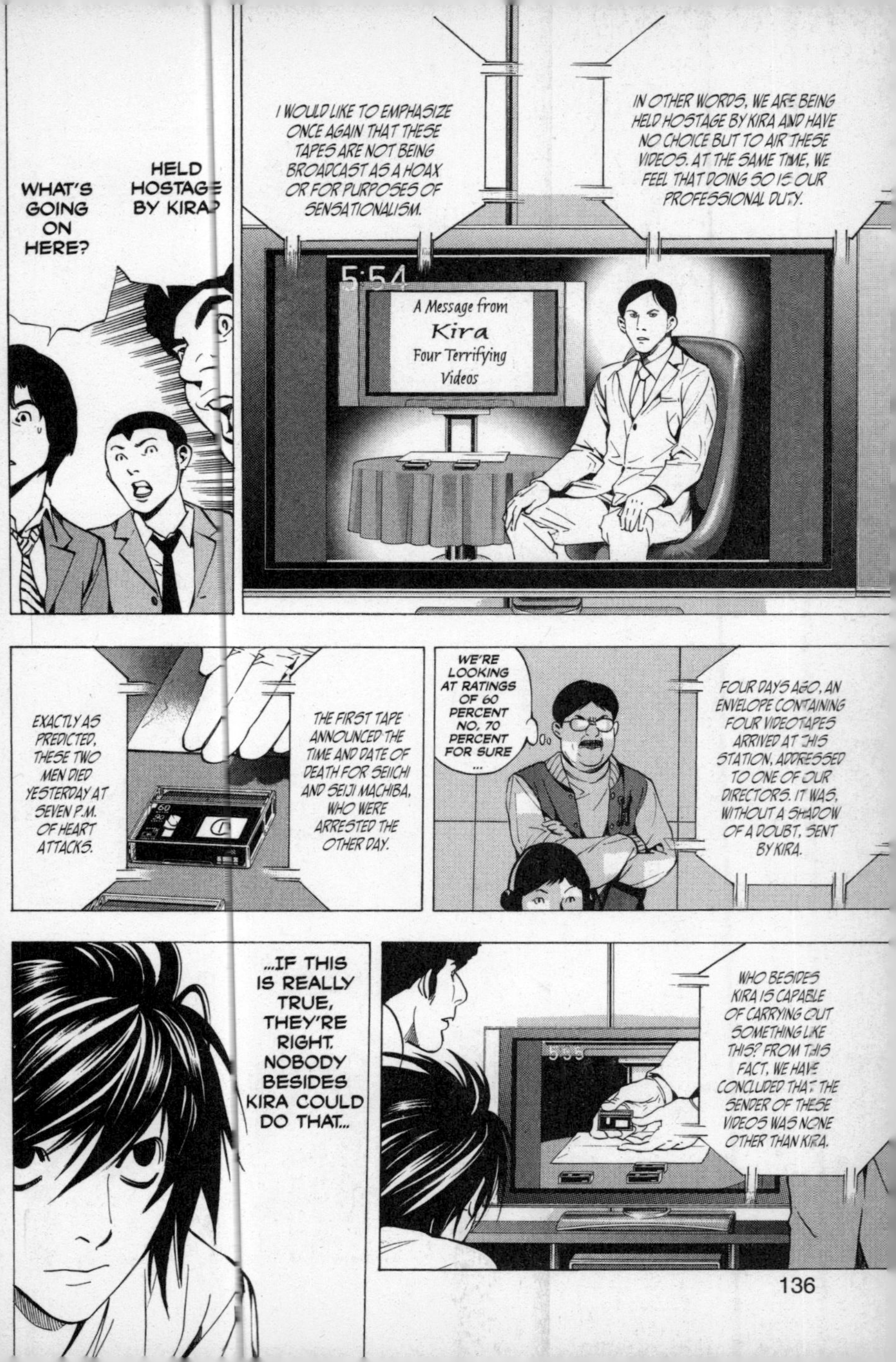
IN OTHER WORDS, WE ARE BEING HELD HOSTAGE BY KIRA AND HAVE NO CHOICE BUT TO AIR THESE VIDEOS. AT THE SAME TIME, WE FEEL THAT DOING SO IS OUR PROFESSIONAL DUTY.
I WOULD LIKE TO EMPHASIZE ONCE AGAIN THAT THESE TAPES ARE NOT BEING BROADCAST AS A HOAX OR FOR PURPOSES OF SENSATIONALISM.
5:54
A Message from
Kira
Four Terrifying Videos
HELD HOSTAGE BY KIRA?
WHAT'S GOING ON HERE?
FOUR DAYS AGO, AN ENVELOPE CONTAINING FOUR VIDEOTAPES ARRIVED AT THIS STATION, ADDRESSED TO ONE OF OUR DIRECTORS. IT WAS, WITHOUT A SHADOW OF A DOUBT, SENT BY KIRA.
WE'RE LOOKING AT RATINGS OF 60 PERCENT NO, 70 PERCENT FOR SURE ...
THE FIRST TAPE ANNOUNCED THE TIME AND DATE OF DEATH FOR SEIICHI AND SEIJI MACHIBA, WHO WERE ARRESTED THE OTHER DAY.
EXACTLY AS PREDICTED, THESE TWO MEN DIED YESTERDAY AT SEVEN P.M. OF HEART ATTACKS.
WHO BESIDES KIRA IS CAPABLE OF CARRYING OUT SOMETHING LIKE THIS? FROM THIS FACT, WE HAVE CONCLUDED THAT THE SENDER OF THESE VIDEOS WAS NONE OTHER THAN KIRA.
...IF THIS IS REALLY TRUE, THEY'RE RIGHT. NOBODY BESIDES KIRA COULD DO THAT...

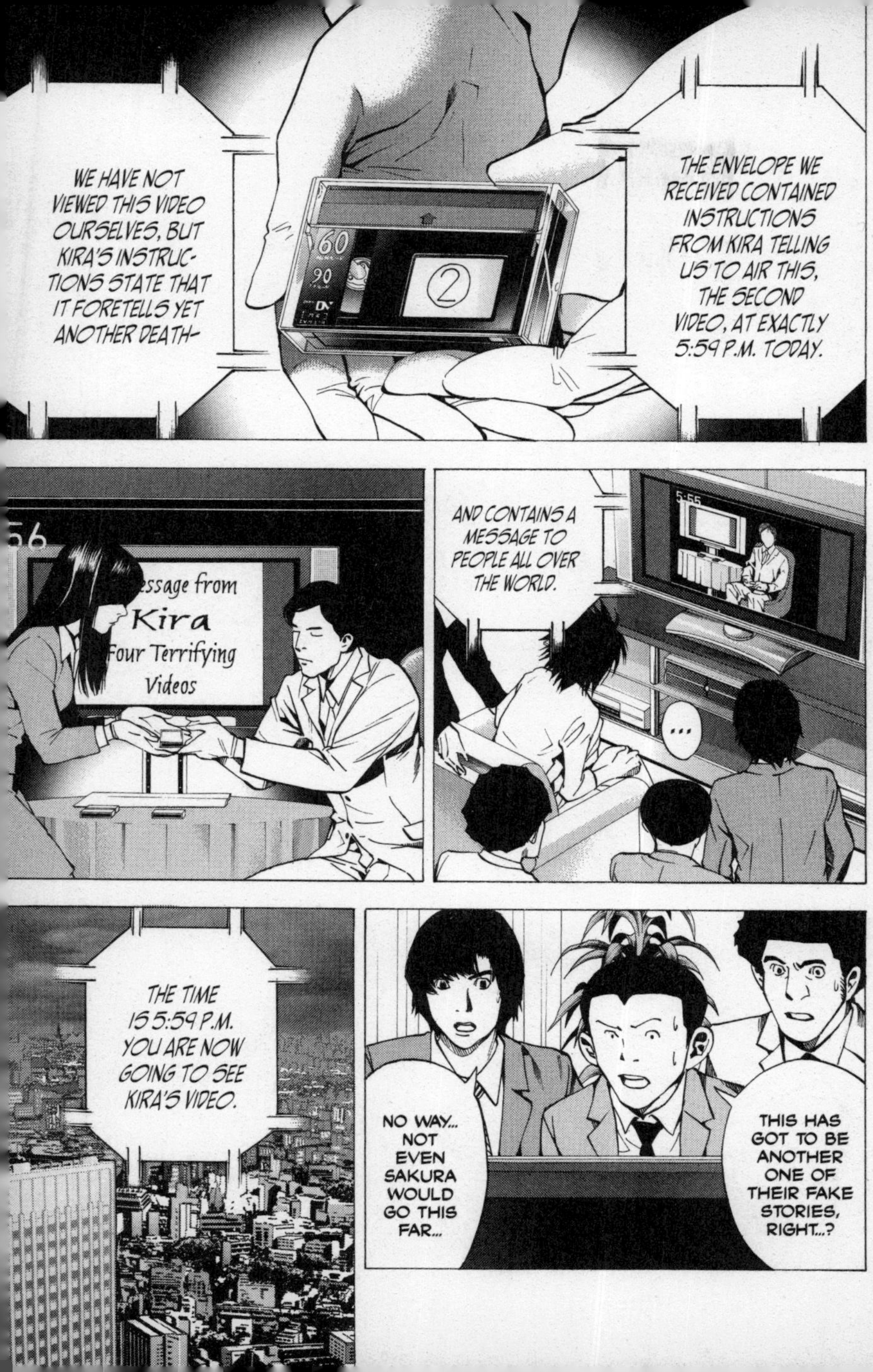
THE ENVELOPE WE RECEIVED CONTAINED INSTRUCTIONS FROM KIRA TELLING US TO AIR THIS, THE SECOND VIDEO, AT EXACTLY 5:59 P.M. TODAY.
WE HAVE NOT VIEWED THIS VIDEO OURSELVES, BUT KIRA'S INSTRUCTIONS STATE THAT IT FORETELLS YET ANOTHER DEATH-
60
90
2
5:55
AND CONTAINS A MESSAGE TO PEOPLE ALL OVER THE WORLD.
...
essage from
Kira
Four Terrifying
Videos
THIS HAS GOT TO BE ANOTHER ONE OF THEIR FAKE STORIES, RIGHT...?
NO WAY... NOT EVEN SAKURA WOULD GO THIS FAR...
THE TIME IS 5:59 P.M. YOU ARE NOW GOING TO SEE KIRA'S VIDEO.

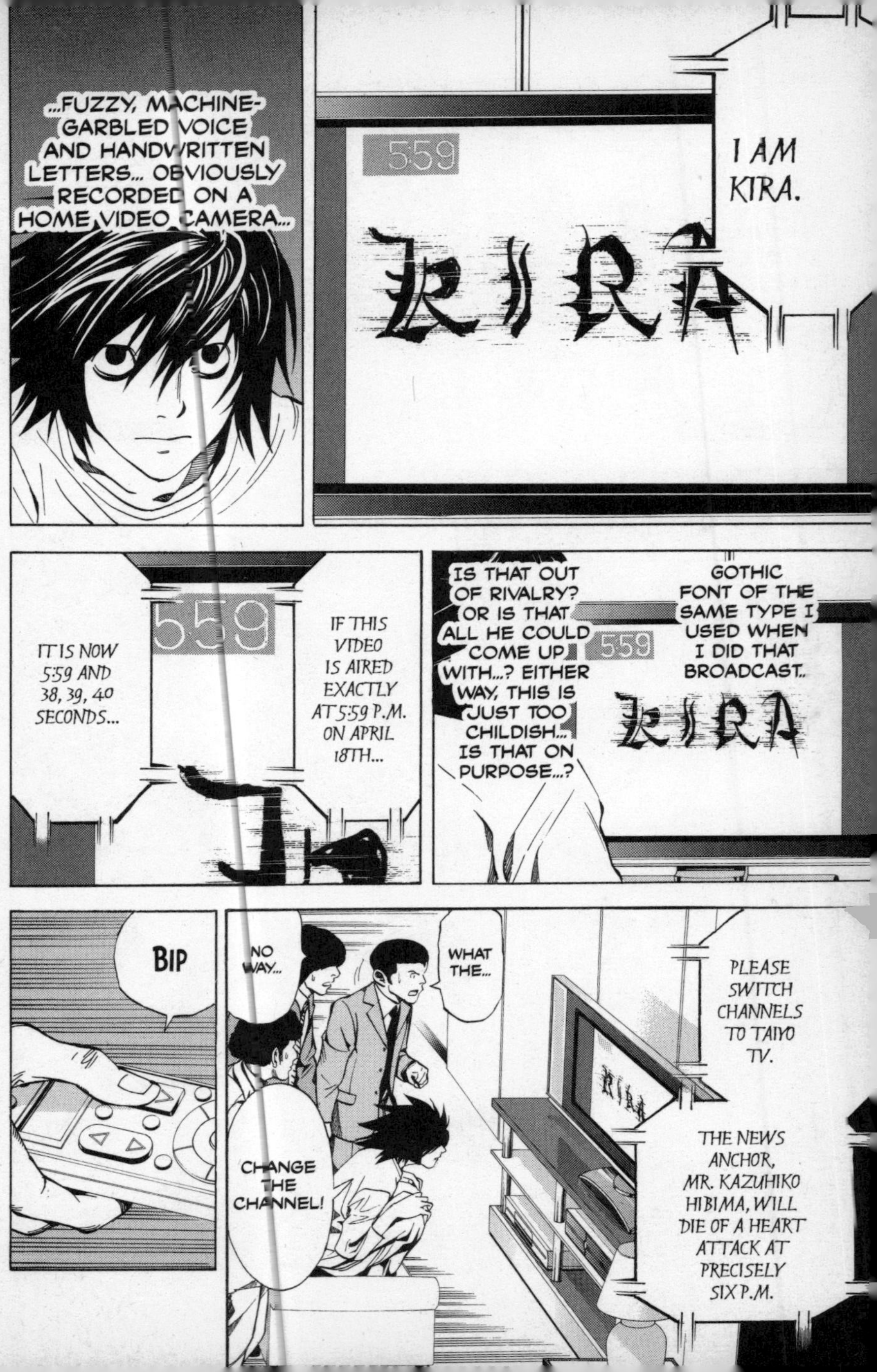
559
KIRA
I AM KIRA.
...FUZZY, MACHINE-GARBLED VOICE AND HANDWRITTEN LETTERS... OBVIOUSLY RECORDED ON A HOME VIDEO CAMERA...
559
KIRA
GOTHIC FONT OF THE SAME TYPE I USED WHEN I DID THAT BROADCAST..
IS THAT OUT OF RIVALRY? OR IS THAT ALL HE COULD COME UP WITH...? EITHER WAY, THIS IS JUST TOO CHILDISH... IS THAT ON PURPOSE...?
559
IF THIS VIDEO IS AIRED EXACTLY AT 5:59 P.M. ON APRIL 18TH...
IT IS NOW 5:59 AND 38, 39, 40 SECONDS...
PLEASE SWITCH CHANNELS TO TAIYO TV.
THE NEWS ANCHOR, MR. KAZUHIKO HIBIMA, WILL DIE OF A HEART ATTACK AT PRECISELY SIX P.M.
WHAT THE...
NO WAY...
CHANGE THE CHANNEL!
BIP

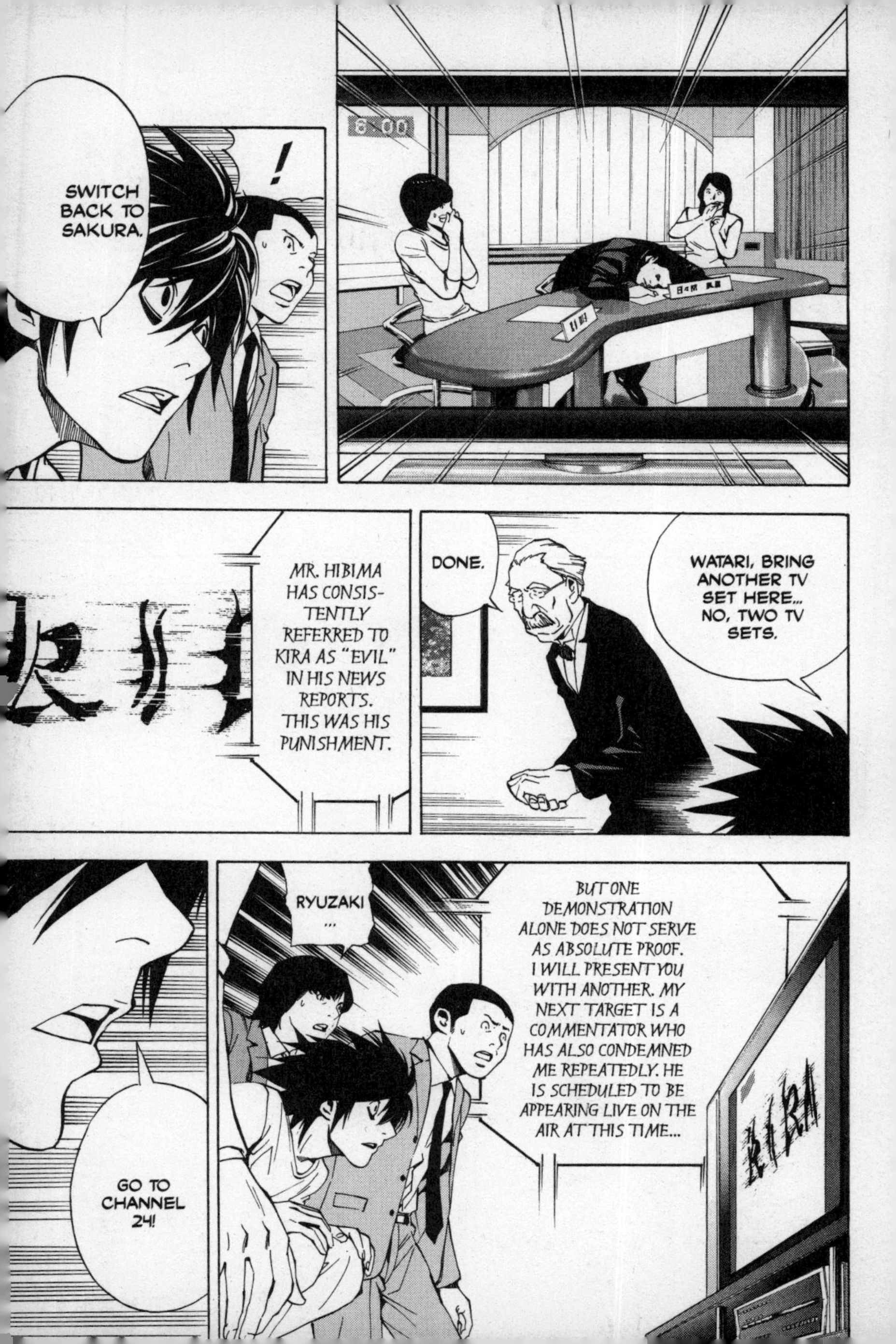
6:00
!
SWITCH BACK TO SAKURA.
WATARI, BRING ANOTHER TV SET HERE... NO, TWO TV SETS.
DONE.
MR. HIBIMA HAS CONSISTENTLY REFERRED TO KIRA AS "EVIL" IN HIS NEWS REPORTS. THIS WAS HIS PUNISHMENT.
KIRA
BUT ONE DEMONSTRATION ALONE DOES NOT SERVE AS ABSOLUTE PROOF. I WILL PRESENT YOU WITH ANOTHER. MY NEXT TARGET IS A COMMENTATOR WHO HAS ALSO CONDEMNED ME REPEATEDLY. HE IS SCHEDULED TO BE APPEARING LIVE ON THE AIR AT THIS TIME...
RYUZAKI ...
GO TO CHANNEL 24!

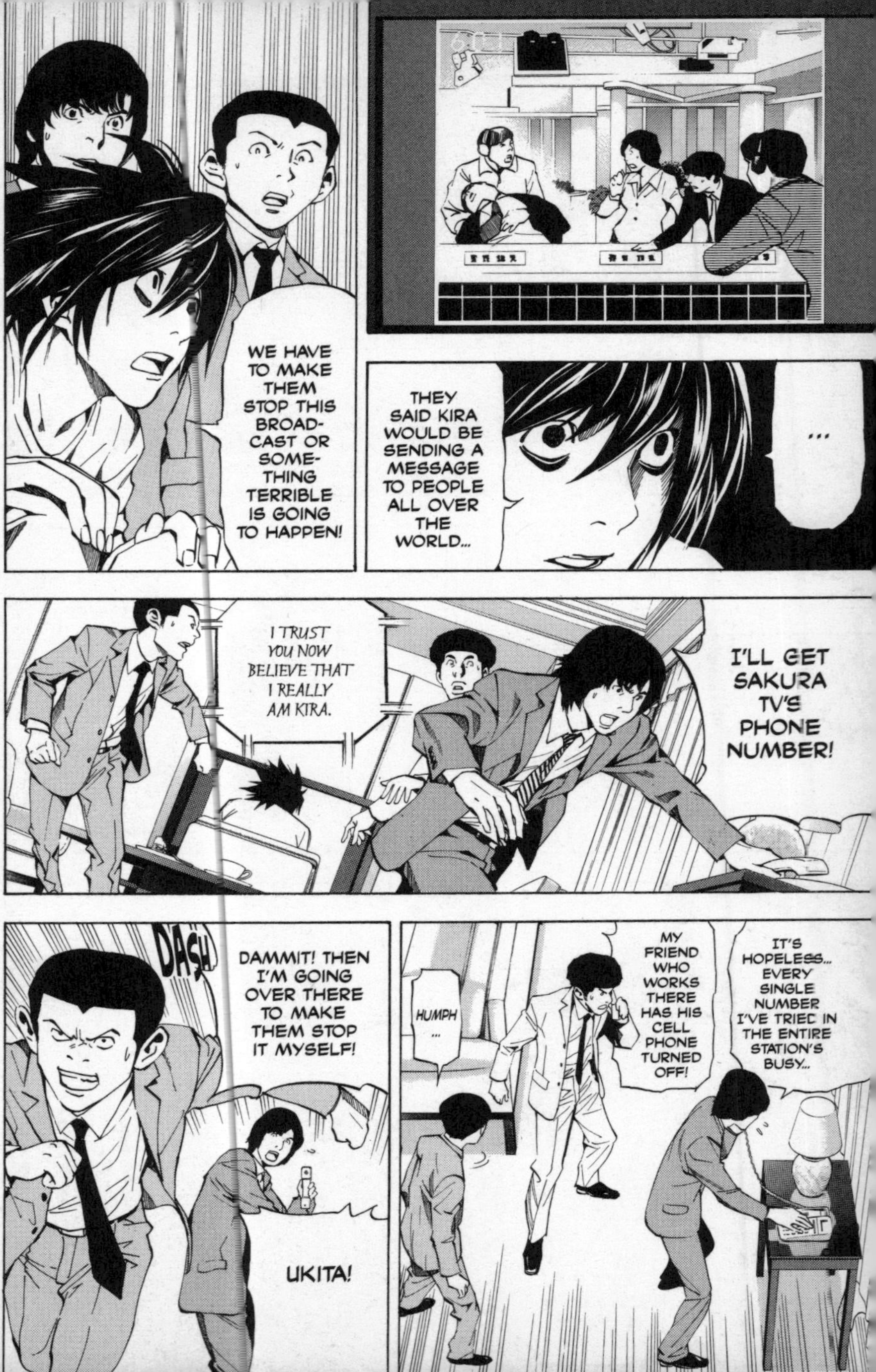
...
THEY SAID KIRA WOULD BE SENDING A MESSAGE TO PEOPLE ALL OVER THE WORLD...
WE HAVE TO MAKE THEM STOP THIS BROAD-CAST OR SOME-THING TERRIBLE IS GOING TO HAPPEN!
I'LL GET SAKURA TV'S PHONE NUMBER!
I TRUST YOU NOW BELIEVE THAT I REALLY AM KIRA.
IT'S HOPELESS... EVERY SINGLE NUMBER I'VE TRIED IN THE ENTIRE STATION'S BUSY...
MY FRIEND WHO WORKS THERE HAS HIS CELL PHONE TURNED OFF!
HUMPH...
DASH
DAMMIT! THEN I'M GOING OVER THERE TO MAKE THEM STOP IT MYSELF!
UKITA!

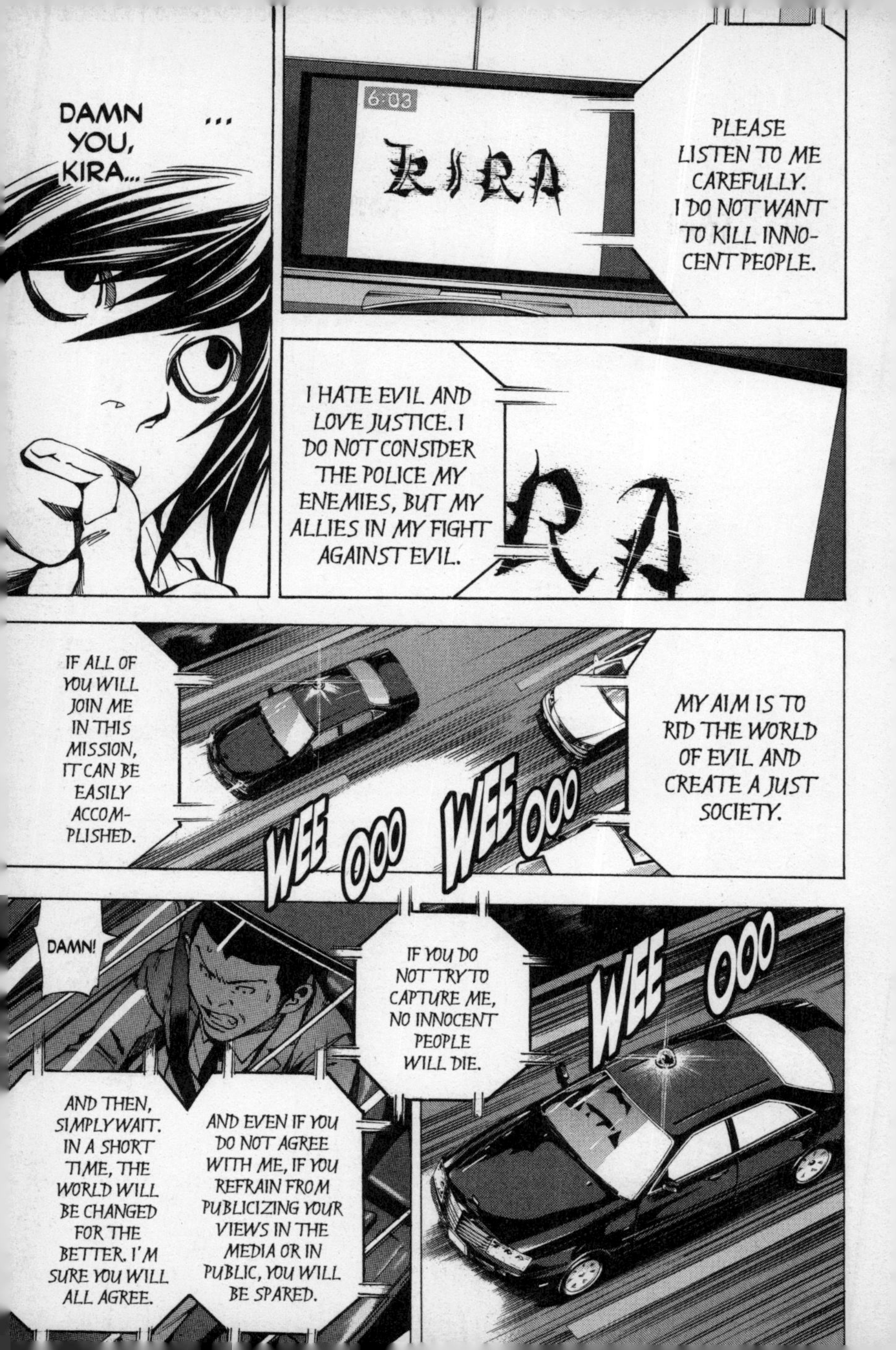
6:03
KIRA
PLEASE LISTEN TO ME CAREFULLY. I DO NOT WANT TO KILL INNOCENT PEOPLE.
I HATE EVIL AND LOVE JUSTICE. I DO NOT CONSIDER THE POLICE MY ENEMIES, BUT MY ALLIES IN MY FIGHT AGAINST EVIL.
...
DAMN YOU, KIRA...
MY AIM IS TO RID THE WORLD OF EVIL AND CREATE A JUST SOCIETY.
WEE OOO WEE OOO
IF ALL OF YOU WILL JOIN ME IN THIS MISSION, IT CAN BE EASILY ACCOMPLISHED.
WEE OOO
IF YOU DO NOT TRY TO CAPTURE ME, NO INNOCENT PEOPLE WILL DIE.
DAMN!
AND EVEN IF YOU DO NOT AGREE WITH ME, IF YOU REFRAIN FROM PUBLICIZING YOUR VIEWS IN THE MEDIA OR IN PUBLIC, YOU WILL BE SPARED.
AND THEN, SIMPLY WAIT. IN A SHORT TIME, THE WORLD WILL BE CHANGED FOR THE BETTER. I'M SURE YOU WILL ALL AGREE.

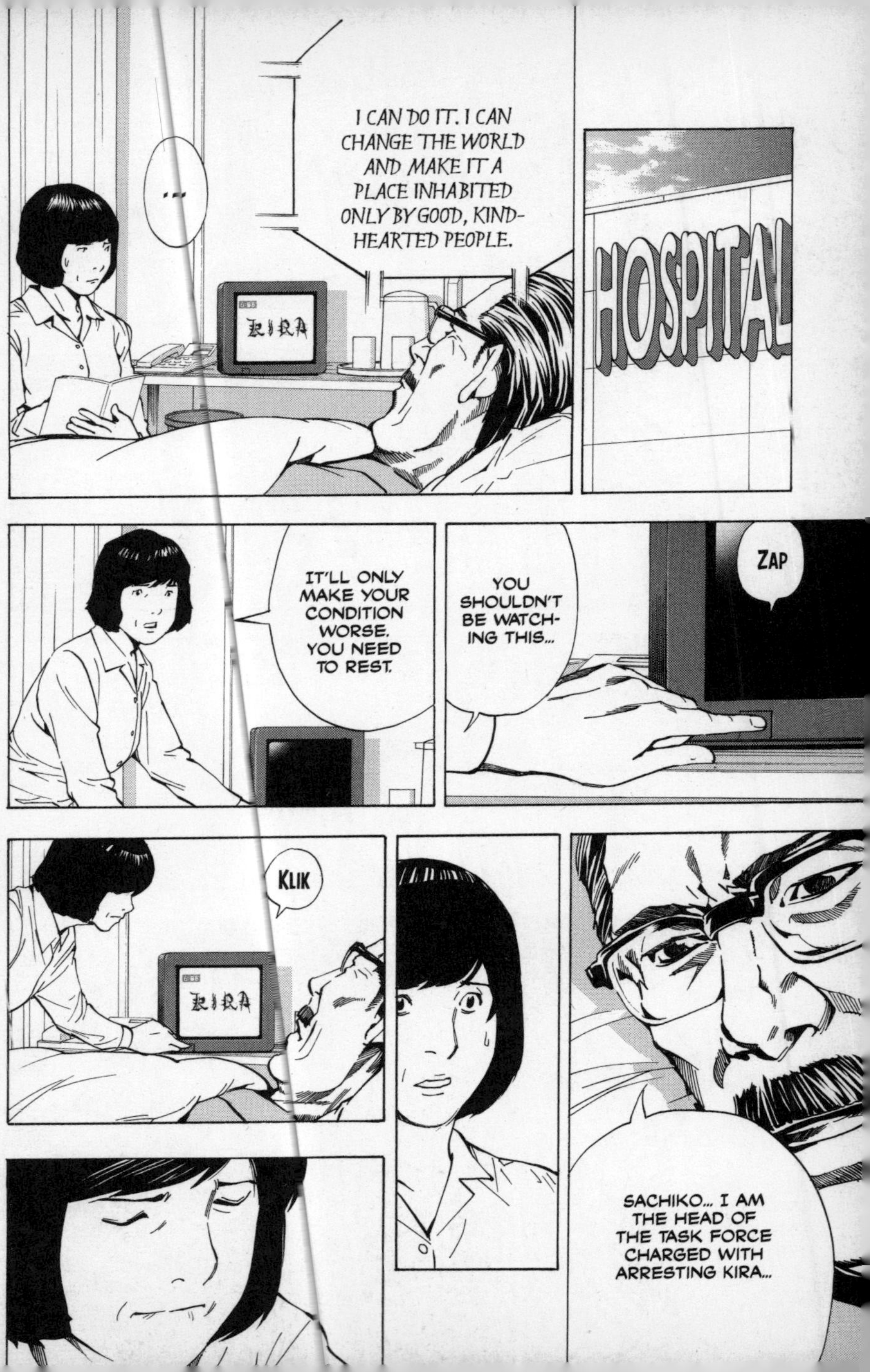
HOSPITAL
I CAN DO IT. I CAN CHANGE THE WORLD AND MAKE IT A PLACE INHABITED ONLY BY GOOD, KIND-HEARTED PEOPLE.
...
KIRA
ZAP
YOU SHOULDN'T BE WATCHING THIS...
IT'LL ONLY MAKE YOUR CONDITION WORSE. YOU NEED TO REST.
SACHIKO... I AM THE HEAD OF THE TASK FORCE CHARGED WITH ARRESTING KIRA...
KLIK
KIRA

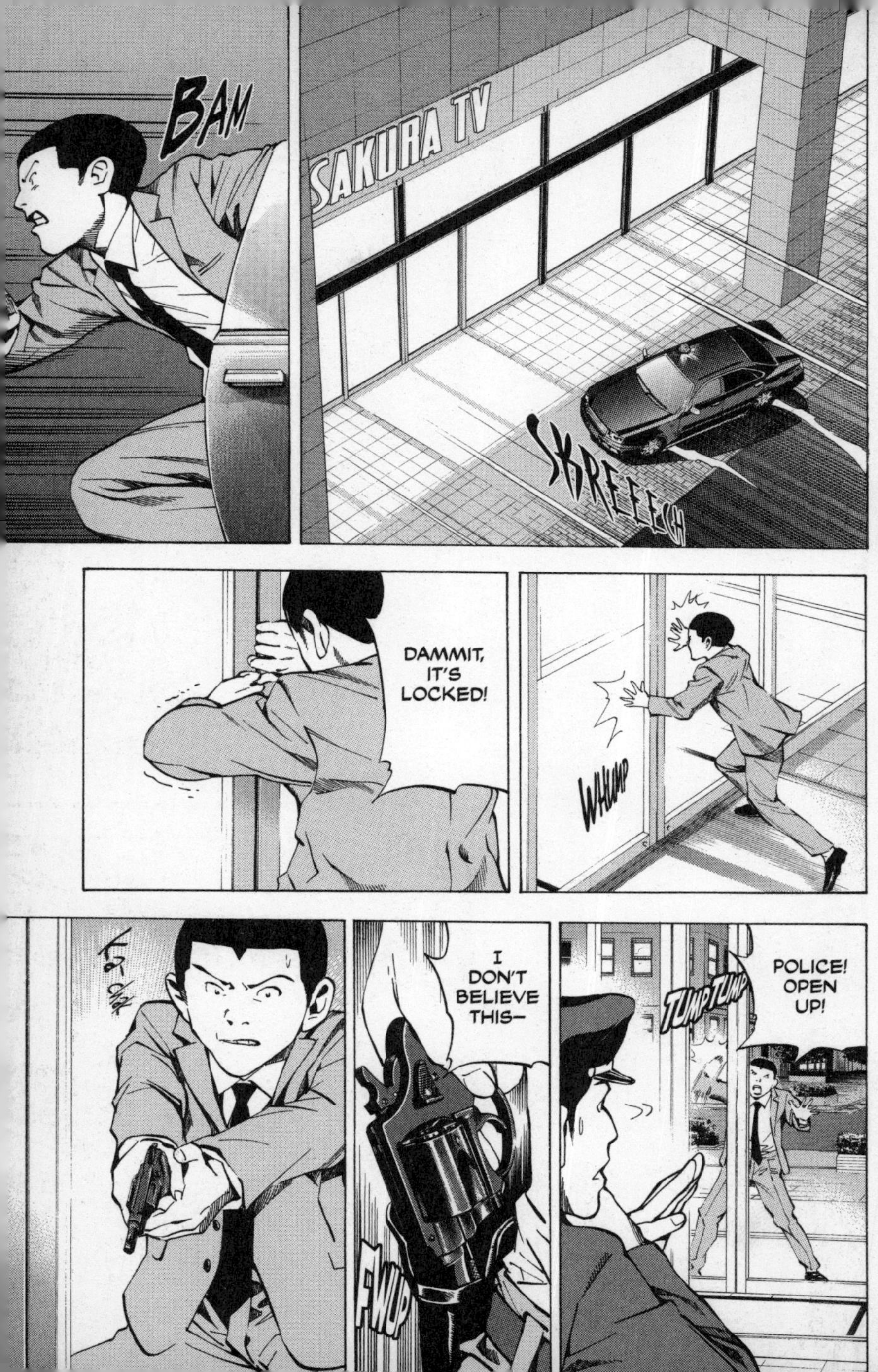
SAKURA TV
SKREEECH
BAM
WHUMP
DAMMIT, IT'S LOCKED!
POLICE! OPEN UP!
TUMP TUMP
I DON'T BELIEVE THIS—
FWUP

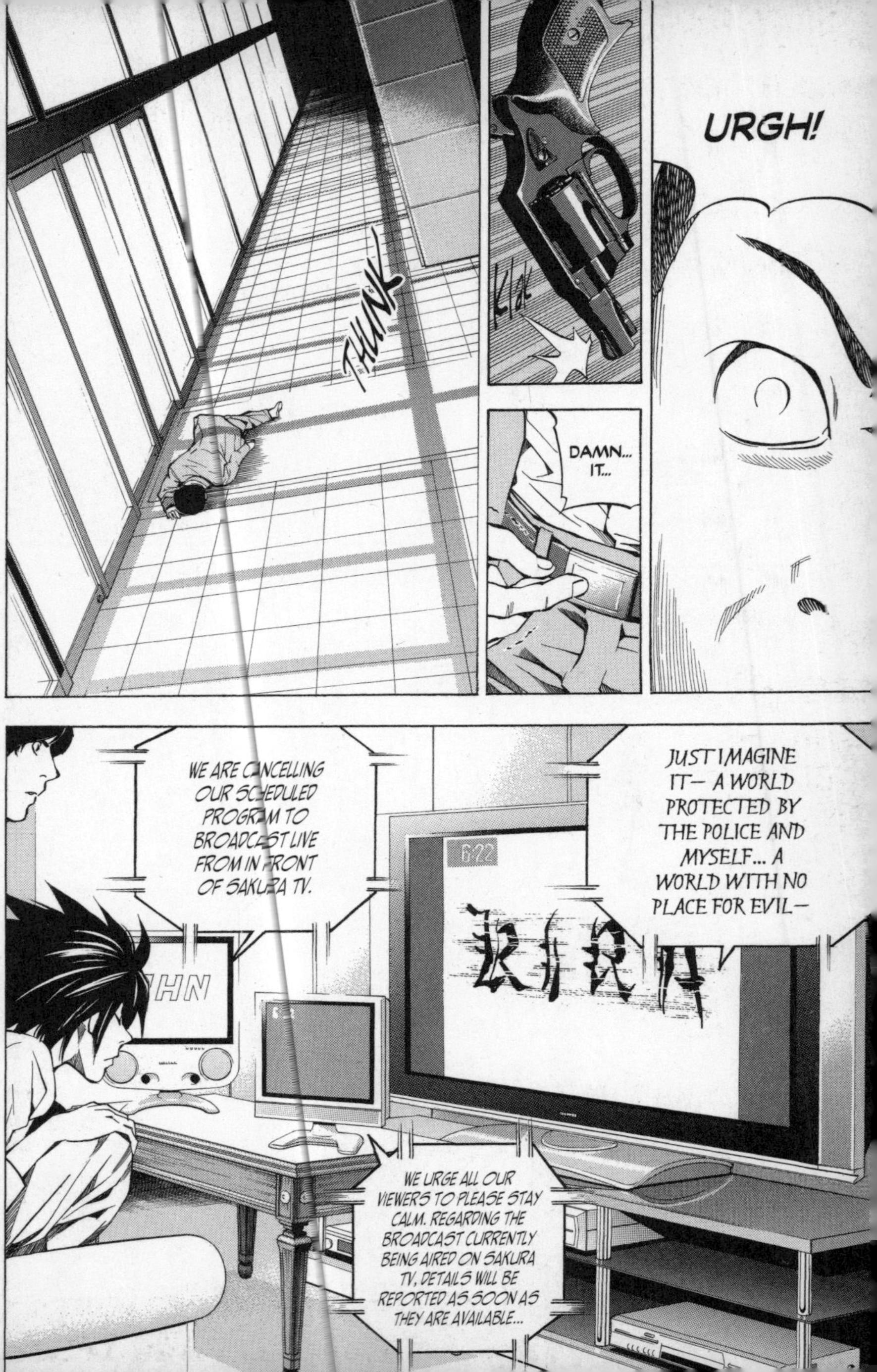
URGH!
KLAK
DAMN... IT...
THUNK
JUST IMAGINE IT— A WORLD PROTECTED BY THE POLICE AND MYSELF... A WORLD WITH NO PLACE FOR EVIL—
WE ARE CANCELLING OUR SCHEDULED PROGRAM TO BROADCAST LIVE FROM IN FRONT OF SAKURA TV.
WE URGE ALL OUR VIEWERS TO PLEASE STAY CALM. REGARDING THE BROADCAST CURRENTLY BEING AIRED ON SAKURA TV, DETAILS WILL BE REPORTED AS SOON AS THEY ARE AVAILABLE...

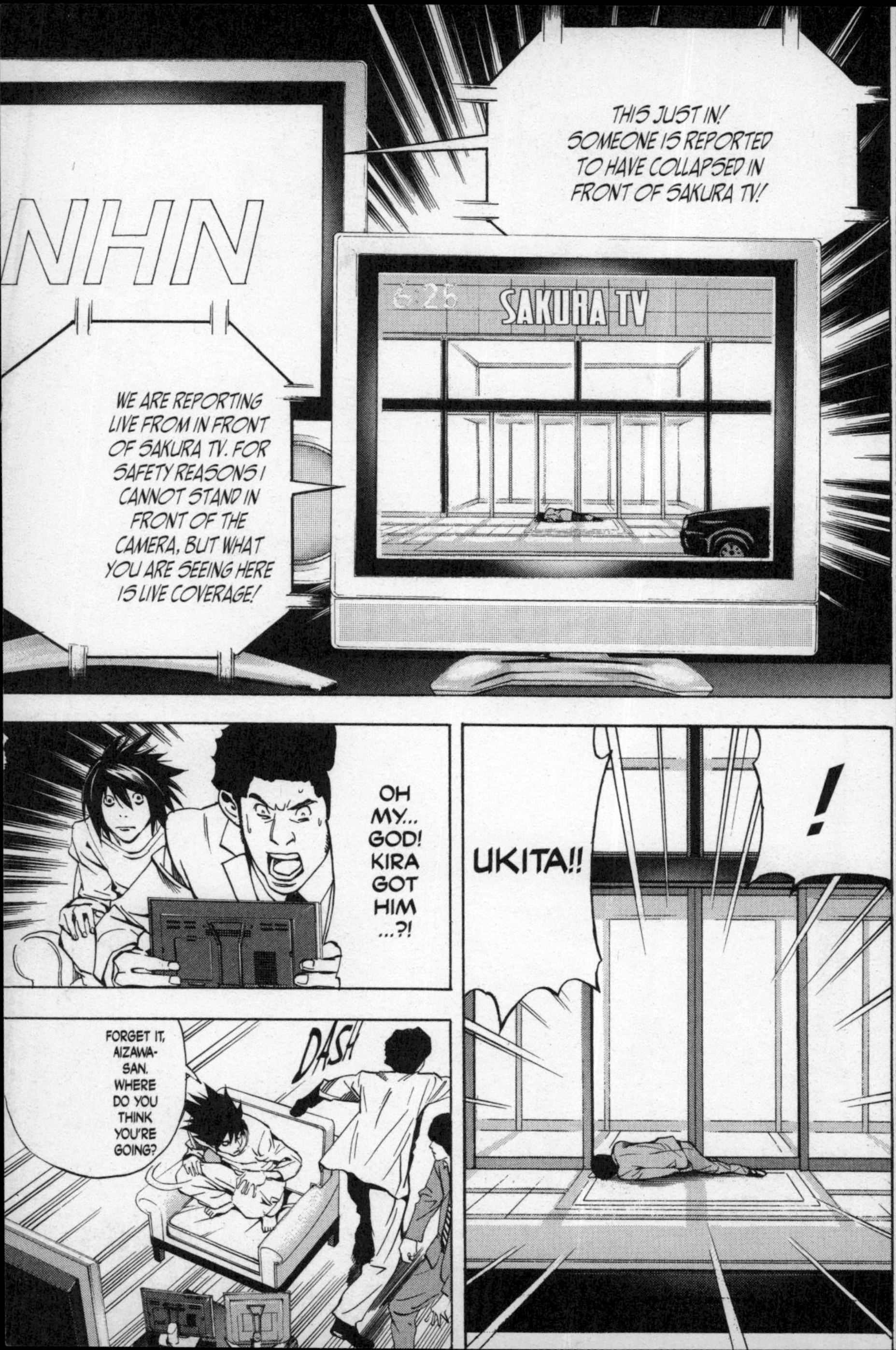
THIS JUST IN! SOMEONE IS REPORTED TO HAVE COLLAPSED IN FRONT OF SAKURA TV!
NHN
WE ARE REPORTING LIVE FROM IN FRONT OF SAKURA TV. FOR SAFETY REASONS I CANNOT STAND IN FRONT OF THE CAMERA, BUT WHAT YOU ARE SEEING HERE IS LIVE COVERAGE!
SAKURA TV
!
UKITA!!
OH MY... GOD! KIRA GOT HIM ...?!
DASH
FORGET IT, AIZAWA-SAN. WHERE DO YOU THINK YOU'RE GOING?

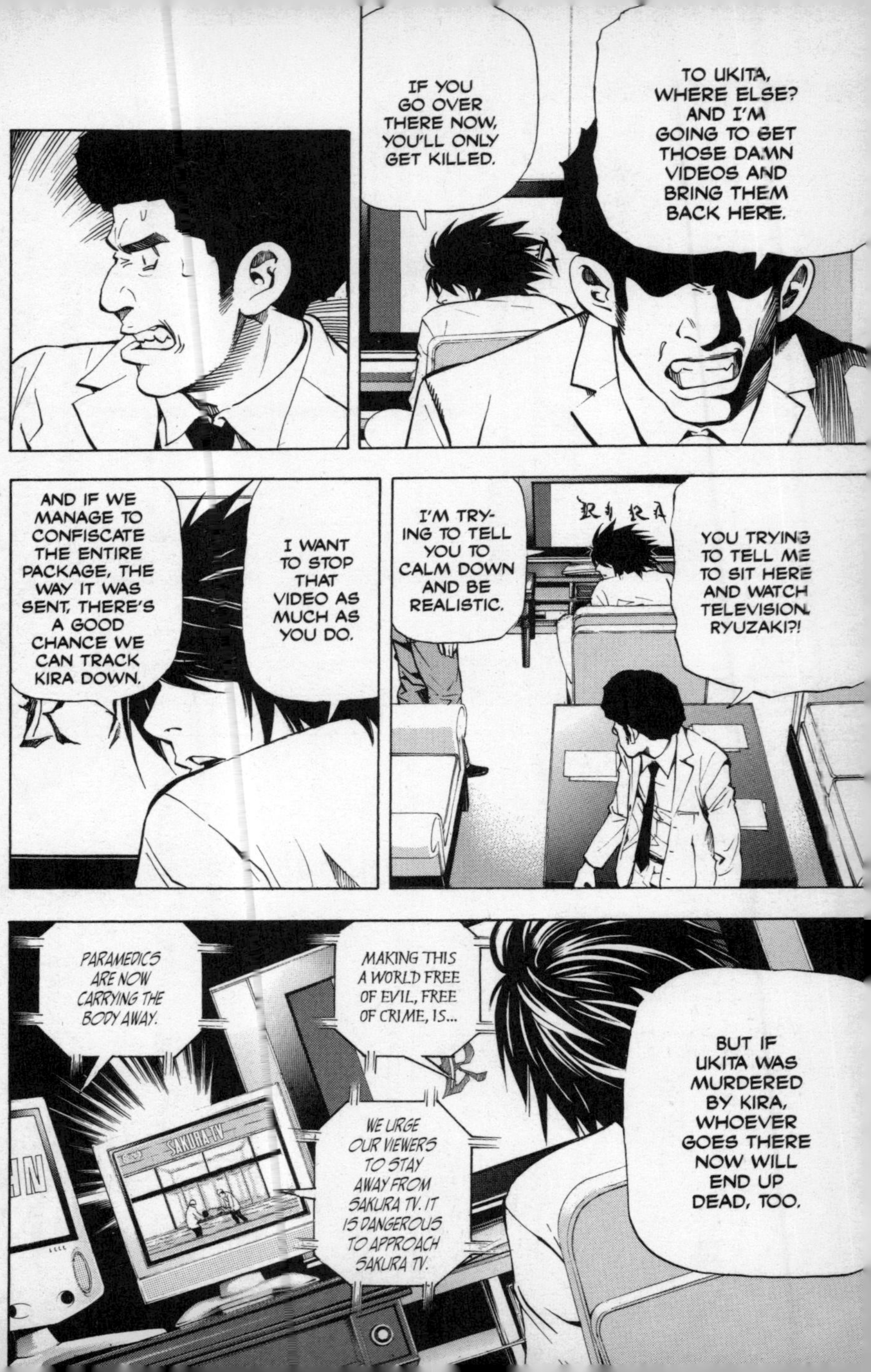

TO UKITA, WHERE ELSE? AND I'M GOING TO GET THOSE DAMN VIDEOS AND BRING THEM BACK HERE.
IF YOU GO OVER THERE NOW, YOU'LL ONLY GET KILLED.
YOU TRYING TO TELL ME TO SIT HERE AND WATCH TELEVISION, RYUZAKI?!
I'M TRYING TO TELL YOU TO CALM DOWN AND BE REALISTIC.
I WANT TO STOP THAT VIDEO AS MUCH AS YOU DO.
AND IF WE MANAGE TO CONFISCATE THE ENTIRE PACKAGE, THE WAY IT WAS SENT, THERE'S A GOOD CHANCE WE CAN TRACK KIRA DOWN.
BUT IF UKITA WAS MURDERED BY KIRA, WHOEVER GOES THERE NOW WILL END UP DEAD, TOO.
MAKING THIS A WORLD FREE OF EVIL, FREE OF CRIME, IS...
PARAMEDICS ARE NOW CARRYING THE BODY AWAY.
SAKURA-TV
WE URGE OUR VIEWERS TO STAY AWAY FROM SAKURA TV. IT IS DANGEROUS TO APPROACH SAKURA TV.

READ THIS WAY

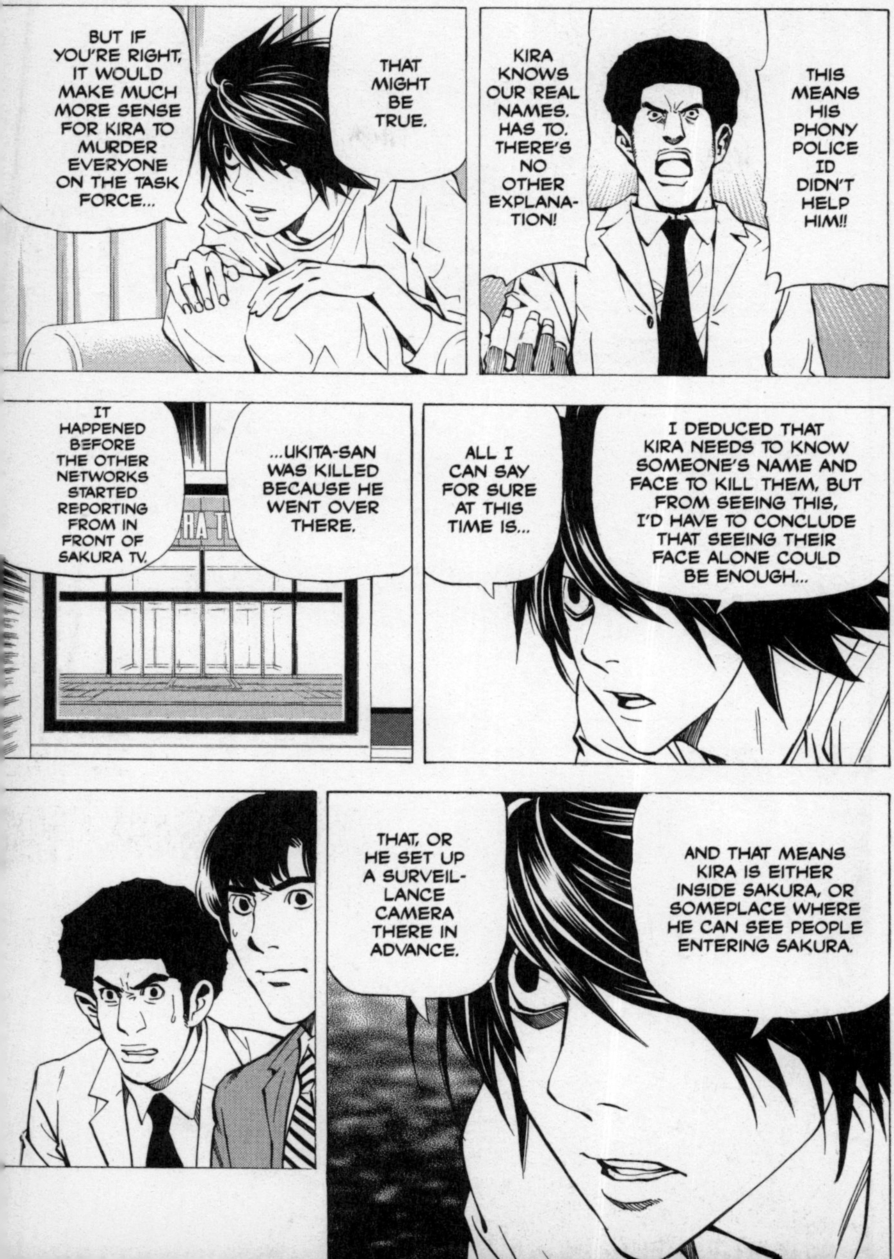

THIS MEANS HIS PHONY POLICE ID DIDN'T HELP HIM!!
KIRA KNOWS OUR REAL NAMES. HAS TO. THERE'S NO OTHER EXPLANATION!
THAT MIGHT BE TRUE.
BUT IF YOU'RE RIGHT, IT WOULD MAKE MUCH MORE SENSE FOR KIRA TO MURDER EVERYONE ON THE TASK FORCE...
I DEDUCED THAT KIRA NEEDS TO KNOW SOMEONE'S NAME AND FACE TO KILL THEM, BUT FROM SEEING THIS, I'D HAVE TO CONCLUDE THAT SEEING THEIR FACE ALONE COULD BE ENOUGH...
ALL I CAN SAY FOR SURE AT THIS TIME IS...
...UKITA-SAN WAS KILLED BECAUSE HE WENT OVER THERE.
IT HAPPENED BEFORE THE OTHER NETWORKS STARTED REPORTING FROM IN FRONT OF SAKURA TV.
AND THAT MEANS KIRA IS EITHER INSIDE SAKURA, OR SOMEPLACE WHERE HE CAN SEE PEOPLE ENTERING SAKURA.
THAT, OR HE SET UP A SURVEIL-LANCE CAMERA THERE IN ADVANCE.

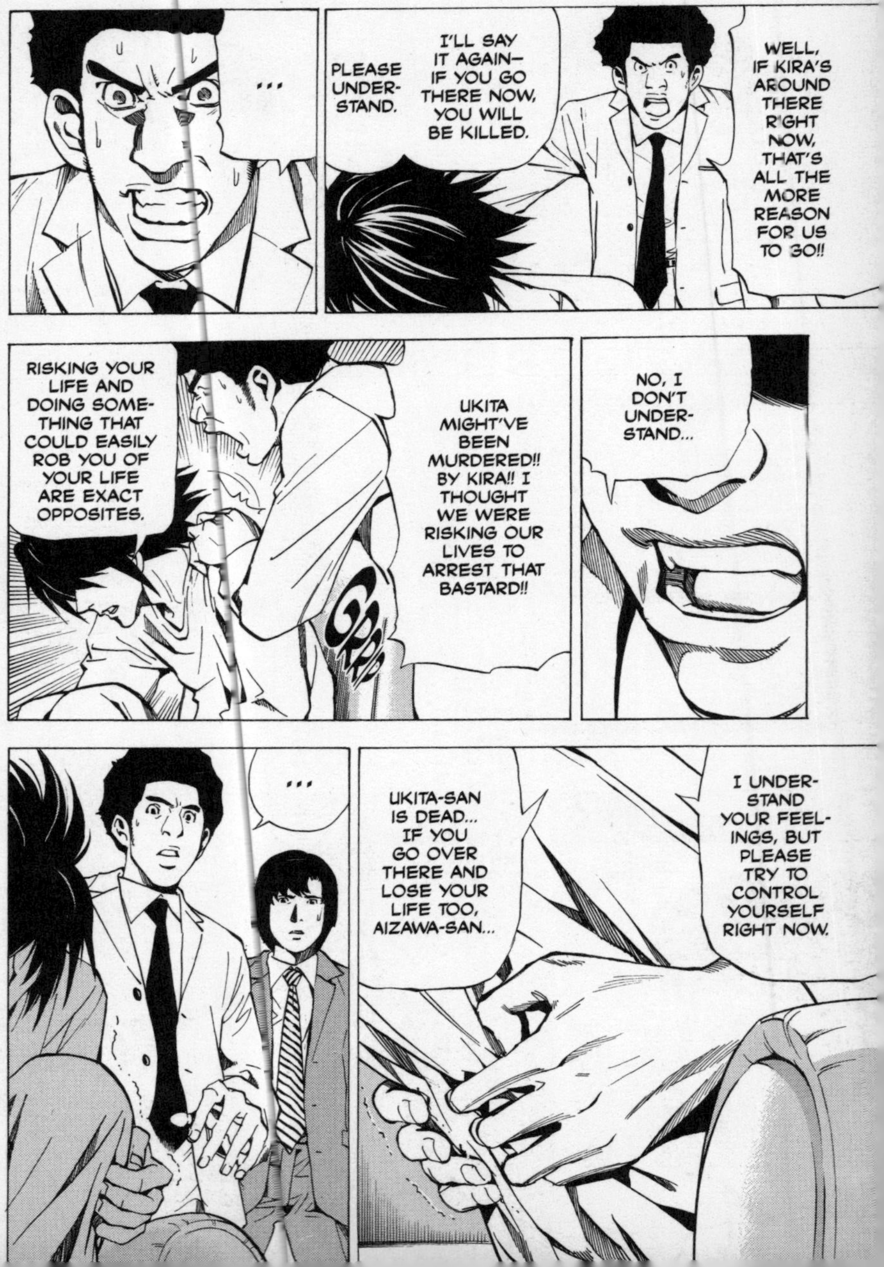
WELL, IF KIRA'S AROUND THERE RIGHT NOW, THAT'S ALL THE MORE REASON FOR US TO GO!!
I'LL SAY IT AGAIN— IF YOU GO THERE NOW, YOU WILL BE KILLED.
PLEASE UNDER-STAND.
...
NO, I DON'T UNDER-STAND...
UKITA MIGHT'VE BEEN MURDERED!! BY KIRA!! I THOUGHT WE WERE RISKING OUR LIVES TO ARREST THAT BASTARD!!
GRIP
RISKING YOUR LIFE AND DOING SOME-THING THAT COULD EASILY ROB YOU OF YOUR LIFE ARE EXACT OPPOSITES.
I UNDER-STAND YOUR FEEL-INGS, BUT PLEASE TRY TO CONTROL YOURSELF RIGHT NOW.
UKITA-SAN IS DEAD... IF YOU GO OVER THERE AND LOSE YOUR LIFE TOO, AIZAWA-SAN...
...

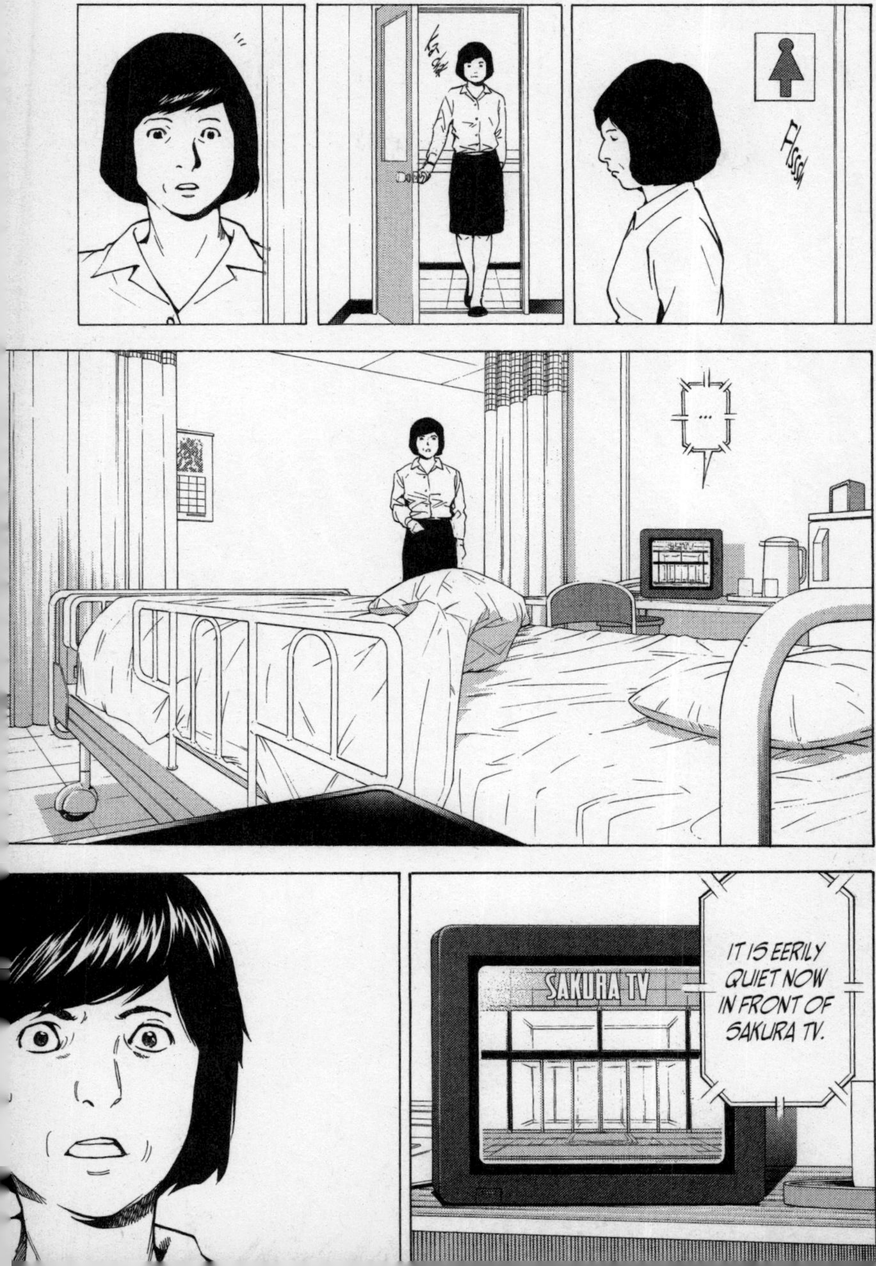
Flssh
...
SAKURA TV
IT IS EERILY QUIET NOW IN FRONT OF SAKURA TV.

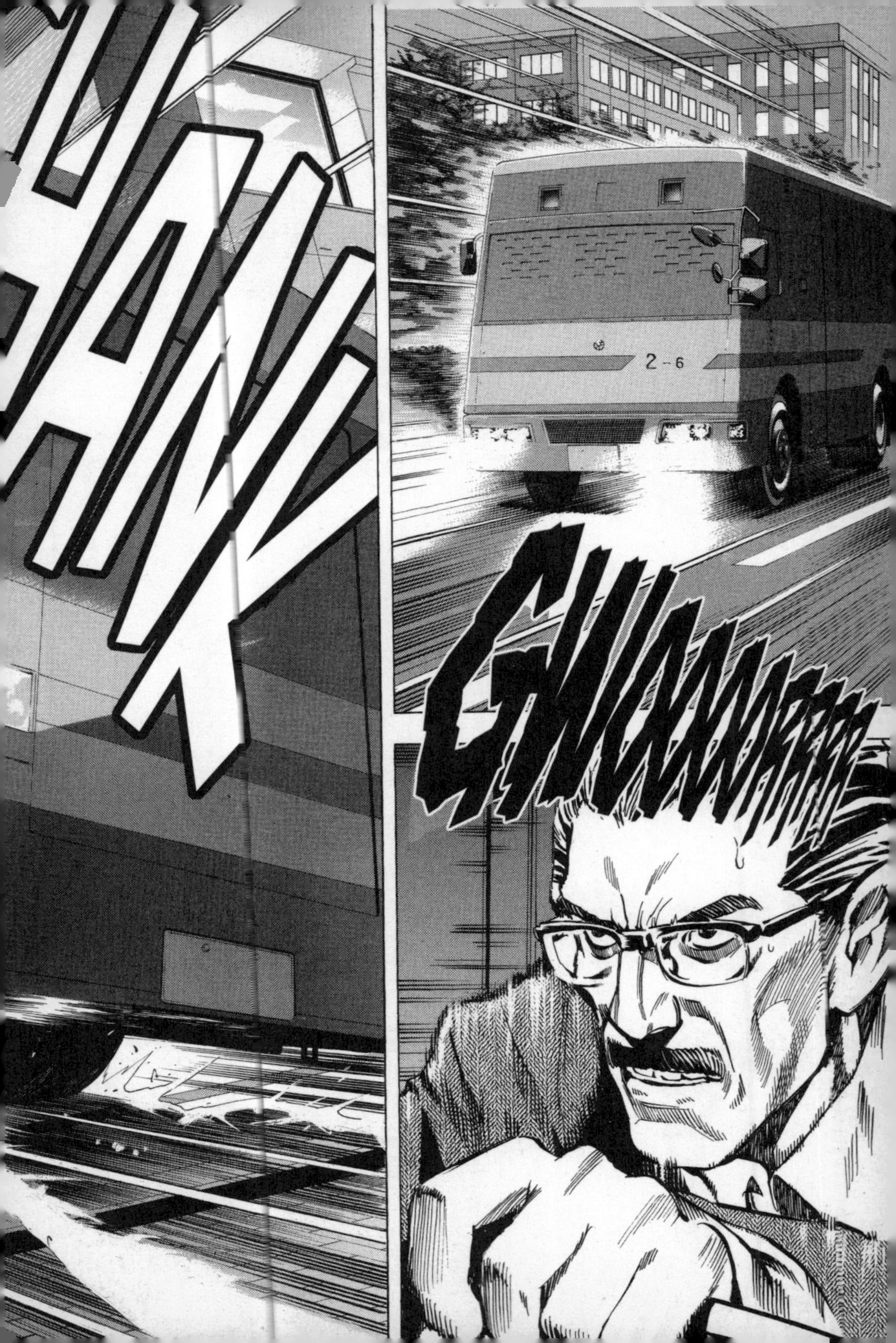
2-6
CHAK

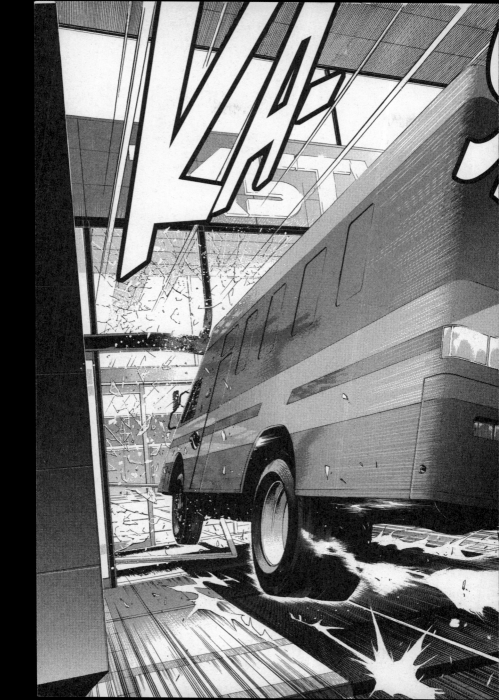

DEATH NOTE
How to use it
XIV

○ When the owner of the DEATH NOTE dies while the
  Note is being lent, its ownership will be transferred
  to the person who is holding it at that time.

デスノートを貸している時に所有者が死んだ場合、
所有権は、その時、手にしている者に移る。

○ If the DEATH NOTE is stolen and the owner is killed
  by the thief, its ownership will automatically be transferred
  to the thief.

デスノートを盗まれ、その盗んだ者に所有者が殺された場合、
所有権は自動的にその者に移る。

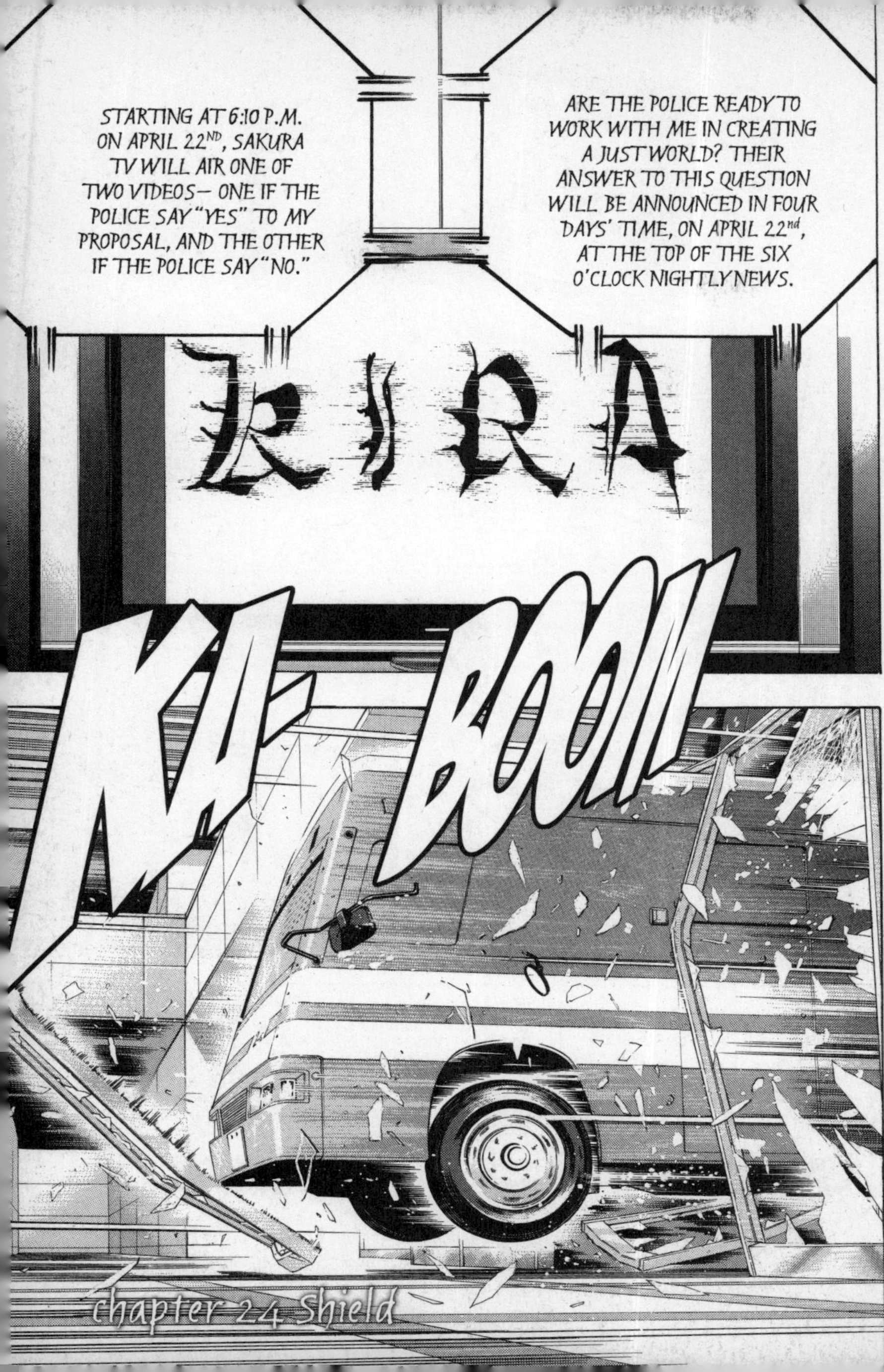
ARE THE POLICE READY TO WORK WITH ME IN CREATING A JUST WORLD? THEIR ANSWER TO THIS QUESTION WILL BE ANNOUNCED IN FOUR DAYS' TIME, ON APRIL 22nd, AT THE TOP OF THE SIX O'CLOCK NIGHTLY NEWS.
STARTING AT 6:10 P.M. ON APRIL 22ND, SAKURA TV WILL AIR ONE OF TWO VIDEOS— ONE IF THE POLICE SAY "YES" TO MY PROPOSAL, AND THE OTHER IF THE POLICE SAY "NO."
KIRA
KA-BOOM
chapter 24 Shield

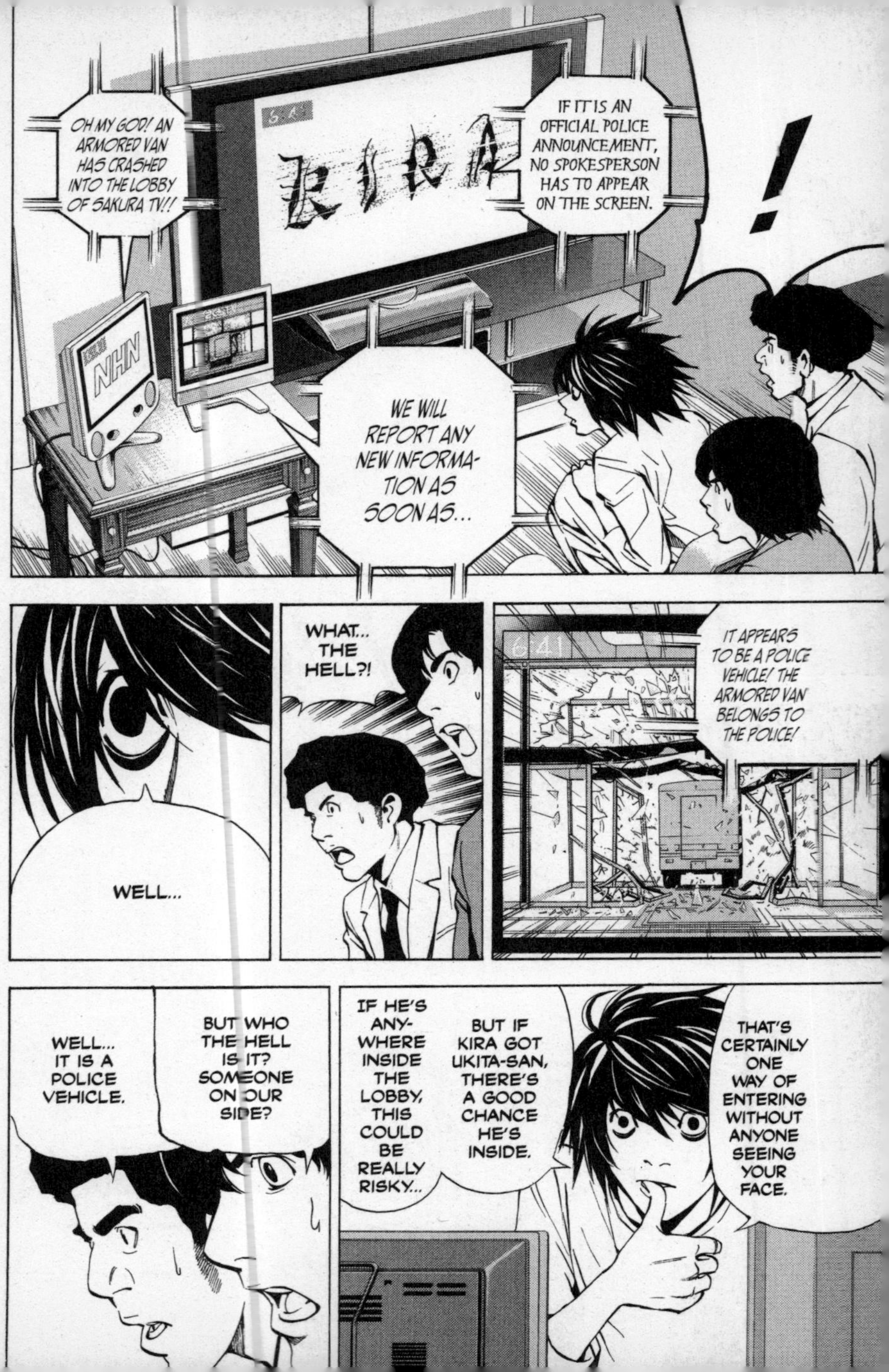
IF IT IS AN OFFICIAL POLICE ANNOUNCEMENT, NO SPOKESPERSON HAS TO APPEAR ON THE SCREEN.
!
KIRA
OH MY GOD! AN ARMORED VAN HAS CRASHED INTO THE LOBBY OF SAKURA TV!!
NHN
WE WILL REPORT ANY NEW INFORMATION AS SOON AS...
IT APPEARS TO BE A POLICE VEHICLE! THE ARMORED VAN BELONGS TO THE POLICE!
WHAT... THE HELL?!
WELL...
THAT'S CERTAINLY ONE WAY OF ENTERING WITHOUT ANYONE SEEING YOUR FACE.
BUT IF KIRA GOT UKITA-SAN, THERE'S A GOOD CHANCE HE'S INSIDE.
IF HE'S ANYWHERE INSIDE THE LOBBY, THIS COULD BE REALLY RISKY...
BUT WHO THE HELL IS IT? SOMEONE ON OUR SIDE?
WELL... IT IS A POLICE VEHICLE.

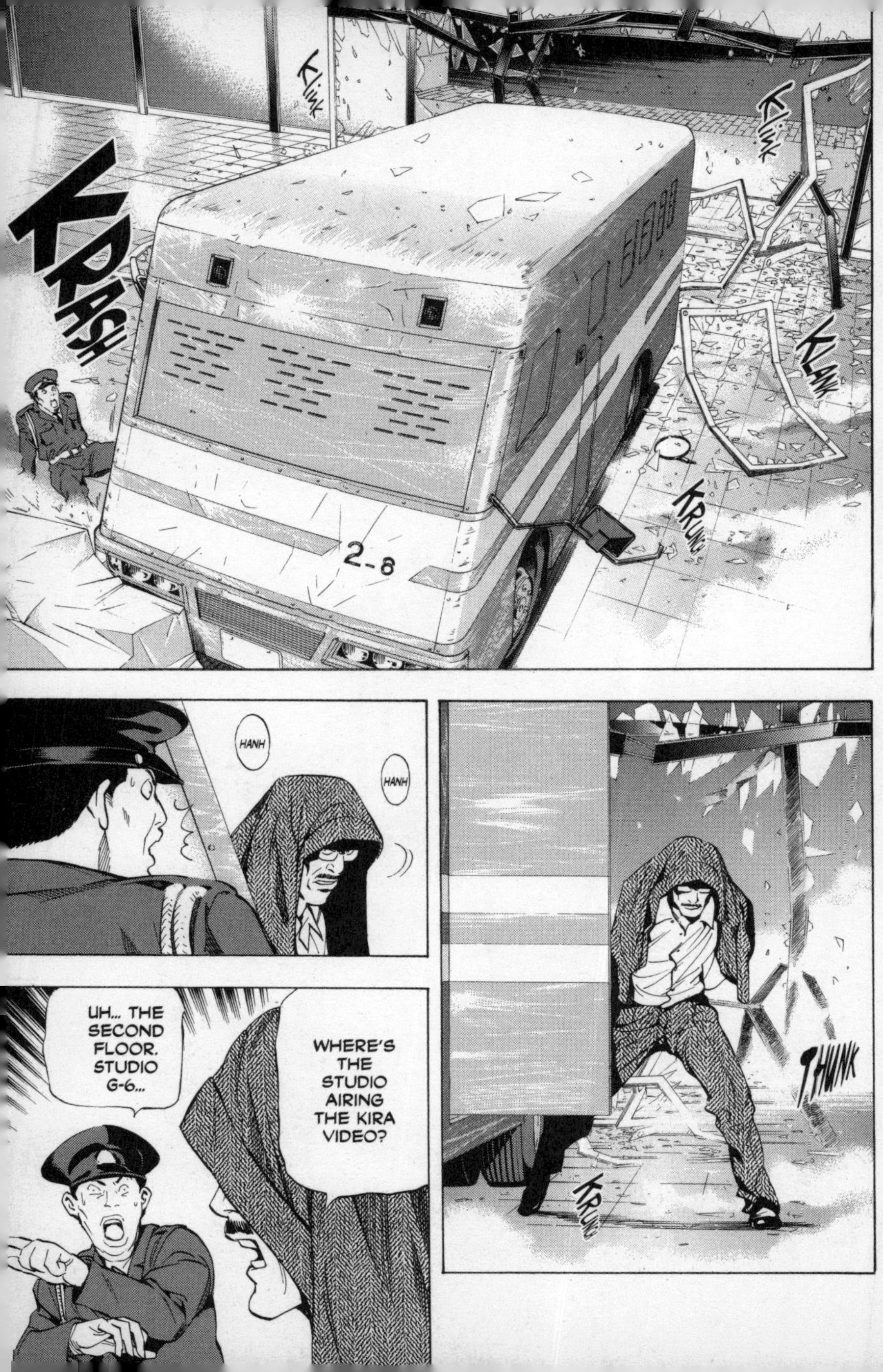
Klink
Klink
KLANK
KRUNCH
KRASH
THUNK
KRUNG
HANH
HANH
WHERE'S THE STUDIO AIRING THE KIRA VIDEO?
UH... THE SECOND FLOOR. STUDIO G-6...

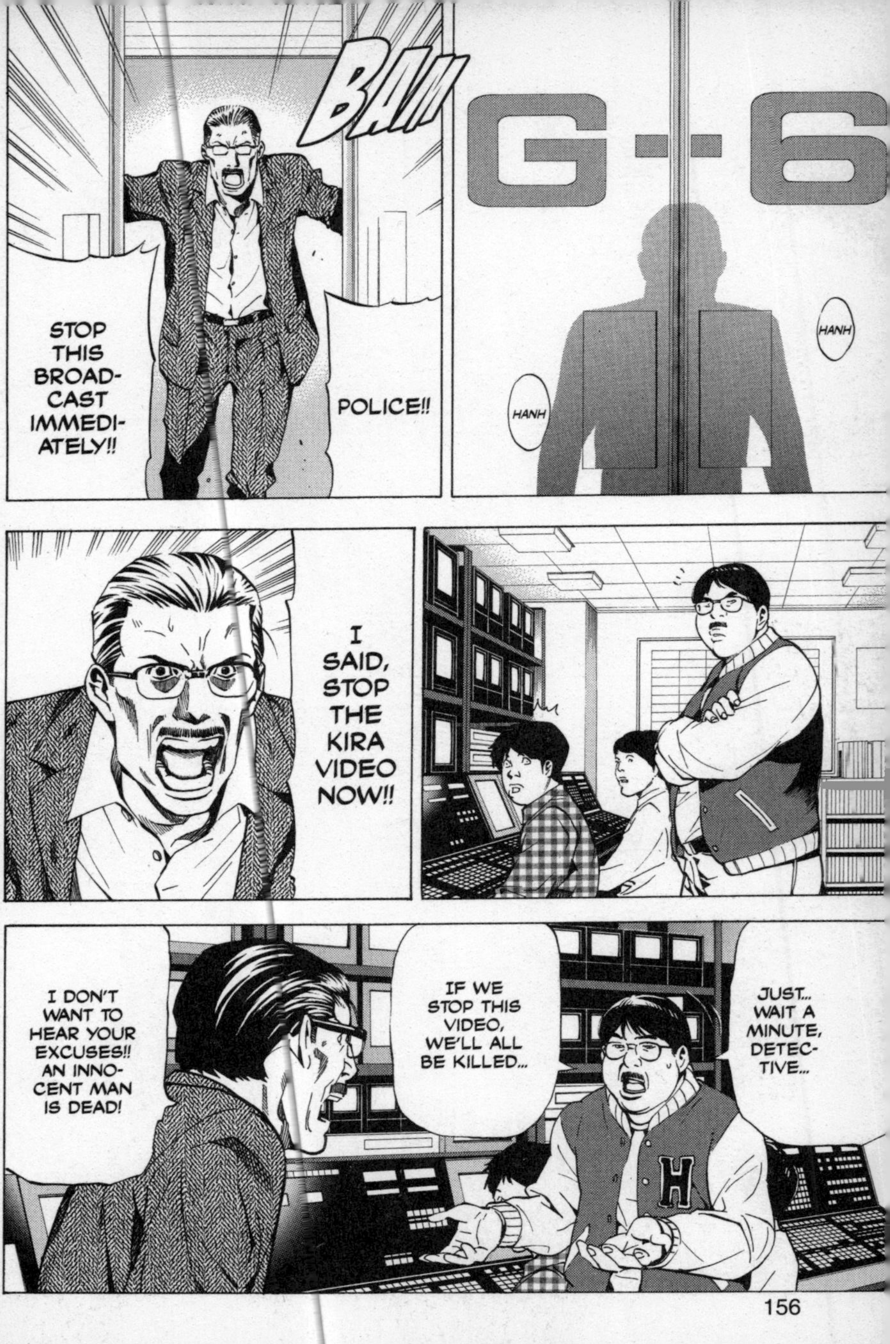
G-6
HANH
HANH
BAM
POLICE!!
STOP THIS BROADCAST IMMEDIATELY!!
I SAID, STOP THE KIRA VIDEO NOW!!
JUST... WAIT A MINUTE, DETECTIVE...
IF WE STOP THIS VIDEO, WE'LL ALL BE KILLED...
I DON'T WANT TO HEAR YOUR EXCUSES!! AN INNOCENT MAN IS DEAD!

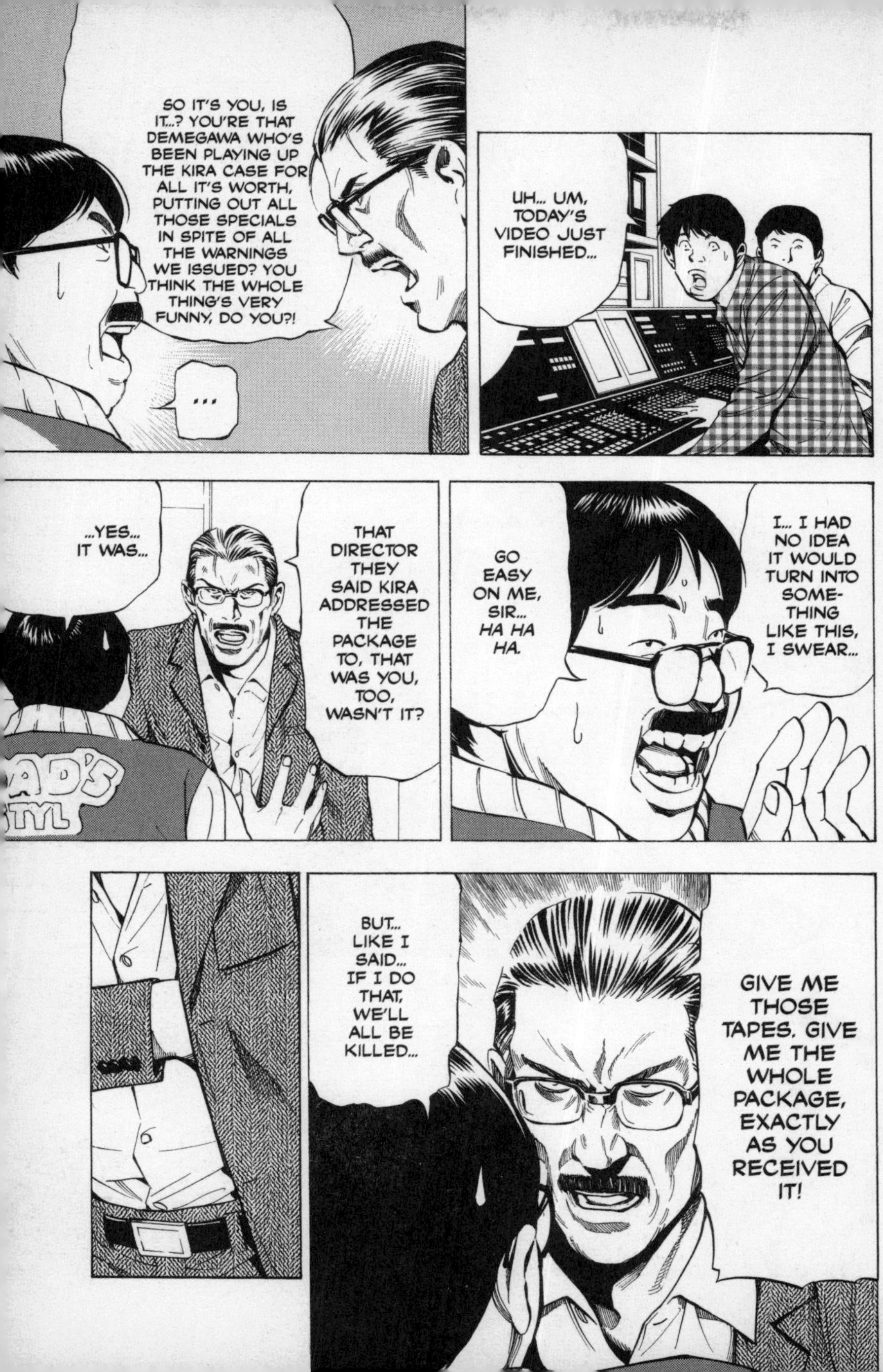
UH... UM, TODAY'S VIDEO JUST FINISHED...
SO IT'S YOU, IS IT...? YOU'RE THAT DEMEGAWA WHO'S BEEN PLAYING UP THE KIRA CASE FOR ALL IT'S WORTH, PUTTING OUT ALL THOSE SPECIALS IN SPITE OF ALL THE WARNINGS WE ISSUED? YOU THINK THE WHOLE THING'S VERY FUNNY, DO YOU?!
...
I... I HAD NO IDEA IT WOULD TURN INTO SOME-THING LIKE THIS, I SWEAR...
GO EASY ON ME, SIR... *HA HA HA.*
THAT DIRECTOR THEY SAID KIRA ADDRESSED THE PACKAGE TO, THAT WAS YOU, TOO, WASN'T IT?
...YES... IT WAS...
GIVE ME THOSE TAPES. GIVE ME THE WHOLE PACKAGE, EXACTLY AS YOU RECEIVED IT!
BUT... LIKE I SAID... IF I DO THAT, WE'LL ALL BE KILLED...

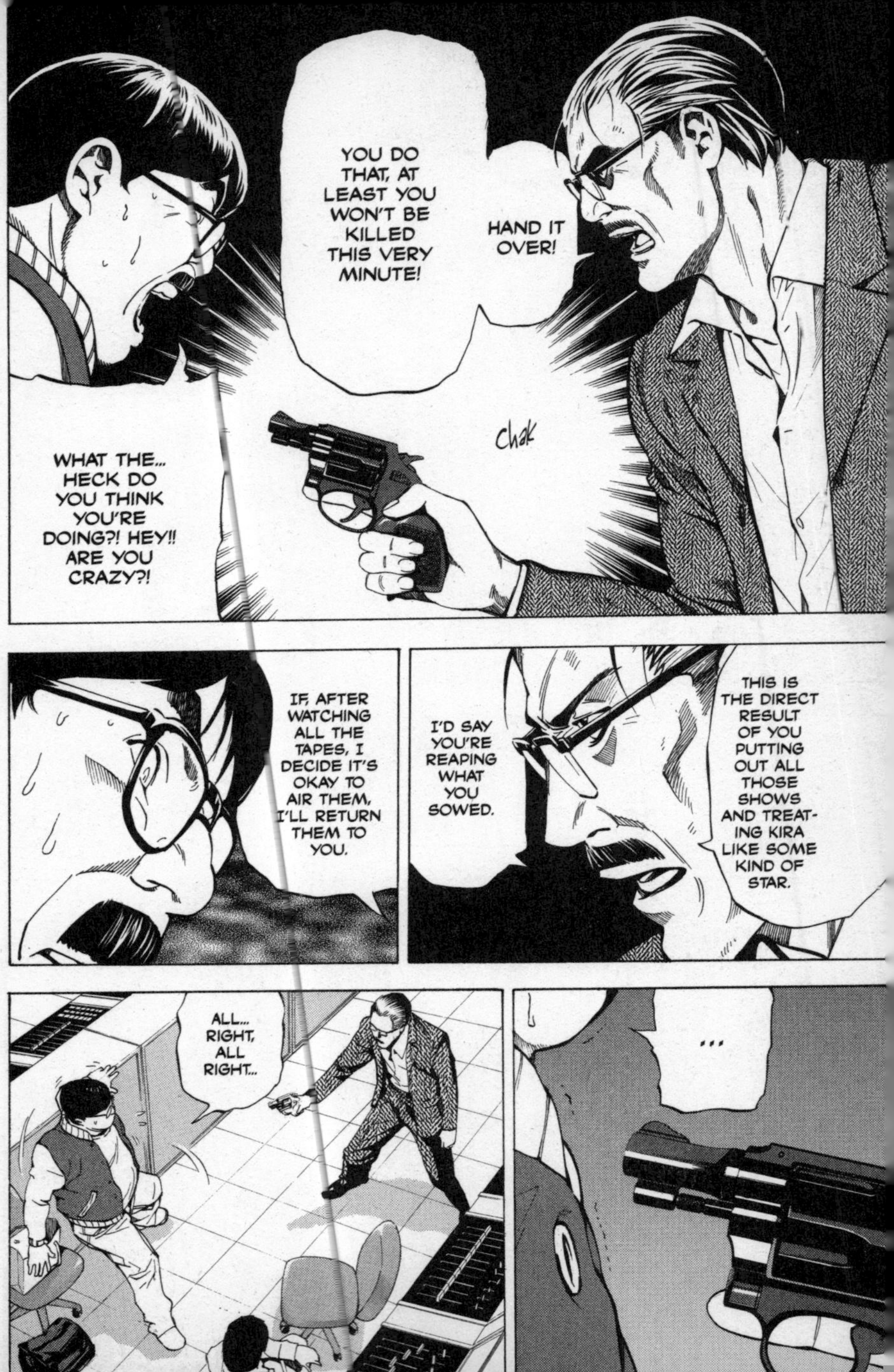
HAND IT OVER!
YOU DO THAT, AT LEAST YOU WON'T BE KILLED THIS VERY MINUTE!
Chak
WHAT THE... HECK DO YOU THINK YOU'RE DOING?! HEY!! ARE YOU CRAZY?!
THIS IS THE DIRECT RESULT OF YOU PUTTING OUT ALL THOSE SHOWS AND TREATING KIRA LIKE SOME KIND OF STAR.
I'D SAY YOU'RE REAPING WHAT YOU SOWED.
IF, AFTER WATCHING ALL THE TAPES, I DECIDE IT'S OKAY TO AIR THEM, I'LL RETURN THEM TO YOU.
...
ALL... RIGHT, ALL RIGHT...

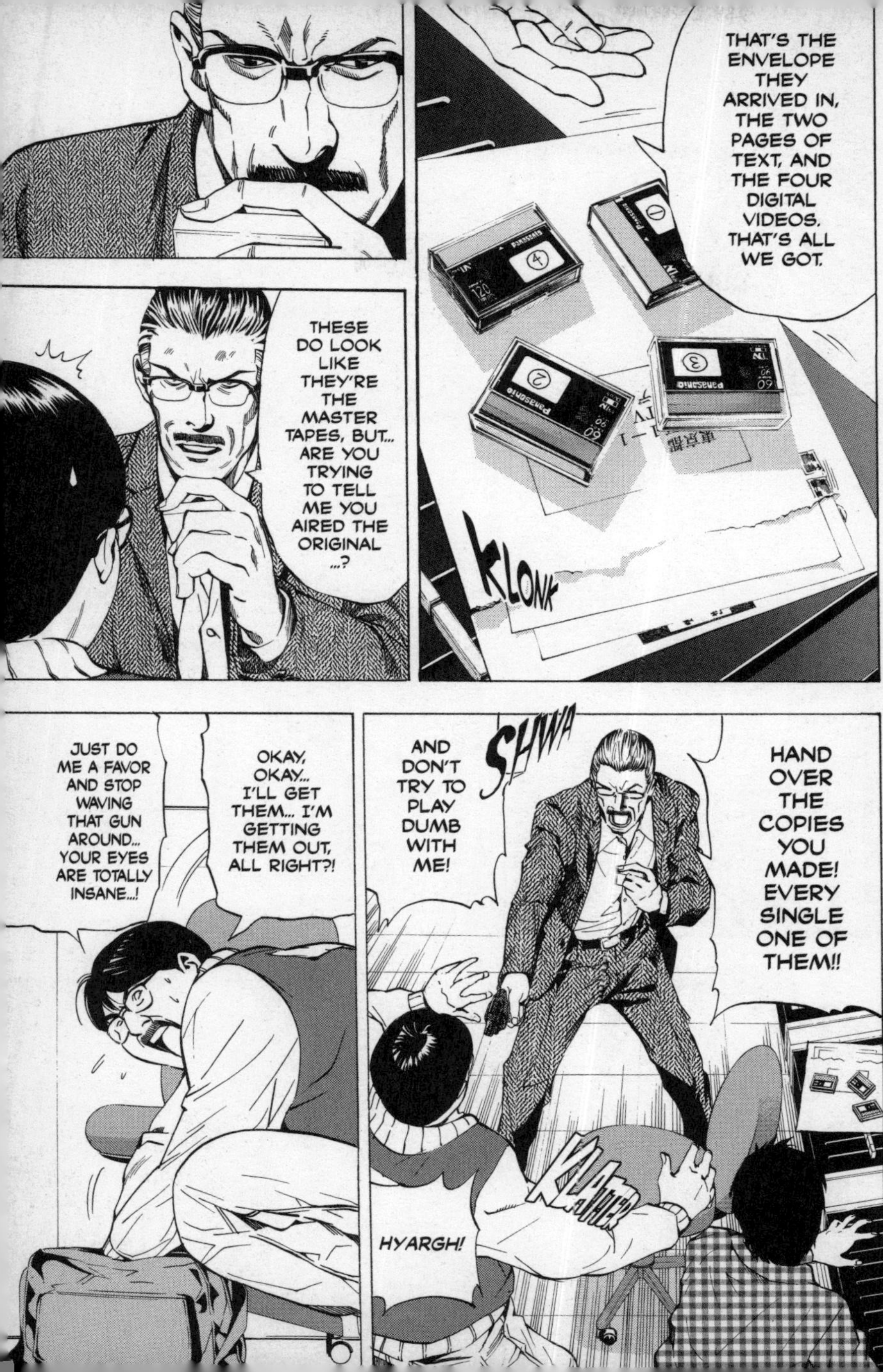
THAT'S THE ENVELOPE THEY ARRIVED IN, THE TWO PAGES OF TEXT, AND THE FOUR DIGITAL VIDEOS. THAT'S ALL WE GOT.
KLONK
THESE DO LOOK LIKE THEY'RE THE MASTER TAPES, BUT... ARE YOU TRYING TO TELL ME YOU AIRED THE ORIGINAL ...?
HAND OVER THE COPIES YOU MADE! EVERY SINGLE ONE OF THEM!!
SHWA
AND DON'T TRY TO PLAY DUMB WITH ME!
HYARGH!
OKAY, OKAY... I'LL GET THEM... I'M GETTING THEM OUT, ALL RIGHT?!
JUST DO ME A FAVOR AND STOP WAVING THAT GUN AROUND... YOUR EYES ARE TOTALLY INSANE...!

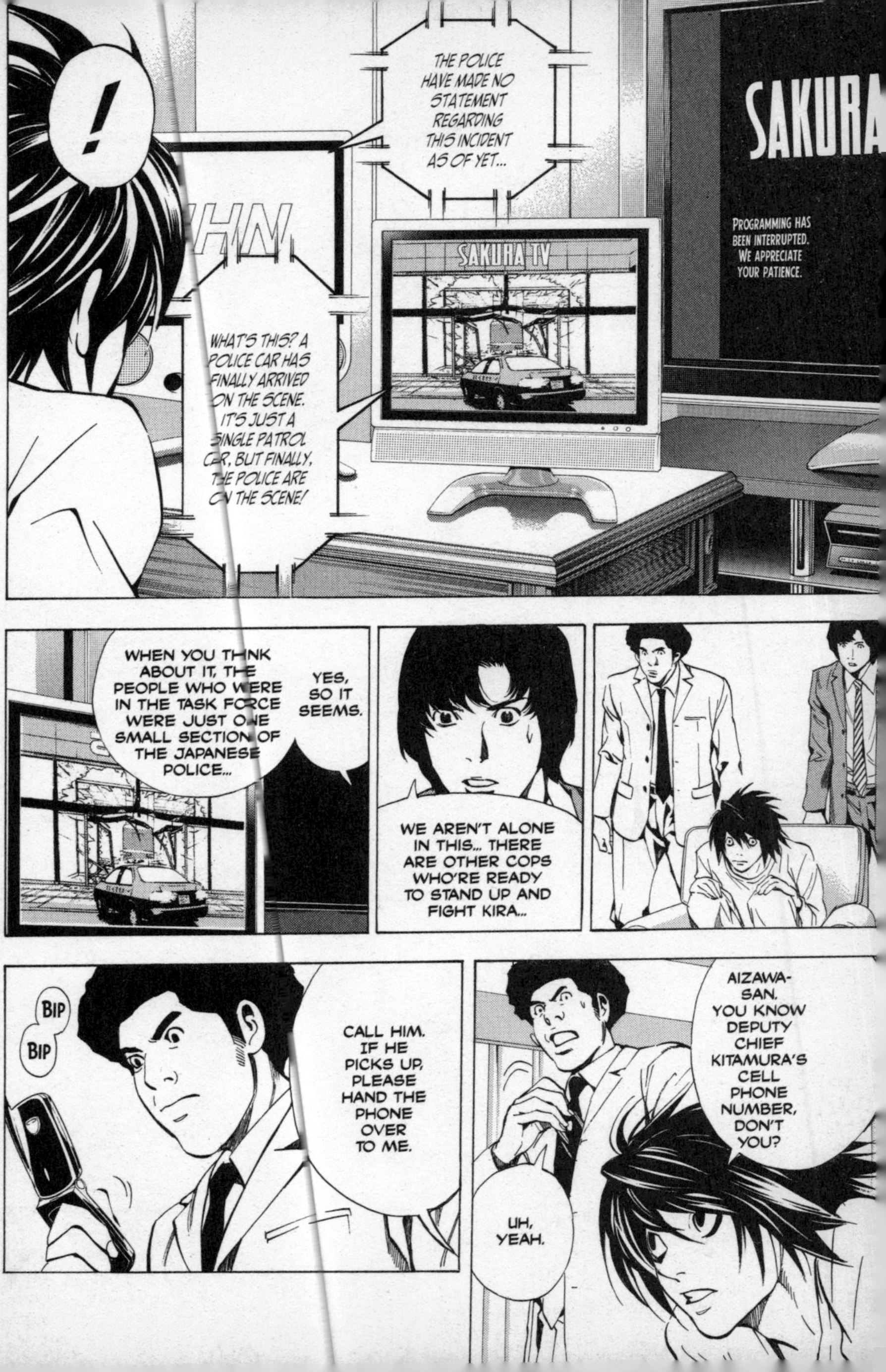
SAKURA
PROGRAMMING HAS BEEN INTERRUPTED. WE APPRECIATE YOUR PATIENCE.
THE POLICE HAVE MADE NO STATEMENT REGARDING THIS INCIDENT AS OF YET...
SAKURA TV
!
WHAT'S THIS? A POLICE CAR HAS FINALLY ARRIVED ON THE SCENE. IT'S JUST A SINGLE PATROL CAR, BUT FINALLY, THE POLICE ARE ON THE SCENE!
WE AREN'T ALONE IN THIS... THERE ARE OTHER COPS WHO'RE READY TO STAND UP AND FIGHT KIRA...
WHEN YOU THINK ABOUT IT, THE PEOPLE WHO WERE IN THE TASK FORCE WERE JUST ONE SMALL SECTION OF THE JAPANESE POLICE...
YES, SO IT SEEMS.
AIZAWA-SAN. YOU KNOW DEPUTY CHIEF KITAMURA'S CELL PHONE NUMBER, DON'T YOU?
UH, YEAH.
CALL HIM. IF HE PICKS UP, PLEASE HAND THE PHONE OVER TO ME.
BIP
BIP

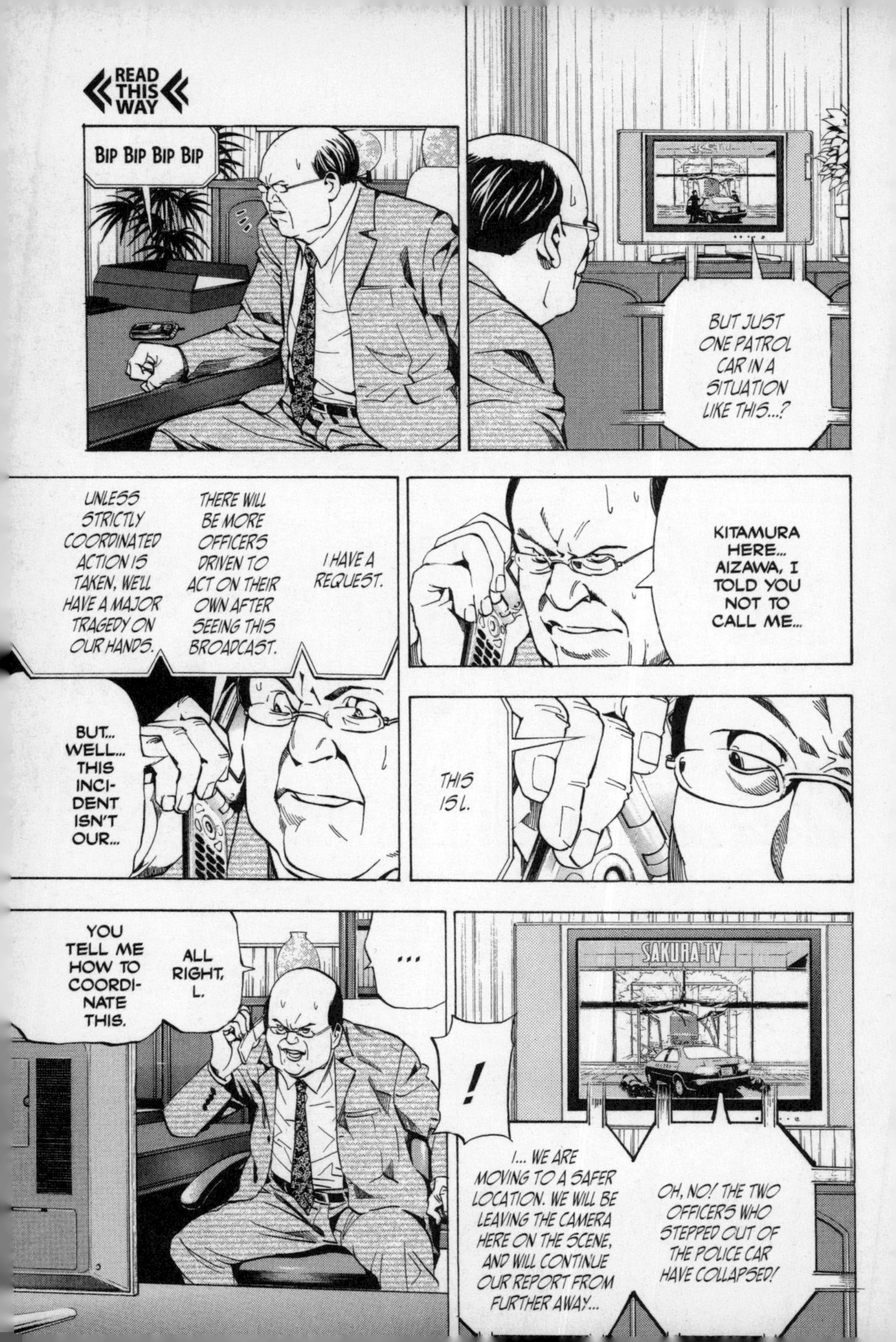
READ THIS WAY
BUT JUST ONE PATROL CAR IN A SITUATION LIKE THIS...?
BIP BIP BIP BIP
KITAMURA HERE... AIZAWA, I TOLD YOU NOT TO CALL ME...
I HAVE A REQUEST.
THERE WILL BE MORE OFFICERS DRIVEN TO ACT ON THEIR OWN AFTER SEEING THIS BROADCAST.
UNLESS STRICTLY COORDINATED ACTION IS TAKEN, WE'LL HAVE A MAJOR TRAGEDY ON OUR HANDS.
THIS IS L.
BUT... WELL... THIS INCI-DENT ISN'T OUR...
SAKURA TV
OH, NO! THE TWO OFFICERS WHO STEPPED OUT OF THE POLICE CAR HAVE COLLAPSED!
I... WE ARE MOVING TO A SAFER LOCATION. WE WILL BE LEAVING THE CAMERA HERE ON THE SCENE, AND WILL CONTINUE OUR REPORT FROM FURTHER AWAY...
!
...
ALL RIGHT, L.
YOU TELL ME HOW TO COORDI-NATE THIS.

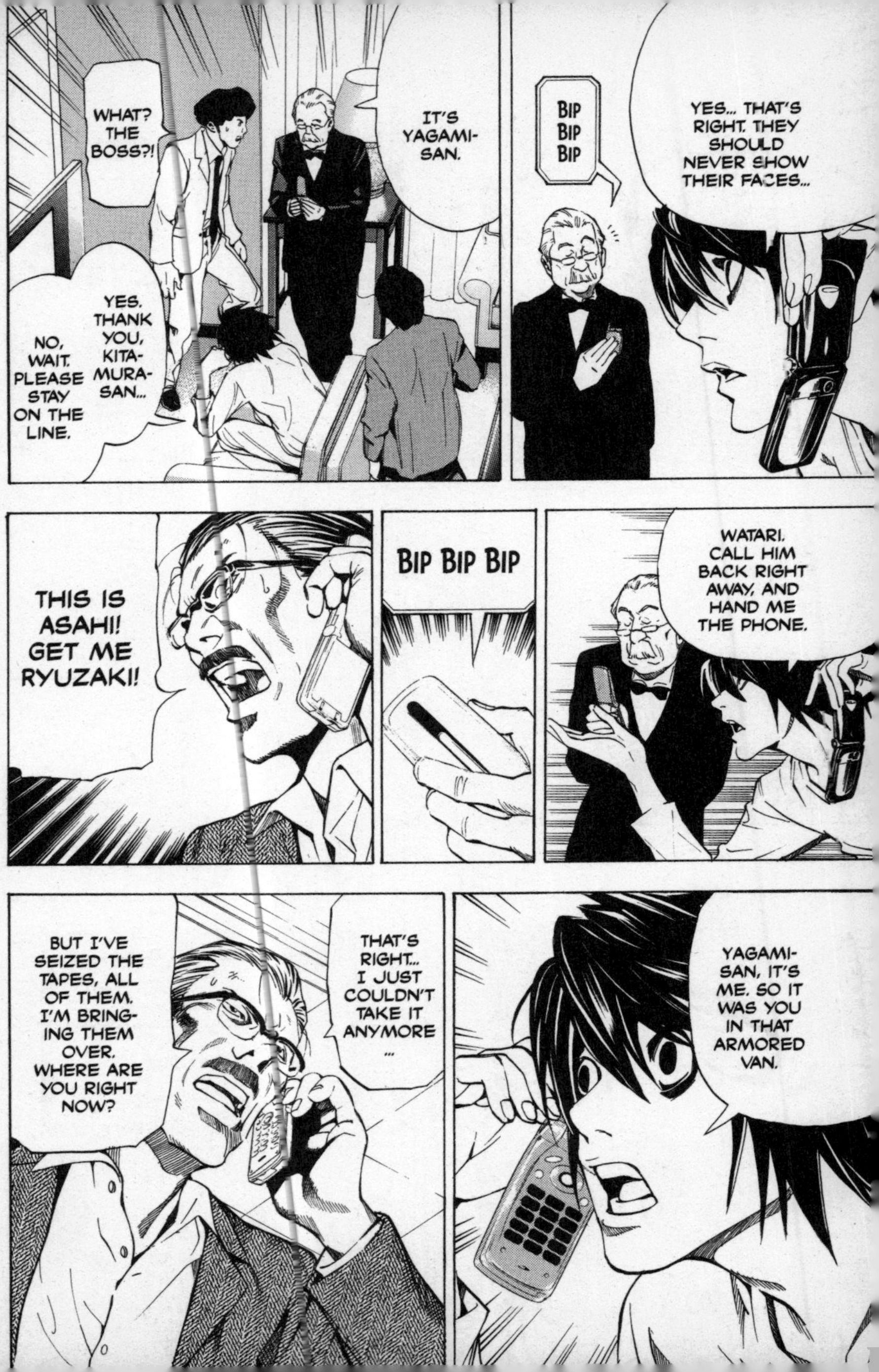
YES... THAT'S RIGHT. THEY SHOULD NEVER SHOW THEIR FACES...
BIP BIP BIP
IT'S YAGAMI-SAN.
WHAT? THE BOSS?!
YES. THANK YOU, KITA-MURA-SAN...
NO, WAIT. PLEASE STAY ON THE LINE.
WATARI. CALL HIM BACK RIGHT AWAY, AND HAND ME THE PHONE.
BIP BIP BIP
THIS IS ASAHI! GET ME RYUZAKI!
YAGAMI-SAN, IT'S ME. SO IT WAS YOU IN THAT ARMORED VAN.
THAT'S RIGHT... I JUST COULDN'T TAKE IT ANYMORE ...
BUT I'VE SEIZED THE TAPES, ALL OF THEM. I'M BRING-ING THEM OVER. WHERE ARE YOU RIGHT NOW?

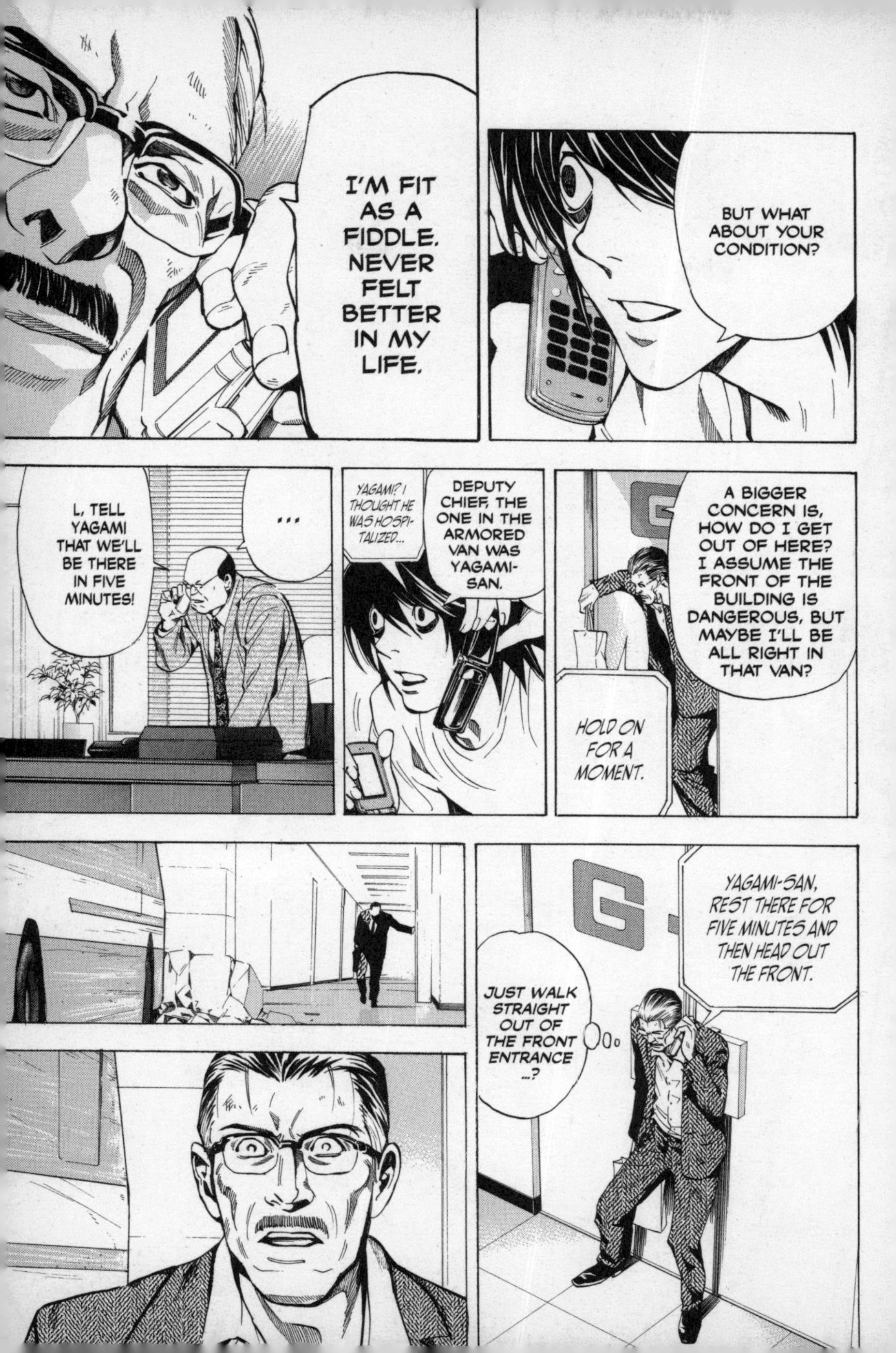
BUT WHAT ABOUT YOUR CONDITION?
I'M FIT AS A FIDDLE. NEVER FELT BETTER IN MY LIFE.
A BIGGER CONCERN IS, HOW DO I GET OUT OF HERE? I ASSUME THE FRONT OF THE BUILDING IS DANGEROUS, BUT MAYBE I'LL BE ALL RIGHT IN THAT VAN?
HOLD ON FOR A MOMENT.
DEPUTY CHIEF, THE ONE IN THE ARMORED VAN WAS YAGAMI-SAN.
YAGAMI? I THOUGHT HE WAS HOSPITALIZED...
...
L, TELL YAGAMI THAT WE'LL BE THERE IN FIVE MINUTES!
YAGAMI-SAN, REST THERE FOR FIVE MINUTES AND THEN HEAD OUT THE FRONT.
JUST WALK STRAIGHT OUT OF THE FRONT ENTRANCE ...?

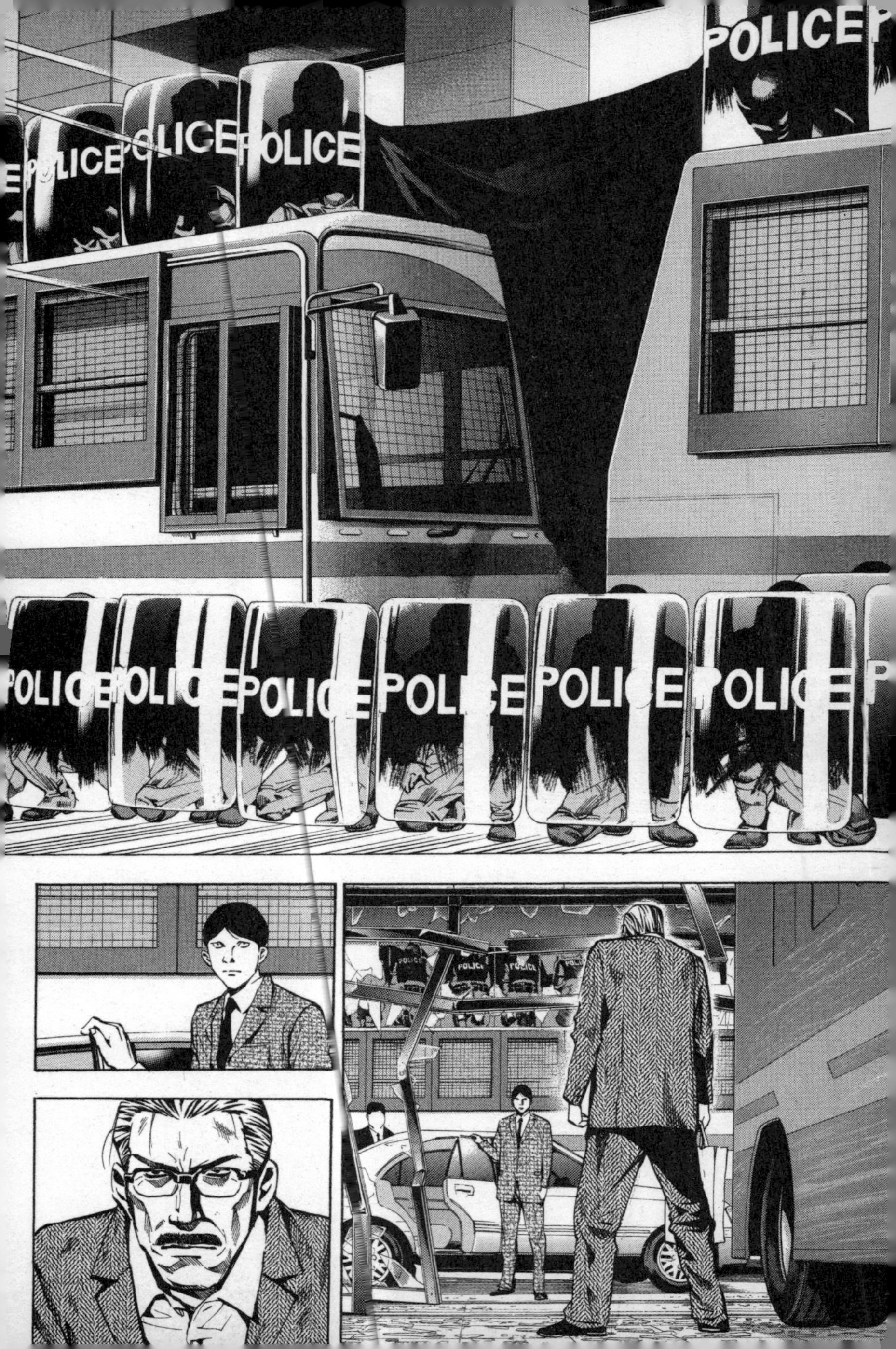
POLICE
POLICE
POLICE
POLICE
POLICE
POLICE
POLICE
POLICE

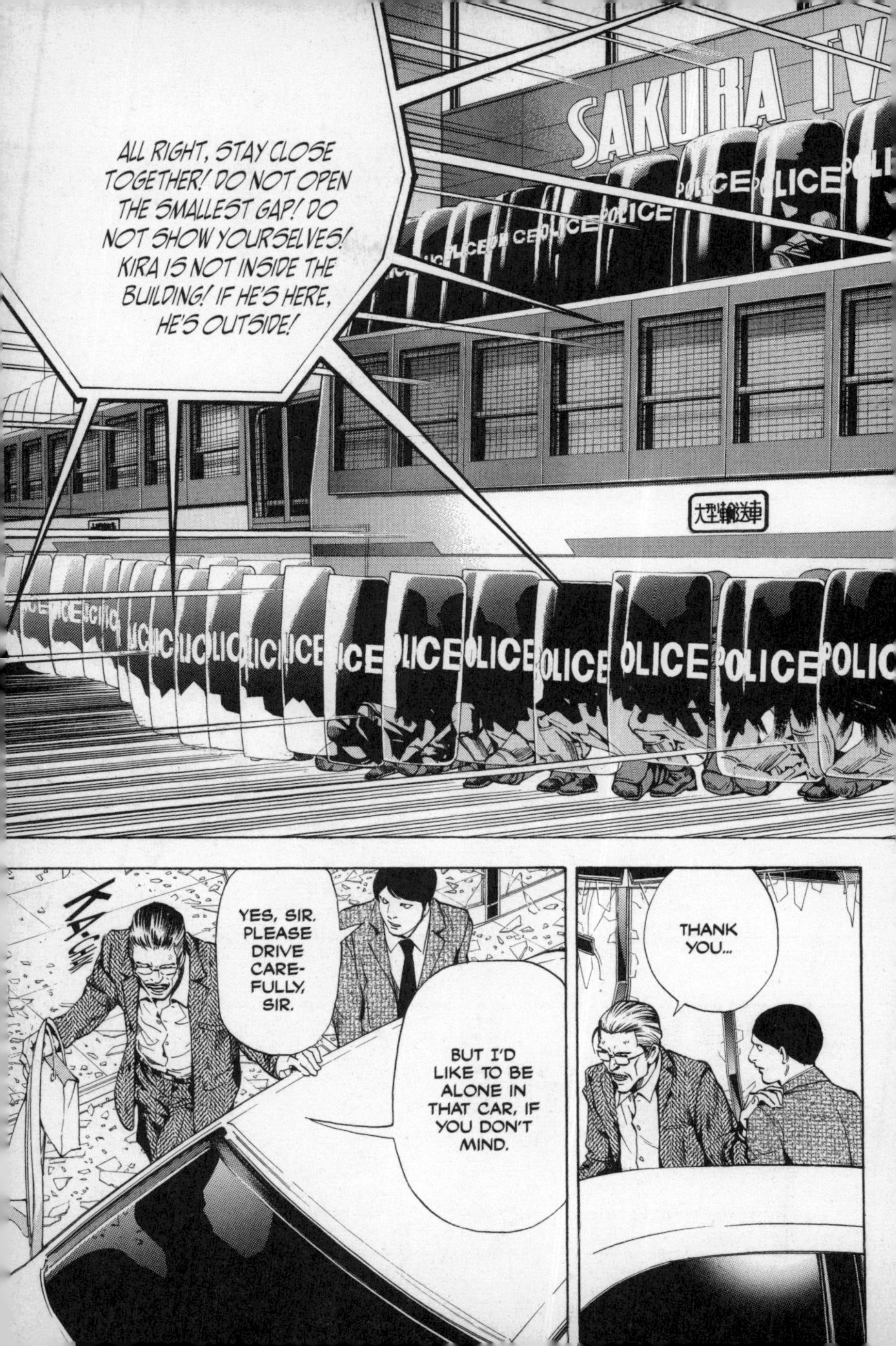
ALL RIGHT, STAY CLOSE TOGETHER! DO NOT OPEN THE SMALLEST GAP! DO NOT SHOW YOURSELVES! KIRA IS NOT INSIDE THE BUILDING! IF HE'S HERE, HE'S OUTSIDE!
SAKURA TV
POLICE
大型輸送車
THANK YOU...
BUT I'D LIKE TO BE ALONE IN THAT CAR, IF YOU DON'T MIND.
YES, SIR. PLEASE DRIVE CAREFULLY, SIR.
KA-CHH

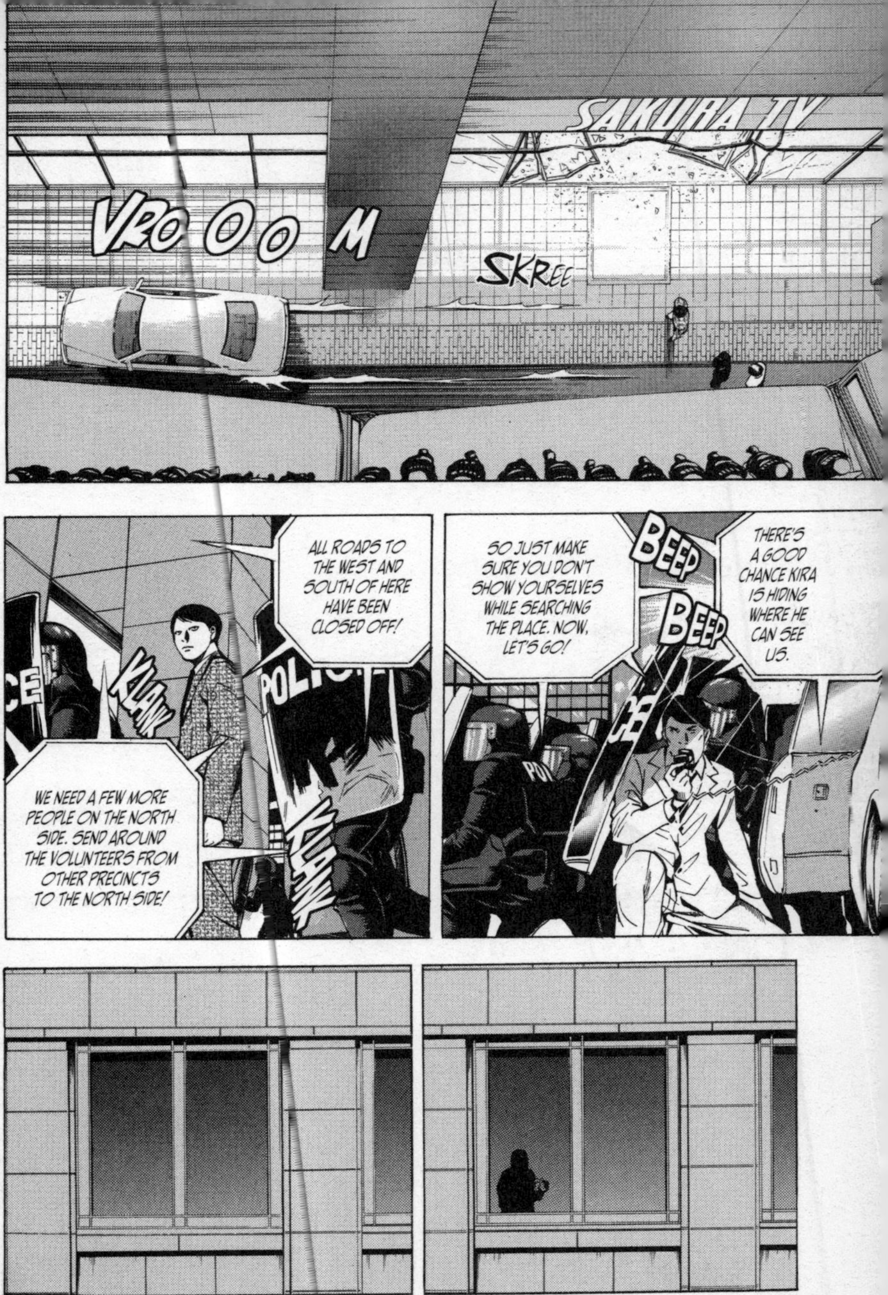
SAKURA TV
VROOOOM
SKREE
THERE'S A GOOD CHANCE KIRA IS HIDING WHERE HE CAN SEE US.
BEEP
BEEP
SO JUST MAKE SURE YOU DON'T SHOW YOURSELVES WHILE SEARCHING THE PLACE. NOW, LET'S GO!
ALL ROADS TO THE WEST AND SOUTH OF HERE HAVE BEEN CLOSED OFF!
KLANK
WE NEED A FEW MORE PEOPLE ON THE NORTH SIDE. SEND AROUND THE VOLUNTEERS FROM OTHER PRECINCTS TO THE NORTH SIDE!
KLANK

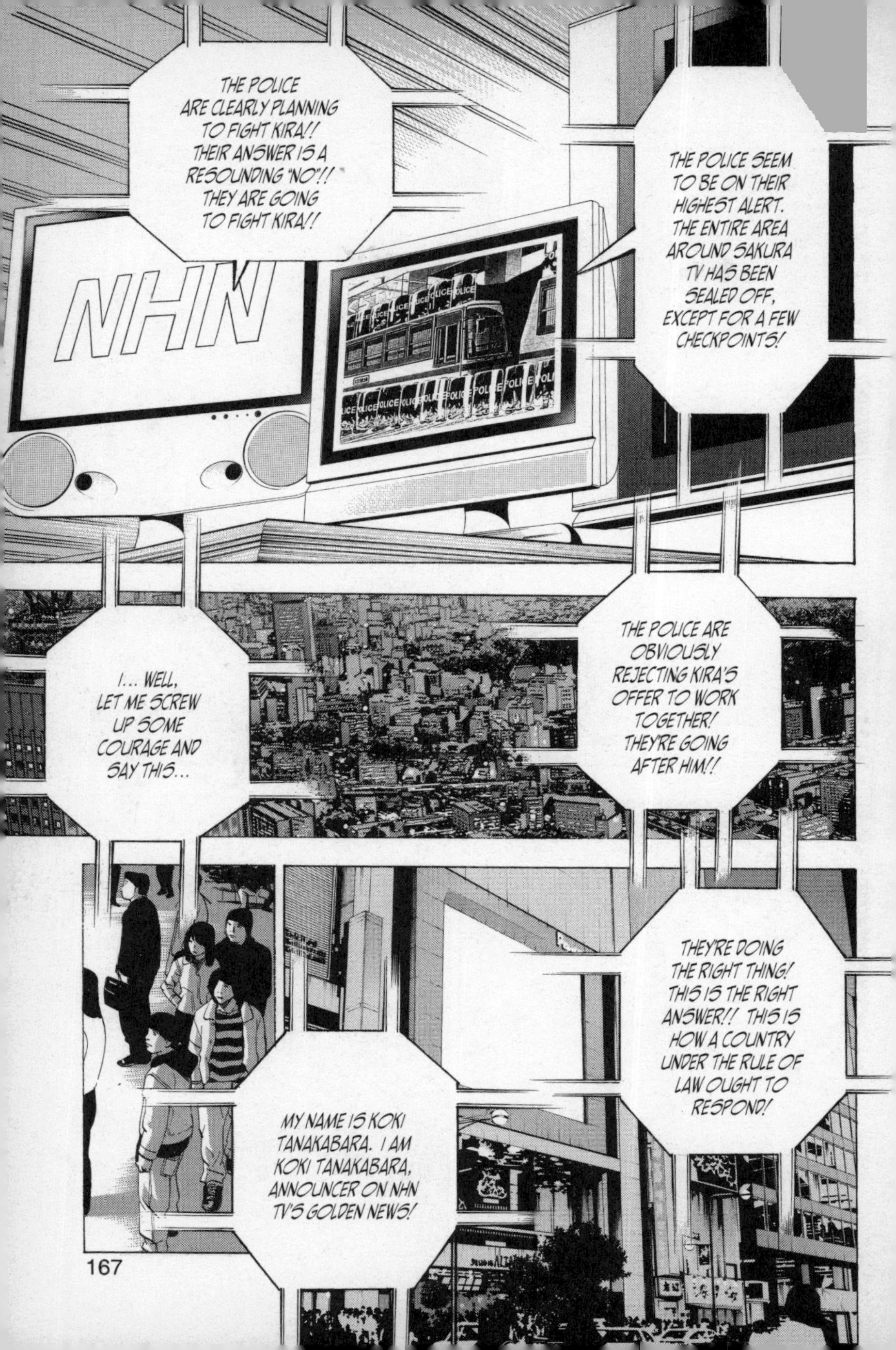
THE POLICE SEEM TO BE ON THEIR HIGHEST ALERT. THE ENTIRE AREA AROUND SAKURA TV HAS BEEN SEALED OFF, EXCEPT FOR A FEW CHECKPOINTS!
THE POLICE ARE CLEARLY PLANNING TO FIGHT KIRA!! THEIR ANSWER IS A RESOUNDING "NO"!! THEY ARE GOING TO FIGHT KIRA!!
NHN
POLICE
THE POLICE ARE OBVIOUSLY REJECTING KIRA'S OFFER TO WORK TOGETHER! THEY'RE GOING AFTER HIM!!
I... WELL, LET ME SCREW UP SOME COURAGE AND SAY THIS...
THEY'RE DOING THE RIGHT THING! THIS IS THE RIGHT ANSWER!! THIS IS HOW A COUNTRY UNDER THE RULE OF LAW OUGHT TO RESPOND!
MY NAME IS KOKI TANAKABARA. I AM KOKI TANAKABARA, ANNOUNCER ON NHN TV'S GOLDEN NEWS!

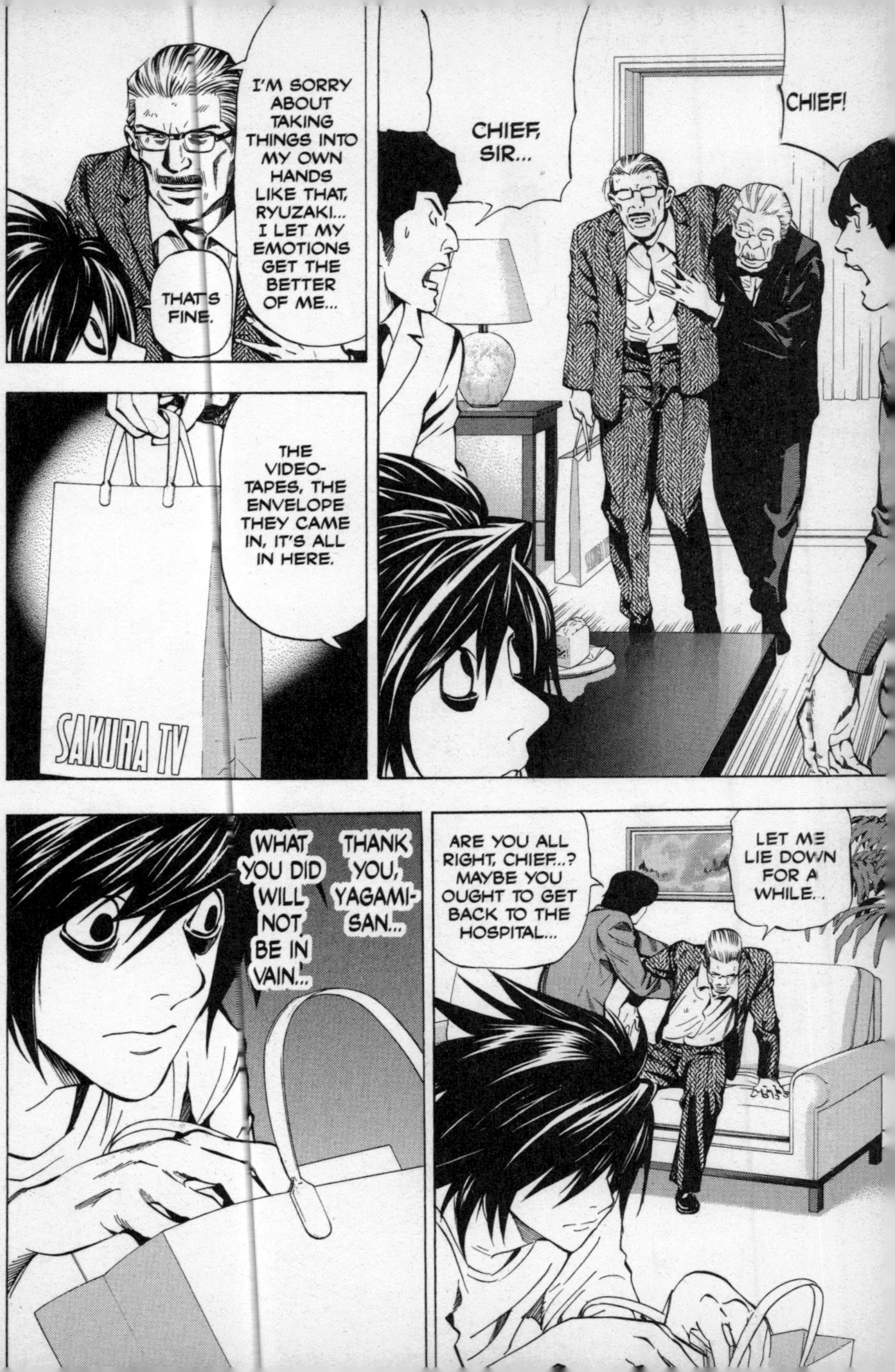
CHIEF!
CHIEF, SIR...
I'M SORRY ABOUT TAKING THINGS INTO MY OWN HANDS LIKE THAT, RYUZAKI... I LET MY EMOTIONS GET THE BETTER OF ME...
THAT'S FINE.
THE VIDEO-TAPES, THE ENVELOPE THEY CAME IN, IT'S ALL IN HERE.
SAKURA TV
LET ME LIE DOWN FOR A WHILE...
ARE YOU ALL RIGHT, CHIEF..? MAYBE YOU OUGHT TO GET BACK TO THE HOSPITAL...
THANK YOU, YAGAMI-SAN...
WHAT YOU DID WILL NOT BE IN VAIN...

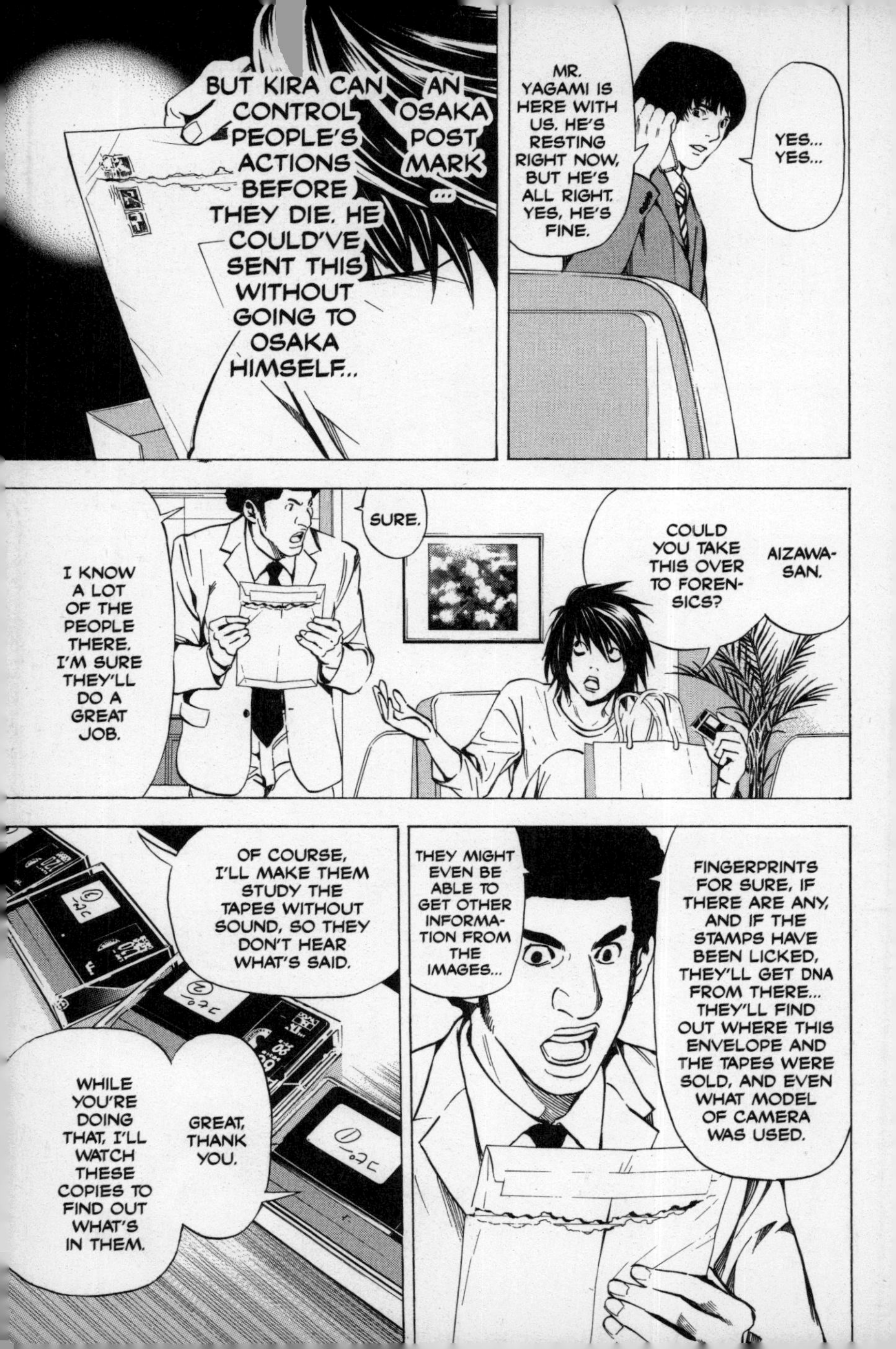
YES... YES...
MR. YAGAMI IS HERE WITH US. HE'S RESTING RIGHT NOW, BUT HE'S ALL RIGHT. YES, HE'S FINE.
AN OSAKA POSTMARK...
BUT KIRA CAN CONTROL PEOPLE'S ACTIONS BEFORE THEY DIE. HE COULD'VE SENT THIS WITHOUT GOING TO OSAKA HIMSELF...
AIZAWA-SAN.
COULD YOU TAKE THIS OVER TO FORENSICS?
SURE.
I KNOW A LOT OF THE PEOPLE THERE. I'M SURE THEY'LL DO A GREAT JOB.
FINGERPRINTS FOR SURE, IF THERE ARE ANY, AND IF THE STAMPS HAVE BEEN LICKED, THEY'LL GET DNA FROM THERE... THEY'LL FIND OUT WHERE THIS ENVELOPE AND THE TAPES WERE SOLD, AND EVEN WHAT MODEL OF CAMERA WAS USED.
THEY MIGHT EVEN BE ABLE TO GET OTHER INFORMATION FROM THE IMAGES...
OF COURSE, I'LL MAKE THEM STUDY THE TAPES WITHOUT SOUND, SO THEY DON'T HEAR WHAT'S SAID.
GREAT, THANK YOU.
WHILE YOU'RE DOING THAT, I'LL WATCH THESE COPIES TO FIND OUT WHAT'S IN THEM.

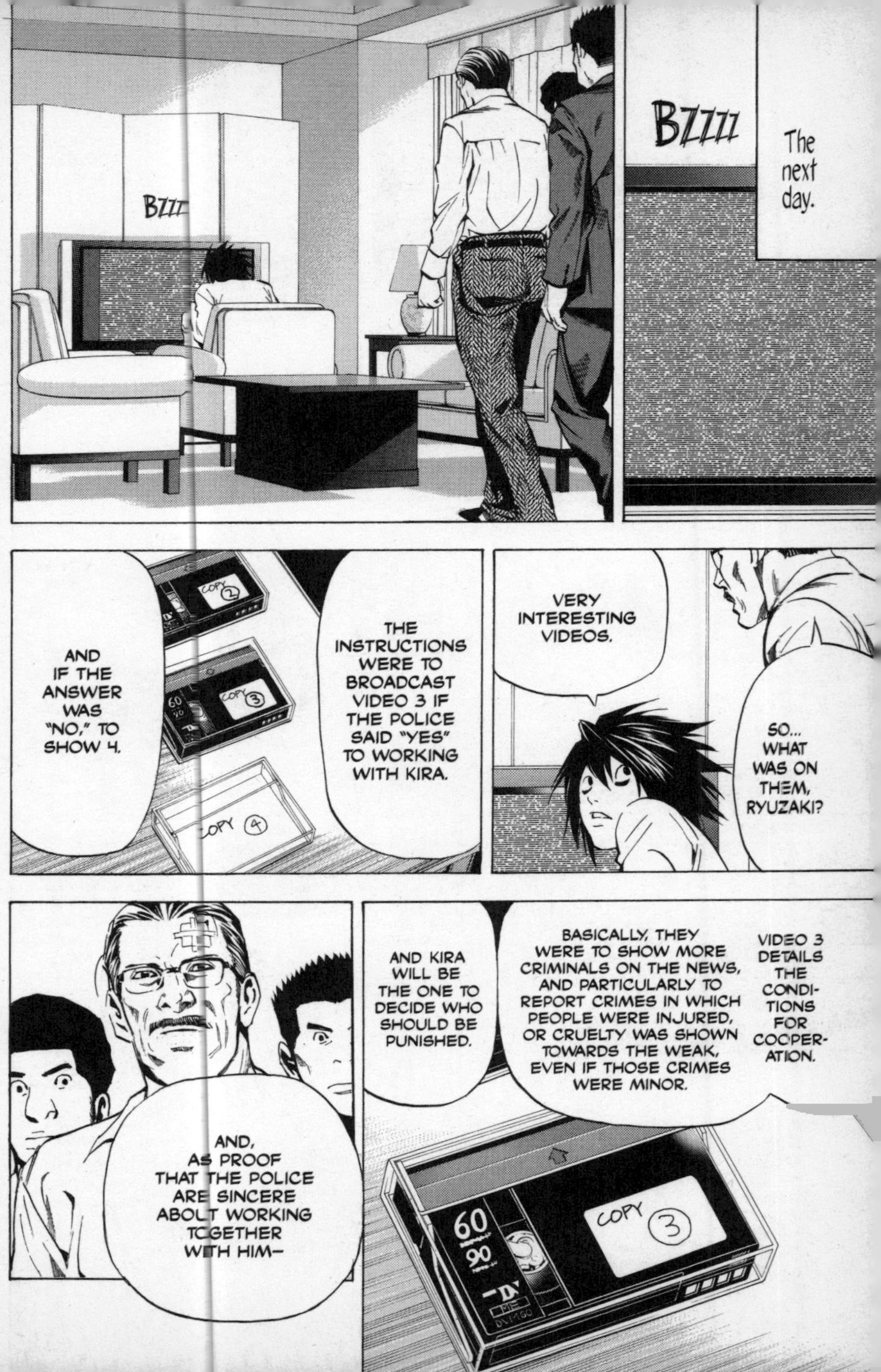
BZZZZ
The next day.
BZZZ
SO... WHAT WAS ON THEM, RYUZAKI?
VERY INTERESTING VIDEOS.
THE INSTRUCTIONS WERE TO BROADCAST VIDEO 3 IF THE POLICE SAID "YES" TO WORKING WITH KIRA.
AND IF THE ANSWER WAS "NO," TO SHOW 4.
COPY 2
COPY 3
COPY 4
VIDEO 3 DETAILS THE CONDITIONS FOR COOPERATION.
BASICALLY, THEY WERE TO SHOW MORE CRIMINALS ON THE NEWS, AND PARTICULARLY TO REPORT CRIMES IN WHICH PEOPLE WERE INJURED, OR CRUELTY WAS SHOWN TOWARDS THE WEAK, EVEN IF THOSE CRIMES WERE MINOR.
AND KIRA WILL BE THE ONE TO DECIDE WHO SHOULD BE PUNISHED.
COPY 3
AND, AS PROOF THAT THE POLICE ARE SINCERE ABOUT WORKING TOGETHER WITH HIM—

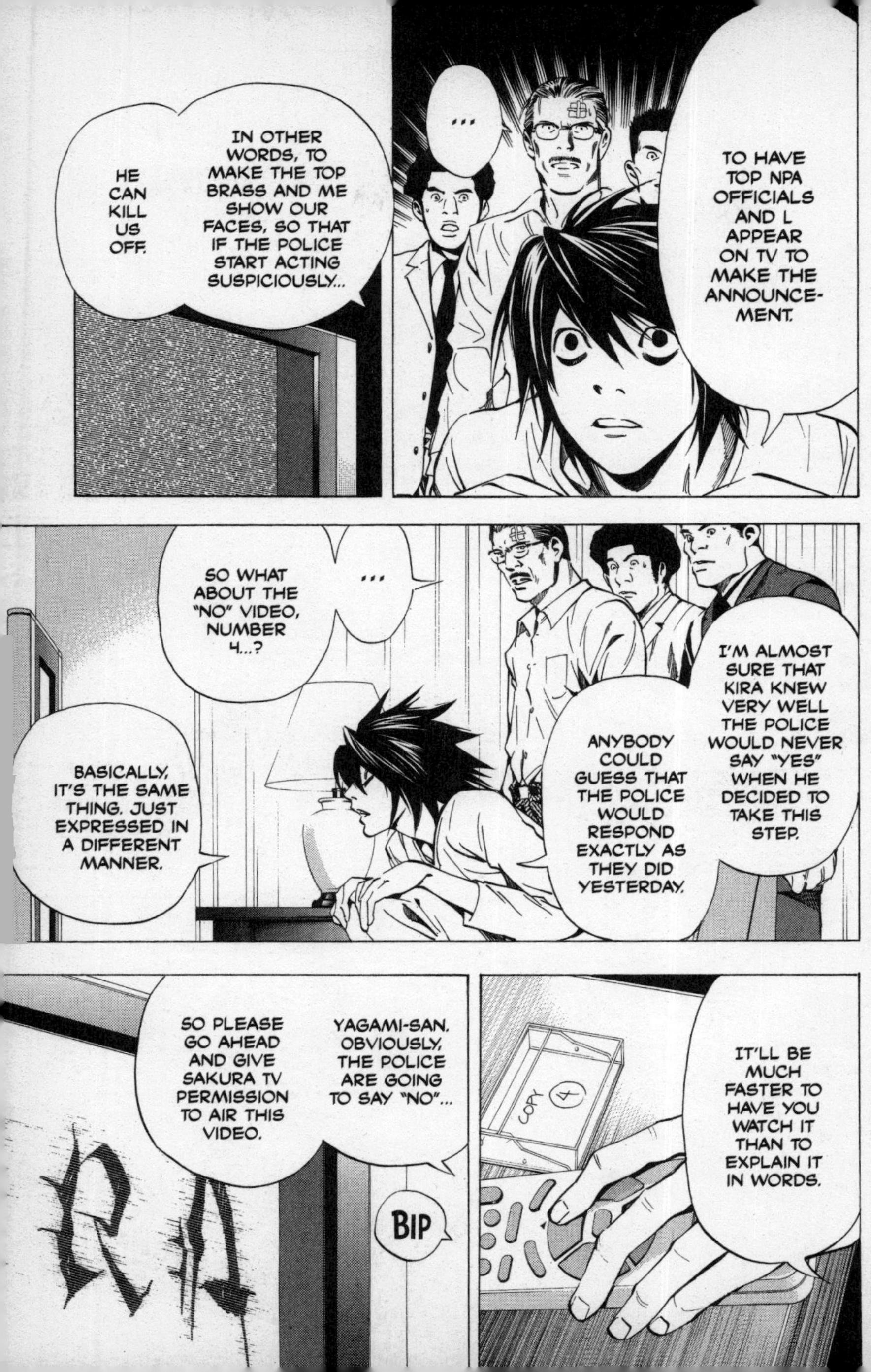

TO HAVE TOP NPA OFFICIALS AND L APPEAR ON TV TO MAKE THE ANNOUNCEMENT.
...
IN OTHER WORDS, TO MAKE THE TOP BRASS AND ME SHOW OUR FACES, SO THAT IF THE POLICE START ACTING SUSPICIOUSLY...
HE CAN KILL US OFF.
I'M ALMOST SURE THAT KIRA KNEW VERY WELL THE POLICE WOULD NEVER SAY "YES" WHEN HE DECIDED TO TAKE THIS STEP.
ANYBODY COULD GUESS THAT THE POLICE WOULD RESPOND EXACTLY AS THEY DID YESTERDAY.
...
SO WHAT ABOUT THE "NO" VIDEO, NUMBER 4...?
BASICALLY, IT'S THE SAME THING. JUST EXPRESSED IN A DIFFERENT MANNER.
IT'LL BE MUCH FASTER TO HAVE YOU WATCH IT THAN TO EXPLAIN IT IN WORDS.
COPY 4
YAGAMI-SAN. OBVIOUSLY, THE POLICE ARE GOING TO SAY "NO"...
SO PLEASE GO AHEAD AND GIVE SAKURA TV PERMISSION TO AIR THIS VIDEO.
BIP

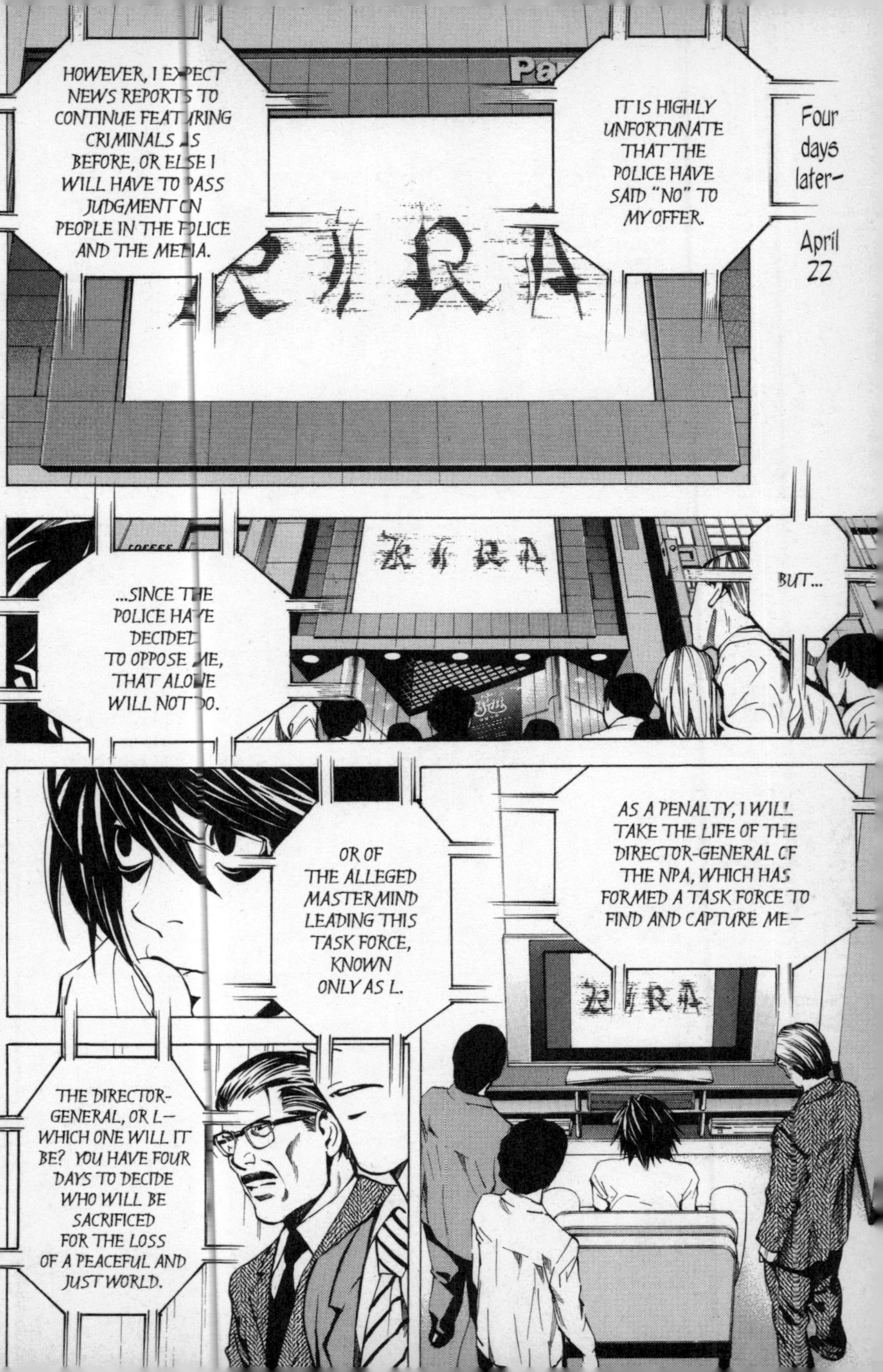
Four days later—
April 22
IT IS HIGHLY UNFORTUNATE THAT THE POLICE HAVE SAID "NO" TO MY OFFER.
HOWEVER, I EXPECT NEWS REPORTS TO CONTINUE FEATURING CRIMINALS AS BEFORE, OR ELSE I WILL HAVE TO PASS JUDGMENT ON PEOPLE IN THE POLICE AND THE MEDIA.
KIRA
BUT...
...SINCE THE POLICE HAVE DECIDED TO OPPOSE ME, THAT ALONE WILL NOT DO.
AS A PENALTY, I WILL TAKE THE LIFE OF THE DIRECTOR-GENERAL OF THE NPA, WHICH HAS FORMED A TASK FORCE TO FIND AND CAPTURE ME—
OR OF THE ALLEGED MASTERMIND LEADING THIS TASK FORCE, KNOWN ONLY AS L.
THE DIRECTOR-GENERAL, OR L— WHICH ONE WILL IT BE? YOU HAVE FOUR DAYS TO DECIDE WHO WILL BE SACRIFICED FOR THE LOSS OF A PEACEFUL AND JUST WORLD.

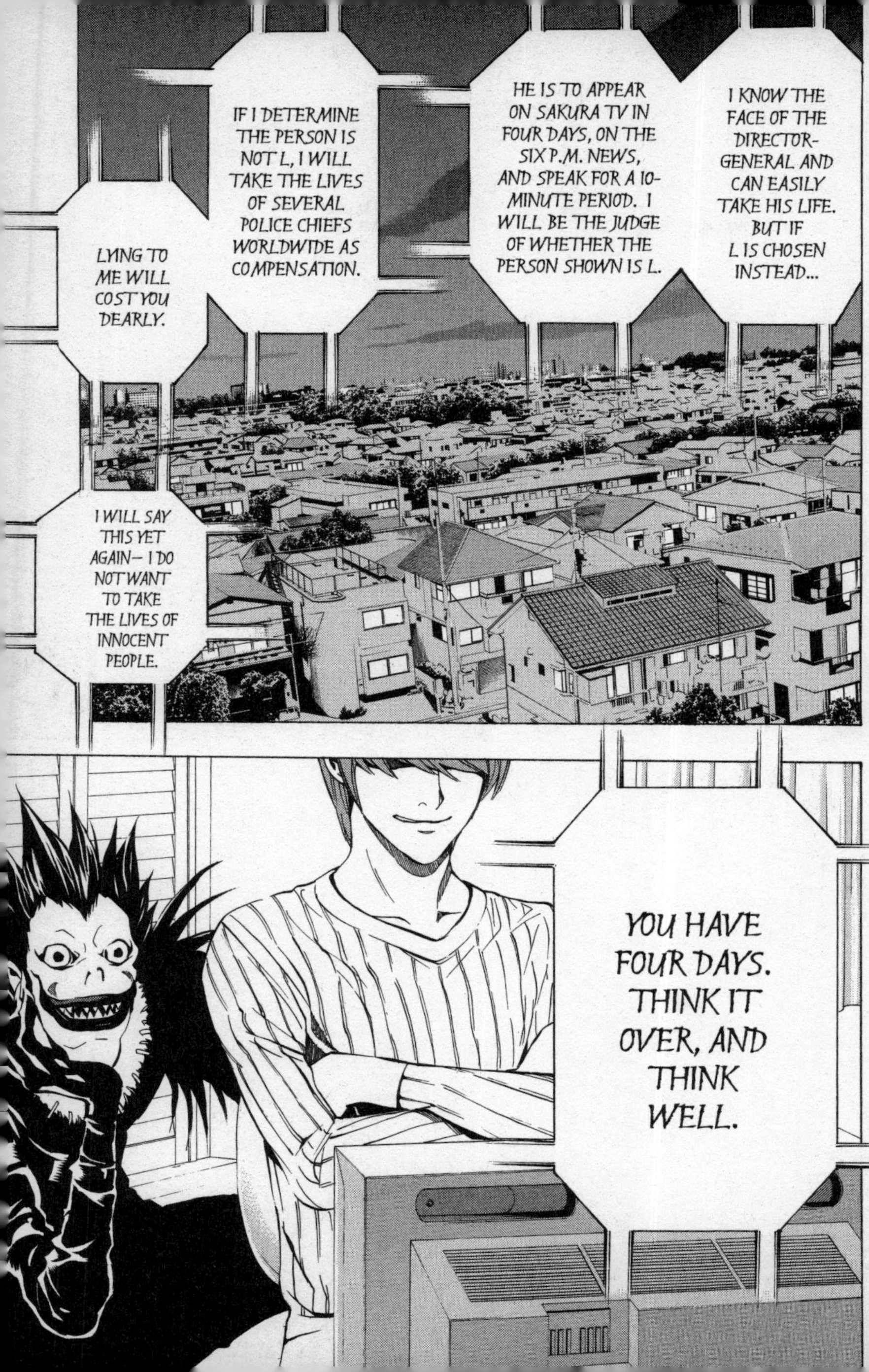
I KNOW THE FACE OF THE DIRECTOR-GENERAL AND CAN EASILY TAKE HIS LIFE. BUT IF L IS CHOSEN INSTEAD...
HE IS TO APPEAR ON SAKURA TV IN FOUR DAYS, ON THE SIX P.M. NEWS, AND SPEAK FOR A 10-MINUTE PERIOD. I WILL BE THE JUDGE OF WHETHER THE PERSON SHOWN IS L.
IF I DETERMINE THE PERSON IS NOT L, I WILL TAKE THE LIVES OF SEVERAL POLICE CHIEFS WORLDWIDE AS COMPENSATION.
LYING TO ME WILL COST YOU DEARLY.
I WILL SAY THIS YET AGAIN— I DO NOT WANT TO TAKE THE LIVES OF INNOCENT PEOPLE.
YOU HAVE FOUR DAYS. THINK IT OVER, AND THINK WELL.

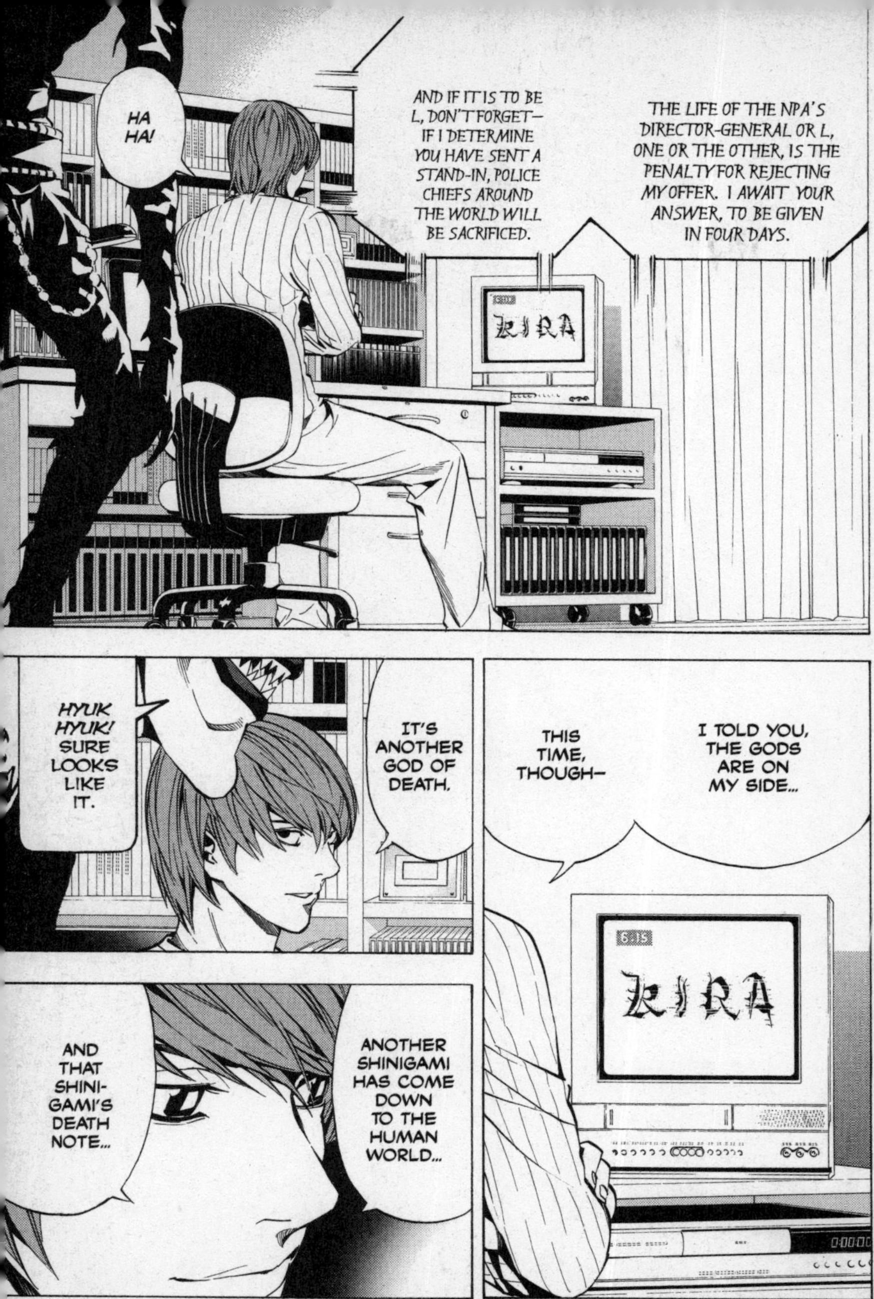
THE LIFE OF THE NPA'S DIRECTOR-GENERAL OR L, ONE OR THE OTHER, IS THE PENALTY FOR REJECTING MY OFFER. I AWAIT YOUR ANSWER, TO BE GIVEN IN FOUR DAYS.
AND IF IT IS TO BE L, DON'T FORGET—IF I DETERMINE YOU HAVE SENT A STAND-IN, POLICE CHIEFS AROUND THE WORLD WILL BE SACRIFICED.
HA HA!
KIRA
I TOLD YOU, THE GODS ARE ON MY SIDE...
THIS TIME, THOUGH—
KIRA
IT'S ANOTHER GOD OF DEATH.
HYUK HYUK! SURE LOOKS LIKE IT.
ANOTHER SHINIGAMI HAS COME DOWN TO THE HUMAN WORLD...
AND THAT SHINIGAMI'S DEATH NOTE...

chapter 25 Fool

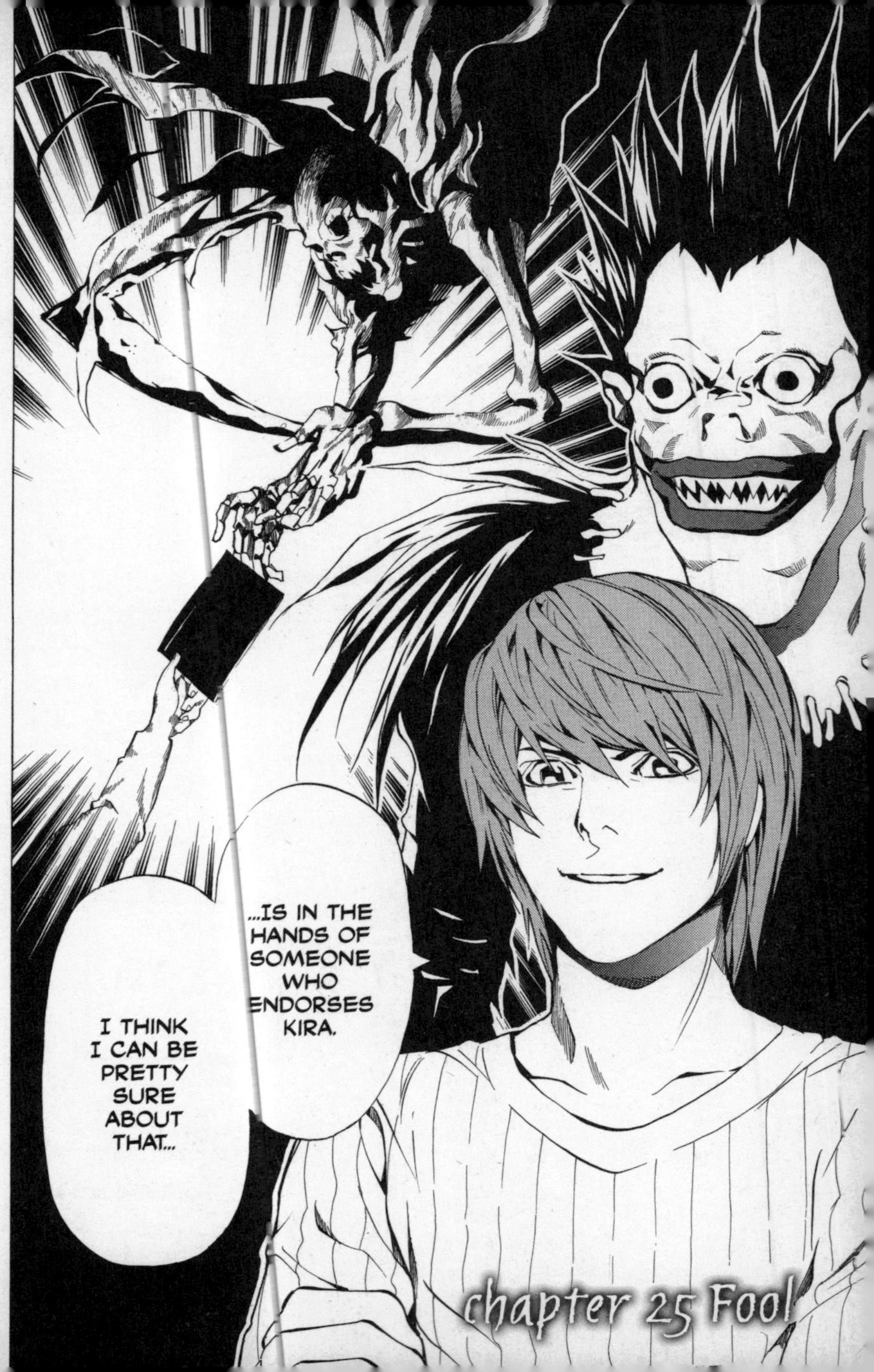
...IS IN THE HANDS OF SOMEONE WHO ENDORSES KIRA.
I THINK I CAN BE PRETTY SURE ABOUT THAT...
chapter 25 Fool

READ THIS WAY

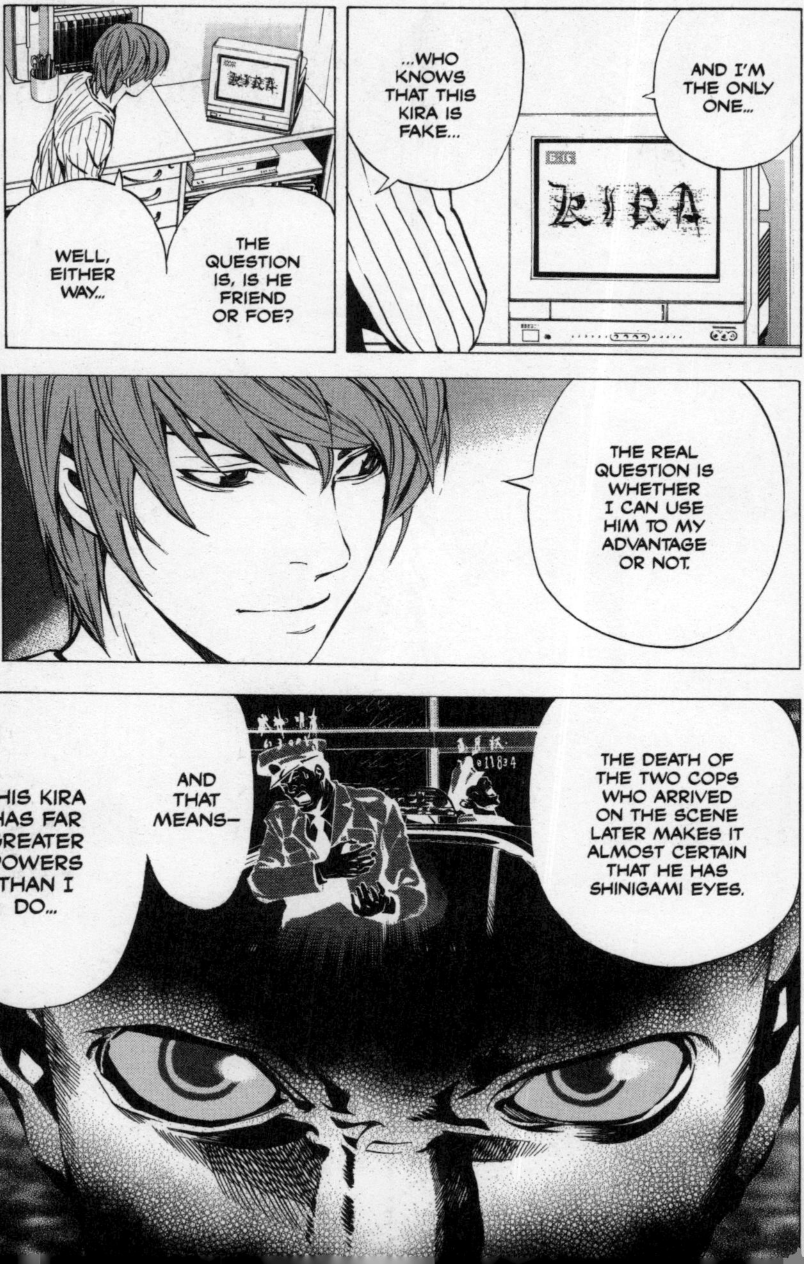

AND I'M THE ONLY ONE...
...WHO KNOWS THAT THIS KIRA IS FAKE...
THE QUESTION IS, IS HE FRIEND OR FOE?
WELL, EITHER WAY...
THE REAL QUESTION IS WHETHER I CAN USE HIM TO MY ADVANTAGE OR NOT.
THE DEATH OF THE TWO COPS WHO ARRIVED ON THE SCENE LATER MAKES IT ALMOST CERTAIN THAT HE HAS SHINIGAMI EYES.
AND THAT MEANS—
THIS KIRA HAS FAR GREATER POWERS THAN I DO...

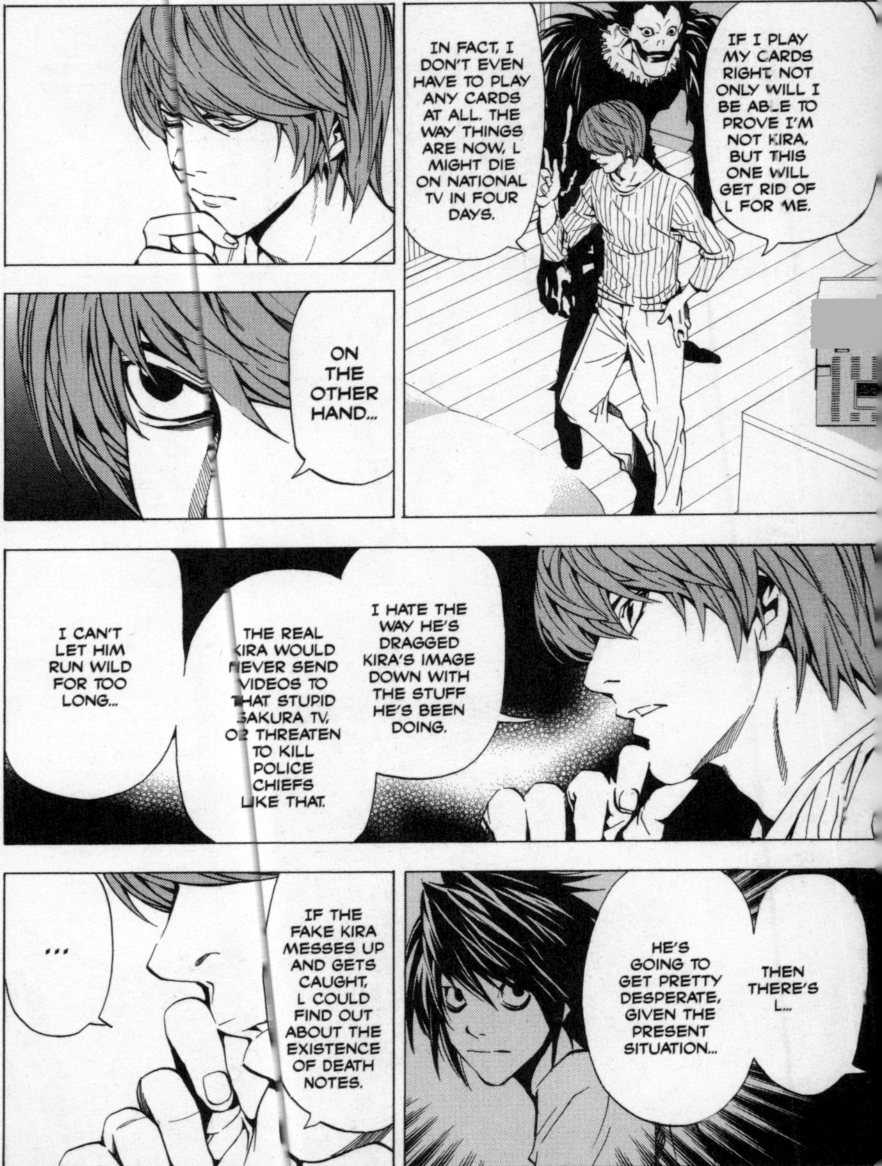
IF I PLAY MY CARDS RIGHT, NOT ONLY WILL I BE ABLE TO PROVE I'M NOT KIRA, BUT THIS ONE WILL GET RID OF L FOR ME.
IN FACT, I DON'T EVEN HAVE TO PLAY ANY CARDS AT ALL. THE WAY THINGS ARE NOW, L MIGHT DIE ON NATIONAL TV IN FOUR DAYS.
ON THE OTHER HAND...
I HATE THE WAY HE'S DRAGGED KIRA'S IMAGE DOWN WITH THE STUFF HE'S BEEN DOING.
THE REAL KIRA WOULD NEVER SEND VIDEOS TO THAT STUPID SAKURA TV, OR THREATEN TO KILL POLICE CHIEFS LIKE THAT.
I CAN'T LET HIM RUN WILD FOR TOO LONG...
THEN THERE'S L...
HE'S GOING TO GET PRETTY DESPERATE, GIVEN THE PRESENT SITUATION...
IF THE FAKE KIRA MESSES UP AND GETS CAUGHT, L COULD FIND OUT ABOUT THE EXISTENCE OF DEATH NOTES.
...

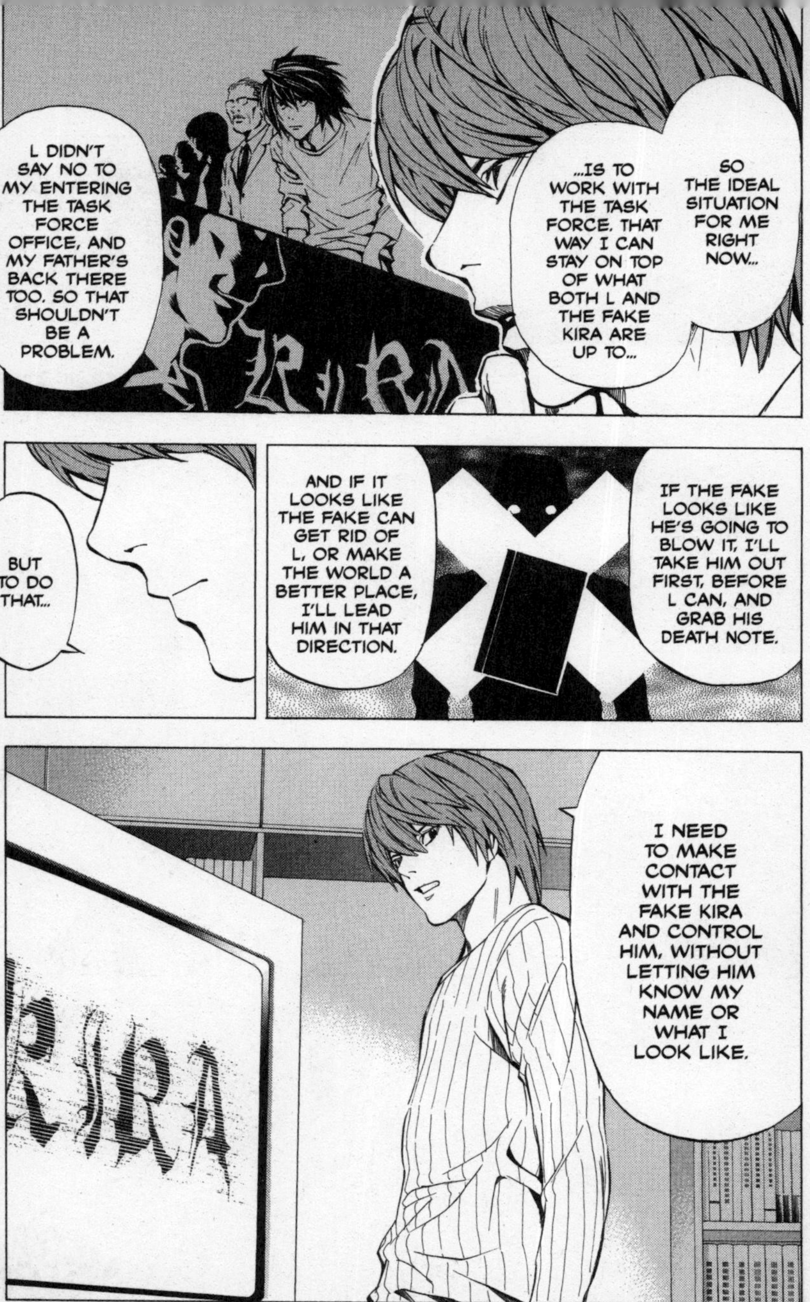
SO THE IDEAL SITUATION FOR ME RIGHT NOW...
...IS TO WORK WITH THE TASK FORCE. THAT WAY I CAN STAY ON TOP OF WHAT BOTH L AND THE FAKE KIRA ARE UP TO...
L DIDN'T SAY NO TO MY ENTERING THE TASK FORCE OFFICE, AND MY FATHER'S BACK THERE TOO, SO THAT SHOULDN'T BE A PROBLEM.
IF THE FAKE LOOKS LIKE HE'S GOING TO BLOW IT, I'LL TAKE HIM OUT FIRST, BEFORE L CAN, AND GRAB HIS DEATH NOTE.
AND IF IT LOOKS LIKE THE FAKE CAN GET RID OF L, OR MAKE THE WORLD A BETTER PLACE, I'LL LEAD HIM IN THAT DIRECTION.
BUT TO DO THAT...
I NEED TO MAKE CONTACT WITH THE FAKE KIRA AND CONTROL HIM, WITHOUT LETTING HIM KNOW MY NAME OR WHAT I LOOK LIKE.

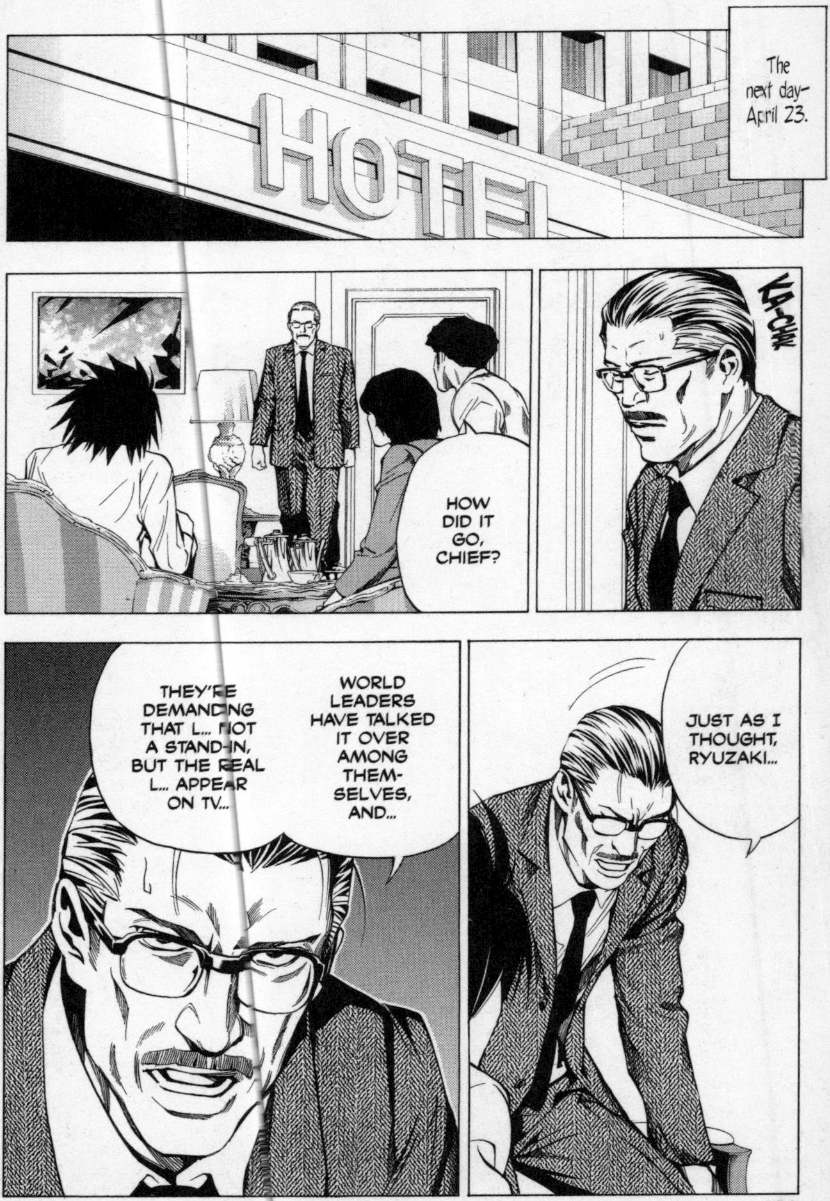

The next day— April 23.
KA-CHAK
HOW DID IT GO, CHIEF?
JUST AS I THOUGHT, RYUZAKI...
WORLD LEADERS HAVE TALKED IT OVER AMONG THEM-SELVES, AND...
THEY'RE DEMANDING THAT L... NOT A STAND-IN, BUT THE REAL L... APPEAR ON TV...

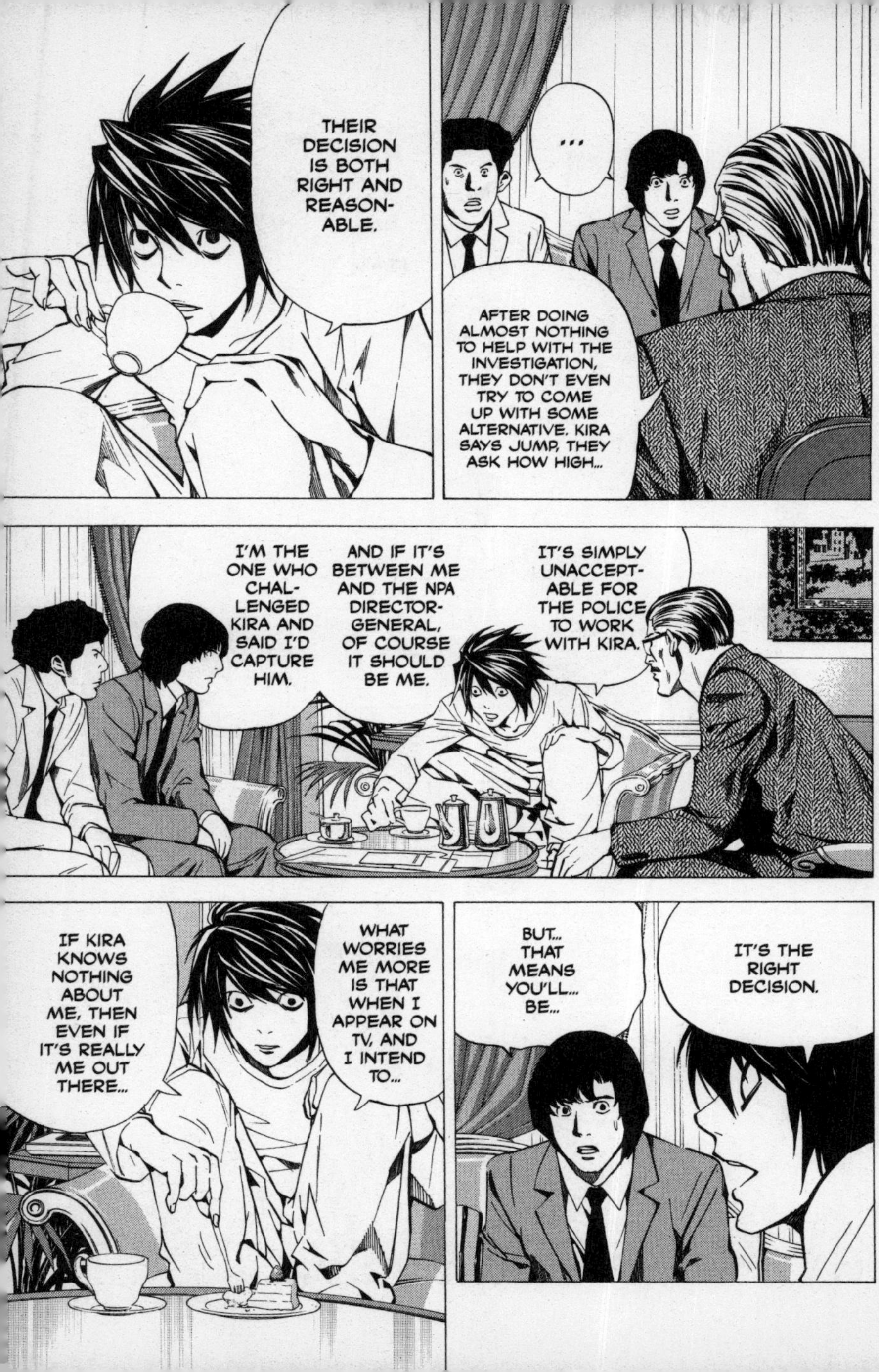
...
AFTER DOING ALMOST NOTHING TO HELP WITH THE INVESTIGATION, THEY DON'T EVEN TRY TO COME UP WITH SOME ALTERNATIVE. KIRA SAYS JUMP, THEY ASK HOW HIGH...
THEIR DECISION IS BOTH RIGHT AND REASON-ABLE.
IT'S SIMPLY UNACCEPT-ABLE FOR THE POLICE TO WORK WITH KIRA.
I'M THE ONE WHO CHAL-LENGED KIRA AND SAID I'D CAPTURE HIM.
AND IF IT'S BETWEEN ME AND THE NPA DIRECTOR-GENERAL, OF COURSE IT SHOULD BE ME.
IT'S THE RIGHT DECISION.
BUT... THAT MEANS YOU'LL... BE...
WHAT WORRIES ME MORE IS THAT WHEN I APPEAR ON TV, AND I INTEND TO...
IF KIRA KNOWS NOTHING ABOUT ME, THEN EVEN IF IT'S REALLY ME OUT THERE...

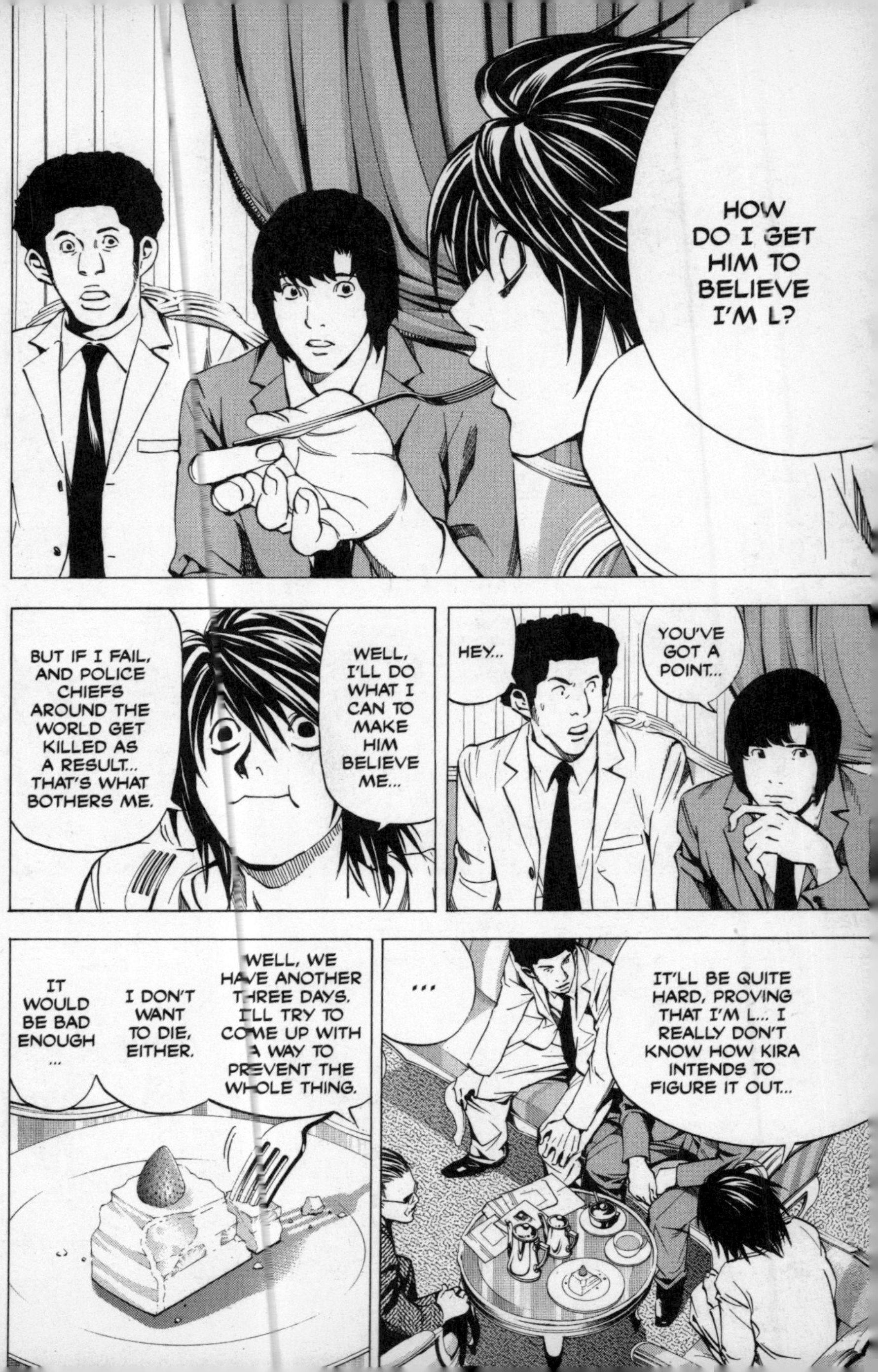
HOW DO I GET HIM TO BELIEVE I'M L?
YOU'VE GOT A POINT...
HEY...
WELL, I'LL DO WHAT I CAN TO MAKE HIM BELIEVE ME...
BUT IF I FAIL, AND POLICE CHIEFS AROUND THE WORLD GET KILLED AS A RESULT... THAT'S WHAT BOTHERS ME.
IT'LL BE QUITE HARD, PROVING THAT I'M L... I REALLY DON'T KNOW HOW KIRA INTENDS TO FIGURE IT OUT...
...
WELL, WE HAVE ANOTHER THREE DAYS. I'LL TRY TO COME UP WITH A WAY TO PREVENT THE WHOLE THING.
I DON'T WANT TO DIE, EITHER.
IT WOULD BE BAD ENOUGH ...

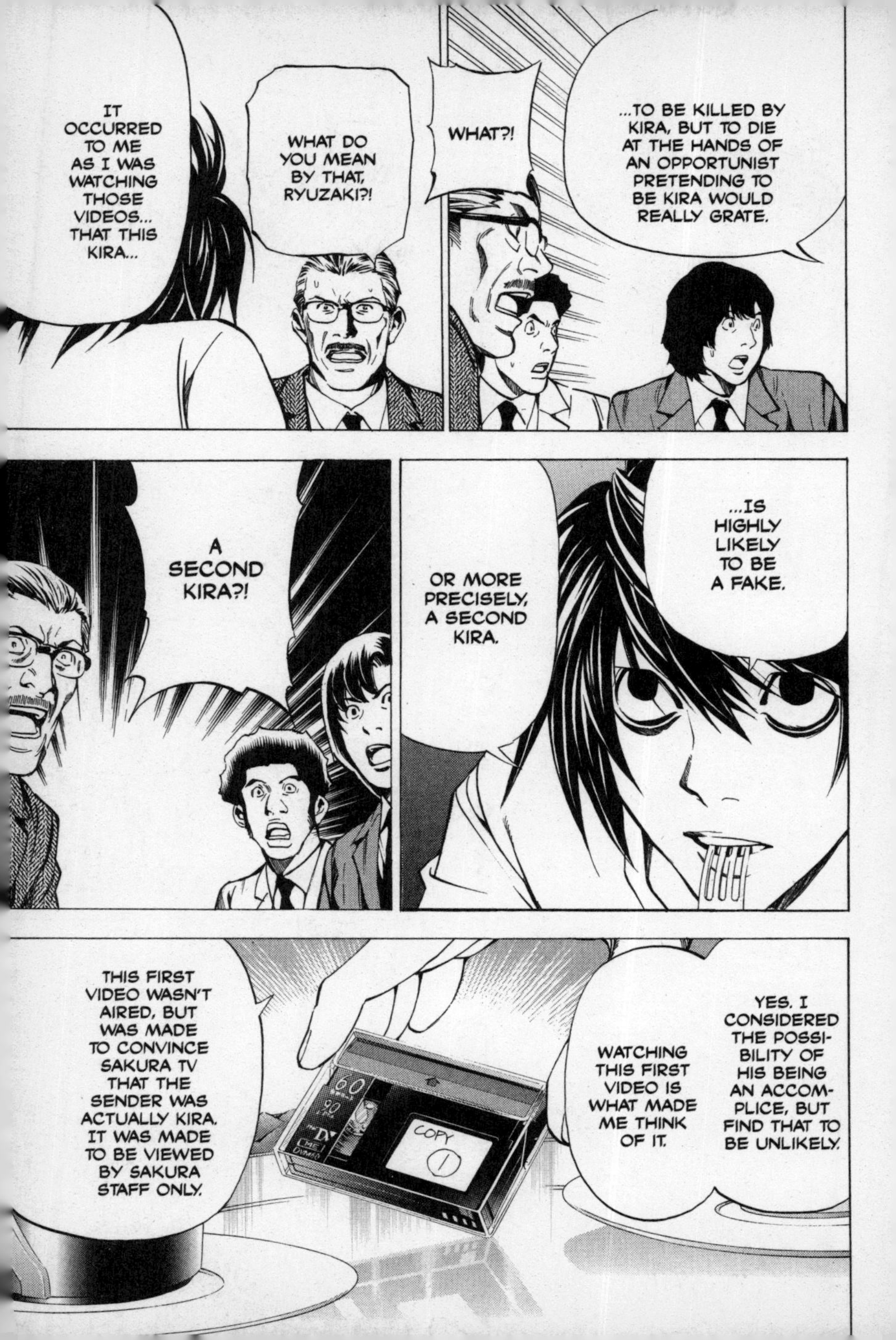
...TO BE KILLED BY KIRA, BUT TO DIE AT THE HANDS OF AN OPPORTUNIST PRETENDING TO BE KIRA WOULD REALLY GRATE.
WHAT?!
WHAT DO YOU MEAN BY THAT, RYUZAKI?!
IT OCCURRED TO ME AS I WAS WATCHING THOSE VIDEOS... THAT THIS KIRA...
...IS HIGHLY LIKELY TO BE A FAKE.
OR MORE PRECISELY, A SECOND KIRA.
A SECOND KIRA?!
YES. I CONSIDERED THE POSSI-BILITY OF HIS BEING AN ACCOM-PLICE, BUT FIND THAT TO BE UNLIKELY.
WATCHING THIS FIRST VIDEO IS WHAT MADE ME THINK OF IT.
COPY 1
THIS FIRST VIDEO WASN'T AIRED, BUT WAS MADE TO CONVINCE SAKURA TV THAT THE SENDER WAS ACTUALLY KIRA. IT WAS MADE TO BE VIEWED BY SAKURA STAFF ONLY.

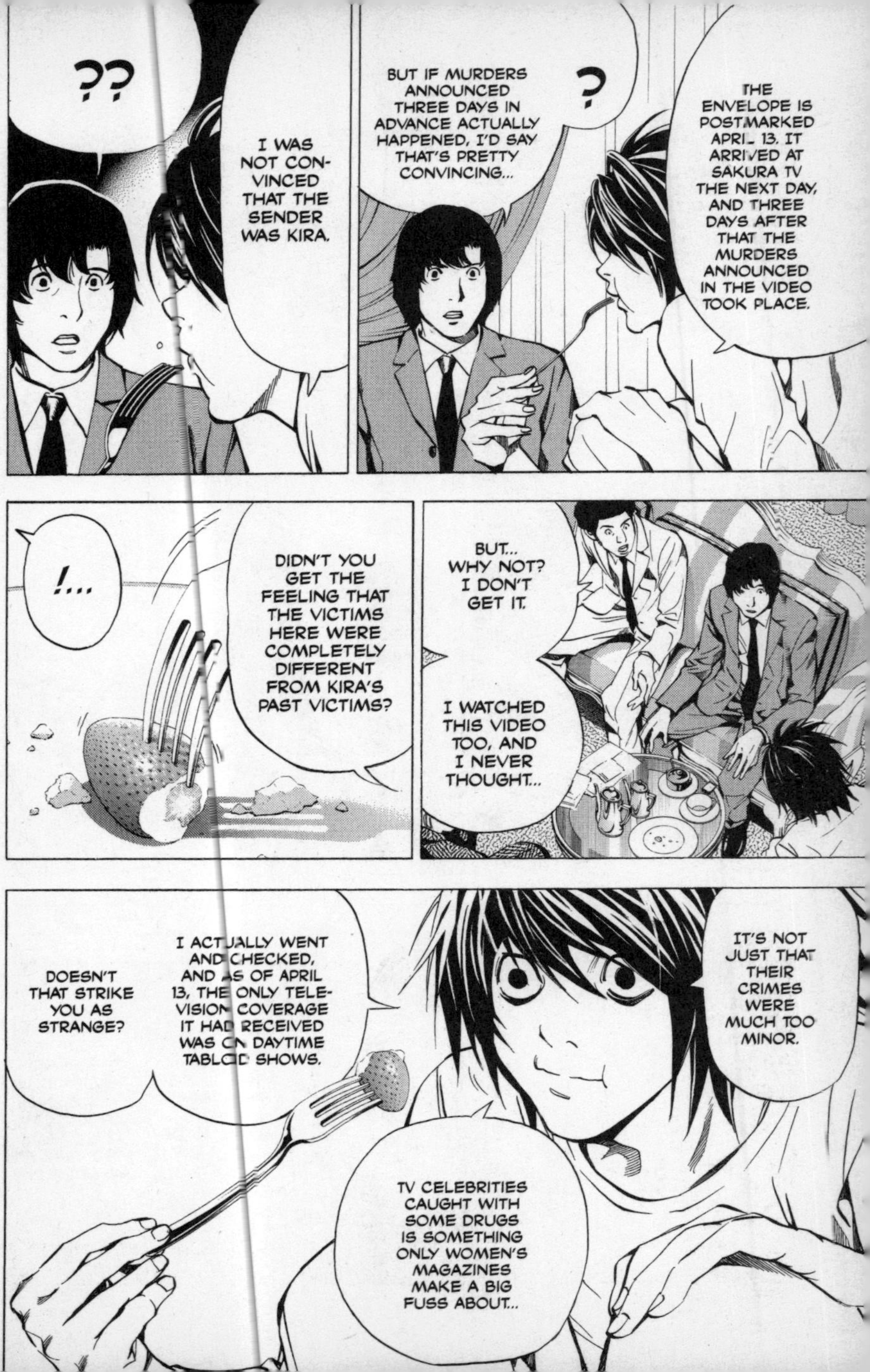
THE ENVELOPE IS POSTMARKED APRIL 13. IT ARRIVED AT SAKURA TV THE NEXT DAY, AND THREE DAYS AFTER THAT THE MURDERS ANNOUNCED IN THE VIDEO TOOK PLACE.
?
BUT IF MURDERS ANNOUNCED THREE DAYS IN ADVANCE ACTUALLY HAPPENED, I'D SAY THAT'S PRETTY CONVINCING...
I WAS NOT CONVINCED THAT THE SENDER WAS KIRA.
??
BUT... WHY NOT? I DON'T GET IT.
I WATCHED THIS VIDEO TOO, AND I NEVER THOUGHT...
DIDN'T YOU GET THE FEELING THAT THE VICTIMS HERE WERE COMPLETELY DIFFERENT FROM KIRA'S PAST VICTIMS?
!...
IT'S NOT JUST THAT THEIR CRIMES WERE MUCH TOO MINOR.
TV CELEBRITIES CAUGHT WITH SOME DRUGS IS SOMETHING ONLY WOMEN'S MAGAZINES MAKE A BIG FUSS ABOUT...
I ACTUALLY WENT AND CHECKED, AND AS OF APRIL 13, THE ONLY TELEVISION COVERAGE IT HAD RECEIVED WAS ON DAYTIME TABLOID SHOWS.
DOESN'T THAT STRIKE YOU AS STRANGE?

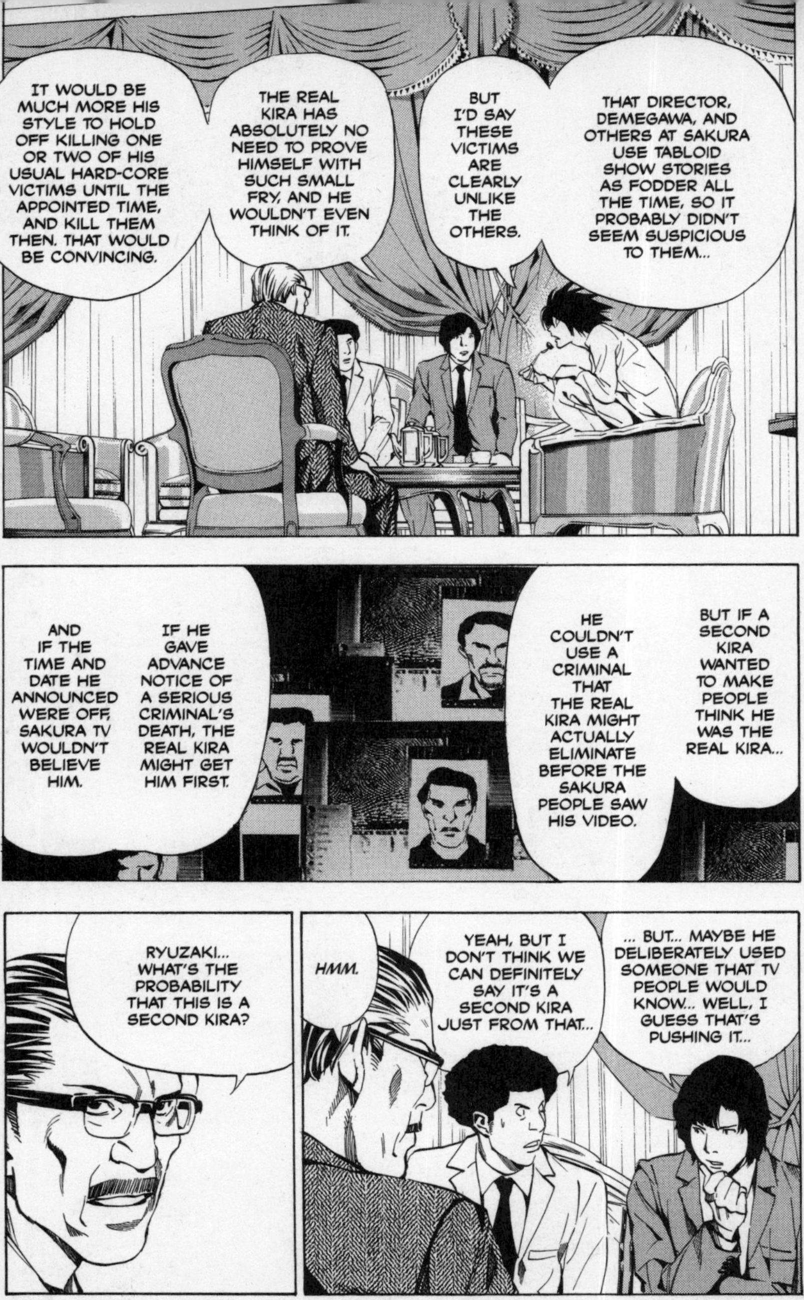

THAT DIRECTOR, DEMEGAWA, AND OTHERS AT SAKURA USE TABLOID SHOW STORIES AS FODDER ALL THE TIME, SO IT PROBABLY DIDN'T SEEM SUSPICIOUS TO THEM...
BUT I'D SAY THESE VICTIMS ARE CLEARLY UNLIKE THE OTHERS.
THE REAL KIRA HAS ABSOLUTELY NO NEED TO PROVE HIMSELF WITH SUCH SMALL FRY, AND HE WOULDN'T EVEN THINK OF IT.
IT WOULD BE MUCH MORE HIS STYLE TO HOLD OFF KILLING ONE OR TWO OF HIS USUAL HARD-CORE VICTIMS UNTIL THE APPOINTED TIME, AND KILL THEM THEN. THAT WOULD BE CONVINCING.
BUT IF A SECOND KIRA WANTED TO MAKE PEOPLE THINK HE WAS THE REAL KIRA...
HE COULDN'T USE A CRIMINAL THAT THE REAL KIRA MIGHT ACTUALLY ELIMINATE BEFORE THE SAKURA PEOPLE SAW HIS VIDEO.
IF HE GAVE ADVANCE NOTICE OF A SERIOUS CRIMINAL'S DEATH, THE REAL KIRA MIGHT GET HIM FIRST.
AND IF THE TIME AND DATE HE ANNOUNCED WERE OFF, SAKURA TV WOULDN'T BELIEVE HIM.
... BUT... MAYBE HE DELIBERATELY USED SOMEONE THAT TV PEOPLE WOULD KNOW... WELL, I GUESS THAT'S PUSHING IT...
YEAH, BUT I DON'T THINK WE CAN DEFINITELY SAY IT'S A SECOND KIRA JUST FROM THAT...
HMM.
RYUZAKI... WHAT'S THE PROBABILITY THAT THIS IS A SECOND KIRA?

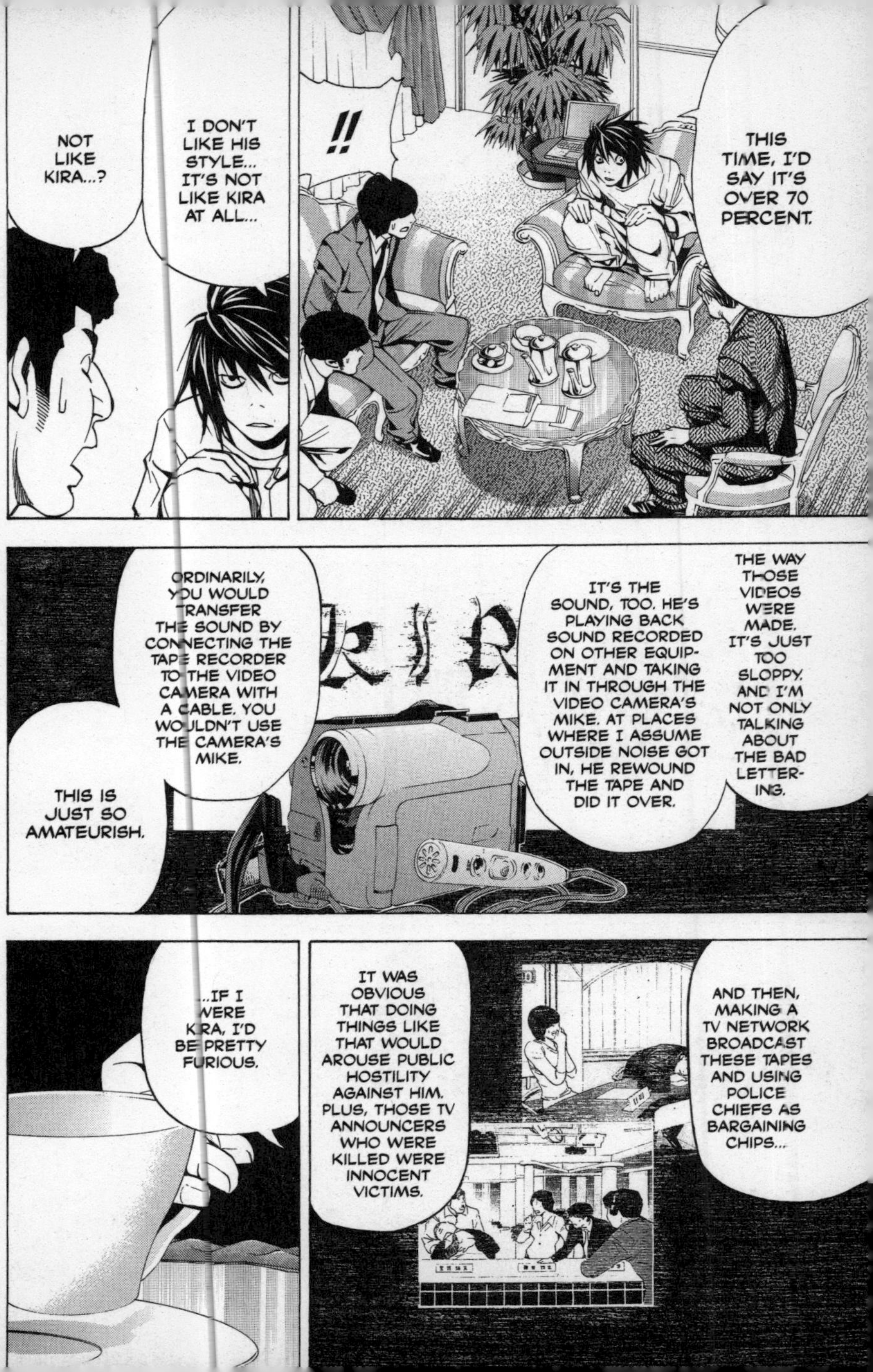
THIS TIME, I'D SAY IT'S OVER 70 PERCENT.
!!
I DON'T LIKE HIS STYLE... IT'S NOT LIKE KIRA AT ALL...
NOT LIKE KIRA...?
THE WAY THOSE VIDEOS WERE MADE. IT'S JUST TOO SLOPPY. AND I'M NOT ONLY TALKING ABOUT THE BAD LETTERING.
IT'S THE SOUND, TOO. HE'S PLAYING BACK SOUND RECORDED ON OTHER EQUIPMENT AND TAKING IT IN THROUGH THE VIDEO CAMERA'S MIKE. AT PLACES WHERE I ASSUME OUTSIDE NOISE GOT IN, HE REWOUND THE TAPE AND DID IT OVER.
ORDINARILY, YOU WOULD TRANSFER THE SOUND BY CONNECTING THE TAPE RECORDER TO THE VIDEO CAMERA WITH A CABLE. YOU WOULDN'T USE THE CAMERA'S MIKE.
THIS IS JUST SO AMATEURISH.
AND THEN, MAKING A TV NETWORK BROADCAST THESE TAPES AND USING POLICE CHIEFS AS BARGAINING CHIPS...
IT WAS OBVIOUS THAT DOING THINGS LIKE THAT WOULD AROUSE PUBLIC HOSTILITY AGAINST HIM. PLUS, THOSE TV ANNOUNCERS WHO WERE KILLED WERE INNOCENT VICTIMS.
...IF I WERE KIRA, I'D BE PRETTY FURIOUS.

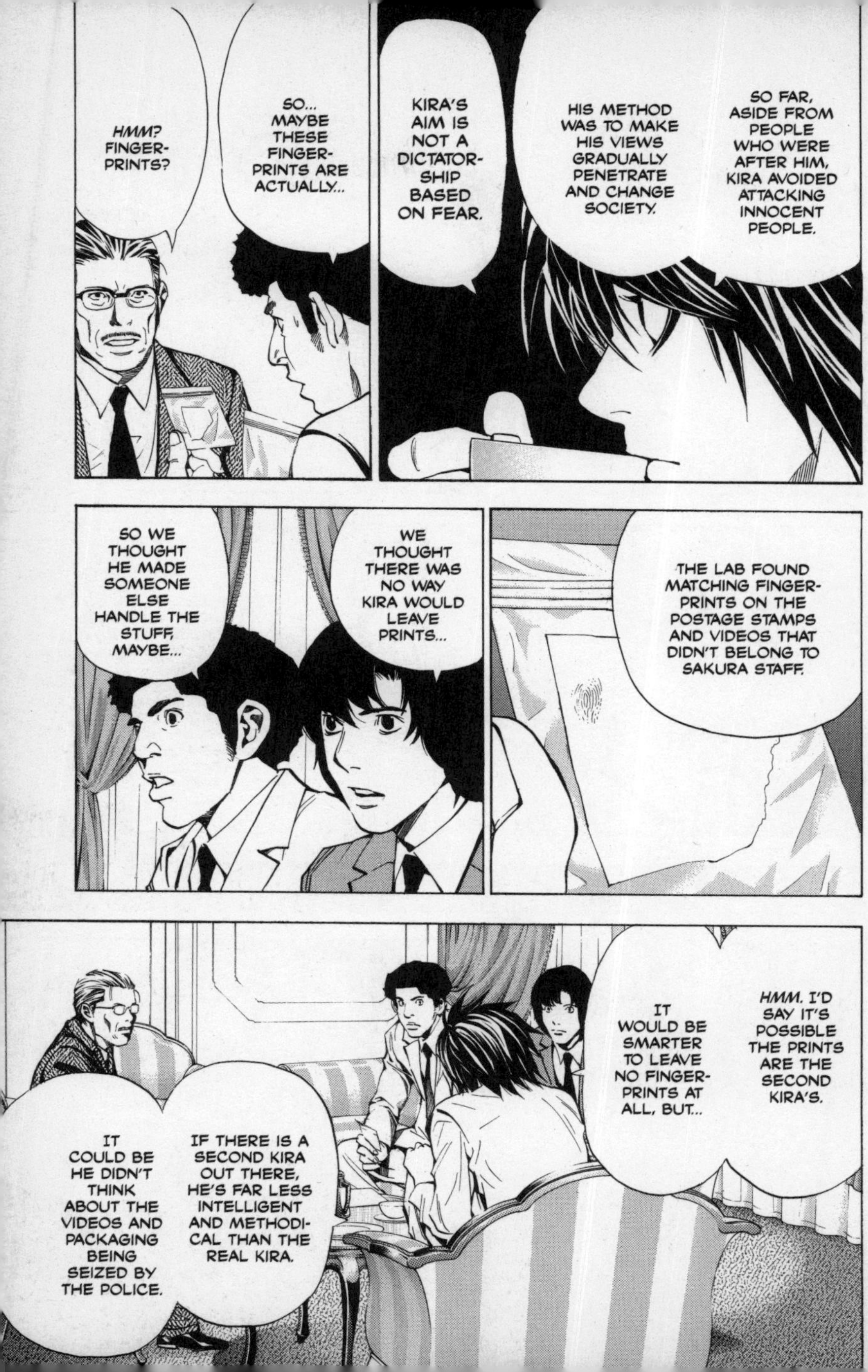
SO FAR, ASIDE FROM PEOPLE WHO WERE AFTER HIM, KIRA AVOIDED ATTACKING INNOCENT PEOPLE.
HIS METHOD WAS TO MAKE HIS VIEWS GRADUALLY PENETRATE AND CHANGE SOCIETY.
KIRA'S AIM IS NOT A DICTATORSHIP BASED ON FEAR.
SO... MAYBE THESE FINGERPRINTS ARE ACTUALLY...
HMM? FINGERPRINTS?
THE LAB FOUND MATCHING FINGERPRINTS ON THE POSTAGE STAMPS AND VIDEOS THAT DIDN'T BELONG TO SAKURA STAFF.
WE THOUGHT THERE WAS NO WAY KIRA WOULD LEAVE PRINTS...
SO WE THOUGHT HE MADE SOMEONE ELSE HANDLE THE STUFF, MAYBE...
HMM. I'D SAY IT'S POSSIBLE THE PRINTS ARE THE SECOND KIRA'S.
IT WOULD BE SMARTER TO LEAVE NO FINGERPRINTS AT ALL, BUT...
IF THERE IS A SECOND KIRA OUT THERE, HE'S FAR LESS INTELLIGENT AND METHODICAL THAN THE REAL KIRA.
IT COULD BE HE DIDN'T THINK ABOUT THE VIDEOS AND PACKAGING BEING SEIZED BY THE POLICE.

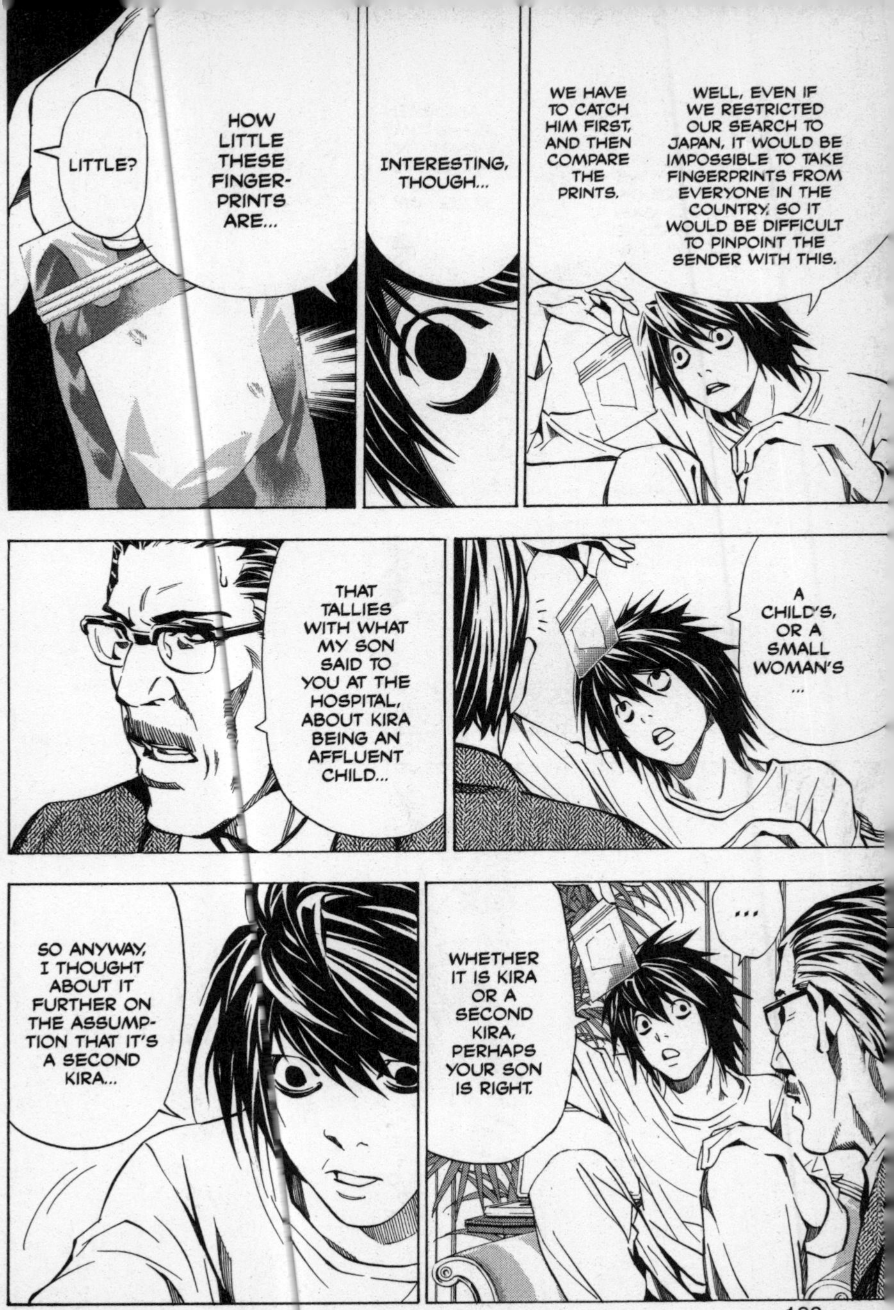
WELL, EVEN IF WE RESTRICTED OUR SEARCH TO JAPAN, IT WOULD BE IMPOSSIBLE TO TAKE FINGERPRINTS FROM EVERYONE IN THE COUNTRY, SO IT WOULD BE DIFFICULT TO PINPOINT THE SENDER WITH THIS.
WE HAVE TO CATCH HIM FIRST, AND THEN COMPARE THE PRINTS.
INTERESTING, THOUGH...
HOW LITTLE THESE FINGER-PRINTS ARE...
LITTLE?
A CHILD'S, OR A SMALL WOMAN'S ...
THAT TALLIES WITH WHAT MY SON SAID TO YOU AT THE HOSPITAL, ABOUT KIRA BEING AN AFFLUENT CHILD...
...
WHETHER IT IS KIRA OR A SECOND KIRA, PERHAPS YOUR SON IS RIGHT.
SO ANYWAY, I THOUGHT ABOUT IT FURTHER ON THE ASSUMP-TION THAT IT'S A SECOND KIRA...

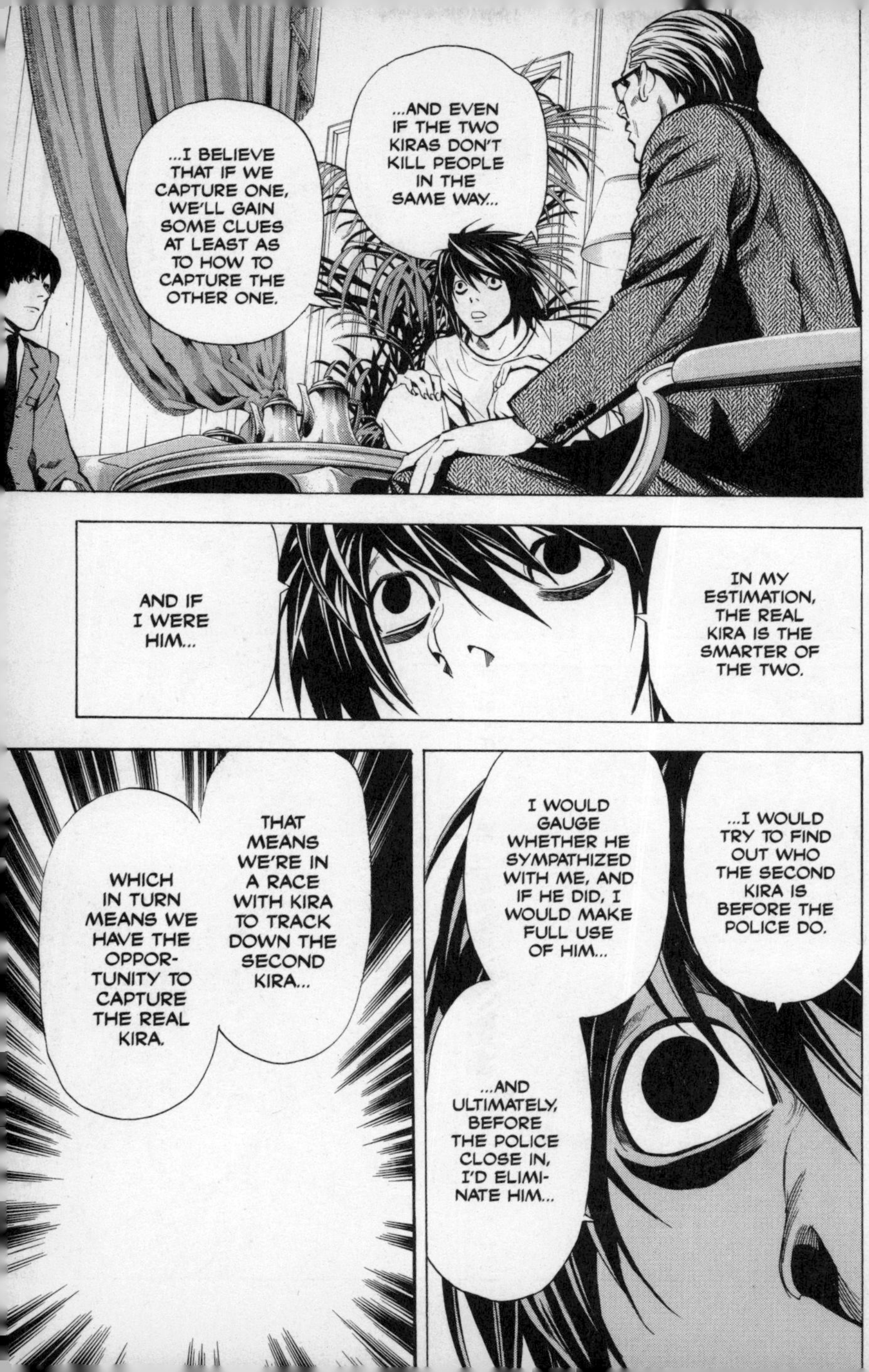
...AND EVEN IF THE TWO KIRAS DON'T KILL PEOPLE IN THE SAME WAY...
...I BELIEVE THAT IF WE CAPTURE ONE, WE'LL GAIN SOME CLUES AT LEAST AS TO HOW TO CAPTURE THE OTHER ONE.
IN MY ESTIMATION, THE REAL KIRA IS THE SMARTER OF THE TWO.
AND IF I WERE HIM...
...I WOULD TRY TO FIND OUT WHO THE SECOND KIRA IS BEFORE THE POLICE DO.
I WOULD GAUGE WHETHER HE SYMPATHIZED WITH ME, AND IF HE DID, I WOULD MAKE FULL USE OF HIM...
...AND ULTIMATELY, BEFORE THE POLICE CLOSE IN, I'D ELIMI-NATE HIM...
THAT MEANS WE'RE IN A RACE WITH KIRA TO TRACK DOWN THE SECOND KIRA...
WHICH IN TURN MEANS WE HAVE THE OPPOR-TUNITY TO CAPTURE THE REAL KIRA.

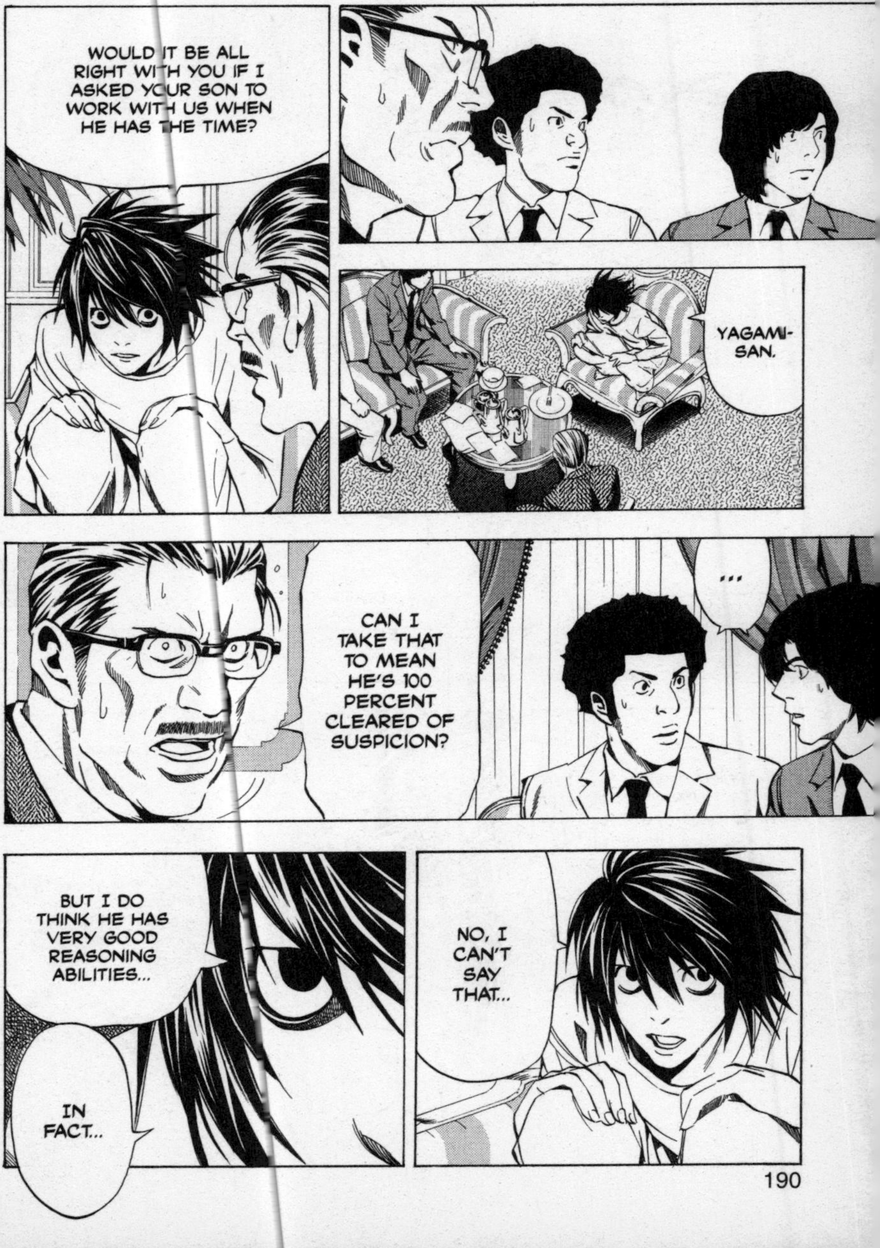
YAGAMI-SAN.
WOULD IT BE ALL RIGHT WITH YOU IF I ASKED YOUR SON TO WORK WITH US WHEN HE HAS THE TIME?
...
CAN I TAKE THAT TO MEAN HE'S 100 PERCENT CLEARED OF SUSPICION?
NO, I CAN'T SAY THAT...
BUT I DO THINK HE HAS VERY GOOD REASONING ABILITIES...
IN FACT...

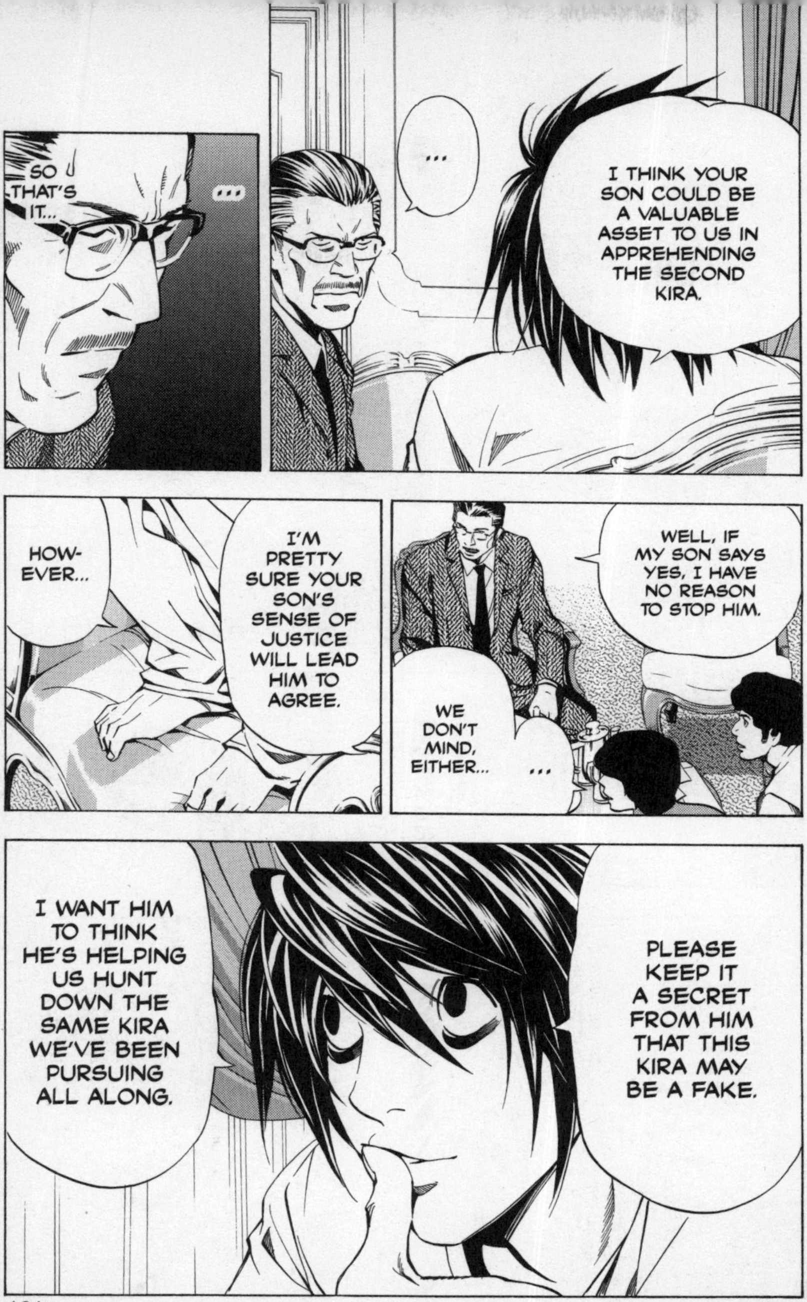
I THINK YOUR SON COULD BE A VALUABLE ASSET TO US IN APPREHENDING THE SECOND KIRA.
...
...
SO THAT'S IT...
WELL, IF MY SON SAYS YES, I HAVE NO REASON TO STOP HIM.
WE DON'T MIND, EITHER...
...
I'M PRETTY SURE YOUR SON'S SENSE OF JUSTICE WILL LEAD HIM TO AGREE.
HOW-EVER...
PLEASE KEEP IT A SECRET FROM HIM THAT THIS KIRA MAY BE A FAKE.
I WANT HIM TO THINK HE'S HELPING US HUNT DOWN THE SAME KIRA WE'VE BEEN PURSUING ALL ALONG.

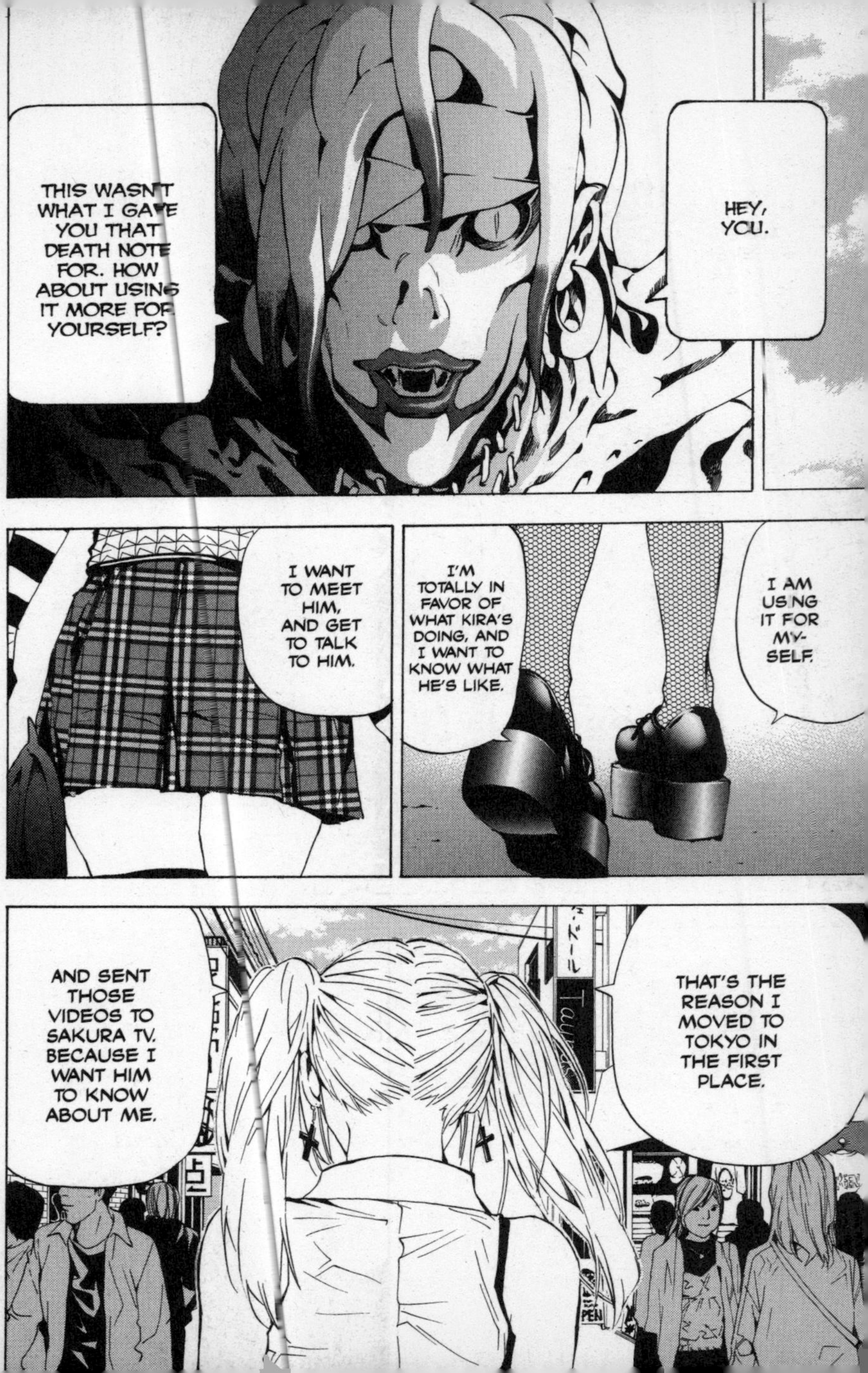
HEY, YOU.
THIS WASN'T WHAT I GAVE YOU THAT DEATH NOTE FOR. HOW ABOUT USING IT MORE FOR YOURSELF?
I AM USING IT FOR MY-SELF.
I'M TOTALLY IN FAVOR OF WHAT KIRA'S DOING, AND I WANT TO KNOW WHAT HE'S LIKE.
I WANT TO MEET HIM, AND GET TO TALK TO HIM.
THAT'S THE REASON I MOVED TO TOKYO IN THE FIRST PLACE.
AND SENT THOSE VIDEOS TO SAKURA TV. BECAUSE I WANT HIM TO KNOW ABOUT ME.

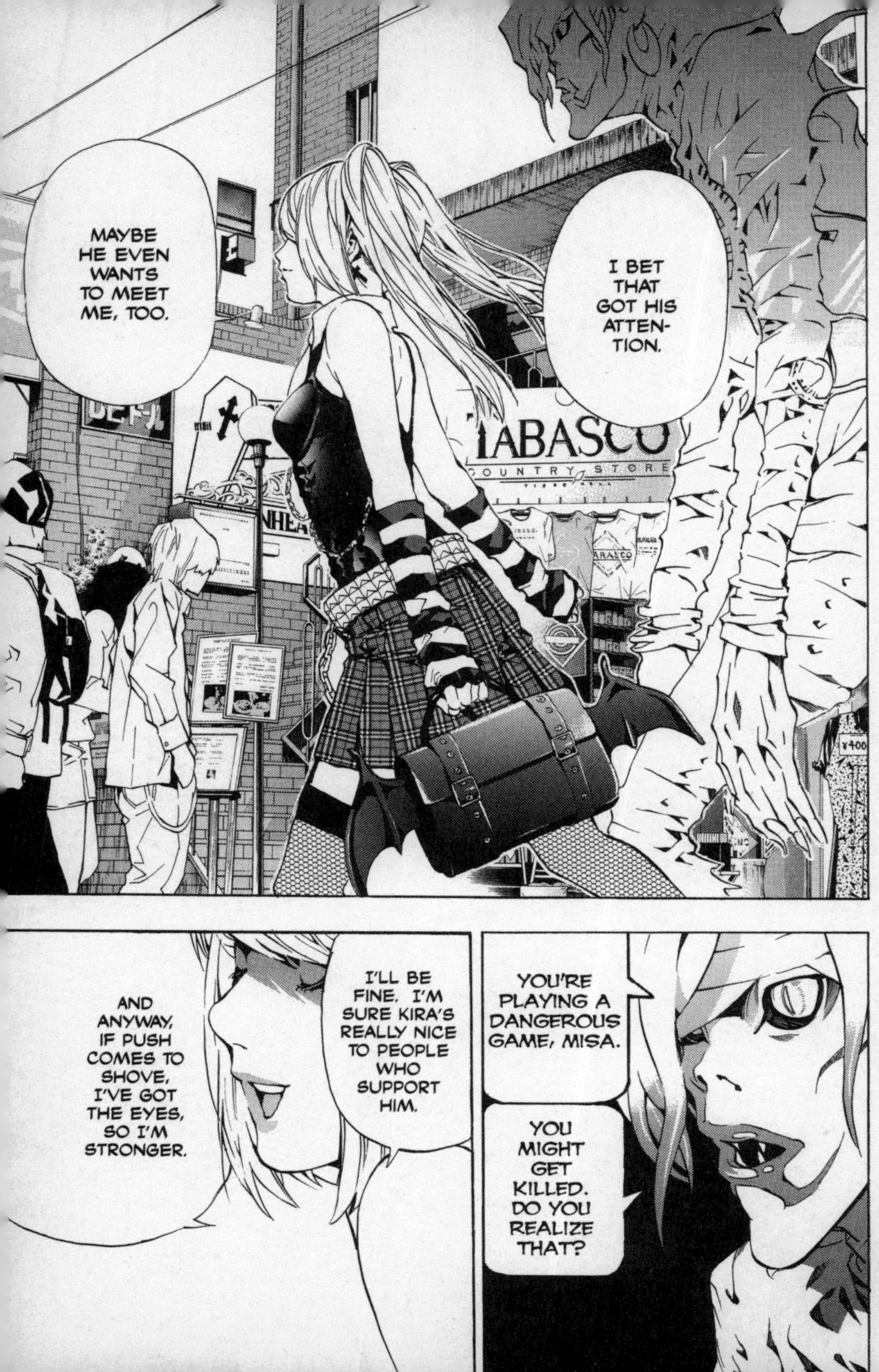
I BET THAT GOT HIS ATTENTION.
MAYBE HE EVEN WANTS TO MEET ME, TOO.
YOU'RE PLAYING A DANGEROUS GAME, MISA.
YOU MIGHT GET KILLED. DO YOU REALIZE THAT?
I'LL BE FINE. I'M SURE KIRA'S REALLY NICE TO PEOPLE WHO SUPPORT HIM.
AND ANYWAY, IF PUSH COMES TO SHOVE, I'VE GOT THE EYES, SO I'M STRONGER.

DEATH NOTE
How to use it
XV

○ When the same name is written on more than two DEATH NOTES, the Note which was first filled in will take effect, regardless of the time of death,.

二冊以上のデスノートに同じ人間の名前が書かれた場合、
記してある死亡時刻には関係なく、一番先に書かれたものが優先される。

○ If writing the same name on more than two DEATH NOTES is completed within a 0.06-second difference, it is regarded as simultaneous; the DEATH NOTE will not take effect and the individual written will not die.

二冊以上のデスノートで名前を書き終える時間の差が
０.０６秒以内の場合は同時とみなされ、
それらのノートに書かれた事は無効になり、
名前を書かれた人間は死なない。

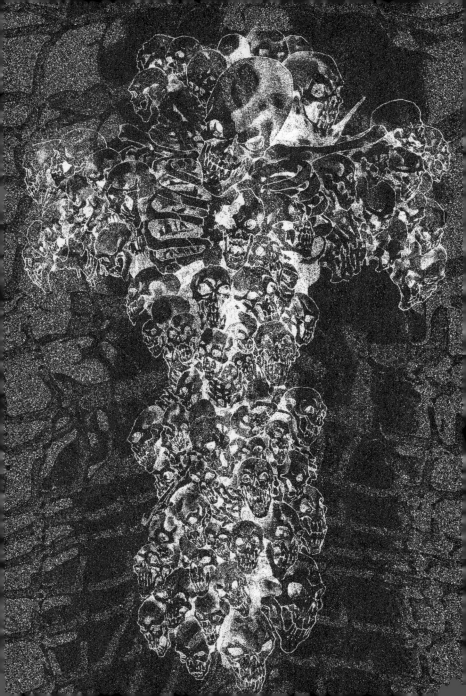

In the Next Volume

There's a new Kira in town, and Light has been invited to help L track him down.
But it looks like this Kira made the bargain for Shinigami eyes—half a lifespan for
the ability to know anyone's name, just by looking at them! Can Light use his rival's
powers to finally kill L? Or does the second Kira have other plans for Light?

Available Now!

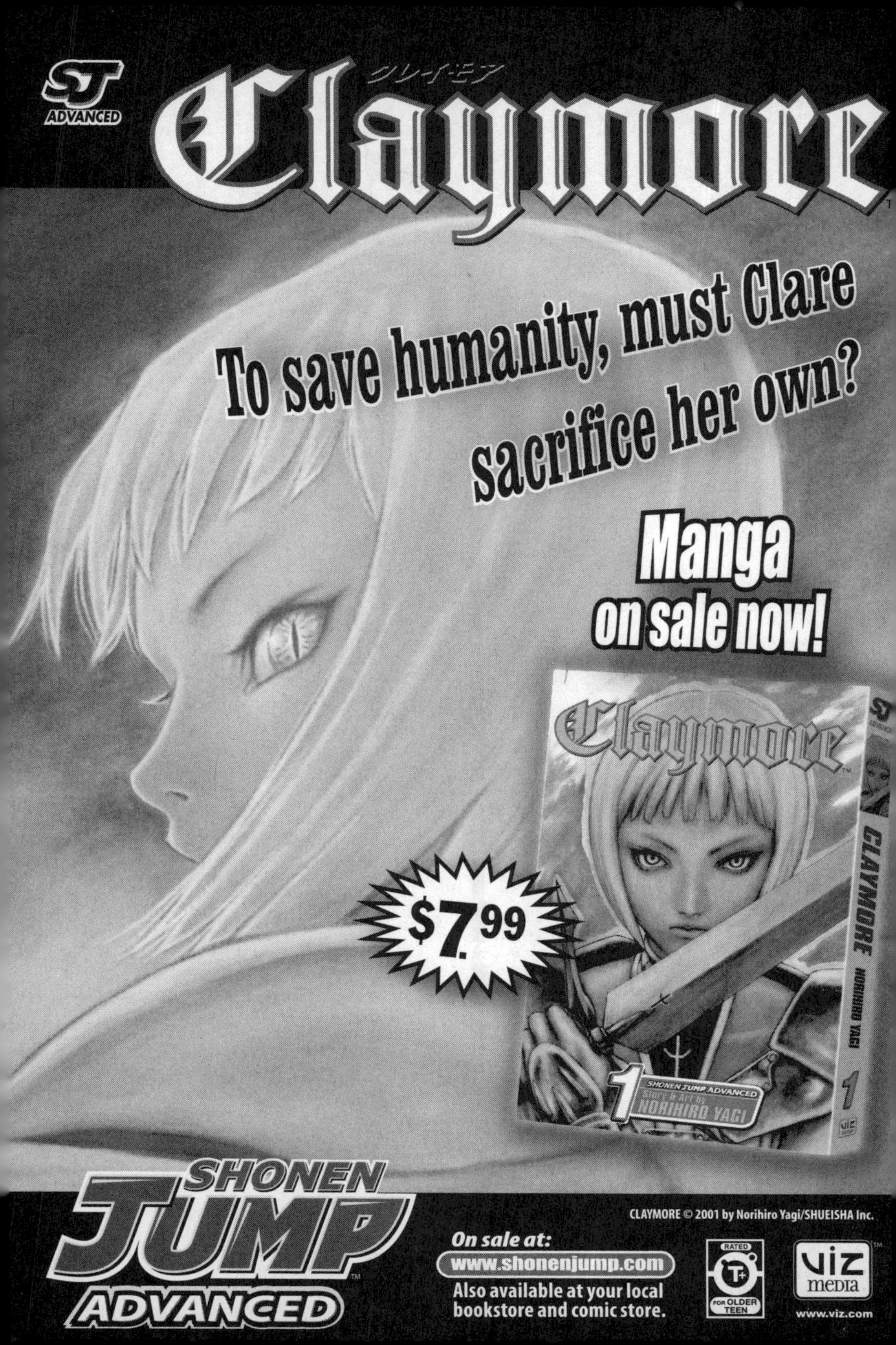
SJ ADVANCED
クレイモア
Claymore
To save humanity, must Clare sacrifice her own?
Manga on sale now!
$7.99
Claymore
CLAYMORE
NORIHIRO YAGI
1
SHONEN JUMP ADVANCED
Story & Art by
NORIHIRO YAGI
SHONEN JUMP ADVANCED
CLAYMORE © 2001 by Norihiro Yagi/SHUEISHA Inc.
On sale at:
www.shonenjump.com
Also available at your local bookstore and comic store.
RATED T+ FOR OLDER TEEN
viz media
www.viz.com

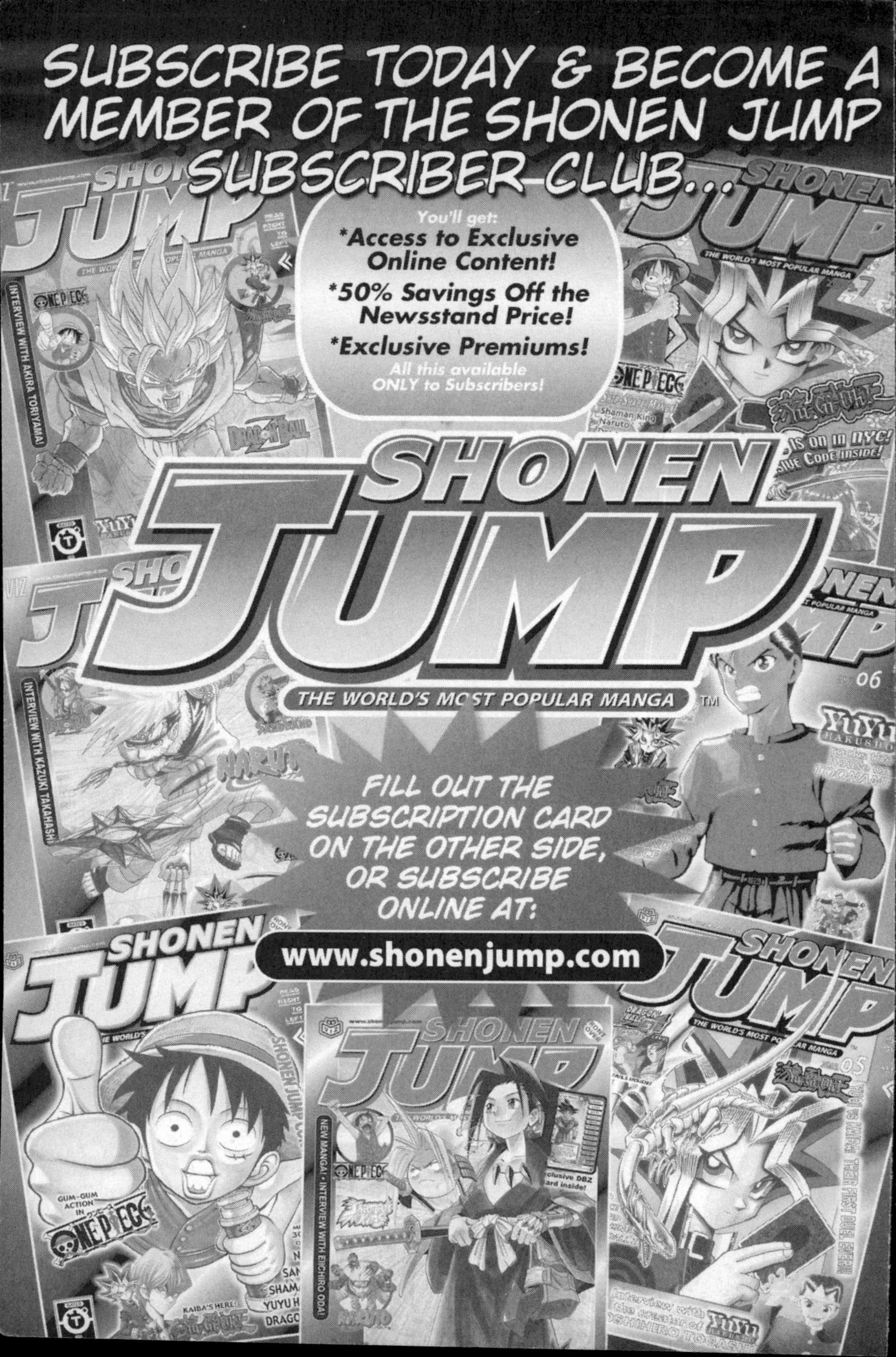
SUBSCRIBE TODAY & BECOME A MEMBER OF THE SHONEN JUMP SUBSCRIBER CLUB...
You'll get:
*Access to Exclusive Online Content!
*50% Savings Off the Newsstand Price!
*Exclusive Premiums!
All this available ONLY to Subscribers!
SHONEN JUMP
THE WORLD'S MOST POPULAR MANGA™
FILL OUT THE SUBSCRIPTION CARD ON THE OTHER SIDE, OR SUBSCRIBE ONLINE AT:
www.shonenjump.com